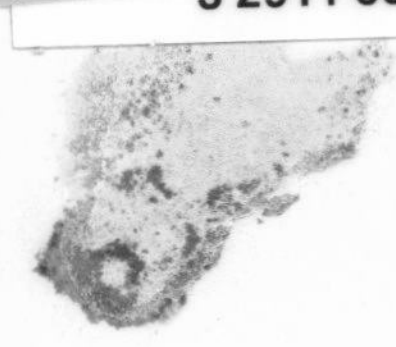

LIFE INSURANCE COMPANIES IN THE CAPITAL MARKET

MSU Business Studies

ELECTRONICS IN BUSINESS
Gardner M. Jones

EXPLORATIONS IN RETAILING
Stanley C. Hollander

ELEMENTARY MATHEMATICS OF LINEAR PROGRAMMING AND GAME THEORY
Edward G. Bennion

MARGINAL ASPECTS OF MANAGEMENT PRACTICES
Frederic N. Firestone

HISTORY OF PUBLIC ACCOUNTING IN THE UNITED STATES
James Don Edwards

CONTRIBUTIONS OF FOUR ACCOUNTING PIONEERS
James Don Edwards
Roland F. Salmonson

LIFE INSURANCE COMPANIES IN THE CAPITAL MARKET
Andrew F. Brimmer

LIFE INSURANCE COMPANIES
IN THE
CAPITAL MARKET

ANDREW F. BRIMMER

MSU BUSINESS STUDIES 1962

Bureau of Business and Economic Research
Graduate School of Business Administration
Michigan State University, East Lansing

ACKNOWLEDGMENTS

The author gratefully acknowledges the kindness of the publishers in giving permission to quote from the following:

The National Debt in War and Transition by Henry C. Murphy. Copyright 1950. McGraw-Hill Book Company, Inc.

Business Week, June 30, 1956.

Investment of Life Insurance Funds, edited by David McCahan. Copyright 1953. Richard D. Irwin, Inc.

American Economic Review, May, 1954.

Federal Reserve Bulletin, January, 1942; January, 1958; March, 1951; and the Federal Reserve System *Annual Report*, 1947.

Concerning U. S. Government Securities, by C. F. Childs. Copyright 1947. C. F. Childs and Company.

"Changing Concepts of Central Banking," by Allen Sproul in *Money, Trade and Economic Growth, Essays in Honor of John Henry Williams*. Copyright 1951. The Macmillan Company.

Library of Congress Catalog Card Number 62-62788

Preface

This book is the result of two essentially separate investigations. The initial study was undertaken in connection with a dissertation, "Some Studies in Monetary Policy, Interest Rates, and the Investment Behavior of Life Insurance Companies," presented to Harvard University in 1956. In that study, the objective was to test the relevance of the so-called "theory of credit availability" as an explanation of the influence of monetary policy on a set of financial intermediaries other than commercial banks. Subsequently, an opportunity arose to publish the dissertation. However, it was thought advisable to revise the study—not only to extend the coverage along the same lines of analysis on the basis of recent material but to acquire an additional perspective by the inclusion of data for companies differing with respect to size and other characteristics. For this purpose, the 200 largest life insurance companies in the United States (176) and Canada (24) were surveyed in the Spring of 1959 through a mail questionnaire (supplemented by a small number of personal interviews). Slightly more than three-fifths of the companies completed the questionnaire. The intent was to use the results of the mail survey to expand the original findings. Later it was decided to change drastically the orientation of the analysis, so the outcome was substantially a new study, although it rests heavily on the information from the first investigation.

The present examination focuses on fluctuations in the availability of life insurance funds in five sectors of the capital market in response to changes in the structure of interest rates. The five sectors are the markets for United States government securities, corporate bonds, real estate mortgages, state and local government securities, and equity capital. While the impact of monetary policy on life insurance companies' investment portfolios is clearly visible, the analysis goes much beyond explaining the mechanics of this influence. An attempt is made to trace the ebb and flow of life insurance funds among the sectors of the capital market and to appraise the consequences resulting from the marked shifts in investment behavior. The companies' capital market participation since World War II is the primary object of scrutiny, but historical data from earlier periods add perspective to the more recent pattern. The method of analysis and mode of data presentation were dictated by the desire to illuminate the conduct of these institutions in the capital market and to present the statistical and other evidence to document this role. While much of the evidence describing their investment activities is amenable to examination with the aid of the powerful tools of modern statistical analysis, such techniques were used sparingly. Given the goals outlined above, it was unnecessary to rely heavily on sophisticated quantitative methods.

In the course of this study, I have benefited from the aid and advice of numerous persons and institutions. I will always be grateful for the guidance and assistance of Professor John H. Williams when I was preparing the dissertation mentioned above. Moreover, since I completed the dissertation after I joined the Research Department of the Federal Reserve Bank of New York, I am indebted to that institution for the facilities and generous work schedule which allowed me to speed the conclusion of the project. At Michigan State University (where I formerly taught), the Bureau of Business and Economic Research supplied financial assistance in connection with the mail survey, research, and clerical assistance and also undertook the burden of publication. The Economics Department at Michigan State relieved me of teaching responsibilities for one quarter and also provided research assistance over several years. For anyone investigating the life insurance industry, the Institute of Life Insurance and the Life Insurance Association of America are indispensable. I have relied heavily on them—especially on the work of the latter, much of which reflected the efforts of Dr. James J. O'Leary (Director of Economic Research) and Dr. Kenneth M. Wright (formerly Assistant Director of Economic Research). The investment officers in the large number of life insurance companies who completed and returned the mail questionnaire made a major contribution, and those few who granted personal interviews as well, contributed even more. I appreciate their help.

In addition to those already named, numerous other persons aided the project at various stages. My wife, Doris M. S. Brimmer, compiled a large share of the statistics on which the dissertation was based, and she also prepared much of the index for the present volume. I also benefited from the stimulating conversation and ideas of my former colleagues at the Federal Reserve Bank of New York—among whom Jack Guttentag must be mentioned individually. At Michigan State University, Thomas Mayer and John P. Henderson read much of the manuscript at different stages of preparation and offered helpful criticism. Carl Brehm, Max G. Mueller and Herbert Kisch also made many useful suggestions.

The most sustained aid, in the form of editorial criticism and substantive comment on the revised version of the manuscript, came from Professors Eli P. Cox and John L. O'Donnell (respectively, Director and Assistant Director of the Bureau of Business and Economic Research at Michigan State University). I wish to thank Mrs. June Beeson, Assistant Editor of the Bureau, for her excellent editorial work which greatly improved the presentation. Dr. Anne C. Garrison, Bureau Editor, also helped with the editorial work at various points.

Several graduate and undergraduate research assistants at Michigan State University carried out most of the statistical computations required for the analysis and incorporation of material from the mail survey. Among these, Miss Joan Romans devoted the longest and most conscientious effort to the assignment. I have benefited from the published work of many scholars; I have made an effort to identify them at the appropriate places. Other persons, whom I cannot mention explicitly either by name or reference to their publications, have also furthered the study in different ways, and I wish to thank them also.

Finally, I assume all responsibility for the analysis and conclusions presented, and no person or institution mentioned above should be charged with any of the weaknesses which necessarily remain.

Andrew F. Brimmer
Wharton School of Finance and Commerce
University of Pennsylvania
May, 1962

Contents

LIFE INSURANCE COMPANIES IN THE CAPITAL MARKET

Part I Framework of Life Insurance Development

List of Tables

List of Charts

PART I

Framework of Life Insurance Investment

CHAPTER I

Life Insurance Companies as Financial Intermediaries

SECTION I
RISE OF FINANCIAL INTERMEDIARIES

This examination of the investment behavior of life insurance companies was undertaken with several objectives in mind. The first aim is to trace the impact of changes in the structure of interest rates on the flow of investment funds from these institutions to the capital market. Secondly, an appraisal is made of the part played by life insurance companies in facilitating several fundamental changes during the last three decades in the structure and functioning of the market for long-term funds. Finally, some of the implications of life insurance companies' investment behavior for the growth and stability of the economy as a whole are evaluated.

The study was prompted by the fact that, while an ample body of information exists pertaining to both the underwriting business of life insurance companies and the types of financial assets held by them, few investigations have focused specifically on the changing role of these institutions as financial intermediaries. It is true that this aspect of life insurance companies' activities has been surveyed by numerous students in studies of other financial institutions.[1] It is also true that a small number of articles in professional journals and periodicals have assayed their performance from time to time.[2] Moreover, at least one volume[3] has provided a comprehensive survey of some of the major legal and institutional problems faced by life insurance companies in managing an investment operation. However, while these projects have added to the body of knowledge relating to these investors, their specific role as financial intermediaries remains to be more fully illuminated.

That nonbank financial intermediaries should be studied more closely in relation to the general economy has been suggested by many students of monetary economics, and several pioneering ventures primarily of a theoretical nature have attracted considerable attention in recent years.[4] The nonbank financial intermediaries most frequently discussed are life insurance companies, savings and loan associations, mutual savings banks, corporate pension funds, credit unions, and similar savings institutions. While they exhibit much diversity in their sources and uses of funds, they have several characteristics in common. They do not create money, which is the exclusive function of commercial banks and the Federal Reserve System. On the other hand, they mobilize a vast amount of savings originating with individuals and business firms seeking a variety of income, safety, and other objectives. At the same time, through the acquisition of different types of financial assets, they channel these savings into numerous sectors of the economy to enable other individuals, business firms, and governmental units to spend for consumption and capital formation in excess of their current incomes. Thus, these intermediaries contribute in a substantial way to bridging the gap between borrowers and lenders, many of whom would hesitate (because of risk and other reasons) to deal directly with each other. Furthermore, by helping to enlarge the secondary market for securities, they enhance the liquidity of the entire economy and greatly increase the efficiency of money and credit.

There is, however, another side to the matter. Because of either legal or customary restrictions, most of these intermediaries limit their investment activities to a relatively narrow range of financial assets. With few exceptions, these consist almost wholly of various types of debt. Some of them (for example, savings and loan associations) specialize in real estate mortgages, while others (for example, mutual savings banks) concentrate on mortgages and federal government securities. Credit unions limit themselves primarily to the extension of consumer credit. Among all of these, life insurance companies and noninsured corporate pension funds have the greatest relative freedom in selecting investment outlets. However, while life insurance companies must choose high-grade debt obligations, pension funds can acquire significant amounts of equities as well. Nevertheless, the ability of life insurance companies and other financial institutions to switch their investment activities from one sector of the capital market to another in response to changes in the structure of interest rates, gives them considerable influence over the total volume, rate, and direction of credit flows in the economy. Decisions to shift the flow of funds over relatively short time periods can thus increase the instability inherent in aggregate output and employment.

This possibility is aggravated by the fact that these financial intermediaries are not directly affected by the traditional controls exercised by the monetary authorities. Such controls (changes in discount rates, reserve requirements, and open market operations) have been aimed at commercial banks and designed to influence the volume of bank reserves. The latter in turn would determine the availability and cost of credit and directly affect the level of economic activity and prices.

The growth of nonbank financial intermediaries has transformed this view of the financial system in a number of ways. First, currency and deposits, the leading form of bank debt, constitute a declining share of total debt, and the proportion of total financial assets held by the banking system is also decreasing. Similarly, there is a secular decline in the fraction of their financial assets that business firms and consumers hold in the form of money, and banks are declining relatively as sources of loanable funds. This means that an increasing share of financial assets and liabilities is only indirectly responsive to banking policies and the traditional technique of monetary controls. It has been observed that

> traditional controls are more appropriate to competitive loanable-funds markets than to markets that are dominated by a few large institutional lenders such as insurance companies. In imperfectly competitive markets, where a few nonbank institutional lenders are important market forces, capital rationing may become the critical medium for enforcing financial control.[5]

Other evidence could be cited to document the growing importance of financial intermediaries in the American economy and to justify the expenditure of effort to chart their course of development.[6] However, assuming that the merit of such an investigation has now been established, the focus can be shifted to an examination of the investment behavior of life insurance companies, the largest of the nonbank financial institutions.

Section II
Data and Method of Approach

Both data and the technique of employing them in this investigation of life insurance companies' investment behavior were dictated by the objectives outlined above. Throughout, however, an attempt was made to examine the companies' activities in the context of prevailing economic conditions. While reliance had to be placed primarily on data available from public sources, a considerable amount of crucial information was obtained through a confidential questionnaire and personal interviews with representatives of a number of companies. These are discussed below. The analysis was conducted at both the industry level and at the level of companies grouped by size and type (mutual vs. stock).

All legal reserve life insurance companies in the United States are included. Statistics for these companies are reported by the Institute of Life Insurance. There were 1,407 such companies registered at the end of 1959, of which about 90 percent were stock and the rest mutual. Because the mutual companies are generally older, they account for over three-fifths of the total life insurance in force. The statistics for these companies cover the operations of the health and accident departments of life insurance companies as well as those activities associated purely with their life insurance business. It was not possible to separate these. On the other hand, the life insurance activities of fraternal orders, savings banks, and various governmental programs are not included.

The statistics used most frequently relate to changes in the assets of life insurance companies during three time periods: Pre-World War II (roughly 1920-40, although some discussions reach back beyond 1920), World War II (1941-45), and Post-World War II (1945-59). Net changes in assets were arranged to produce abbreviated sources and uses of funds tables.[7] From the point of view of the investment behavior of life insurance companies, the part of the flow of funds system of most interest relates to the financial uses of funds. In some instances, however, certain items in the nonfinancial sources of funds accounts are also employed. These consist primarily of premium receipts and investment income, but receipts from sales of foreclosed properties, insurance benefits, and miscellaneous sources are also included. In Chapter II the relative sizes of these various income sources are discussed in detail. Premiums are recorded gross of dividends to policyholders and of commissions. Investment earnings, mainly interest, dividends, and rental income, are also recorded gross of investment expenses. Because the main focus is on the uses which life insurance companies make of their net income, nonfinancial uses (chiefly payroll and other operating expenses) are not analyzed in detail. Instead, attention is concentrated on the use of funds to acquire financial assets, such as United States government securities, corporate bonds, real estate mortgages, state and local government obligations, and corporate stocks. While net changes in these assets over specified time periods yield the main statistical series employed in the study, gross flows are also examined in some instances; also statistics relating to the companies' forward commitments to purchase securities and mortgages are used where they were available for certain of the postwar years.

Several problems arise in using life insurance data to study capital market flows. In the first place, financial assets of life insurance companies are recorded at amortized value or market prices in published sources such as the *Life Insurance Fact Book.* Thus, changes in assets computed from these figures reflect bookkeeping revaluations as well as real changes in the volume of funds reaching the capital markets from life insurance companies. In order to appraise the magnitude of this distortion, the valuation adjustments reported in the annual flow of funds series covering 1946-59 published by the Board of Governors of the Federal Reserve System were used to compute ratios of such adjustments to total changes in specific types of assets. For the change in total assets, the ratio was only .001 percent; in relation to the net change in total financial assets the ratio was .002 percent. Practically all of the latter was accounted for by the bookkeeping revaluation of common stocks owned. Since these represented an average of 2 percent of total assets, and because the study of life insurance companies' investment behavior in the stock market is confined to Chapter IX, the small errors introduced by changes in the book value of assets were ignored.

Another problem which had to be faced with the life insurance data was raised by the timing of transactions. Beginning with 1951, life insurance assets presented in the *Life Insurance Fact Book* are on an accrual basis rather than a cash basis. Thus, income and other nonfinancial flows in the flow of funds accounts derived from these statistics are to some extent on an accrual basis but the corresponding accrual assets and liability items (due and deferred premiums and interest and investment income accrued, and due and accrued expenses) are not recorded among the financial transactions. This inconsistent timing in the accounts, due to lack of information on which to base the appropriate adjustments, is reflected in a discrepancy between total sources and total uses. Again, since the accounts employed in this survey are an abbreviated version of the flow of funds system, this problem does not create a major obstacle.

The second substantial body of information on life insurance companies' investment activities was obtained in a mail questionnaire sent out in mid-March, 1959. The survey was sponsored by the Bureau of Business and Economic Research of Michigan State University (referred to in the text as BBER-MSU Survey, 1959). Before the questionnaire was mailed, a draft of the questions was prepared and circulated among a few industry representatives for criticism. The final version (consisting of 23 questions) asked for the following types of information, on a confidential basis, relating to life insurance companies' investment policies and opinions. They were asked to submit a copy of their annual statement and accompanying schedules of investments covering business for 1958. These are the statements submitted to state supervisory officials. Otherwise, they were asked to complete a table summarizing their assets as of December 31, 1958. Sixty-five companies enclosed statements and schedules, and 62 were used in a special study reported in Chapter VIII. Companies were asked to identify the main factors they consider in diversifying their investments and to indicate whether the distribution of their assets as of December 31, 1958, was broadly in line with the long-run desired distribution; if not, they were asked to indicate which categories they wish to increase or decrease. Five questions were devoted to the nature and process of investment decisions in life insurance companies. Respondents were asked to indicate who (from directors down through the officer in charge of investments) is mainly responsible for setting the overall investment policies of the company. Where investment policies are determined by a group, information was requested on the frequency of meetings to discuss such policies. The questionnaire also sought to discover the extent to which investment operations in securities and mortgages are handled as a single function under the immediate control of one officer or as separate functions. Finally, the companies were asked whether investment funds are budgeted for particular types of assets during a given time period. Where this is the case, they were asked to specify the length of the budget period and to describe the way in which funds can be transferred from one heading to another within the budget period. A related question concerned the extent to which life insurance companies employ investment advisory firms to give advice on portfolio management. The aim was primarily to determine whether smaller institutions have access to expert guidance in investment matters although they may not themselves be able to maintain professional staffs.

Two questions were devoted to an inquiry concerning objectives (other than that of obtaining interest income) of the companies in holding United States government and state and local government securities. The aim with respect to federal government issues was to discover whether the companies consider this part of their portfolio to be in balance with the rest of their assets; the target for state and local issues was to find out how much weight life insurance companies assign to tax-exempt income.

Two questions were asked about the companies' use of forward commitments and direct placement of corporate securities and mortgages. The respondents were asked to describe the average length of existing commitments for corporate securities and mortgages and to indicate the maximum length of commitments they were prepared to make for each type of obligation. They were also asked to describe whether and how the length of commitments varies with changes in the level of interest rates. Finally, they were asked to report the usual percentage range of the commitment fee (if charged) for corporate bonds and real estate mortgages.

To obtain information on the flexibility of their mortgage lending activities, they were asked to indicate the primary source of residential mortgages and to describe briefly their policies toward investing in federally-underwritten mortgages (FHA and VA) compared with investing in conventional mortgages.

The final questions concerned the companies' investment policies and attitudes relating to common stocks. A brief description of current policies was requested. Then they were asked whether they believe that the present legal restrictions (in their state of domicile and in New York State if they are licensed to do business there but domiciled elsewhere) on investing in common stocks by life insurance companies should be liberalized; what limit (defined as a percentage of assets or surplus) they would recommend on the ownership of common stocks; whether life insurance companies should invest in common stock other than the so-called blue chip stocks, and if so under what conditions. Finally, they were asked whether they believe that detailed legal restrictions on the investment activities of life insurance companies should be eliminated and such activity left to each company to be guided by the so-called prudent man rule. A brief comment on the whole issue was also requested.

The questionnaire was mailed in mid-March, 1959, and a follow-up letter went out in April explaining more fully the sponsorship of the survey and assuring the companies of the intent to treat the replies confidentially. The list of companies to receive the questionnaire was taken from *Bests Insurance News, Life Edition*, July, 1958. This showed, by size of assets as of December, 1957, the 200 largest life insurance companies in the United States and Canada; 176 were American and 24 were Canadian. The largest company had total assets of $15,536,144 thousand, and the smallest had total assets of $22,580 thousand.[8] Of the 176 questionnaires sent to American companies, 117 were returned and 111 of these contained complete information. Thus, the effective returns amounted to about 63 percent. Seventeen of the 24 Canadian companies returned the questionnaires; ten of these could have been used. However, the Canadian replies were set aside after the decision was made to restrict the survey to American companies. The pattern of response by size of company is shown in Table I-1. It will be noted that the response rate was heaviest among the largest companies, so the information obtained gives a fairly comprehensive coverage of a substantial proportion of the

TABLE I-I

PATTERN OF RESPONSE OF AMERICAN LIFE INSURANCE COMPANIES
TO THE SURVEY MADE BY THE BUREAU OF BUSINESS AND ECONOMIC RESEARCH,
MICHIGAN STATE UNIVERSITY, MARCH, 1959
(Responding Companies are Underlined)

Rank of Companies, by Size of Assets, from Largest to Smallest

1	**2**	**3**	4	**5**	**6**	**7**	**8**	**9**	**10**
11	**12**	13	**14**	**15**	**16**	**17**	18	**19**	**20**
21	**22**	**23**	24	**25**	**26**	**27**	**28**	**29**	30
31	**32**	33	34	**35**	36	**37**	**38**	**39**	**40**
41	**42**	**43**	**44**	**45**	**46**	**47**	**48**	49	50
51	**52**	**53**	**54**	55	**56**	**57**	**58**	**59**	**60**
61	**62**	**63**	**64**	**65**	66	**67**	68	**69**	**70**
71	72	**73**	74	**75**	**76**	**77**	**78**	79	80
81	82	**83**	**84**	85	**86**	**87**	**88**	89	90
91	**92**	**93**	**94**	**95**	96	97	**98**	**99**	100
101	**102**	**103**	104	**105**	**106**	**107**	108	109	110
111	112	113	**114**	115	116	**117**	**118**	**119**	**120**
121	**122**	**123**	**124**	125	**126**	**127**	128	129	**130**
131	132	133	134	135	**136**	137	138	139	140
141	**142**	143	**144**	**145**	146	**147**	148	149	150
151	**152**	**153**	154	155	156	157	**158**	159	**160**
161	**162**	163	**164**	165	166	**167**	**168**	169	**170**
171	**172**	173	174	**175**	**176**				

Size Grouping of Companies Replying

Size Group		Number of Companies	Asset Range, December, 1957 ($ Thousands)
I		28	359,134 — 13,919,133
II		28	121,258 — 357,469
III		28	52,287 — 111,326
IV		27	22,580 — 51,603
	Total Companies	111	

industry's assets. Table I-1 also shows the size grouping of the companies replying.

In addition to the above sources, information was used from a variety of public documents, books, and articles. These are identified in the bibliographical references.

Section III
Organization and Content of the Study

The behavior of life insurance companies in five main sectors of the capital market is examined in Chapters V through IX of Part II. The material in Chapters II through IV of Part I, however, is essential because it provides the framework required for the subsequent analysis.

In Chapter II, the economic framework of life insurance companies' investment activities is shown. The main emphasis is on the following factors: the persistent inflow of funds due to the rising demand for life insurance protection; the relation among accumulated savings in the form of reserves, the rate of earnings on invested reserves, and the net cost of life insurance; the slowdown in recent years in the annual rate of growth of savings through life insurance companies; and the slightly weakening competitive position of life insurance companies in the capital market compared with other institutional investors, especially noninsured corporate pension funds and savings and loan associations. In Chapter III, the legal framework governing life insurance companies' investment activities is sketched. It is shown that, although considerable diversity prevails among the various states, the laws of New York and five other states are the most crucial. The moderately liberal trend in investment laws during the last decade is traced, and attention is also called to the severity of the remaining restrictions. The typical internal organization of life insurance companies to handle investment operations is also described. Although numerous factors influence the decisions of life insurance companies to invest in any particular financial asset, it is shown in Chapter IV that, in general, such decisions are primarily a function of the structure of interest rates. The pattern of response to changes in the structure of interest rates on a small range of assets is shown to be consistent with the behavior expected of a rational long-term investor—given the legal framework and the chief investment targets for which these institutions aim. Simultaneously, however, the role of custom in shaping investment decisions is recognized.

Within the above framework, the companies' investment behavior in five sectors of the capital market is analyzed in Part II. The analysis begins in Chapter V with the market for United States government securities. Although life insurance companies hold only a small proportion of their assets in the form of government securities, this market exerts a strategic influence on their overall investment activities. Such issues serve the liquidity needs of the institutions, which are related to portfolio management rather than to insurance operations, and provide a certain amount of diversification. The interest rates on Governments are usually too low to make them attractive as permanent investment outlets; nevertheless, these rates are the key to the entire rate structure because of the absence of credit risk in the ownership of Governments. Thus, government securities are the benchmark against which to judge the investment qualities of all other types of earning assets. Variations in the prices and yields on government securities are instrumental in determining the availability of life insurance funds to other sectors of the capital market.

The overwhelming preference of most life insurance companies for corporate bonds is shown in Chapter VI. The rise of these institutions to a position of dominance in the corporate bond market is traced to the development of the direct placement technique as an alternative to public sale of securities. The differences in the companies' share of sub-parts of the corporate bond market are explained. In addition, the growing competition from pension funds is appraised. The investment behavior of life insurance companies in the mortgage market is reviewed in Chapter VII. The extent of the companies' reliance on federally-underwritten mortgages is pointed out, but the main story centers in the sharply defined contracyclical pattern of their mortgage lending. While their participation in the mortgage market is clearly destabilizing in the flow of investment funds, it is highly stabilizing from the point of view of real capital formation in residential construction and aggregate economic activity. This result has been mainly caused by the companies' shift to federally-underwritten mortgages during recessions and away from them with the revival of corporate demand for funds on the eve of prosperity. However, with the spread of discounts, the rigidity of the rate ceilings on federally-underwritten mortgages has been weakened, and this may reduce the influence of life insurance companies on the rate of real investment in the economy. Finally, the major role of life insurance companies in the farm mortgage market is outlined.

The state and local government securities market is shown in Chapter VIII to receive only a meager share of life insurance funds. The main reason is that the relatively light burden of federal taxation carried by life insurance companies severely reduces the advantage of tax-exempt income to them. Nevertheless, they do play a significant role in the market for revenue bonds secured by earnings of business-type publicly owned enterprises. The main features of revenue bonds which make them attractive to life insurance companies are discussed, and the growth of revenue bond financing by special authorities is explained. Finally, in Chapter IX the minor role of life insurance companies in supplying funds to small businesses is appraised. The extent to which these loans take the form of mortgages is also shown. The relatively insignificant place of common stocks as an investment outlet is discussed, and a case is made for life insurance companies investing much more heavily in common stocks. It is argued that not only should legal restrictions be eased further, but the unfavorable attitudes of most company officials should be modified to take account of the special attributes of life insurance companies as institutional investors which make common stocks an appropriate investment outlet.

Chapter X provides a summary of the major findings of the study; some of the main implications of these findings for several more general questions of economic analysis and public policy are also discussed.

Footnotes

1. See, for example, Raymond Goldsmith, *Financial Intermediaries in the American Economy Since 1900,* a study sponsored by the National Bureau of Economic Research (Princeton: Princeton University Press, 1958); Houghton Bell and Harold G. Fraine, "Legal Framework, Trends and Developments in Investment Practices of Life Insurance Companies," *Law and Contemporary Problems,* Winter, 1952, pp. 46-87.

2. One of the best is James J. O'Leary, "The Institutional Savings-Investment Process and Current Economic Theory," *American Economic Review,* May, 1954, pp. 454-70.

3. David McCahan (ed.), *Investment of Life Insurance Funds* (Philadelphia: University of Pennsylvania Press, 1953).

4. John G. Gurley and Edward S. Shaw, *Money in a Theory of Finance* (Washington, D.C.: The Brookings Institutions, 1960). Warren L. Smith, "Financial Intermediaries and Monetary Controls," *Quarterly Journal of Economics,* November, 1959, pp. 533-53. D. A. Alhadeff, "Credit Controls and Financial Intermediaries," *American Economic Review,* September, 1960, pp. 655-71.

5. John G. Gurley and Edward S. Shaw, "Financial Aspects of Economic Development," *American Economic Review,* September, 1955, p. 537.

6. I have examined some of the problems posed by life insurance companies for monetary management in some detail. See *Some Studies in Monetary Policy, Interest Rates and the Investment Behavior of Life Insurance Companies,* a dissertation presented to Harvard University, 1956. Also, much of the work of the Commission on Money and Credit has bearing on this subject. However, the present study was virtually completed when the Commission's report appeared; cf. *Money and Credit, Their Influence on Jobs, Prices and Growth* (Englewood Cliffs, N.J.: Prentice-Hall, 1961). For an excellent summary of the Commission's findings see Arthur Smithies, "The Commission on Money and Credit," *Quarterly Journal of Economics,* November, 1961, pp. 544-68.

7. This accounting technique is explained in a number of places. See Morris Copeland, *A Study of Money Flows in the United States* (New York: National Bureau of Economic Research, 1952); *Flow of Funds in the United States, 1939-1953* (Washington, D.C.: Board of Governors of the Federal Reserve System, 1955).

8. It should be noted that the asset range of companies receiving the questionnaire differs from that of the companies replying. The largest company did not reply, but the smallest one did.

CHAPTER II

Economic Background of Capital Market Activities

SECTION I
DEMAND FOR PROTECTION

The persistent search for personal and family security has made the life insurance industry, at least until the last few years, one of the leading growth sectors in the American economy. This steady expansion, in addition to providing increased protection to millions of policyholders and their dependents, generated about $108 billion of savings by the end of 1959. These savings in turn were used to finance capital formation by business, consumers, and governmental units. In this chapter, the economic framework of the life insurance industry is analyzed with special reference to the investment problems which these companies face.

At the end of 1959, life insurance owned in the United States totaled $542.1 billion.[1] This represented a gain of 9.8 percent over 1958; this rate of increase was somewhat larger than that achieved in the previous year but was again below the average annual increase registered in the postwar period. (See Chart II-1.) The slower rate of expansion is partly attributable to the incomplete recovery from the 1957-58 recession (the rate of growth also slowed down in the previous two postwar recessions), but as explained below, other factors were also at work. The amount of life insurance in force at the end of 1959 was about three and one-half times that at the end of 1945, and the annual rate of expansion during the postwar period is the second highest on record, being exceeded only by that achieved in the decade 1915-25.

As shown in Chart II-1, the growth of life insurance in force is closely

CHART II-1

Annual Percentage Changes in Disposable Personal Income, Life Insurance in Force, and Assets of Life Insurance Companies, 1930-1959

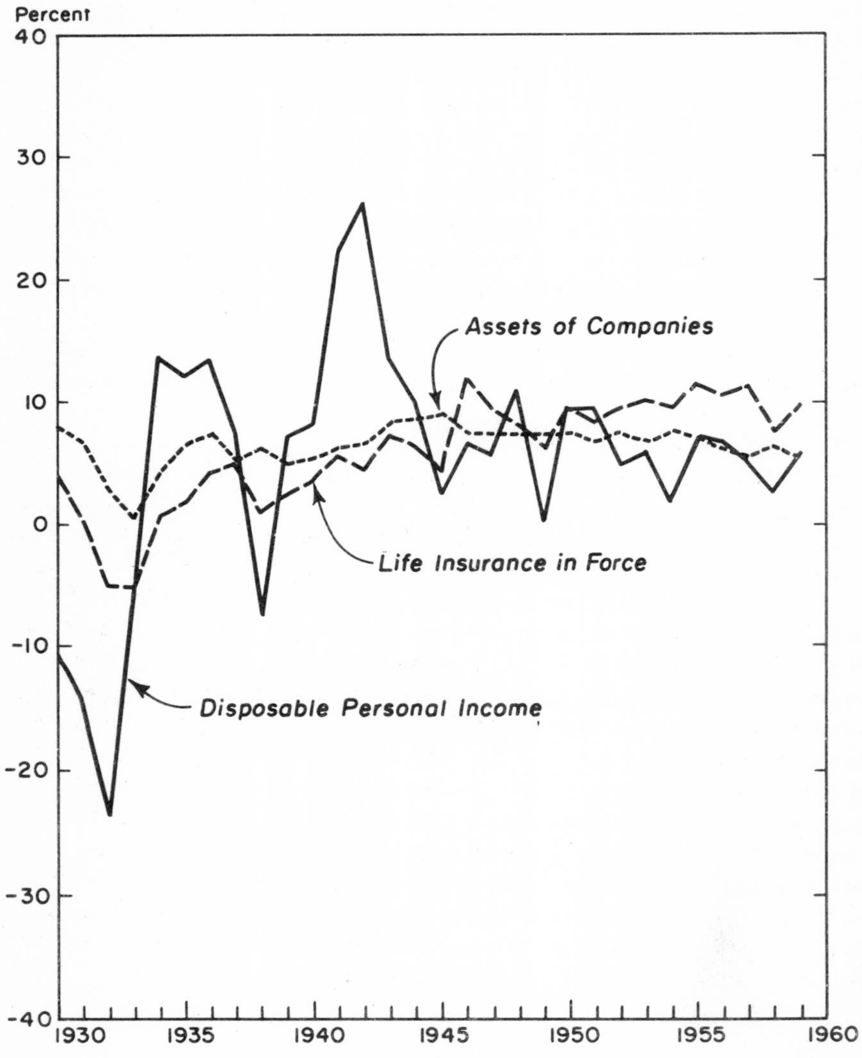

SOURCE: Appendix Table II-1, p. 385.

related to the level and rate of growth of disposable personal income. However, the volume of insurance shows a much stronger secular expansion and greater cyclical stability than income. The major contours of business cycles since 1929 are clearly identifiable in the pattern of income changes. In contrast, considerable drops in income are registered as only moderate declines in the rate of growth of insurance in force, but slackening of the pace of income expansion is hardly noticeable in the trend of life insurance outstanding. The high degree of stability in the life insurance business is derived chiefly from the widespread ownership of life policies. At the end of 1959, the $542.1 billion of life insurance in force was owned by 115 million policyholders. This represented 64 percent of the total United States population and an even higher proportion (about four-fifths) of the men who are more likely to be heads of households. Life insurance owned during 1959 amounted to $9,500 per family, or around three times the 1945 figure. Moreover, the average amount of insurance was two-fifths greater than the average family disposable income of $5,900.

The full scope of life insurance ownership is clearly shown in the Survey of Consumer Finances conducted by the Survey Research Center, University of Michigan, for the Board of Governors of the Federal Reserve System. The survey showed that 79 percent of the spending units in the United States owned life insurance in 1956.[2] It also revealed that the ownership of life insurance and the average premium payment rise steeply with the level of family income; while only 43 percent of the families with incomes under $1,000 were insured and paid an average premium of $60 in 1956, the ratio of coverage jumped to 96 percent among families whose income was $7,500 or over, and their premium averaged $440. Moreover, life insurance ownership varies directly with the degree of urbanization. People of the Northeast region of the country are far more frequently insured than those living in the North Central and West (taken together), while a larger percentage of the latter is insured than one finds in the South. This pattern of coverage has considerable bearing on the regional distribution of life insurance investments, since it enables these companies to mobilize funds in the more developed parts of the country to transfer to areas having the highest rates of expansion.

Section II
Growth of the Industry Since World War II

The profile of expansion in the life insurance industry in the postwar period is sketched in Table II-1. It will be noted that, when measured by

TABLE II-I

SELECTED INDICATORS OF GROWTH IN THE
LIFE INSURANCE INDUSTRY, 1945-1959
(In Millions of Dollars, Except Where Indicated)

Item	1945	1959	Annual Compound Rate of Growth Percent
1. Number of Life Insurance Companies: Total	463	1,407	8.3
Mutual		151	
Stock		1,256	
2. Life Insurance Personnel: Total	261,200	450,000	4.0
Full-time agents	128,700	200,000	3.2
Other personnel	132,500	250,000	4.6
3. Life Insurance in Force: Total	151,762	542,128	9.5
Ordinary	101,550	315,953	8.4
Group	22,172	159,807	15.1
Industrial	27,675	39,688	2.6
Credit	365	26,680	35.9
4. Life Insurance Purchases: Total	14,554	70,854	12.0
Ordinary	9,859	51,678	12.6
Group	1,265	12,317	17.7
Industrial	3,430	6,859	5.1
5. Life Insurance and Disposable Personal Income Per Family (Dollars)			
Life insurance	3,200	9,500	8.1
Disposable personal income	3,200	5,900	4.5
6. Life Insurance Benefit Payments: Total	2,667	7,531	7.7
Death benefits	1,280	3,110	6.6
Matured endowments	407	632	3.2
Disability payments	87	119	2.3
Annuity payments	216	656	8.3
Surrender values	211	1,493	15.0
Policy dividends	466	1,521	8.8
7. Income of Life Insurance Companies: Total	7,674	21,790	7.7
Premium income	5,159	16,622	8.7
Investment and other income	2,515	5,168	5.3
8. Cost Factors in Life Insurance			
Death rate (per 1,000 lives exposed)	7.9	6.0	−2.0
Earnings rate (percent)	3.11	3.96	1.8
Ratio of operating expenses to total income (percent)	13.7	17.6	1.8
Taxes, licenses, and fees	153	958	14.0
9. Policy Reserves	38,667	93,975	6.6
10. Total Assets	44,797	113,650	6.9
11. Memorandum: Gross National Product (Billions of dollars)	213.6	479.5	5.9

SOURCE: Institute of Life Insurance, **Life Insurance Fact Book**, various years.

almost any of the indexes, the industry achieved growth rates well in excess of the rate of expansion for the economy as a whole. While gross national product, the most comprehensive measure of overall economic activity, increased about 6 percent at an annual rate, the annual increment in most of the industry categories was considerably more.

The mounting demand for insurance services was met not only by the enlargement of existing companies but by the establishment of new firms as well. By 1959 there were three times as many life insurance companies in operation as in 1945. The emergence of new companies was especially marked in some of the most rapidly developing sections of the country, and this resulted in a radical shift in the industry's geographical distribution. Well over one-third of the life insurance companies in 1959 had their head offices in the Southwest Central region (comprising Arkansas, Louisiana, Texas, and Oklahoma) compared with just over one-quarter in 1945. New England, the Middle Atlantic states, the West Coast, and the Middle West, while making sizable gains in the absolute number of companies, still lost relatively because of the much faster pace of expansion in the Southwest and the Mountain states. The Southeast region barely maintained its position over the period. Texas, Louisiana, and Arizona were the states with the largest number of companies in 1959, with 314, 122, and 108, respectively. Texas, with 55 companies, and Louisiana, with 54, were also in the lead in 1945, but in the earlier year Arizona had only one company. The mushrooming of companies in these states in the postwar period is probably more a reflection of somewhat less demanding registration requirements than of the actual strength of the market for life insurance. To some extent, the spectacular growth in the number of companies listing Delaware as the site of their head offices is due to a similar situation. During the postwar period, there was also a striking change in the preference of company promoters as to type of organization. Stock companies have far outstripped those established as mutual concerns, and the greater number of these have been launched in states with corporation laws less stringent than those in states such as New York and Massachusetts. Data are not readily available for early postwar years on the breakdown of companies between stock and mutual forms of organization, but evidence does suggest a marked swing toward stock companies in recent years. For example, in 1954 the 708 stock companies accounted for about 80 percent of the total number and for about one-third of the total assets held by all companies. By 1959, there were 1,256 stock companies, representing 90 percent of the total, and they held two-fifths of the assets. Thus, while the much older mutual companies still conducted the bulk of the business, the trend to the stock form of organization is also clear. In fact, the number of mutual companies actually decreased from 169 in 1954 to 151 in 1959. The tendency to launch stock companies no doubt sprang from the relatively high profit rates available as the insurance industry expanded to meet the growing demand for insurance. However, an incentive was probably also provided by the low rates of federal taxation which applied to investment and operating income originating in insurance companies until 1959.

The typical life insurance company greatly improved the efficiency of its operations in the postwar period. This is shown in the fact that life insurance personnel increased much more slowly than the total volume of business—even after allowing for the impact of higher prices on the face value of insurance in force. Moreover, the ratio of operating expenses to total income rose only moderately. The advance in output per man-hour was not uniform for all phases of the business. The gains were apparently greatest among professional personnel (exemplified by full-time agents); the latter were able to handle about 2.3 times the volume of business per man in 1959 as in 1945; for all other personnel the corresponding ratio was only 1.9 times that at the end of the war. This divergent trend among employees is partly accounted for by the rapid expansion of group policies because these require much less time per dollar of insurance than do ordinary policies. Credit insurance, the use of which is also spreading rapidly, likewise entails relatively few man-hours in relation to the volume of business. Both group and credit insurance registered percentage gains considerably in excess of those achieved in the ordinary category. As a result, ordinary insurance, which accounted for two-thirds of the total life insurance in force in 1945, had shrunk to less than three-fifths by 1959; over the same period, the face value of group contracts doubled as a percentage of the total, and credit insurance rose from less than one-tenth of one percent to about 5 percent. To some extent the latter advances were carved out at the expense of industrial insurance which increased by less than 3 percent per year, and whose share was squeezed from almost one-fifth of the total to only 7 percent; the slower pace of ordinary type policies is also evident. However, one should not conclude that sales of ordinary insurance were stagnant throughout the period. On the contrary, there were wide swings in the composition of new purchases of insurance, and in 1959 ordinary policies represented nearly three-quarters of the total. While group policies rose steadily—and even accelerated after the mid-1950's—there was a sharp pick up in sales of ordinary insurance in the closing years of the decade. This spurt came partly from the introduction of new types of contracts, among which family plans were especially important.

But whatever the soil which nourished the growth of insurance in force, the impact of this growth in relation to family income was marked. In 1945, insurance and after-tax income per family both amounted to about $3,200. Over the ensuing 14 years, however, disposable personal income per family rose 1.8 times for an annual increase of 4.5 percent, while the average amount of life insurance owned by each family rose three times, or by 8 percent per year. Of course, the gains in family income and insurance in force were partly a result of higher prices, but there is no doubt that by the end of the 1950's families were holding a far greater amount of protection in relation to annual income than they were at the end of the war. Nevertheless, insurance per family was still equivalent to only 19 months of family income, and there was strong evidence suggesting that the ratio would rise further.

Benefits paid to American policyholders and their families in 1959 amounted to $7.5 billion. This was 2.8 times the payments made in 1945 and represented a rate of increase of 7.7 percent each year. The increase in benefits during these years, while marked, was primarily a result of the expanding volume of insurance in force. Benefits grew more slowly than insurance in force chiefly because of declining death rates among policyholders, but the relative newness of a large share of policies was also a factor. For example, in 1959 more than half of the life insurance in force had been taken out since 1950, and benefits under these would not begin to accrue on a large scale for a number of years. Death benefits remained the single most important type of payment in 1959 and accounted for two-fifths of aggregate benefits. Over the postwar period, such benefits were dampened somewhat by the lower death rates, and the annual increment averaged about 6.6 percent per year. Death benefits paid under group contracts, however, rose substantially because of the spreading coverage of this type of insurance.

Payments to policyholders themselves registered sizable gains during the postwar years, although trends diverged significantly for different classes of benefits. In 1959, living benefits amounted to $4.4 billion and accounted for almost three-fifths of total benefit payments. Included in such benefits are matured endowments, annuity payments, disability payments, surrender values, and policy dividends. Matured endowments, at $632 million in 1959, were 1.6 times the payments at the close of the war. Such payments registered only modest increases in the postwar period partly because there was no radical change in policyholders' preferences for policies of this type. Moreover, toward the end of the 1950's, there was a substantial decrease in matured endowment payments under industrial policies. In 1959, life insurance companies paid out $119 million as compensation under disability policies (excluding disability payments which arose as contingencies of ordinary life policies). This was approximately one-third greater than in 1945. The bulk of disability payments (about 83 percent) represented income benefits, and the remainder was paid under premium waiver provisions. Payments made in 1959 by life insurance companies as annuities came to $656 million, a threefold increase compared with 1945. While the annual rate of growth in all types of annuities between these years was about 8.3 percent, the rate of advance for those originating in group policies was considerably higher. Of the annuities paid in 1959, individual contracts accounted for 54 percent compared with 46 percent for group policies. Comparable figures for 1945 are unavailable, but the proportion was undoubtedly much more in favor of individual contracts.

Cash surrender values climbed more steeply than any other type of benefit in the postwar years. By 1959 the withdrawals of accumulated savings (especially those left under supplementary contracts) were more than seven times the outflow in 1945, equivalent to an increase of 15 percent each year. Traditionally, such payments arise in the surrender of policies to obtain emergency funds, but other forces also exerted a strong undertow. For example, many policyholders became increasingly willing over the period to draw down savings through life insurance to make payments on homes and durable consumer goods while others used the proceeds in business ventures. In addition, policies were frequently turned in, and the savings were reinvested in stocks and other types of equities. But whatever the reasons behind the advance in surrender values, the trend was still strong at the end of the decade. Dividends paid to holders of participating policies rose somewhat ahead of insurance in force during the postwar period. This was due almost entirely to the substantial expansion in investment income because nonparticipating policies increased more rapidly than those enjoying dividend rebates. The uses policyholders made of dividends changed significantly during the period under review. For example, there was a marked rise in the proportion left with the companies to collect interest and to add to insurance; the share used to pay premiums dropped sharply, and cash withdrawals remained about unchanged in relation to total dividends.

Income of life insurance companies rose by about 7.7 percent per year between 1945 and 1959 and amounted to $21.8 billion in the latter year. Premium income advanced somewhat ahead of that from investment earnings, but the rate of increase fell short of that for total life insurance in force. This suggests that there was a sizable gain in the amount of protection provided per premium dollar; underlying this relative decrease in cost is the increased emphasis on group insurance and term policies involving lower average premiums for a given face amount of insurance. Investment income in 1959 amounted to $3.9 billion, and income from other sources (mainly representing policy proceeds left with the companies under supplementary contracts) totaled $1.3 billion. Together these sources of income registered an increase of 184 percent over the 1945 level. While the bulk of the advance in investment income can be attributed to the expansion in savings through life insurance and the simultaneous rise in investible funds, it is also partly due to the uptrend in yields since 1945. The effects of this improvement in the rate of return on the net cost of life insurance to policyholders are discussed more fully in Section III of this chapter.

The major factors determining the cost of life insurance diverged somewhat during the postwar period. As mentioned previously, the death rate declined appreciably over these years (by almost one-quarter), and this helped to keep down the cost of protection while prices for goods and services in general were rising steadily. However, the improvement in the mortality experience from some diseases (including tuberculosis, diabetes, pregnancy, and childbirth) was partly offset by the unfavorable effects on death rates caused by other diseases (especially heart disease and cancer). The tendency for operating expenses to rise in relation to income of the life insurance companies was partially offset by the improvement in investment earnings, both of which rose at the same annual rate in percentage terms.

One type of operating expense, however, rose sharply during the postwar period. This is the amount paid by life insurance companies for taxes, licenses, and fees, which in 1959 was almost six times the 1945 level. Almost three-fifths of the total tax payments in 1959 (mainly covering 1958 operations) represented federal income taxes; one-quarter was state taxes on premiums, and 16 percent was accounted for by other taxes, licenses, and fees. However, the outstanding change in the tax area was the Life Insurance Company Income Tax Act of 1959. The new law, passed in June, was not only designed to replace the temporary measure adopted in 1955 but was also intended to bring the taxation of life insurance companies more into line with that of other businesses. For example, on their 1957 investment income, these institutions paid federal income taxes equal to about 8.7 percent; the revised legislation was expected to lift the ratio to somewhat more than 12 percent on their 1958 operations. Although both the executive and legislative branches of the federal government made numerous attempts to revamp the tax formula applicable to life insurance companies, the 1959 act was the first to pass successfully through Congress since 1942. The legislation is extremely complicated, and the effects of some of its provisions will not be clear for some time.

Nevertheless, its main features can be summarized briefly. The law was made retroactive to cover the companies' income for 1958. It is estimated that federal income taxes paid on operations for 1958 amounted to between $450 and $500 million, compared with $288 million for 1957; the burden for 1959 apparently climbed further to approximately $535 million. Higher investment income was partly responsible for the increased tax payments, but the more fundamental cause was the radical redefinition of the tax base. Under the old law, 85 percent of life insurance companies' earnings from invested assets was exempt from any federal taxes, and the remaining 15 percent was taxed at the regular 52 percent corporate rate. The 1959 act lifts the taxable proportion to 21 or 22 percent—depending on the extent of investment losses in recent years. Secondly, underwriting income, virtually all of which emerges from premiums collected in excess of the amount required for protection, was subjected to income taxes for the first time since 1921. This source of income has been growing rapidly in recent years. The gains are due mainly to increasing life expectancy which is reflected in the mortality tables only after a considerable time lag, and to the reducing of operating expenses. In the future, underwriting income is to be divided roughly into two equal parts. One-half will be taxed in the year earned at the 52 percent rate applicable to ordinary income. The remainder will not be taxed at all unless it is distributed to stockholders, at which time it will be subject to the 52 percent rate. Underlying this treatment is the assumption that so long as such income is held by the life insurance company, it is part of the reserves held to guarantee payment of policyholders' claims.

This new definition of taxable income affects stock companies more adversely than those organized as mutual institutions. Stock companies receive a relatively large proportion of their income from underwriting profits while the bulk of the mutuals' income arises from investment earnings. Consequently, the old tax scheme imposed on the mutual companies about three-quarters of the federal income taxes paid by the industry although they have about two-thirds of the insurance business. Under the 1959 legislation, their share of total income taxes is expected to decline to about 65 percent. Furthermore, the "specialty companies" (e.g., those which write credit insurance and other types of term policies) are typically owned by stockholders and derive their income primarily from underwriting since they accumulate a rather small volume of reserves. This type of business has usually been quite profitable, and the major part of its profits has escaped taxation by the federal government. This will no longer be true.

The reaction of life insurance companies to the heavier incidence of taxation will not be fully known for several years. In the meantime, the first year's experience under the act suggests that most companies adjusted to the higher taxes (which had been long expected) without either greatly reducing dividends to policyholders or radically shifting their investment portfolios to absorb higher-yielding assets. On the other hand, it seems evident that more companies will be induced to acquire relatively more equities and state and local government securities; otherwise the net cost of insurance to policyholders would probably rise appreciably and seriously impair the companies' competitive position.

Policy reserves accumulated by life insurance companies more than doubled between 1945 and 1959, representing an annual increase of 6.6 percent. As explained more fully in Section IV of this chapter, these reserves constitute the main source of investible funds controlled by these institutions and have given them a premier position in several sectors of the capital market. However, the annual rate of growth in reserves began to slow down in the 1950's, and this has serious implications for their future investment activities. Total assets of the life insurance companies registered an increase of more than 140 percent between 1945 and 1959, a rate of increase somewhat faster than that experienced by reserves. The differential growth rate primarily reflected the accumulation of surplus funds, but the expansion of nonfinancial assets and fluctuations in market prices or other valuations of securities also played a part.

Because reserves originate through the insurance side of the companies' operations—and are the main source of their investible funds—they constitute the common frontier between the life insurance industry and the capital market. The nature of this relation is discussed more fully in Section IV. In Section III, the link between the rate of return on invested assets and the net cost of life insurance is examined.

Section III
Investment Earnings and Net Cost of Insurance

Life insurance is sold primarily on a net cost basis. Policyholders expect, and usually receive, dividends which reduce the gross premiums.[3] Interest earned on invested reserves is one of the chief sources of funds used to pay dividends, and the higher the yield the lower the cost of insurance.

Because of technical difficulties, it is not possible to obtain information directly of the effects on insurance cost of variations in investment yields. The main obstacle arises from the numerous changes in actuarial assumptions that have been used at various times in life insurance accounting. Yet, certain general statements can be made about the impact of investment yields on net cost. It is evident that this effect is especially important with respect to those types of insurance (such as endowment policies) which have a high reserve in relation to the face value of the policy. At the opposite extreme, interest earnings are of little significance in the net cost of term insurance which carries virtually no reserve. Ordinary policies stand in an intermediate position between endowment and term plans. Under all plans, however, interest is a more important influence on cost when the protection is paid for in advance by a single premium than when level annual premiums are used, since such payments create a relatively large fund on which interest can accumulate.

An idea of the relation of investment yields to cost of insurance can be obtained indirectly through the following means: (1) the dividends that could have been paid if invested assets had yielded a higher rate of return than that actually achieved can be estimated, (2) the effects of changes in the rate of return on the respective costs of endowment and ordinary policies can be compared, and (3) the net cost of a particular type of insurance can be estimated on the basis of an elementary statistical analysis. The results of these three explorations indicate that an increase of one percent (i.e., from 3 to 4 percent) in the average yield earned by a life insurance company would generally make possible a reduction of about 10 percent in the net cost of ordinary policies and would permit an even greater decrease in the cost of endowment insurance. Each of the above approaches will now be illustrated.

If interest rates in the postwar period had been as high as those prevailing just prior to the depression of the 1930's, earnings of life insurance companies would have run between two-fifths and three-fifths above what they actually averaged. As a first approximation, it seems reasonable to suppose that all the additional income would have been reflected either in larger dividends to policyholders or lower gross premiums. In either case, the net cost of insurance would probably have been reduced by almost as much as the increase in investment earnings.

This prospect is illustrated in the computation shown in Table II-2. The net cost of insurance in 1949 would have been 18 percent lower than it actually was in that year if the twenty companies studied had been able to invest their assets at the average yield prevailing in 1930. By 1956, the net cost would have been reduced by 15 percent if assets had earned the 1930 rate. The slightly smaller potential decrease in the latter year

TABLE II-2

NET RATE OF INTEREST EARNED ON INVESTED FUNDS
AND THE NET COST OF INSURANCE TO POLICYHOLDERS
EXPERIENCE OF TWENTY COMPANIES, 1949 AND 1956
(In Millions of Dollars)

	1949	1956
Gross Premiums	5,280	7,726
Policy Dividends	615	1,194
Aggregate Net Cost	4,665	6,532
Net Investment Income:		
Assume 1930 rate (4.81 percent) were applied to assets held in 1949 and 1956	2,152	3,254
Actual at 1949 rate (2.98 percent) and at 1956 rate (3.33 percent)	1,331	2,253
Potential Increase in Dividends:		
Assume return to 1930 rate	821	1,001
Potential Increase in Dividends as Percent of Net Cost of Insurance	17.6	15.3
Actual Increase in Dividends:		
Corresponding to improvement in yield, 1949-1956	—	237
Actual Increase in Dividends as Percent of Net Cost of Insurance, 1949-1956	—	3.6

SOURCE: Data for 1949 are from a report by the Life Insurance Association of America in support of proposed amendments to Article 5, Section 81, of the New York Insurance Law, submitted to the Joint Legislative Committee on Insurance Rates and Regulations of New York State, January 30, 1951. Data for 1956 were compiled from **Best's Life Insurance Reports, 1957.** In each year, statistics are for the 20 largest companies whose combined assets were 80 percent of the industry total in 1949 and 67 percent in 1956.

reflects the sizable recovery in yields since 1949. This advance in the rate of return between 1949 and 1956 meant that actual earnings on invested assets were boosted by approximately 18 percent, and this in turn enabled the net cost of insurance to be reduced by almost 4 percent.

As already mentioned, variations in the rate of earnings have a bigger impact on the cost of endowment than on the cost of ordinary policies. While such costs are affected by factors other than yield (such as changes in mortality and operating expenses), the rate of return has been the primary source of differences; changes in mortality, expenses, and miscellaneous factors have generally had the same impact on both types of policies. The influence of earnings on the net cost for ordinary and endowment policies is illustrated in Table II-3. These figures show that, for the twenty largest companies discussed above, the net cost of endowment insurance averaged about 10 percent higher in the period 1928-48 than it did in 1908-28. On the other hand, the net cost of ordinary insurance was virtually unchanged, advancing by less than 1 percent. Undoubtedly, the greater rise in the net cost of endowment policies was due primarily to the decline in gross yields on invested reserves, which fell from an average of 5 percent in the earlier period to 4.2 percent in the later years.[4] The net cost of ordinary insurance was held down primarily because there is a considerable time lag between actual mortality improvements and the changes made in life insurance mortality tables from which actuarial rates are computed. These improvements in mortality tended to offset the decline in interest earnings. If yields had continued to average 5 percent, combined with the steady decline in mortality rates, both types of insurance would have shown substantial reductions in net cost.

TABLE II-3

INTEREST RATES AND THE NET COST OF ORDINARY AND ENDOWMENT INSURANCE

Type of Insurance	Average Annual Net Cost (Premium Less Dividend) of a $1,000 Policy Issued at Age 35	
	In Force During	
	1908-28	1928-48
Ordinary	$20.10	$20.24
20-Year Endowment	38.58	42.49

SOURCE: LIAA study cited in the footnote to Table II-2.

The influence of investment earnings on the net cost of insurance has been illustrated further through a statistical regression analysis made by the Life Insurance Association of America and reported as part of their presentation before the New York Joint Legislative Committee on Insurance Rates and Regulations. The analysis presupposes that the net cost varies directly with operating expenses and mortality, and inversely with the rate of return. The study assumed that all gains are returned as policyholders' dividends and no portion is retained in surplus. Also, it was assumed that actual rates of mortality are identical with the rates tabulated in the Commissioner's 1941 Standard Ordinary Table. It was further assumed that, on the average, actual expenses applicable to ordinary policies amounted to $3.65 per $1,000 of insurance. Under these assumptions, the net cost of ordinary insurance issued at age 35 would depend upon the rate of return earned on invested reserves as shown in Table

II-4. These figures indicate that the net cost should be $4.32 less when 5 percent is earned than when 3 percent is the yield obtainable on investments. This reduction in cost amounts to about one-fifth of the cost under the 3 percent assumption. Similarly, net cost would decrease about 10 percent if the rate of return were 4 percent rather than 3 percent. Thus, for an equal change in yield, the percentage reduction in the cost of ordinary life insurance at age 35 is about the same as the estimated average reduction in cost of all kinds of insurance in force in 1949 (as shown above). Reductions in costs of endowment policies would be greater, and reductions in term policies would be less, than the percentage calculated for ordinary insurance using a regression analysis.

TABLE II-4

ESTIMATED NET ANNUAL COST PER $1,000 OF ORDINARY LIFE INSURANCE ISSUED AT AGE 35: REGRESSION ANALYSIS

Assumed Rate of Return on Invested Reserves (Percent)	Net Annual Cost
2.5	$24.15
3.0	22.78
3.5	21.55
4.0	20.45
4.5	19.39
5.0	18.46

SOURCE: LIAA study cited in the footnote to Table II-2.

The actual yield experience of life insurance companies has varied markedly. The highest annual rate of return earned since 1915 was 5.18 percent obtained in 1923. After that year, and especially after 1930, the yield dropped persistently until 1947, when the trough was reached at 2.88 percent. By 1959, the rate of return had climbed to 3.96 percent; while federal income taxes shaved this rate somewhat (figures are not available showing the latest after-tax yields) the gain over 1947 is still appreciable. The decline in the rate of earnings on invested assets from 1923 through 1947, particularly after the early 1930's, was the result of an insufficient demand for investible funds as well as the monetary policy of the federal government which sought to make bank reserves abundant. Actually, however, considerable weakness, from the perspective of the financial investor, was already evident throughout most of the decade of the 1920's. This gradual deterioration in investment outlets centered mainly in farm mortgages and railroad securities, but it was also discernible in other sectors. The situation was aggravated with the onset of the depression, despite the ample supply of bank reserves, since the private demand for capital did not respond to the incentive of extremely low interest rates. Instead, large-scale refunding of corporate securities previously issued at the high yields prevailing in the 1920's led to a greatly augmented supply of funds in the hands of life insurance companies. As a result these institutions found themselves investing, in addition to their newly acquired funds, a swelling inflow of cash arising from the turnover of their existing mortgages and securities.

In addition to the direct adverse effect on interest rates, the relatively small demand for investment funds in the private economy caused the life insurance companies to invest a rising proportion of their assets in United States government bonds, the volume of which was being expanded by deficit financing, thus reducing still more the yield on their funds. The entry of the United States into World War II in 1941 greatly speeded up this process. By the end of the war, almost one-half of the assets held by all life insurance companies was in United States government obligations, and this had depressed the rate of return on their whole portfolio to 3.05 percent. The subsequent decline in 1959 to around 6 percent in the ratio of Governments to total assets, coupled with the enormous demand for capital funds from private sectors of the economy in the postwar period, was largely responsible for the noticeable improvement realized in investment yields.

SECTION IV
ORIGIN AND TREND OF SAVINGS THROUGH LIFE INSURANCE

As a by-product of the demand for life insurance, and because of the widespread use of the level-premium plans in most life contracts, life insurance companies have become some of the most important savings institutions in the American economy. Their position as savings intermediaries rests on the special nature of the level-premium plan used in computing the cost of protection. Ordinary and endowment policies involve considerable savings, but term insurance generates only negligible amounts. Because the probability of death increases with age, the annual cost would soon become prohibitive if the required premium were to rise along with the risk involved—as in the case of term contracts. To counteract this tendency, the level-premium scheme was evolved; in this type of policy the size of the premium remains the same throughout the premium-paying period. Thus, for a given group of insured lives, the death rate is low in the early years of the policy, and the premiums collected are more than sufficient to cover the claims which materialize; the reverse is true as the members of the group advance in age. The surplus in the early stages of the plan is added to reserves and invested so that the accumulated total plus investment earnings will be available to offset the rising burden of claims. The level-premium plan is used for all ordinary and endowment policies (and the rate of savings is even larger for the latter than for the former), but most term policies also assume that a modest amount of reserves will be accumulated.

While most life insurance policies can be viewed as providing a combination of pure protection each year and a systematic savings schedule, the bulk of policyholders probably do not consider their accumulated savings as readily available. Nevertheless, the reserves are a source of liquidity, and policy loans (the borrowing of part of the reserves built up under the policy) have always been used by policyholders. Moreover, most states now have laws requiring life insurance companies to make such loans with ceilings closely approximating the amounts accumulated. Reserves (or virtually all of them) can also be withdrawn if the policy is cancelled. On the whole, however, the vast bulk of savings accumulated through life insurance remains with the companies and constitutes the main source of funds which these institutions invest in the capital market.

The long-run trend of savings and reserves is shown in Chart II-2 and Appendix Table II-2. The origin of savings in reserves is clearly evident. The fact that the savings curve lies slightly above that for reserves is explained primarily through the existence of capital gains (included in savings but excluded from reserves) in the companies' investment portfolios—except for a few years during the depression of the 1930's when the curves were reversed. These savings data represent the net increase in total admitted assets of all United States life insurance companies, less the increase in policy loans and after adjustment for net capital gains and losses.

The statistics tell the following story: Until the 1950's, savings accumulated in life insurance companies just about doubled every decade. For example, between 1899 and 1909, savings rose from $1.5 billion to $3.3 billion, an increase of 120 percent. By 1919 the level stood at $6.2 billion, or 90 percent above that ten years earlier. The decade of the 1920's brought the largest increase (147 percent) for any of the ten-year periods as the amount accumulated advanced to $15.3 billion in 1929. As one would expect, the rate of growth declined somewhat during the depression decade of the 1930's, but even so policyholders boosted their savings in life insurance by 80 percent, lifting the amount to $27.3 billion in 1939. World War II and the years immediately following brought an extremely favorable environment to the life insurance industry, and this was clearly reflected in the expansion of savings in this form. Between 1939 and 1949, the total increased to $57.8 billion, a gain of 112 percent. However, in the decade ending in 1959, the rate of growth in savings through life insurance slackened appreciably. In these years, the accumulated volume advanced to $108.0 billion, or by only 80 percent.

Against this rising trend the short-run variations in the annual additions to accumulated savings are also shown in Chart II-2. From an increase of

CHART II-2
Trend of Savings Through Life Insurance Companies, and Policy Reserves, 1896-1959
(Ratio Scales)

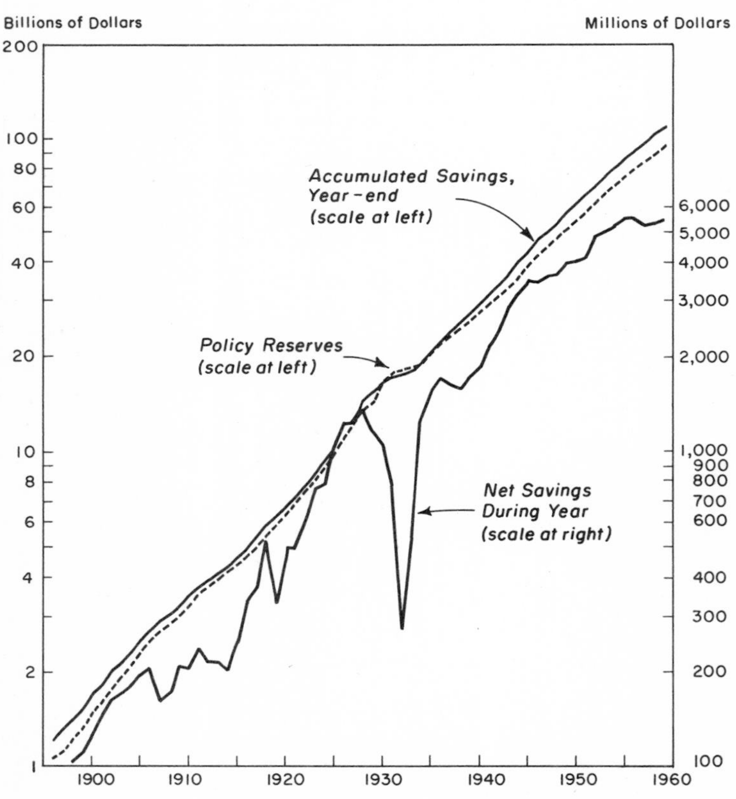

SOURCE: Appendix Table II-2, p. 386.

$83 million in 1897, net savings rose sharply to $206 million in 1906, and the percentage change climbed from 6.7 percent to 8.2 percent. In 1907, both the amount and rate of savings declined, but the previous annual growth was reattained three years later. While the dip was undoubtedly partly attributable to the financial panic of 1907 and the subsequent depression, the adverse publicity of the Armstrong or Hughes investigation of life insurance companies in New York in 1905 may also have contributed to the slower rate of growth. The sluggish performance of the life insurance industry between 1907 and 1914, when viewed in terms of the annual increase of savings, was probably a mirror of the general slowdown of the economy as a whole, because the path of national income over these years displays essentially the same profile. World War I affected the expansion of savings through life insurance in the way one would normally expect. The yearly addition rose from $202 million in 1914 to $519 million in 1918; moreover, the drop to $328 million during the next year was clearly related to the reconversion of the economy from war to peacetime production.

This interruption in the pace of expansion in life insurance savings proved only temporary. Even the depression of 1921, while sharp and severe for the economy as a whole, did no more than slow the rate of growth in this form of savings. In fact, the upsurge of life insurance sales (especially of the ordinary and endowment types which involve large accumulations of reserves) between 1921 and 1928 was so strong that the industry experienced the highest annual growth rates on record; in 1925-28 the rate exceeded 10 percent and actually amounted to 12 percent in 1926. With the onset of the depression, savings through life insurance shrank along with other types of savings. By 1932, when the trough was reached, the annual increase was only $274 million, representing a gain of 1.6 percent. On the other hand, the figure was still positive—in sharp contrast with the absolute shrinkage in the amount of savings accumulated in many other types of institutions. Toward the end of the depression, policyholders not only reduced drawings against accumulated life insurance savings but also began to buy new insurance in increasing volume. By 1935, the annual increase in savings through this medium had surpassed the previous peak set in 1928; while the secondary depression of 1936 again dampened the trend, this was quickly reversed by the economic buoyancy generated by war preparation and subsequently by World War II itself. The annual dollar volume of new savings through life insurance climbed from $1.8 billion in 1940 to $3.4 billion in 1945; over the same period the growth rate advanced from 6.7 percent to 8.7 percent.

From this peak, the rate of growth in savings through life insurance receded steadily to 6.7 percent in 1951; for the next two years the high level of economic activity during the Korean War sparked a revival in the rate of accumulation. Nevertheless, industry observers were gradually beginning to realize that several fundamental changes were occurring in the composition of life insurance savings which adversely affected the rate of savings itself. The emergence of these developments was partly obscured by the recessions of 1953-54 and 1957-58, but their presence was becoming increasingly evident. It is not surprising to observe that each of the first three postwar recessions dampened the rate of growth in savings through life insurance, but contrary to expectations, the subsequent recoveries failed to restore the previous pace of growth. The factors accounting for this relative stagnation in savings in this form are complex and still somewhat obscure. Because the economy as a whole has been slowing down since the early 1950's, it is not unreasonable to attribute part of the lessened vigor in the growth of life insurance savings to the slack in the general economy. On the other hand, several specific developments within the life insurance industry itself seem to have played the major role. It is, of course, difficult to disentangle these influences, but the following factors stand out: (1) there has been a substantial shift to group and term (as opposed to ordinary) insurance policies necessitating a smaller accumulation of reserves; (2) policyholders have been drawing more heavily against the liquidity of their policies as shown in the acceleration of policy loans and the increase in surrender values; (3) partly because of the uptrend in interest rates, beneficiaries have become increasingly reluctant to leave dividends and proceeds of policies on deposit with insurance companies; (4) operating expenses of life insurance companies have risen sharply. All of these developments have dampened the growth of savings through life insurance companies, but at least one of them (the rise in interest rates) has also lifted the companies' net investment income which in turn has stimulated the accumulation of savings through life insurance. A brief summary of the impact of these influences on the rate of savings in this form will now be given. The discussion is based on work done in the Institute of Life Insurance and the Life Insurance Association of America and reported by Kenneth M. Wright.[5]

Before examining the details underlying the decline in the rate of growth of savings through life insurance since the early 1950's, it would be helpful to view the recent changes in historical perspective. Statistics in Table II-5 show the composition of life insurance in force, by type of insurance, in selected years since 1920; also shown are changes in the

TABLE II-5

COMPOSITION OF LIFE INSURANCE IN FORCE, BY TYPE OF INSURANCE, WITH U. S. LIFE INSURANCE COMPANIES, 1920-1958

(In Billions of Dollars)

Amount in Force	1920		1930		1940		1950		1958	
Type of Insurance	Amount	Percent of Total	Amount	Percent of Total	Amount	Percent of Total	Amount	Percent of Total	Amount	Percent of Total
Total in Force	42.3	100.0	107.9	100.0	117.8	100.0	242.1	100.0	521.9	100.0
Ordinary life and endowment[1]	31.0	73.3	72.4	67.1	75.1	63.8	137.0	56.6	246.8	47.3
Industrial	7.2	17.0	18.3	17.0	21.3	18.1	34.4	14.2	40.6	7.8
Ordinary term[2]	2.5	5.9	7.3	6.8	6.0	5.1	18.1	7.5	59.7	11.4
Group[3]	1.6	3.8	9.9	9.1	15.4	13.0	52.6	21.7	174.8	33.5

Changes in the Composition of Life Insurance in Force	1920-30		1930-40		1940-50		1950-58	
Type of Insurance	Amount	Percent of Total	Amount	Percent of Total	Amount	Percent of Total	Amount	Percent of Total
Total in Force	65.6	100.0	9.9	100.0	124.3	100.0	279.8	100.0
Ordinary life and endowment[1]	41.4	63.1	2.7	27.3	61.9	49.8	109.8	39.2
Industrial	11.1	16.9	3.0	30.3	13.1	10.6	6.2	2.2
Ordinary term[2]	4.8	7.3	−1.3	−13.1	12.1	9.7	41.6	14.9
Group[3]	8.3	12.7	5.5	55.5	37.2	29.9	122.2	43.7

1. All ordinary life insurance except term.
2. Includes individual credit life insurance.
3. Includes group credit life insurance.

SOURCE: Institute of Life Insurance.

composition between these years. The most striking feature of this table is the acceleration of the relative shift of consumers' preferences away from ordinary and endowment insurance (involving large reserves) to group policies and term contracts (with relatively small or no reserves). For example, the first type of insurance declined from just under three-quarters of the total in force in 1920 to less than one-half in 1958; moreover, industrial insurance which accounted for almost one-sixth of the total in 1920 declined even more sharply in relation to the face value of all contracts. On the other hand, ordinary term insurance virtually doubled as a proportion of the total volume, and group policies increased nearly tenfold. The same tendencies are shown in the distribution of changes in the composition of life insurance in force. Decade by decade, with the exception of the period covering the World War II years, ordinary and endowment policies have accounted for a declining share of the net increase in life insurance in force. In contrast, ordinary term (excluding the understandable drop during the depression of the 1930's) and group policies mounted steadily over the same period. In fact, the pace of the latter types quickened appreciably during the last decade: while their combined share of the total life insurance in force in 1950 amounted to somewhat less than three-tenths, the proportion had risen to nearly 45 percent by 1958, and represented approximately three-fifths of the net gain in all types of life insurance in the same period.

Data in Table II-6 summarize some of the more specific influences depressing the rate of growth of savings through life insurance companies in recent years. The first thing to note is the substantial change in the structure of premium payments. Because all types of premiums, except those for industrial policies, have grown year by year, a common base is required to enable comparisons over time. For this purpose premiums (and other data in the table) are expressed as a percentage of gross inflow of life insurance funds. It is evident that the gradual but steady decline in premiums as a source of funds is due primarily to the drop in industrial premiums (reflecting the more or less secular decline in this type of insurance), but the slower expansion of ordinary insurance has also been a drag on the inflow of funds. Simultaneously, the shift to group policies has lifted premium receipts of this type, and this factor has partially compensated for the decline in industrial and ordinary premiums. Another way to emphasize the shift is to compare premiums with the net inflow of savings shown in the memorandum at the bottom of Table II-6. In 1952, it required $174 of premiums to generate $100 of net savings; by 1958 the figure had climbed by more than one-quarter to $228.

TABLE II-6

SELECTED ITEMS: GROSS FLOW OF FUNDS THROUGH LIFE INSURANCE COMPANIES, 1952-1958

(In Millions of Dollars)

	1952	1953	1954	1955	1956	1957	1958
Life and Annuity Premiums							
Total (amount)	8,322	8,968	9,448	10,191	10,885	11,649	12,177
Percent of gross inflow	62.0	61.2	60.1	59.8	59.2	58.5	58.2
Ordinary (amount)	5,362	5,747	6,045	6,477	6,961	7,489	7,905
Percent of gross inflow	39.9	39.2	38.4	38.0	37.9	37.6	37.8
Industrial (amount)	1,404	1,467	1,508	1,548	1,571	1,531	1,511
Percent of gross inflow	10.5	10.0	9.6	9.1	8.5	7.7	7.2
Group (amount)	1,556	1,754	1,895	2,166	2,353	2,629	2,761
Percent of gross inflow	11.6	12.0	12.1	12.7	12.8	13.2	13.2
Surrender Values and Policy Loan							
Extensions: Total (amount)	1,150	1,293	1,530	1,591	1,768	2,207	2,465
Percent of gross inflow	8.6	8.8	9.7	9.3	9.6	11.1	11.8
Surrender values (amount)	644	714	869	922	1,024	1,291	1,457
Percent of gross inflow	4.8	4.9	5.5	5.4	5.6	6.5	7.0
Policy loans (amount)	506	579	661	669	744	916	1,008
Percent of gross inflow	3.8	3.9	4.2	3.9	4.0	4.6	4.8
Payments on Supplementary Contracts and Dividends Left on Deposit							
Total (amount)	732	792	846	907	1,000	1,137	1,155
Percent of gross inflow	5.5	5.4	5.4	5.3	5.4	5.7	5.5
Supplementary contracts (amount)	621	666	693	738	808	902	881
Percent of gross inflow	4.6	4.5	4.4	4.3	4.4	4.5	4.2
Disbursement of dividends left on deposit (amount)	111	126	153	169	192	235	274
Percent of gross inflow	0.9	0.9	1.0	1.0	1.0	1.2	1.3

TABLE II-6 (cont.)

	1952	1953	1954	1955	1956	1957	1958
Insurance Commissions, Expenses, Taxes							
Total (amount)	2,265	2,498	2,699	2,932	3,240	3,631	3,864
Percent of gross inflow	16.8	17.0	17.1	17.2	17.6	18.2	18.5
Commissions (amount)	941	1,050	1,102	1,189	1,307	1,446	1,495
Percent of gross inflow	7.0	7.2	7.0	7.0	7.1	7.3	7.1
Expenses (amount)	1,082	1,200	1,328	1,440	1,597	1,820	1,962
Percent of gross inflow	8.0	8.1	8.4	8.4	8.7	9.1	9.4
Taxes, licenses, fees (amount)	242	248	269	303	336	365	407
Percent of gross inflow	1.8	1.7	1.7	1.8	1.8	1.8	2.0
Memorandum:							
Gross inflow	13,422	14,649	15,727	17,051	18,380	19,899	20,937
Gross outflow	8,625	9,649	10,509	11,540	12,811	14,698	15,598
Net savings	4,797	5,000	5,218	5,511	5,569	5,201	5,339
Plus: net increase in policy loans	123	201	213	163	229	350	319
Plus: net capital gains	177	—	522	272	—	—	613
Minus: net capital losses	—	43	—	—	219	253	—
Net increase in total assets	5,097	5,158	5,953	5,946	5,579	5,298	6,271

SOURCE: Computed from Kenneth M. Wright, "Gross Flow of Funds Through Life Insurance Companies," **Journal of Finance,** May 1960, pp. 140-56.

The adverse impact of policyholders' drawings against the savings accumulated in their policies can be easily traced in the trend of surrender values, policy loans, and payments on supplementary contracts and dividends left on deposit with the companies. All of these drains absorbed 14 percent of the gross inflow of life insurance funds in 1952, but the proportion had risen to 17 percent by 1958. While some of the increased outflow was undoubtedly induced by the recessions of 1953-54 and 1957-58, the more general rise throughout the period is also unmistakable. The volume of funds paid out by life insurance companies to policyholders who turn in their policies to obtain the accumulated savings (surrender values) rose from less than 5 percent of gross inflow in 1952 to 7 percent in 1958. Such payments show a strong cyclical pattern, with two-thirds of the total percentage advance during this period occurring in the recession years 1954 and 1957. Apparently many holders of life insurance policies chose to withdraw their savings to finance necessary family expenditures while they were temporarily unemployed. The same profile is mirrored in the statistics for policy loans, and probably for the same reason.

The next category of outflows is of special importance for the present discussion. Many beneficiaries of life insurance policies have historically left the proceeds with the institutions to administer under supplementary contracts. The latter have typically been a net source of funds for the companies. In recent years, however, the contribution of such contracts to net savings through life insurance has been sharply reduced. In fact, one type of supplementary contract has actually produced a net drain. This situation has arisen because beneficiaries have the option of (1) receiving the policy proceeds in terms of a fixed number of payments over a definite number of years, or (2) having the size of the payments adjusted in such a way that the proceeds will be paid out over the expected life of the beneficiary. In the first type of contract, the interest rate employed in determining the size of payments is of crucial importance, and the life expectancy of the beneficiary is the strategic variable in the second type of contract. Since 1952, these different contracts have had a divergent impact on net savings through life insurance. While the agreement involving life contingencies continued to attract funds every year, the other type consistently lost ground. This apparently was due primarily to the fact that many people increasingly considered such deposits with life insurance companies a poor form of investment. As more profitable investment outlets expanded (especially the opportunities afforded in equities), such funds were withdrawn on a large scale. In fact, the outflow of funds under supplementary contracts without life contingencies actually exceeded the inflow in each of the three years 1956-58, although in the last year the size of the drain was somewhat smaller. The disbursement of policy dividends left with life insurance companies (and of interest on such deposits) reflects the same set of factors and has also adversely affected the rate of savings through insurance. By 1958, such payments accounted for 1.3 percent of the gross inflow of funds compared with 0.9 percent in 1952, a relative gain of more than two-fifths.

In addition to the above influences, which are primarily the by-products of recessions and shifts in savings patterns, the accumulation of savings through life insurance has also been eroded by the rising costs of conducting the life insurance business. These costs consist mainly of commissions paid to salesmen, operating expenses, and taxes. The advance in operating expenses is easily understandable in view of the steadily increasing cost of labor and materials in the economy as a whole during the last decade. Moreover, the heavier burden of taxes is also basically a reflection of the general tendency for state and local governments to collect larger fees for licenses and to impose larger business taxes. On the other hand, the impact of federal income taxes was about the same during this period; as already mentioned, the amendment to the internal revenue code resulting in substantially higher federal taxes was adopted in 1959. Higher commissions, however, did make a much bigger dent in the inflow of funds. These rose sharply in 1957, and the increase seems to have been related to stepped-up sales of "family-plan" types of policies under which salesmen received a somewhat larger share of the initial premium.

From the above discussion, it is evident that in recent years the rate of savings through life insurance has been adversely affected by factors internal to the industry as well as by developments in the economy as a whole. But on balance, the result has been a significant lag, relative to other institutions, in the mobilization of savings by these companies. Nevertheless, life insurance companies remain a dominant force in certain sectors of the capital market. The contours of their competitive position are outlined in Section V.

Section V
Competition in the Mobilization and Investment of Savings

The relative decline in the rate of savings through life insurance companies has somewhat weakened their competitive position in the mobilization of savings. This deterioration, however, has been far less than that experienced by commercial and mutual savings banks; on the other hand, life insurance companies have fallen short of the growth rates achieved by noninsured corporate pension funds and savings and loan associations.

The changing status of the major savings institutions during the postwar period is shown in Table II-7. These intermediaries serve as mobilizers of savings and as depositaries for the public's surplus funds; they also transfer these financial resources into particular sectors of the capital market in whose securities they specialize. In this context, the time deposits (but not the demand deposits) of commercial banks are included, because they are an approximate indication of the savings part of their business.

TABLE II-7

ASSETS OF LEADING SAVINGS INSTITUTIONS
IN THE UNITED STATES, 1945 AND 1959
(In Billions of Dollars)

	1945		1959		Distribution of Change: 1945-59	
Type of Institution	Amount	Percent of Total	Amount	Percent of Total	Amount	Percent of Total
Life Insurance Companies	44.8	43.2	113.7	36.6	68.9	33.2
Savings and Loan Associations	8.7	8.4	63.5	20.4	54.8	26.5
Noninsured Corporate Pension Funds	2.9	2.8	25.3	8.1	22.4	10.8
Credit Unions	0.1	0.1	3.3	1.1	3.2	1.5
Commercial Banks: Time Deposits	30.2	29.1	66.2	21.3	36.0	17.4
Mutual Savings Banks	17.0	16.4	38.9	12.5	21.9	10.6
Total	103.7	100.0	310.9	100.0	207.2	100.0

SOURCE: **Life Insurance Fact Book; Savings and Loan Fact Book**; Securities and Exchange Commission; **Federal Reserve Bulletin.**

These data show that life insurance companies have lagged in the relative growth of the major savings institutions. They had slightly more than two-fifths of the total assets of the group in 1945, but this proportion was 37 percent in 1959. Moreover, they accounted for only one-third of the net expansion during these years in the total assets held by the six types of financial institutions. While some of the newer life insurance companies (especially those organized on the basis of stock ownership rather than as mutual companies) have registered growth rates exceeding those achieved by pension funds, the industry as a whole has lost ground relatively. This comparative lag holds serious implications for the capital market because life insurance companies are the only major savings institutions able to invest in a wide range of financial instruments. While savings and loan associations specialize in mortgages, and pension funds absorb an increasing proportion of the new corporate bonds and stocks, life insurance companies stand astride virtually all of the markets for long-term debt and are also making some gains in the market for equity capital. Because of their combined size and strategic position, when they enter a particular sector of the capital market, the availability of funds in that sector expands enormously; the reverse also holds.

Perhaps the strongest competitors of life insurance companies in the postwar period have been the savings and loan associations. Since the end of World War II, these institutions have made an impressive recovery from the severe damage done by the depression of the 1930's. For example, during the years 1933-39, more than one-third of the savings and loan associations collapsed with accumulated losses of $179 million; moreover, those which continued to operate suffered losses of $373 million. Thus, the combined losses amounted to over $550 million, about one-twelfth of the total assets of all associations at the end of 1932. While savings and loan associations as a group began to revive during the war years, phenomenal strides were made after 1945. At the end of the war, they had only 8 percent of the assets owned by savings institutions; the proportion had climbed to one-fifth by 1959, and the net increase in their holdings accounted for about one-quarter of the total expansion. These associations mobilize savings through the issuance of shares which are technically not convertible into cash on demand. While the actual rate of withdrawal of savings may be rather high at times, the associations have generally experienced a sustained and sizable inflow. Thus, they are ideal long-term lenders. Partly because of their historic origin in the home-building industry, but also because of the high rates of return, they have concentrated on supplying funds to the mortgage market. It is in this area that they have posed stiff competition for life insurance companies.

Noninsured corporate pension funds have also grown at a phenomenal rate during the last decade, and by 1959 their $25.3 billion of assets represented 8 percent of the total. The institutions shown in Table II-7 do not account for all pension plans in existence on the dates indicated. The federal and state governments, as well as many local units, maintain pension systems. The civil service retirement system, the Social Security system, and railroad retirement systems are examples at the federal level. These trust funds, which are managed by the United States Treasury Department, are absorbing an increasing share of the public debt which is their sole investment outlet. State and local employees' pension plans have also traditionally invested mainly in government securities, but they are beginning to branch out into areas such as mortgages and housing projects. At the end of 1959, major pension and retirement programs in the United States had accumulated about $95.5 billion of assets, of which $44.7 billion (or 47 percent) represented private retirement funds. The private plans were further divided into those insured with life insurance companies and the noninsured plans managed by trustees (among which banks and trust companies predominate). Insured pension reserves accounted for about $17.5 billion of the assets held by life insurance companies in 1959. These funds are commingled with the companies' other resources and invested under the same restrictions which regulate their overall investment activities.

This latter situation has resulted in a number of complaints by life insurance companies that they are at a disadvantage in the competition with banks and trust companies for corporate pension business. Trustees of noninsured pension plans can invest the accumulated funds under the same regulations which govern ordinary trusts. This latitude has enabled them to solicit new business on the promise of higher earnings to be derived from the ownership of corporate stocks and bonds—and especially common stocks. However, the Life Insurance Company Income Tax Act of 1959 made possible lower premium rates and higher interest guarantees, and this change has reduced the competitive disadvantage under which insured pension plans had previously operated.

The $25.3 billion of assets held by corporate pension plans in 1959 accounted for 93 percent of total noninsured pension funds. Moreover, the growth of their holdings in the postwar years represented about 11 percent of the total expansion in the assets of savings institutions—although they owned less than 3 percent of the amount outstanding in 1945. The chief mechanism underlying this meteoric advance was the inclusion of pensions as a target in collective bargaining by trade unions following a National Labor Relations Board ruling in 1949. Subsequently, in addition to bargaining for wages, hours, and working conditions, trade union officials began to press for pension rights along with other types of fringe benefits. While the rate of growth in pension fund assets has been slackening somewhat in recent years, the outlook is for considerable further expansion. Many unions failed to win pension plans in the 1950's, but toward the end of the decade they were returning to the issue. Furthermore, many corporations are granting pensions on a voluntary basis. While the change in the income tax law mentioned above will allow life insurance companies to garner a greater share of the new pension business, they will continue to encounter vigorous competition from non-insured plans in both the mobilization and investment of savings in this form.

The postwar expansion of credit unions is striking, but this has had little effect on life insurance companies. At the end of 1959, they owned about 1 percent of the total assets held by the leading savings institutions, compared with only one-tenth of 1 percent in 1945. Credit unions, which are a major source of consumer credit, are of some importance in local areas and frequently reduce some of the market traditionally enjoyed by small loan companies and more recently by commercial banks.

The remaining institutions shown in Table II-7 have lagged considerably behind the rest, and this has probably eased somewhat the investment problem of life insurance companies. Commercial and mutual savings banks have both fallen behind in the competitive race for savings in the postwar period. Commercial banks' time deposits represented 29 percent of the total assets of savings intermediaries at the end of World War II, reflecting their absorption of a sizable share of the large volume of savings during the war itself. By the end of 1959, however, their stake in the total had shrunk to just over one-fifth. They registered the smallest percentage gain among the types of institutions shown and accounted for only 17 percent of the net increase in the combined assets. This relative stagnation can be attributed to legal restrictions on investment activities as well as to limitations on the area in which they can do business. Aside from the severe restraints which virtually close off many investment outlets for the banks, the vast majority of them are also subject to ceilings on the interest rates they can pay to attract savings. Because practically all the banks are insured with the Federal Deposit Insurance Corporation, the maximum rate they can offer on savings deposits is 4 percent.[6] Savings and loan associations, the banks' leading competitors in mobilizing savings, have no ceilings. They can offer whatever rate their earnings enable them to sustain, and this gives them a considerable advantage over the banks. In addition, limitations on branch banking in most states have pinned commercial banks within the limits of the central city in virtually all the metropolitan areas. This inability to penetrate into the suburbs, where the fastest rates of population growth are ocurring, has seriously hampered large commercial banks in their efforts to tap the expanding volume of savings. In many cases this situation has produced a haven for savings and loan associations. From the point of view of life insurance companies, the lessened role of commercial banks in gathering time deposits has meant that the banks have offered less competition in the mortgage market, because many banks use their time deposit liabilities as a rough guide to the amount of real estate mortgages they can acquire.

Mutual savings banks have also fallen behind relative to other institutions in the postwar years. They had more than twice as many assets in 1959 as in 1945, but they accounted for only 13 percent of the total at the later date compared with 16 percent at the earlier one. They also accounted for just 11 percent of the net expansion in total assets of the group. These institutions have suffered from their concentration in New England and the Middle Atlantic states where the rate of economic growth has been considerably below that for the rest of the country. Nevertheless, the absolute volume of savings in their home territories has traditionally been large and is continuing to grow. Furthermore, many of the mutual savings banks have begun to emphasize both mortgages and corporate bonds more heavily, and this shift in investment policy has brought them into sharper competition with life insurance companies.

From this discussion, it is evident that life insurance companies have come under strong pressure in the postwar period—not only because of the decline in the rate of savings through life insurance—but also because of the more intensive competition among financial institutions for investment outlets.

The impact of this competition, as well as other factors, on the redistribution of financial assets among life insurance companies and other types of financial intermediaries since the end of World War II is clearly outlined in Tables II-8, II-9, II-10. In examining these figures, one can also detect the main contours of life insurance companies' investment policies in the postwar period.

The outstanding feature of these tables is the decline of overall liquidity of financial assets resulting from the enormous expansion of long-term private debt since 1945. While cash and United States government securities (the chief sources of liquidity) constituted three-fifths of all financial assets in 1945, the ratio had shrunk to one-third by 1959. Simultaneously, the share of corporate bonds and real estate mortgages almost doubled, rising from 9 percent to 17 percent; other loans to the private sector (especially loans to businesses and consumers) also increased sharply in relation to the total volume of financial assets. These marked swings in the structure of financial assets—generated by the shifting demand for loanable funds—created favorable investment opportunities for some lending institutions and disadvantages for others. As a rule, the major financial intermediaries shown in the tables attempt to cover their principal liabilities with assets of comparable liquidity and maturity Thus, the growth of long-term private debt relative to other types of

TABLE II-8

OWNERSHIP OF SELECTED FINANCIAL ASSETS IN THE UNITED STATES, 1945 AND 1959

(In Billions of Dollars)

Institutions	Total Financial Assets		Currency and Deposits[1]		U.S. Government Securities		State and Local Government Securities		Corporate and Foreign Bonds		Real Estate Mortgages		Corporate Stocks[2]		Other Financial Assets[3]	
	1945	1959	1945	1959	1945	1959	1945	1959	1945	1959	1945	1959	1945	1959	1945	1959
Federal Reserve Banks	45.1	53.6	20.5	20.1	24.3	26.6	—	—	—	—	—	—	—	—	0.3	6.9
Commercial Banks	159.3	240.8	34.8	49.5	90.6	59.8	4.0	17.0	3.0	1.2	4.8	28.1	0.3	—	21.8	85.2
Mutual Savings Banks	16.9	38.4	0.6	0.8	10.7	6.8	0.1	0.7	1.0	3.6	4.2	25.0	0.2	0.8	0.1	0.7
Life Insurance Companies	43.9	110.0	0.8	1.3	20.6	6.9	0.7	3.2	11.2	46.7	6.6	39.2	1.0	4.6	3.0	8.1
Savings and Loan Associations	8.5	62.6	0.5	2.2	2.4	4.5	—	—	—	—	5.4	53.1	—	—	0.2	2.8
Corporate Pension Funds	2.9	25.3	0.1	0.4	1.3	2.1	—	—	1.0	12.8	—	0.6	0.3	8.5	0.2	0.9
Other Insurance Companies	7.9	29.0	0.6	1.8	4.0	5.4	0.6	7.2	0.2	3.1	0.2	1.0	2.2	9.4	0.1	1.1
Other Financial Institutions[4]	9.9	49.4	1.6	3.1	3.1	2.1	0.4	0.3	0.4	1.8	0.1	1.7	1.3	14.5	2.7	25.9
Total Above Financial Institutions	294.4	609.1	59.5	79.2	157.3	114.2	5.8	28.4	16.8	69.2	21.3	148.7	5.3	37.8	28.4	131.6
All Other Holders	389.5	1,025.2	119.5	216.5	95.6	127.3	13.7	35.3	9.7	16.1	14.2	42.3	113.7	417.2	23.1	170.4
Total Financial Assets	683.9	1,634.3	179.0	295.7	252.9	241.5	19.5	63.7	26.5	85.3	35.5	191.0	119.0	455.0	51.5	302.0

Note: Figures are rounded and may not add to totals shown.

1. Includes gold certificates and member bank reserves held by Federal Reserve Banks and interbank deposits.

2. Stock at market value.

3. Includes consumer credit, security credit, other bank loans to business, and trade credit.

4. Finance companies, open-end investment companies, security brokers and dealers, banks in U. S. Territories and possessions and U. S. agencies of foreign banks.

SOURCE: Compiled from **Federal Reserve Bulletin; Life Insurance Fact Book**; Securities and Exchange Commission, "Corporate Pension Funds, 1959"; **Savings and Loan Fact Book;** Raymond W. Goldsmith, **Financial Intermediaries in the American Economy Since 1900** (Princeton: Princeton University Press, 1958), Appendix A.

TABLE II-9

OWNERSHIP OF SELECTED FINANCIAL ASSETS IN THE UNITED STATES, 1945 AND 1959

(Percentage Distribution)

Institutions	Total Financial Assets		Currency and Deposits		U.S. Government Securities		State and Local Government Securities		Corporate and Foreign Banks		Real Estate Mortgages		Corporate Stocks		Other Financial Assets	
	1945	1959	1945	1959	1945	1959	1945	1959	1945	1959	1945	1959	1945	1959	1945	1959
Federal Reserve Banks	6.6	3.3	11.5	6.8	9.6	11.0	—	—	—	—	—	—	—	—	0.6	2.3
Commercial Banks	23.3	14.7	19.4	16.7	35.8	24.8	20.5	26.7	11.3	1.4	13.5	14.7	0.3	—	42.3	28.2
Mutual Savings Banks	2.5	2.3	0.3	0.3	4.3	2.8	0.5	1.1	3.8	4.2	11.8	13.1	0.2	0.2	0.2	0.2
Life Insurance Companies	6.5	6.7	0.4	0.4	8.2	2.9	3.6	5.0	42.3	54.8	18.6	20.6	0.8	1.0	5.8	2.7
Savings and Loan Associations	1.2	3.8	0.3	0.7	0.9	1.9	—	—	—	—	15.2	27.8	—	—	0.4	0.9
Corporate Pension Funds	0.4	1.5	0.1	0.1	0.5	0.9	—	—	3.8	15.0	—	0.3	0.3	1.9	0.4	0.3
Other Insurance Companies	1.2	1.8	0.3	0.6	1.6	2.3	3.1	11.3	0.8	3.6	0.6	0.5	1.8	2.1	0.2	0.4
Other Financial Institutions	1.4	3.0	0.9	1.0	1.3	0.9	2.1	0.5	1.6	2.1	0.3	0.9	1.1	3.2	5.2	8.6
Total above Financial Institutions	43.1	37.1	33.2	26.6	62.2	47.3	29.8	44.6	63.4	81.1	60.0	77.9	4.5	8.4	55.1	43.6
All Other Holders	56.9	62.9	66.8	73.4	37.8	52.7	70.2	55.4	36.6	18.9	40.0	22.1	95.5	91.6	44.9	56.4
Total Financial Assets	100.0	100.0	100.0	100.0	100.0	100.0	100.0	100.0	100.0	100.0	100.0	100.0	100.0	100.0	100.0	100.0

SOURCE: Table II-8.

TABLE II-10

PERCENTAGE DISTRIBUTION OF SELECTED TYPES OF ASSETS IN THE PORTFOLIOS OF LEADING FINANCIAL INSTITUTIONS, 1945 AND 1959

Type of Asset	Life Insurance Companies		Commercial Banks		Mutual Savings Banks		Savings and Loan Assoc.		Corporate Pension Funds		Other Insurance Companies		Other Financial Institutions		Total Financial Institutions		All Other Holders		Total Financial Assets	
	1945	1959	1945	1959	1945	1959	1945	1959	1945	1959	1945	1959	1945	1959	1945	1959	1945	1959	1945	1959
Cash	1.8	1.2	21.8	20.6	3.5	2.1	5.9	3.5	3.4	1.6	7.6	6.2	16.2	6.3	20.2	13.0	30.7	21.1	26.2	18.1
U.S. Government Securities	46.9	6.3	56.9	24.8	63.3	17.7	28.2	7.2	44.8	8.3	50.6	18.6	34.4	4.3	53.4	18.8	24.6	12.4	37.0	14.8
State and Local Government Securities	1.6	2.9	2.5	7.1	0.6	1.8	—	—	—	—	7.6	24.8	4.0	0.6	2.0	4.7	3.5	3.4	2.9	3.9
Corporate and Foreign Bonds	25.5	42.5	1.9	0.5	5.9	9.4	—	—	34.5	50.6	2.5	10.7	4.0	3.6	5.7	11.4	2.5	1.6	3.9	5.2
Real Estate Mortgages	15.0	35.6	3.0	11.7	24.9	65.1	63.6	84.9	—	2.4	2.5	3.4	1.0	3.4	7.2	24.4	3.6	4.1	5.2	11.7
Corporate Stocks	2.3	4.2	0.2	—	1.2	2.1	—	—	10.4	33.6	27.9	32.4	13.1	29.4	1.8	6.2	29.2	40.7	17.4	27.8
Other Financial Assets	6.9	7.3	13.7	35.3	0.6	1.8	2.3	4.4	6.9	3.5	1.3	3.9	27.3	52.4	9.7	21.5	5.9	16.7	7.4	18.5
Total Financial Assets	100.0	100.0	100.0	100.0	100.0	100.0	100.0	100.0	100.0	100.0	100.0	100.0	100.0	100.0	100.0	100.0	100.0	100.0	100.0	100.0

SOURCE: Table II-8.

financial assets enhanced the role of long-term lenders, among which life insurance companies occupy a premier position.

These expanding investment opportunities not only provided an outlet for the new savings accumulating in these institutions but also allowed them to liquidate the low-yielding United States government securities which represented such a large proportion of the assets of all financial intermediaries at the end of the war. Life insurance companies led all other institutions in the replacement of United States government issues with private issues. For example, in 1945 their holdings of $21 billion of Governments amounted to 47 percent of their total financial assets, but during the next 14 years they disposed of about two-thirds of these obligations. Thus, by 1959 they owned only $7 billion of United States government debt, which represented just 6 percent of their total portfolio. Among commercial and mutual savings banks, which have a much greater need for liquidity, about one-third of the Governments held at the end of the war had been liquidated by 1959. On the other hand, savings and loan associations, corporate pension funds, and other insurance companies all added to their holdings of Governments in the postwar years. Their net investment in Governments seems to have been primarily for liquidity purposes, because in relation to their total financial assets such holdings also declined drastically. While life insurance companies disposed of such a substantial proportion of their Governments over the postwar period, the rate of liquidation varied greatly; net sales were large when the demand for funds by corporations and home builders was heavy, and tended to slacken during recessions. Within the framework of the business cycle, however, as interest rates advanced in response to rising prosperity, the pace of liquidation was reduced somewhat. Toward the end of the period, moreover, life insurance companies actually turned into net investors in Governments. This development was partly attributable to the impact of the 1957-58 recession (when alternative private outlets were either shrinking or expanding more slowly); it was also partly due to the fact that many institutions apparently felt their government holdings had reached the minimum required for liquidity purposes and built up such holdings as their total assets increased.

Life insurance companies' greatest relative gains centered in corporate bonds. These issues rose from one-quarter to over two-fifths of their total investment portfolio between 1945 and 1959, and the companies' share of the outstanding corporate bonds climbed from 42 percent to 55 percent. While corporate pension funds in the last half of the 1950's became strong competitors in the corporate bond market, life insurance companies enjoyed such a dominant position that they still were able to acquire more than three-fifths of the new issues. Their virtual hegemony in this part of the capital market rests on the considerable advantage they hold in the direct or private placement of corporate issues. After 1951 they concentrated increasingly on industrial and miscellaneous bonds, and they acquired roughly four-fifths of such bond holdings through direct placement.

While life insurance companies as a group showed an overwhelming preference for corporate bonds over real estate mortgages, the rapidly expanding volume of new savings through insurance in the early postwar years enabled them to take up a rising share of corporate issues and still participate in the mortgage market. As mentioned above, these new savings were also frequently supplemented by proceeds from sales of government bonds. However, the unpegging of the government securities market in the spring of 1951 and the reappearance of sizable potential capital losses seriously weakened the incentive to sell Governments. Thus, the slower rate of savings and the fear of capital losses apparently induced many investment managers to be more selective in the types of assets they would acquire. While institutions as a whole continued to purchase mortgages on a large scale, there was an unmistakable shift in favor of corporate bonds. For example, over the 14 years ending in 1959, life insurance companies lifted their share of the outstanding mortgage debt by only 2 percentage points (from 19 percent to 21 percent); in contrast, their share of outstanding corporate bonds advanced by 13 percentage points (from 42 percent to 55 percent). Some of their failure to garner a more sizable piece of the mortgage market may be attributed to the squeeze exerted by other investors, especially savings and loan associations whose portion of the market soared from 15 percent to 28 percent. Commercial and mutual savings banks, corporate pension funds, and other financial institutions also registered modest gains in the mortgage market. While some of the greater absorption of mortgages by all these institutions was at the expense of nonfinancial holders, there is no doubt that the competition among institutions became more stringent each year, and this was a serious bind on the ability of life insurance companies to carve out a larger section of the market. Nevertheless, the suggestion that the companies developed a strong preference for corporate bonds over mortgages still seems to be supported by the acute change in the composition of their investment portfolio. Moreover, the spectacular advances in their mortgage acquisitions (particularly the acquisitions of federally-underwritten loans) occurred during periods of recessions when the corporate demand for funds was restricted.

During the postwar period, life insurance companies made modest gains in the market for equity capital, and the corporate stocks owned by them rose from 0.8 percent to 1.8 percent of the total outstanding. Part of this rise in their holdings (as in the value of the amount outstanding) reflected higher stock prices, but there undoubtedly was some net expansion after allowing for price changes. The liberalization of investment laws in 1951 and 1957 in New York State (whose regulations govern the disposition of about 90 percent of all life insurance assets) provided somewhat greater scope to life insurance companies to participate in the stock market, but the advantages of the less restrictive provisions have been exploited by relatively few institutions. When these companies have entered the stock market, they have concentrated on high grade issues of the most secure corporations, and in pursuing these they have encountered stiff competition from corporate pension funds. For instance, from holding only 0.3 percent of total corporate stocks in 1945, pension funds raised their proportion to 1.9 percent by 1959—nearly twice the share held by life insurance companies. Other financial institutions (notably mutual funds) also entered the stock market on a comprehensive scale in the postwar period; by 1959 they held 3.2 percent of corporate stocks measured by value, which was about three times the percentage in 1945. Nevertheless, individuals and personal trusts remained the dominant forces in the stock market.

Between 1945 and 1959, life insurance companies expanded their holdings from about 3.6 percent to 5 percent of the outstanding long-term debt of state and local governments in the United States. These securities also rose from 1.6 percent to 2.9 percent of the companies' financial assets. Still, unlike rich individuals, banks, and other investors subject to high federal income tax rates, life insurance companies see little advantage in owning tax-exempt securities. As discussed above, prior to the amendment of the Internal Revenue Code in 1959, these companies paid federal income taxes equal to approximately 8 percent of their investment income; in the future this rate may average 12 percent. While the heavier burden of income taxation may induce some life insurance companies (especially stock companies) to build up their ownership of state and local securities, it is most unlikely that any significant number of institutions will swarm into the municipal bond market. The ownership of state and local issues by life insurance companies is centered in revenue bonds rather than general obligations. The rate of return on revenue bonds, even before income tax exemption is considered, is frequently close to that on corporate issues. Moreover, the problems of investment appraisal are similar to those involved in corporate bond analysis, and many of the large companies can use the same facilities to handle the acquisition of both types of securities.

From the foregoing survey, it is easy to identify those sections of the capital market which provide the chief outlets for life insurance companies' investible funds. These are the markets for corporate bonds and real estate mortgages which together account for nearly four-fifths of their financial assets. The United States government securities market is also important because it serves as a residual source or use of funds and, in addition, provides the means to satisfy the relatively small liquidity requirements of these institutions. The markets for state and local government obligations and for corporate stocks are also of limited and specialized interest to them. Consequently, the investment activities of life insurance companies since World War II in these five sub-sectors of the capital market are the main focus of this study.

Footnotes

1. Unless otherwise indicated, life insurance statistics in this section are from the Institute of Life Insurance, *1960 Life Insurance Fact Book*.
2. *Ibid.*, pp. 14-15.
3. Dividends are paid by mutual companies; however, the rates charged by stock companies are virtually the same as the net premium charged by mutual companies.
4. These percentages are averages of gross yields of 100 companies for the years 1909-28 and 1929-48, respectively, as reported in *Spectator Insurance Year Books*.
5. Kenneth M. Wright, "Gross Flow of Funds Through Life Insurance Companies," *Journal of Finance*, May, 1960, pp. 140-56.
6. Until December, 1961, the maximum rate was 3 percent; this became effective January 1, 1957.

CHAPTER III

Legal and Organizational Framework of Life Insurance Investment

SECTION I
INTRODUCTION

The regulation of a life insurance company's investment policies is exclusively the responsibility of the state in which the company is domiciled. All of the states and the District of Columbia have adopted legislation in this area. State laws vary widely in detail, but they are generally aimed at two main objectives: (1) to insure safety of policyholders' reserves and (2) to guarantee diversification in the investment portfolio. To achieve the first purpose, most of the laws establish criteria (exemplified in types of assets authorized and earnings requirements) which life insurance companies must follow in selecting investment outlets. The second objective is sought in the specification of ceilings on the amount or proportion of total assets or capital and/or surplus which each institution can invest in a particular type of asset or in individual issues. Different states stress one or the other of these targets, and the latitude permitted in some instances is wide. Nevertheless, a remarkably uniform set of standards has been achieved despite the multiplicity of regulatory jurisdictions. The National Association of Insurance Commissioners has been mainly responsible for the coordination which has made this possible. Its activities are discussed further below.

The regulation of life insurance companies has historically been a state matter. The United States Supreme Court in 1868 adopted the position that insurance was not "commerce" and therefore not subject to federal government regulation under the interstate commerce clause of the

United States Constitution.[1] However, in June, 1944, the Court reversed its earlier stand and thus opened the way for Congress to establish machinery for federal supervision of the insurance business. The decision caused much anxiety in the industry, and spokesmen for its various branches immediately appealed to Congress to block the entry of the federal government into competition with the states in the regulation of insurance. Congress responded with the passage of Public Law 15, 79th Congress, which took effect on March 9, 1945. The relevant sections of the act held in part:

> The Congress hereby declares that the continued regulation and taxation by the several States of the business of insurance is in the public interest, and that silence on the part of Congress shall not be construed to impose any barrier to the regulation or taxation of such business by the several States. . . . Sec. 2 (a) That the business of insurance, and every person engaged therein, shall be subject to the laws of the several States which relate to the regulation or taxation of such business. (But no Act of Congress shall be construed to invalidate, impair, or supersede any law enacted by any state for the purpose of regulating the business of insurance, or which imposes a fee or tax upon such business, unless such Act specifically relates to the business of insurance. . . .)

This act restored the status quo before the Supreme Court decision, and there the issue remained until 1959. In that year, the Court again had to resolve the conflict of federal and state efforts to regulate the life insurance industry. The latest decision was prompted by the proposal of several companies to sell variable annuity contracts based on reserves invested primarily in common stocks. The United States Securities and Exchange Commission argued that such a contract involved the sale of securities and was therefore subject to federal regulation. The companies concerned challenged this ruling, and the matter was eventually carried to the Supreme Court. The nature of this conflict and its resolution are discussed more fully in Section IV of this chapter.

The machinery employed to regulate the insurance industry is similar in most states. An official (usually titled Superintendent, Commissioner, or Director of Insurance) heads a department charged with the administration of the insurance laws. States with a large number of domestic companies (e.g., those with their legal head offices within the state) frequently establish a separate department while others may include insurance regulation in a department encompassing banking and other financial institutions. A state's insurance department is primarily responsible for the regulation of its domestic companies, but it also has authority over those domiciled elsewhere but licensed to carry on business within the state. In addition to licensing companies, the insurance department also makes periodic examinations of their affairs. In most cases, the examination is triennial, although more frequent reviews may be made under some circumstances.

The examination rests on an annual financial statement submitted by each company not only to the insurance department of its home state but also to other states in which it is authorized to write insurance. The statement shows in considerable detail the accounts relating to the company's underwriting business and its investment activities. For instance, the investment schedules include a listing of each security or other asset acquired or disposed of during the year and provide a detailed description of each security held at the end of the year. The amount and type of information given for each asset is basically the same in virtually all states.

This high degree of uniformity is achieved through the use of a standard reporting blank recommended by the National Association of Insurance Commissioners. This organization has also been primarily responsible for many other unifying features of the regulatory process among the various states. For example, the association's staff frequently drafts model insurance legislation and assists in the preparation of policy statements which in many cases become the basis of insurance department rulings in a number of states. The association, which was launched in 1871, is a voluntary organization of state insurance commissioners and has no legal status. Nevertheless, because all states are represented in its membership, it provides a national forum in which to consider common problems arising in the regulatory process. While the association generally meets at least twice each year, much of its work is done through standing committees, among which two are of major importance from the viewpoint of investment regulation. These are the committee on valuation of securities and the committee on examinations. The former attempts to determine the values to be assigned all securities owned by insurance companies and to be shown in their annual statements.[2] The latter committee develops rules and procedures for the guidance of examiners. The examinations are usually conducted by a team consisting of representatives from the insurance department of the company's home state and from one or more other states in which it is licensed. The association's committee on examinations coordinates these examinations to minimize their impact on the company's normal activities and to reduce the expenses involved—which the company must bear. In the absence of this coordination, the effects on the institutions would be exceedingly disruptive, because each state in which the company engages in business has the right to examine its activities. To prevent this result, the committee on examinations dispatches teams whose reports are accepted by all insurance commissioners concerned—although occasionally additional information may be requested by a particular department.

Section II
Nature and Scope of State Investment Laws

Aside from the common regulatory framework evolved through voluntary cooperation, the high degree of concentration in the life insurance industry makes the bulk of life insurance assets subject to the laws of a few states. Thus a wide range of industry assets is treated consistently. For example, at the end of 1958, the investment laws of six states governed directly the disposition of more than three-quarters of life insurance companies' total resources. These were New York, New Jersey, Massachusetts, Connecticut, Wisconsin, and Pennsylvania. The assets of companies domiciled in these states at selected dates and their share in the industry's total are shown in Table III-1. It is evident that the growth of the industry in the rest of the country has shaved the proportion of total assets held by institutions in these leading states, but their dominance is relatively unchallenged. Consequently, an analysis of the laws of these six states would provide an outline of the legal framework of life insurance investment regulation. Moreover, in addition to the direct effect on domiciled companies, their laws affect indirectly the assets of other companies licensed to do business within their borders. For example, the New York law (which has traditionally been the strictest) requires such companies to comply in substance with the investment regulations and limitations imposed on domestic insurers.

The major provisions of the laws in these six states are summarized in Table III-2. The provisions of the Texas law have been added because it is the only legislation in the country requiring life insurance companies underwriting policies in the state to invest within its borders at least 75 percent of the reserves against policies of persons living in Texas. This unique law is discussed briefly at the end of this section.

In order to minimize the exposure of policyholders' reserves to unreasonable risk, most state laws specify conditions which prospective investments must meet before they are eligible for purchase by life insurance companies. The first part of Table III-2 gives an indication of the content of these clauses. With respect to corporate bonds, only the New York and Wisconsin statutes, among those shown, specify the type of collateral as a condition of eligibility, and the Wisconsin specification is rather vague. However, the New York law stipulates that, of the col-

TABLE III-1

ADMITTED ASSETS OF LIFE INSURANCE COMPANIES DOMICILED IN SIX LEADING STATES AND PERCENTAGE OF INDUSTRY ASSETS REPRESENTED, 1906-1958

(In Millions of Dollars)

State	1906		1928		1940		1950		1958	
	Amount	Percent of Total Industry	Amount	Percent of Total Industry	Amount	Percent of Total Industry	Amount	Percent of Total Industry	Amount	Percent of Total Industry
New York	1,700	58.1	6,470	40.5	12,779	41.5	24,225	37.8	37,027	34.4
New Jersey	234	8.0	2,562	16.1	5,045	16.4	10,304	16.1	16,678	15.5
Massachusetts	178	6.1	1,265	7.9	2,635	8.6	6,269	9.8	11,109	10.3
Connecticut	223	7.6	1,198	7.5	2,595	8.4	6,029	9.4	10,814	10.1
Wisconsin	221	7.6	871	5.5	1,421	4.6	2,705	4.2	4,114	3.8
Pennsylvania	191	6.5	812	5.1	1,495	4.9	2,608	4.1	3,127	2.9
Total Six States	2,747	93.9	13,178	82.6	25,970	84.3	54,140	81.4	82,869	77.0
Industry Total	2,924	100.0	15,961	100.0	30,802	100.0	64,020	100.0	107,580	100.0

SOURCE: Institute of Life Insurance.

lateral required to secure the bond issue, no more than one-third can consist of common or non-eligible preferred stock, and in a subsequent section the eligibility of preferred stock is itself defined. Several states not shown in Table III-2 specify that corporate bonds must be secured by a mortgage on assets with a value considerably exceeding the amount of the bond issue.

Earnings requirements, however, are more prevalent than those relating to collateral in determining the eligibility of corporate bonds. All states shown in Table III-2 (except New Jersey) have set such tests, and many other states have taken similar action. The provisions listed are typical. In New York an obligation can be acquired by a life insurance company if the corporation in the previous year earned at least one and one-fourth times its fixed charges and had funds available during the last five years from which it could have paid interest. The Massachusetts requirement is identical except for a slightly higher ratio of earnings to fixed charges. Pennsylvania's provision is similar, although it does not specify that interest must have been actually paid. This section of the laws in Connecticut and Wisconsin simply stipulates that principal and interest on the bonds must not have been in default for five and three years, respectively. The Texas law also contains a default clause, specifies a minimum ratio of earnings to fixed charges, and requires that interest must have been paid during each of the previous five years. Similar provisions, with some variation, are found in the investment laws of a number of other states. In addition to secured obligations, earnings standards are frequently set for unsecured and contingent interest bonds.

The eligibility of real estate mortgages is almost universally defined in terms of the loan-to-value ratio, although the minimum term of the lease may be set for loans against leasehold property. The typical ceiling on conventional mortgage loans seems to be two-thirds of the appraised value of the property. The objective here is to provide a cushion to absorb fluctuation in the market value of the property and thus protect the lender in case the mortgage has to be foreclosed. In recent years, however, there has been a growing tendency among states to raise the loan-to-value ratio to 75 percent, and New York, New Jersey, Pennsylvania, and Texas are among the states with the higher limit. This liberalization allows life insurance companies to compete on more equal terms with savings and loan associations, mutual savings banks, and commercial banks. Many of these other institutions benefit from relatively less stringent rules under either federal or state regulation. Moreover, in the case of mortgages underwritten by the Federal Housing Administration or the Veterans Administration, the effective loan-to-value ratio may be well

TABLE III-2

MAJOR PROVISIONS IN SELECTED STATE LAWS REGULATING INVESTMENT ACTIVITIES OF LIFE INSURANCE COMPANIES

Nature of Provision and Type of Asset	New York	New Jersey	Massachusetts	Connecticut	Wisconsin	Pennsylvania	Texas
I Standards Designed to Insure Safety							
Corporate Bonds							
Type of Collateral	Not more than ⅓ of required collateral can be in common or non-eligible preferred stock	No provision	No provision	No provision	Adequate property held in trust	No provision	No provision
Earnings requirements		No provision					
Years available to pay interest	5		5			5	
Years interest actually paid	3		3				5
Minimum: earnings times fixed charges	1¼		1½			1½	3
Years principal or interest not in default				5	3		5
Mortgage Loans							
Type of property							
Fee	Yes	Yes		Yes	Yes	Yes	Yes
Leasehold	Yes	Yes		Yes	Yes	Yes	Yes
Minimum lease term (years)	21, amortized within 35 years	Amortized within 9/10 of unexpired term of leasehold	21, amortized within ⅘ of unexpired term	No provision	No provision	Amortized Within 30 Years	Amortized within ⅘ term of lease; lease term 10 years beyond loan term
Location of property	U.S.	U.S. and Canada	U.S., Puerto Rico, Canada	No provision	U.S. and Canada	U.S.	No provision

TABLE III-2 (cont.)

MAJOR PROVISIONS IN SELECTED STATE LAWS REGULATING INVESTMENT ACTIVITIES OF LIFE INSURANCE COMPANIES

Nature of Provision and Type of Asset	New York	New Jersey	Massachusetts	Connecticut	Wisconsin	Pennsylvania	Texas
Loan-to-value ratio							
Fee	75	75	66⅔	66⅔	66⅔	75	75
Leasehold	66⅔	66⅔	66⅔	66⅔	66⅔	66⅔	
United States			Limited to amount of premium from insurance on Canadian lines and amounts from authorized Canadian investments				
Canada							
Preferred Stocks							
Prohibited types	Own, except for mutualization	Own, except for retirement	Own, or other insurers assessable	Mining companies	Holding companies	Own, or other insurers assessable	Own, assessable minimum size of corporation
Earnings requirements			No provision			No provision	
Years earnings requirement fully met	1 of last 2						Last 5
Years available to pay dividends	5				5		
Years dividends actually paid		5		5			
Minimum ratio of earnings in previous year to par (or stated) value of stock				3¼% of par or stated value			
Net earnings times: average annual fixed charges maximum contingent interest preferred dividend requirements	1½				2		

TABLE III-2 (cont.)

MAJOR PROVISIONS IN SELECTED STATE LAWS REGULATING INVESTMENT ACTIVITIES OF LIFE INSURANCE COMPANIES

Nature of Provision and Type of Asset	New York	New Jersey	Massachusetts	Connecticut	Wisconsin	Pennsylvania	Texas
Stock not in default	Must be income paying						Within last 5 years
Common Stocks							
Marketability requirement		No provision	No provision	No provision	No provision	No provision	No provision
Listed on recognized exchange	Yes						
Prohibited types				Mining and manufacturing other than gas and electric	Holding companies		
Own	Yes, except for mutualization	Yes, except for retirement	Yes			Yes	Yes
Other insurers			Yes			Yes	Yes
Assessable			Yes			Yes	
Minimum size of issuer							
Capital stock							Mfg. $25,000 Oil, $500,000 (also applies to preferred stock)
Earnings requirements			No provision			No provision	
Number of years dividend paid	10	5		5			
Number of years earnings available	10				3		
Minimum percent of earnings in previous year to par (or stated) value of stock	4%			4%	10%		
Must be dividend paying and not in default	Must be income paying						Within Last 5 years

TABLE III-2 (cont.)

MAJOR PROVISIONS IN SELECTED STATE LAWS REGULATING INVESTMENT ACTIVITIES OF LIFE INSURANCE COMPANIES

Nature of Provision and Type of Asset	New York	New Jersey	Massachusetts	Connecticut	Wisconsin	Pennsylvania	Texas
Income-producing Real Estate							
Types authorized					Leeway provision; real estate limited to 8% of assets	Real estate (including leasehold) within continental U.S. or Canada	No provision
Industrial or commercial	Yes	Yes	Yes			Yes	
Residential Housing	Yes	Yes	Yes			Yes	
Types prohibited							
Agricultural and mining	Yes	No	Yes				
Other	Yes		Yes				
Amortization or depreciation requirements							
Percent per year	2%	Smaller of 40 years or 8/10 of unexpired term of at least 20 years	2%			2%	
Time limit							
Transfer provision	Yes	Yes	Yes			Yes	
II Standards Designed to Insure Diversification and Limits on Concentration							
Corporate Bonds							
Total holdings		Up to $50,000, par value, of bonds of any corporation may be held if none of its stock is held				Railroad and public utility corporations, capital and ¾ reserves. Other corporations, surplus and ¼ reserves	

TABLE III-2 (cont.)

MAJOR PROVISIONS IN SELECTED STATE LAWS REGULATING INVESTMENT ACTIVITIES OF LIFE INSURANCE COMPANIES

Nature of Provision and Type of Asset	New York	New Jersey	Massachusetts	Connecticut	Wisconsin	Pennsylvania	Texas
Total holdings as percent of:							
Total assets				8%			5%
Capital and/or surplus							100%
Legal reserve			50%				Authorized: Corporate first mortgage bonds or debentures of corporations with $5,000,000 capital stock
Maximum investment in bonds of one issuer as percent of							
Total assets	5%				10%		5%
Capital and/or surplus		10%					
Legal reserve							
Maximum investment in any single issue as percent of total assets	½ of 1%				2% of assets for corporations other than railroads and public utilities		
Leeway provision: maximum percent of total assets	1½% in excess of specific authorization		Leeway allowed for funds in excess of ¾ of reserves	Leeway allowed for 8% of total assets			
Mortgage Loans							
Limit on total holdings		No provision		No provision			No provision
Percent of total assets	40%						
Percent of legal reserve			10%				
Limit on mortgage of one mortgagor: percent of total assets	10%				10%		

TABLE III-2 (cont.)

MAJOR PROVISIONS IN SELECTED STATE LAWS REGULATING INVESTMENT ACTIVITIES OF LIFE INSURANCE COMPANIES

Nature of Provision and Type of Asset	New York	New Jersey	Massachusetts	Connecticut	Wisconsin	Pennsylvania	Texas
Limit on loan secured by a single parcel						Greater of $10,000 or 2% of assets	
Amount	$30,000						
Percent of total assets	2%						
Preferred Stocks							
Maximum holdings							
As percent of total assets	2%	2%		8%	5%		
As percent of capital and/or surplus							100%
Maximum investment in one corporation							
As percent of total assets					½ of 1; 10% for all securities of one corporation	2%	
As percent of capital and/or surplus			10%				10%
Maximum percent of outstanding preferred stock of a single firm	20%	5%	10%				
Leeway provision	Leeway limit 2% of assets but subject to specific authorization provision	Leeway provision subject to 2% of total holdings	Leeway provision (dealing with funds in excess of ¾ reserves) subject to above limits	Leeway provision sets limit of 8% of assets	Leeway provision sets additional limit of 5% of assets		
Common Stocks							
Maximum holdings							
As percent of total assets	5%			8% of assets under leeway provision	5% of assets under leeway provision	5%	

TABLE III-2 (cont.)

MAJOR PROVISIONS IN SELECTED STATE LAWS REGULATING INVESTMENT ACTIVITIES OF LIFE INSURANCE COMPANIES

Nature of Provision and Type of Asset	New York	New Jersey	Massachusetts	Connecticut	Wisconsin	Pennsylvania	Texas
As percent of capital and/or surplus	50%					2%	100%
Maximum investment in one corporation							
As percent of total assets	⅕ of 1%	2%			½ of 1%; 10% for all securities of one corporation		
As percent of capital and/or surplus			10%				10%
Maximum percent of outstanding common stock of a single corporation	2%	5%	10%				
Income-producing Real Estate							
Maximum holdings as percent of total assets	5%	5%	5%	8%	5%	10%	No provision
Maximum loan secured by a single parcel as percent of total assets	.005% of assets to $500 million; .0025% of assets over $500 million		1%				

SOURCE: Insurance codes of the respective states.

above 90 percent. This proportion is justified by the federal backing and the mandatory amortization schedule. While investment laws historically required that borrowers own the mortgaged property outright (i.e., hold it in fee simple) as a condition of eligibility, many states now permit loans secured by leased property where the lease is long-term and greatly exceeds the maturity of the mortgage. For example, Texas requires a minimum unexpired lease of 10 years, and in New York and Massachusetts the minimum term is 21 years. Other states direct that the loan must be fully amortized by the expiration of a specified proportion of the lease. In all these cases, however, the maximum loan-to-value ratio is lower for leased property than for that owned outright. Finally, most laws limit eligible property to that located in the United States and Canada.

Eligibility standards for preferred stock center on earnings tests which differ little from those set for corporate bonds. In some cases, however, laws require that minimum earnings in the previous year must be at least a certain percentage (usually 4 or 5 percent) of the par or stated value of the preferred stock. Another variant of the same principle is the requirement that earnings be a certain multiple of fixed charges, maximum contingent interest, and preferred stock dividend. Common stocks are legal investments for life insurance companies in a large majority of states, but constraints remain rather severe as to the types and quality of issues which the companies can acquire. The existence of a market for the stock in question (indicated by its listing on an organized exchange or being frequently traded in the over-the-counter market) is a precondition in a number of states, although New York is the only state among those shown in Table III-2 with this provision. Virtually all states prohibit outright the ownership of certain types of common stocks; usually included in the prohibition are the company's own stock (except for mutualization —i.e., the shift in ownership of the company from stockholders to policyholders), and some laws preclude the purchase of stocks of other insurance companies. A few states restrain life insurance companies from acquiring stocks of corporations which fall below a designated minimum size. The Texas legislation on this point sets the floor at $25,000 net worth for manufacturing corporations and $500,000 for corporations in the oil industry. In some states, the earnings requirements for common stocks are somewhat more stringent than for preferred issues, but the basic standards are usually similar.

Practically all states permit life insurance companies to hold real estate as an investment. On the other hand, they typically restrict ownership to property used for commercial and industrial purposes or to residential housing. In many statutes, property employed in mining and agricultural activities is specifically excluded—presumably on the grounds that it is exposed to undue risks arising from the inherent instability of these industries. Life insurance companies in many instances are required to amortize or depreciate the income-producing real estate they hold at a specified annual rate (e.g., 2 percent in New York, Massachusetts, and Pennsylvania). Most laws also allow life insurance companies to hold foreclosed property as an investment for a reasonable time period rather than dispose of it immediately when the market may be exceptionally weak.

In addition to setting safety guidelines, most state investment statutes prescribe various types of ceilings on assets eligible for ownership by life insurance companies. Such provisions are designed to insure portfolio diversification and to minimize the possibilities of insurance companies gaining control of the corporations which issued the securities. The types of limitations shown in the second part of Table III-2 are typical of the restraints imposed. Some laws restrict the proportion of total assets which can be invested in a single issue of corporate bonds. For example, New York sets the limit at ½ of 1 percent, and no other state allows more than 2 percent. A few states have established a higher ratio (e.g., Connecticut), but this applies to all securities issued by one corporation. Capital and/or surplus, rather than total assets, is the benchmark in a number of laws. Another variation (illustrated in Wisconsin and Pennsylvania statutes) distinguishes among types of corporate bonds and usually permits life insurance companies to invest a greater proportion of assets or reserves in the obligations of railroads and public utilities than in the debt of other corporations. The maximum percentage of total assets which can be invested in bonds of one issuer varies widely, but most cases fall between 5 and 10 percent. Still another type of quantitative limit on corporate bond holdings is contained in the leeway provision found in many investment laws. These clauses give life insurance companies flexibility in coping with investment problems not anticipated when the laws were drafted. The statutes in New York, Massachusetts, and Connecticut are typical. Under the New York legislation, a company can invest in corporate bonds up to 1½ percent of total assets in excess of the proportion specifically authorized; the Connecticut law allows leeway for up to 8 percent of total assets which covers any eligible investment. Massachusetts gives relative freedom in the disposition of funds in excess of three-fourths of policyholders' reserves.

There is considerable uniformity among states in the maximum limits set on life insurance companies' mortgage holdings. Perhaps the most popular restraint is the proportion of total assets (or capital and/or surplus) which can be represented by loans to one mortgagor; the ceiling is typically 10 percent, although in a few cases it is as low as 4 or 5 percent. A slightly different control establishes the maximum loan the company can make if it is secured by a single parcel of real estate. Less frequently, a state law may simply fix the maximum size of a company's total mortgage portfolio; this is usually expressed as a percentage of total assets or legal reserves and is seldom below 40 percent. In rare cases (such as New York), a state may rely on a combination of these three types of restrictions on mortgage holdings.

The limitations on life insurance companies' ownership of preferred stocks in relation to total assets (or other dimensions of the investment portfolio) are similar to those imposed on corporate bond holdings. The variety shown in Table III-2 is representative. The restraints on common stock ownership are somewhat more elaborate. Here the provision is frequently designed to minimize the chances for life insurance companies to acquire voting control over the issuing corporation. Thus, most state investment laws prohibit insurance companies from owning more than a small proportion of the outstanding common stock of a single corporation. The 2 percent of total assets in New York is among the lowest permitted, and the 10 percent in Massachusetts is about the highest. Moreover, some states fix the limit in terms of a combination consisting of a ceiling on total holdings, on maximum investment in one corporation, and on the share of outstanding common stock which a life insurance company can acquire. Most leeway provisions also apply to common stocks. The restraint on investment in equities by these institutions is one of the most hotly debated issues in the regulation of life insurance companies; because of its significance for the more general equity capital question, the matter is discussed in some detail in Chapter IX.

Income-producing real estate owned by life insurance companies is usually restricted to 5 to 10 percent of total assets. The proportion may be higher in those states where other types of real estate are included. Capital and/or surplus is used as the basis of the limitation in a few states.

As mentioned above, Texas requires that life insurance companies licensed to do business within its borders must invest in Texas securities 75 percent of the reserves accumulated behind policies sold in the state.[3] The main purpose of this legislation (adopted in 1907 and known as the Robertson Law) was not simply to safeguard policyholders' reserves; rather the aim was to capture such funds for the purpose of financing economic development in Texas. A new law in 1909 permitted a reduction in premium taxes (which had been raised in 1907) if the life insurance company met the 75 percent rule. Nevertheless, the basic target remained unchanged.

This severe geographical restriction on the investment of reserves induced many of the largest companies to withdraw from Texas. While most of these re-entered the state during the intervening years, some of them returned only after World War II, and a few still have not done so. The incentives to return have differed widely. The rapid expansion of the market for insurance in Texas probably attracted some of the institutions. On the other hand, the vigorous pace of economic development in Texas in recent decades undoubtedly has generated such a large supply of securities eligible for investment by life insurance companies that the 75 percent requirement could be easily met. Of course, it is impossible to determine how much of the high rate of economic growth in Texas should be attributed to the presence of the law and its dampening effect on the mobility of saving. Nevertheless, while most large life insurance companies, operating in the national savings and investment market, probably encounter no difficulty in complying with the Texas requirement, they remain unequivocally opposed to the adoption of similar statutes by other states.[4] They fear that, if even only a few of the large states institute the scheme, this action would be a heavy blow to the continued emergence of a national capital market.

Another technique also designed to expand the supply of savings within a particular geographic area is to reduce tax rates paid by life insurance companies if they invest within the state a certain percentage of their assets. By 1959, nine states in addition to Texas, had adopted such laws. These were Alabama, Colorado, Georgia, Idaho, Louisiana, Montana, New Mexico, Oklahoma, and South Carolina. As a rule, the relevant provisions of these laws stipulate that the tax rate on premiums collected in the state is to vary inversely with the proportion of a company's total assets invested in specified securities originating in the state. However, to qualify for the tax reduction in Montana, the company must invest at least 50 percent of its capital stock in Montana securities. While the above tax incentives impose less of a burden than the Texas legislation on the investment activities of life insurance companies, they too tend to distort the flow of savings through the capital market in response to variations in the rates of economic growth in different regions of the country.

SECTION III
EVOLUTION OF THE NEW YORK STATE INVESTMENT LAW

The spectrum of life insurance investment regulations discussed in Section II is the product of many years of experimentation. Some of the laws were initially written to correct speculative excesses on the part of a large number of companies and to prevent their recurrence. However, subsequent amendments in many instances were in response to drastic changes in the investment environment. Over the years, some types of long accepted assets became scarce, and new types emerged which were not eligible as life insurance company investments. Many of the important modifications in investment laws were induced by the adversities associated with the depression of the 1930's, but the years after World War II also brought major changes. This pattern is clearly illustrated in the evolution of the New York State statute. The year of key changes in the legislation and the principal types of investments permitted are shown in Table III-3. As already mentioned, the New York law is among the strictest in force, and many of its sections have served as models for other states. Thus, a brief discussion of the New York law will place the current regulations in historical perspective and will simultaneously provide an insight into the general status of investment regulations affecting life insurance companies at different dates since the turn of the century.

The strictness of New York's law stems from its investigation of life insurance companies in 1905. As a result of various abuses, a committee of the state legislature, headed by William W. Armstrong, made an extensive inquiry into the affairs of a number of companies. Charles Evans Hughes was the Armstrong committee's counsel and the outstanding figure in the investigation. On the basis of the committee's report,[5] major changes were made in the legal framework shaping the investment activities of life insurance companies. Before 1906, life insurance companies in New York State were permitted wide latitude. The evidence presented in the investigation disclosed the extent to which this freedom had been misused. Abuses had arisen through the participation of life insurance company officers and directors in underwriting syndicates in which they had employed company funds to finance their private speculations. Moreover, through the ownership of common stocks purchased on behalf of life insurance companies, many officials obtained control over other corporations—including banks and mortgage companies.

Following these exposures, New York State in 1906 enacted a new investment law for life insurance companies. This made the legal framework almost the opposite of what it had been. Life insurance investments were restricted to debt obligations of the federal, state and local governments, and adequately secured corporate bonds; mortgage loans could be made—provided they were secured by improved and unencumbered real estate worth at least 50 percent more than the loan. Real estate needed for company use could be held, but property acquired through

TABLE III-3

EVOLUTION OF THE NEW YORK STATE LAW ON LIFE INSURANCE INVESTMENTS

Year	Principal Types of Investments Permitted
1906	United States Government Obligations
	State and Local Government Securities
	U. S. Corporate Obligations Secured by Adequate Collateral
	Equipment Trust Obligations
	Mortgage Loans on Unencumbered Real Property
	Real Estate for Own Use or Foreclosed
	Foreign Investments
	Policy Loans
	Collateral Loans
1922	Real Estate: Housing Projects
1926	Real Estate: Housing Projects
	Acceptances and Bills of Exchange
1928	U. S. Corporate Obligations Qualified by Earnings Test
	Preferred and Guaranteed Stocks
1933	Federal Agency Issues
1934	Mortgage Loans Insured by FHA
1937	Trustees' or Receivers' Obligations
1938	Real Estate: Housing Projects
1945	Mortgage Loans Guaranteed by the VA
	Federal Agency Issues
1946	Real Estate: Income-producing
1947	Obligations of World Bank
1949	Savings and Loan Association Shares
1951	Common Stocks Other Than Insurer or Bank Stock
	Mortgage Loans or Leasehold Property
1957	Common Stocks: Insurer or Bank Stock
1958	Leeway Provision

SOURCE: Life Insurance Association of America.

foreclosure had to be disposed of within five years from the date of foreclosure unless the superintendent of insurance granted an extension on the ground of hardship.[6] Companies were also required to make loans to policyholders on the security of their policies in amounts not exceeding the accumulated legal reserve. Investments were not permitted in (1) stocks, (2) income-producing real property, (3) unsecured corporate obligations or, (4) obligations of unincorporated organizations or individuals unless secured by a real estate mortgage or by collateral in which investments could be made directly. With only minor amendments in 1922 and 1926 (to permit life insurance companies to hold residential property, bankers acceptances, and bills of exchange), the 1906 provisions froze the investment outlets for the next 22 years.

In the meantime, large sections of the New York legislation were adopted by other states, and because New York required substantial compliance by out of state companies which it licensed to conduct business, the statute had a marked impact on the pattern of investment in the country as a whole. The extent of this effect can be gauged from the distribution of life insurance companies' total assets at the end of 1927 on the eve of the next important amendment in New York State. About 43 percent of the industry's total assets consisted of real estate mortgages, and corporate debt accounted for 28 percent. Policy loans, representing 12 percent of their assets, were the next most important item. Public debt obligations comprised only 9 percent of the total, and United States government securities were less than three-fourths of the amount of state and local government issues. Thus, over 90 percent of all investments were in the form of long-term debt. Real estate represented 2 percent of total assets; stocks (principally common) only 1 percent; cash was slightly below 1 percent, and all other assets (composed mainly of accrued interest, uncollected and deferred premiums, and foreign government bonds) made up the balance.

Up to 1928, the safest corporate investments were generally considered to be the obligations of regulated industries, especially railroads and public utilities. These were traditionally secured by mortgages on physical property. Life insurance companies' investments in both types of corporations go back well beyond the end of the nineteenth century.[7] Railroads had reached their maturity before the financing of public utilities had attained substantial volume, and the bulk of life insurance companies' corporate holdings, even as late as 1927, was concentrated in railroad bonds. Although investments had been made for many years in the bonds of water, gas, and telephone companies, it was in the 1920's that the financing of electric power concerns assumed a role of major importance. By the close of 1927, the companies' public utility portfolio was almost half that represented by railroad issues. But given the bias in most investment laws against nonregulated corporations, one is not surprised to note that life insurance companies held only 1 percent of their total assets in the form of obligations of industrial and commercial enterprises.

As mentioned above, New York State in 1928 took a long step toward liberalizing its law regulating life insurance company investments. These institutions could now invest in unsecured corporate debt and preferred stocks in addition to secured corporate bonds. This was possible if the earnings of the issuer applicable to dividends during each of three years, including two of the five preceding years, were equal to 4 percent of its capital stock. The benefits from this significant modification had only begun to accrue when the depression of the 1930's unfolded, and the full implications of this change were not realized until the postwar years.

In the meantime, the Great Depression imposed severe investment problems on life insurance companies. During this period, there was little demand for funds by industry, and many corporations refunded long-term debt to take advantage of the lower interest rates. The latter half of the 1930's was a period of mortgage foreclosures and of sales by life insurance companies of the real estate acquired in satisfaction of debt. In its efforts to stem the depression and stimulate recovery, the federal government launched many new agencies authorized to issue various types of debt. Because these issues were guaranteed by the federal government (and partly because of a scarcity of alternative outlets), the New York law was amended in 1933 and 1934 to allow life insurance companies to purchase federal agency issues and mortgage loans insured by the FHA. Another legacy of the depression was the introduction in 1937 of the provision permitting the acquisition of trustees' or receivers' obligations, many of which were offered to holders of corporate securities whose issuers had been driven into bankruptcy during the preceding years of economic distress. In the search for wider investment outlets, many life insurance companies saw considerable opportunity in residential housing, especially that built with FHA-insured mortgages. Thus, after some debate, the New York law was broadened in 1938 to allow them to acquire such property.

The next set of amendments to the New York State statute was designed to bring within the eligibility range several new types of assets which were quite similar to some which could already be acquired by life insurance companies. Thus, in 1945 mortgages guaranteed by the VA and other types of securities issued by federal agencies were added. In 1946, income-producing property (in addition to housing) was also included. The appearance of the International Bank for Reconstruction and Development, which was authorized to float obligations with virtually a governmental status, necessitated another modification. Permission for life insurance companies to own savings and loan shares was given in 1949.

By almost any criterion, however, the most important amendment to the New York law since 1906 was made in 1951. In that year, for the first time since 1906, life insurance companies were authorized to purchase common stocks (except those issued by other insurers and commercial banks). Provided that the issues met the earnings tests already described above, a company could invest in common stocks up to 3 percent of its total assets or one-third of surplus, whichever was smaller; because admitted surplus was limited to 10 percent of total assets, both ceilings were equivalent. This change was heralded throughout the industry, but, as discussed in Chapter IX, most life insurance companies were slow in taking advantage of the greater freedom. Also in 1951, a provision was added to the New York legislation allowing mortgage loans on property held through a long-term lease. In many instances, this change opened the way for a method of lending centered in sale-leaseback agreements which are also reviewed in Chapter IX. A further liberalization of the common stock clause was made in 1957; the ceiling was raised to 5 percent of total assets or 50 percent of surplus, and the stocks of other insurers and banks became eligible. By the time the leeway provision was added in 1958, giving life insurance companies relatively free choice in the disposition of up to 2 percent of their total assets (provided the investments in question are otherwise eligible), the New York law had evolved into a far less restrictive statute than it was in 1906. Nevertheless, there is still considerable pressure for further relaxation. Some of this pressure has been directed toward modifying the law to permit the sale of variable annuities by life insurance companies. While the actual battle has been fought outside New York State, the largest company in the state (and in the country) has been leading the opposition to the authorization of variable annuities. The nature of this controversy is discussed in the next section.

SECTION IV
INVESTMENT REGULATION AND THE VARIABLE ANNUITY CONTROVERSY

In 1957, the question of state versus federal regulation of certain aspects of life insurance companies' investment practices was reopened. The re-examination sprang from the proposal of several life insurance companies to sell variable annuity contracts based on investments in common stocks or other types of equities. Because of the strategic role of common stocks in the scheme, the Securities and Exchange Commission (SEC), created by Congress to be the watchdog of the securities markets, ruled that variable annuities fall within its jurisdiction. The life insurance companies involved, emphasizing the annuity feature of the contract, replied that they are in the insurance business whose regulation Congress has left to the states. After a number of legal rounds, the case reached the Supreme Court in 1959; the Court agreed with the SEC that variable annuities are securities and, therefore, within the purview of the Securities and Exchange Act of 1934. Thus, by a rather circuitous route, the federal government again became a party in the regulation of life insurance companies' investment policies.

Another element in the debate was the campaign (fought mainly before the New Jersey legislature) to obtain modification in state investment laws to authorize the sale of variable annuities. While some opposition to the sale of such contracts came from investment bankers, security dealers, and commercial banks, the chief protagonists were the two largest companies in the life insurance industry: Metropolitan and Prudential. At the end of the contest, Prudential carried the day and won the right to sell variable annuities in New Jersey. Immediately the test shifted to other states, and the issue is still joined.[8]

The incentive for life insurance companies to offer variable annuities was provided in the shrinking sales of conventional annuity contracts and the rising tendency for holders of such policies to surrender them for cash. Both developments were said to be closely related to a growing expectation of long-run inflation in the United States which in turn induced many savers to seek a hedge through the ownership of equities, especially common stock. The variable annuity contract struck some life insurance officials as being a close substitute for mutual funds and similar investment media which specialize in common stock portfolios. Moreover, it was thought that such a contract would be particularly appealing to savers accustomed to accumulating funds through an insurance policy with life contingencies.

Although the variable annuity has some features in common with the conventional type, there are also fundamental differences. As in the case of the traditional annuity, the life insurance company stipulates a premium in exchange for which it agrees to guarantee the annuitant a stream of payments for the rest of his life after a certain age has been attained. However, unlike the conventional annuity, which guarantees a fixed dollar income, the variable annuity simply guarantees that upon reaching retirement the annuitant will receive a certain number of units each month for life. The distinction is crucial and derives from the different methods of investing premiums envisaged when the two types of contracts are drawn up. Under the conventional annuity plan, the life insurance company commingles annuity premiums with those from other types of policies and makes no effort to channel them into particular assets. When the contract matures, benefits are paid from the company's income without reference to the source. In contrast, premiums collected under variable annuity policies are generally invested in common stocks. How much stock each premium will purchase depends on the value of the portfolio at the time and is expressed as a certain number of accumulation units. The value of the portfolio in turn depends on the level of stock prices. For instance, let us assume that the variable annuity contract involves a premium of $100 per month. If the value of a unit were $10, the annuitant would accumulate 10 units for each premium; if stock prices fell subsequently so that a unit was valued at $5, the accumulation rate would be 20 units per premium. A rise in stock prices would reduce the number of units purchased with each premium. When the annuitant retires, the life insurance company would compute the total number of units he had accumulated; this sum would be divided by his life expectancy (expressed in months) which would give the number of units he is to be paid each month. However, the actual money value of these units (and consequently the annuitant's monthly income). would vary with the net worth of the life insurance company's common stock holdings. The latter would in turn depend on the level of stock prices. It is from the impact of stock prices on the income stream that the variable annuity derives its potential as a possible hedge against inflation. The basic assumption underlying the scheme is a forecast which asserts that common stock prices and dividends will advance abreast (or ahead) of the general price level for consumer goods and services.

The actual sale of the first variable annuity caused little stir in the life insurance industry or among regulatory officials. This is probably explained by the fact that the plan was first offered to a limited market consisting primarily of college teachers. In 1952, the New York State legislature, through a special act, enabled Teacher's Insurance and Annuity Association (TIAA) to organize a subsidiary to be called College Retirement Equities Fund (CREF) which began operations in the same year. Both organizations are nonprofit corporations offering insurance and retirement benefits to the teaching profession. The program was launched after more than two years of study by TIAA. The investigation focused on the behavior of bond and common stock prices over the 70 years from 1880 to 1950.[9] The results demonstrated that a portfolio divided 50-50 between common stocks and bonds would have yielded an income which varied directly with the general level of consumer prices. Moreover, the date the accumulation began made no important difference in the pattern of the income stream. This study provided the model for the combined contract which TIAA-CREF offers. A member of TIAA can earmark up to 50 percent of his premium for investment in CREF, and the remainder is used by TIAA to accumulate a conventional annuity payable in a fixed number of dollars. In 1959, more than four-fifths of TIAA members had also enrolled in CREF, and over 90 percent of these had chosen to invest in CREF the maximum proportion of their premiums which the company permits.

Given the immediate response to the TIAA-CREF program, it was not long before entrepreneurs in the insurance industry perceived the potentialities in a much wider market. Moreover, a few large corporations adopted pension plans for their employees which involved variable periodic payments. So in 1955, the Variable Annuity Life Insurance Company (VALIC) was incorporated in Washington, D.C., with the objective of selling such contracts to the public at large. This site was chosen for its headquarters because the insurance code in the District of Columbia contains a broad definition of annuities and imposes no ceiling on the proportion of total assets which a life insurance company can hold in common stocks. However, VALIC was promptly challenged by the SEC which argued that a variable annuity contract, rooted in a common stock portfolio, is a security and therefore subject to the SEC regulation within the terms of the Securities and Exchange Act of 1934. The VALIC chose to contest the SEC ruling in the Federal Court in the District of Columbia.[10] In September, 1957, federal Judge Robert N. Wilkin decided that the sale of variable annuities is exempt from the SEC's authority because Congress in 1945 explicitly left to the states and the District of Columbia the responsibility for regulating the insurance business in its entirety. The SEC appealed the decision to the Supreme Court. In March, 1959, with Justice William O. Douglas speaking for the majority in a five to four decision, the Court held that variable annuities are securities and thus within the purview of the SEC. Although the Court supported VALIC's contention that a variable annuity contains some elements common to insurance, Justice Douglas held that these were outweighed by the failure of the life insurance company to assume any "risk in the insurance sense"; rather the company guarantees "nothing to the annuitant except an interest in a portfolio of common stocks or other equities. . . ."

The tactical matter of legal jurisdiction over variable annuities having been settled, the path was now clear for a strategic campaign against the bulwark which posed the greatest obstacle. Thus the point shifted to the state legislatures, and the contest was joined in New Jersey. This state became the testing ground because it is the home of The Prudential Insurance Company of America which quickly assumed the leadership of those companies interested in selling variable annuity contracts. As the SEC-VALIC case was threading its way through the federal courts, Prudential launched a drive to modify the New Jersey statute controlling the investment policies of life insurance companies domiciled in the state. Bills for this purpose were introduced, but without success, in the legislature in 1957 and 1958; in 1959 a measure was passed after a rather long and heated debate.

Prudential's argument in support of the amendment, an argument advanced most vigorously by Carrol M. Shanks who was then president of Prudential, was twofold: variable annuity contracts would provide an adequate hedge against creeping inflation whose shadow lingers perennially on the horizon, and they would also open opportunities for retired people to share in the economic growth of the country. This position was bolstered by a subsidiary argument which held that the risk inherent in common stock ownership has been reduced over the years because the economic policies of the federal government have greatly increased the stability of the economy as a whole. Prudential's stand was strongly opposed by the Metropolitan Life Insurance Company. Metropolitan's criticism was aimed at the very core of the variable annuity scheme and was intended to forestall any compromise of the fundamental principle that inflation is the most implacable enemy the life insurance industry has to face. The criticism was made succinctly by Metropolitan's President, Frederic W. Ecker:

> The variable annuity is advanced as a device whereby an individual can hedge against this future inevitable inflation. This places an insurance company and its agents in a curious dilemma, for if it urges the purchase of a variable annuity as a hedge against inflation, it thereby demonstrates that it no longer has faith in the value of its insurance product offering guaranteed dollars.[11]

Other disadvantages of the variable annuity contract were emphasized in the opposition to the proposed amendment, but these were minor points in skirmishes on the periphery of the main battle. Metropolitan found totally unpalatable the explicit recognition and acceptance of the possibility of long-run inflation. Opposition sprang from other sources as well. For example, as early as 1954, the Investment Bankers Association in its annual meeting endorsed a committee report which objected to the sale of variable annuities by life insurance companies. The committee took the view that such a departure "carries a very distinct threat, not only to the investment company industry, but to the entire investment banking business."[12] However, the stand taken by IBA was not supported universally in the profession; some observers thought that the advent of life insurance companies as sellers of securities would probably strengthen the public's confidence in securities in general. On the other hand, some of the larger commercial banks (especially those which manage sizable pension funds) were apprehensive about the prospect of life insurance companies offering variable annuity contracts. Such a development, many of the banks correctly perceived, would mean more intensive competition for corporate pension funds, because life insurance companies would be able to guarantee higher earnings through plans based more heavily on equities.

As already mentioned, the outcome of the debate favored the sale of variable annuities by life insurance companies. In June, 1959, Governor Robert B. Meyner signed a measure which permits institutions domiciled in New Jersey to sell such contracts. Immediately, Prudential set out to design variable annuity plans. At the same time, the company also tackled the urgent task of educating both its agents and its present and potential policyholders regarding the advantages and disadvantages of the variable annuity contract.

The implications of these fundamental changes in the legal framework affecting the investment activities of life insurance companies are still unfolding. It seems inevitable that other states will follow New Jersey in allowing the sale of variable annuities and thus contribute to a broadening of the companies' investment opportunities. How readily a significant number of these institutions will actually take advantage of such liberalization is another matter.

Section V
Organization of Investment Operations

The typical life insurance company can be viewed as one organization engaged in essentially two separate functions. In the first place, as its name implies, it is an ordinary business firm which, for a premium, assumes the risk of the policyholder's untimely death. In this context, the life insurance company is indistinguishable from casualty, fire, and other types of insurers. However, as explained in Chapter II, life insurance companies differ from other insurers because the level premium method of determining the cost of ordinary policies generates a substantial volume of savings in the form of reserves. The investment of these reserves is the second major function of life insurance companies. Since the focus of this study is on the investment behavior of these institutions, no attention need be given here to their internal organization to handle underwriting activity.

As one would normally expect (given the importance of the investment function), the locus of investment decisions in life insurance companies is at the highest managerial level. Some state insurance laws require that such decisions be made or approved by the directors or trustees of the company. The actual machinery adopted varies widely among institutions, but there appears to be a central tendency in the mode of operation. This fact stands out clearly in the BBER-MSU Survey, 1959. The replies to the question on internal organization are summarized in Table III-4. In about three-fourths of the companies reporting, the shaping of investment policies rests with a finance committee, and the board of directors or trustees makes the ultimate determination. This is generally true among small as well as large companies. There is, of course, some variation in the membership of finance committees. However, in approximately two-thirds of the responding companies, the finance committee consists of a number of trustees or directors plus the president of the company and the officer in charge of investment; in about one-tenth of the cases, only the president sits as a committee member with trustees or directors. A few institutions replied that investment decisions are made by a committee of trustees or directors acting alone; but in most of these instances the president is also a trustee or director of the company, and his role as executive officer is not emphasized. In addition, a few life insurance companies replied that the president and officer in charge of investments have the chief responsibility for investment decisions. About two-thirds of these are small institutions, and on the basis of other evidence relating to some of them, it can be inferred that the president plays the dominant role while board members appear to be little more than prestige figures. On the other hand, this explanation does not account for the few large companies in this category. Since other evidence suggests that trustees or directors exercise considerable influence in the companies' affairs, it seems plausible to assume that the respondents misinterpreted the question as focusing on those officials who actually carry out investment decisions. But the exact explanation of these exceptions is unimportant because the great majority of cases bear upon a common organization in which the locus of investment decisions is in the finance committee.

In general, the finance committee in the typical life insurance company seems to be quite systematic in planning and executing the institution's investment program. While much of this orderliness undoubtedly simply reflects the routine springing from the longevity of the operation itself, most of the decisions are probably reached after methodical analysis of the evidence supporting each major proposal to acquire securities or lend funds against a group of properties. About three-quarters of the life insurance companies have regularly scheduled meetings to consider investment matters; most of those without a regular schedule are among the smaller institutions for whom the investment function is less critical than for the larger companies. The frequency of finance committee meetings varies directly with the urgency of the investment problem which the

TABLE III-4

ORGANIZATION OF INVESTMENT MANAGEMENT IN LIFE INSURANCE COMPANIES, DISTRIBUTION OF REPLIES BY COMPANIES PARTICIPATING IN THE BBER-MSU SURVEY, SPRING, 1959

	Total	Size Group of Companies[1]			
		I	II	III	IV
I Locus of Investment Decisions					
A. Finance Committee (inc. trustees or directors with president and officer in charge of investments)	76	19	19	19	19
B. Finance Committee (inc. trustees or directors with president)	11	4	3	3	1
C. President with officer in charge of investments	9	3	0	2	4
D. Committee of directors or trustees alone	7	2	1	1	3
E. Other arrangements	8	0	5	3	0
Total Companies Replying	111	28	28	28	27
II Schedule of Investment Policy Meetings					
A. No regular schedule	28	3	5	8	12
B. Companies with a regular schedule	83	25	23	20	15
C. Schedule of meetings					
Several times each week	12	4	3	3	2
Weekly	35	15	12	4	4
Semi-monthly	9	2	3	4	0
Monthly	24	4	5	8	7
Quarterly	1	0	0	1	0
Annual	2	0	0	0	2
III Organization of Securities and Mortgage Lending					
A. Single department	48	6	9	16	17
B. Separate departments	63	22	19	12	10
Total	111	28	28	28	27
IV Budgeting of Investible Funds					
A. No budget employed	50	9	12	17	12
B. Budget employed	61	19	16	11	15
C. Budget period					
Three months	4	1	2	0	1
Six months	3	0	1	1	1
One year	54	18	13	10	13
D. Locus of authority to change the allocation of budgeted funds					
1. Finance committee	38	12	9	6	11
2. Officer in charge of investments	11	1	5	2	3
3. President	8	5	1	1	1
4. Other	4	1	1	2	0

TABLE III-4 (cont.)

ORGANIZATION OF INVESTMENT MANAGEMENT IN LIFE INSURANCE COMPANIES, DISTRIBUTION OF REPLIES BY COMPANIES PARTICIPATING IN THE BBER-MSU SURVEY, SPRING, 1959

	Total	Size Group of Companies[1]			
		I	II	III	IV
V Employment of Investment Advisers in Portfolio Management					
A. No advisers employed	78	23	19	20	16
B. Number of life insurance companies employing advisers	33	5	9	8	11
C. Number of advisory firms employed	43	10	11	9	13
D. Number of advisory firms per company:					
1	25	2	7	7	9
2	7	2	2	1	2
3	0	0	0	0	0
4	1	1	0	0	0
E. Percentage of cases in which insurance company initiates service					
0 percent	2	0	1	0	1
5	1	0	1	0	0
10	7	1	1	2	3
25	3	0	1	2	0
30	2	1	0	0	1
40	1	0	0	0	1
50	7	2	1	2	2
60	1	0	0	1	0
75	2	0	1	0	1
90	3	1	1	0	1
100	4	0	2	1	1

1. Size Group of Companies (In Millions of Dollars of Total Assets), December, 1957

I	359-13,919
II	121- 357
III	52- 111
IV	23- 52

SOURCE: BBER-MSU Survey, Spring, 1959.

companies face. While somewhat over half of all companies reported that they schedule such meetings at least weekly, more than three-fourths of the institutions in the largest group meet a minimum of once each week. In contrast, weekly or more frequent meetings are held by only two-fifths of the companies in the smallest group, and almost half of them keep a monthly schedule. The two companies among the smallest group which reported that they meet once a year to discuss investment problems undoubtedly had in mind the annual investment estimates which most life insurance companies make.

The relatively close timetable of finance committee meetings in the typical life insurance company is of some significance in understanding the investment process in these institutions. It suggests that those responsible for investment decisions can quickly appraise changes in economic and credit conditions affecting the capital market. Against this background, previous investment plans can be constantly reviewed, and (within the constraints of prior commitments) the pattern of asset acquisition can be modified to exploit yield advantages as they unfold. Of course, over very short periods of time, these shifts can only occur around the fringes of the outflow of funds because previous commitments, consideration of portfolio balance, and purely administrative difficulties would preclude violent swings in the direction of investment activity. One large New England company reported:

> our investment of new money responds to comparative market conditions in the various categories but with a distinct limitation in that you cannot go out of the mortgage business even temporarily without destroying your mortgage organization and by the same token you don't suddenly stop making direct placements because here also one has valuable relationships with the originators of such loans and with the borrowers who are already on your books. . . .

But the spokesman for this company agreed with others that the scheduling of finance committee meetings at relatively short intervals is essential if they are to keep abreast of capital market developments.

Most life insurance companies establish separate divisions to supervise the details relating to investments in securities and real estate mortgages. At the same time, a senior officer usually has managerial authority over the entire investment function and works directly with the finance committee. Among the largest companies, which handle a heavy volume of loans in each category, the delegation of supervision to separate securities and mortgage divisions is standard practice. There is a steady tendency to merge both types of lending activity into one unit as the size of the company declines, so that among the smallest institutions separate divisions are the exception.

In practice life insurance companies' investment activities in securities and mortgages are not sharply compartmentalized. A sizable number of companies, especially those in the vanguard of the industry, employ an investment budget in which funds are roughly allocated between the two divisions. The budget period typically covers one year, although a few companies plan over a shorter horizon. In all cases, the budget is subject to constant review, and the allocation can be changed at any time by the finance committee. In some cases, funds can be transferred between divisions by the investment officer—within limits set by finance committee policy and subject to the constraint imposed by previous commitments and other operating considerations. A large number of companies reported in the BBER-MSU Survey that they normally reassess their budget allocations during the course of the year. The following description of the process given by a New England company is typical:

> We make estimates each December of expected cash flow, commitments, disbursements, etc., for the ensuing year. Disbursements are generally allocated in round numbers between mortgage loans, real estate and securities. It is recognized that following such a program depends to a considerable extent on the correctness of our estimates of probable opportunities. Occasionally there is cause to reappraise this program during the course of a year. This program is reviewed and approved by the full Board of Directors as well as by the Finance Committee. The investment program for any year is probably not restricted sufficiently by mathematical controls to be called a budget. Probably the strictest sections of it are the minimum allocations announced in advance to our mortgage loan correspondents. Other than these allocations, which are made to permit the correspondents to enjoy a reasonable assurance of continued activity sufficient to maintain effective organizations, we do not "lock up" funds for specific uses. As mentioned before, it is understood by everyone that the investment projections are subject to amendment in the light of changing conditions. Changes would be recommended by the Financial Division and approved by the Finance Committee, normally.

The actual steps in the sequence of investment decisions are traced more fully in the next section. But before taking up that task, attention should be called to the special role of outside investment advisers in portfolio management in some life insurance companies. These advisers are generally firms (a few of them are individuals) employed to give specific guidance in actual investment problems, and they should not be confused with those businesses selling investment information. Moreover, they do not include investment banking firms engaged by life insurance companies in connection with direct placement of corporate securities. In the BBER-MSU Survey, 33 institutions (or 30 percent of those reporting) said they employ investment advisers; 25 of these life insurance companies employed one advisory firm; 7 employed two different advisers, and one had retained 4 firms. Among size groups of life insurance companies, the reliance on outside advisers was heaviest among the smaller institutions. The degree of reliance on advisers varied widely. A few companies (all among the largest group) reported that they ask advisory firms to aid them in the acquisition of specific types of assets. For example, two companies hire advisers to guide them in the purchase of common stocks; two other companies invite advisers to comment on public utility issues. But the main objective of most life insurance companies in employing advisory firms is to obtain assistance in coping with a wide range of investment problems. These include the detailed analysis of specific securities, for which task many companies do not have a competent staff. In some cases, advice on overall portfolio planning is also sought. As a rule, the life insurance companies take the initiative by asking the outside firm for an opinion or to undertake a particular assignment, but in many instances (especially among the smaller companies) the initiative frequently rests with the advisers. Of course, the life insurance companies' own officials retain the ultimate responsibility for investment decisions. Nevertheless, the influence of outside advisers on the investment process is strategic in some institutions. Through these advisory firms, some of the smaller life insurance companies are not only brought into closer contact with current capital market developments, but they also receive expert guidance in shaping their response to the changing investment scene. Thus, investment decisions in many of the smaller companies are probably much more sophisticated than some observers may have supposed when their capacity for portfolio management is judged in terms of their own rather slender investment staffs.

SECTION VI
ORIGINATION OF INVESTMENTS

The finance committee in most cases enters the scene at the last stages of the investment process. While it is the chief designer of the company's overall investment policies in day to day operations, its main task is to decide which current alternatives presented by the investment staff will actually be chosen. But before discussing the factors which typically influence the finance committee's choice, it may be well to trace the usual routes by which investment proposals reach the committee.

Applications for business loans or recommendations to purchase securities usually originate in the bond or investment division. The bulk of the typical life insurance company's activities in this area consists of loans rather than stock acquisitions, so the organization for business lending will be emphasized. Loans to business are based primarily on a credit analysis of the borrower in which the life insurance company's investment staff appraises his financial structure, earning power, capacity of management, and future prospects. The mechanics of security analysis differ substantially among companies, and to some extent there are noticeable differences in procedures for handling public acquisitions and privately placed securities. This latter distinction generally holds although lending directly to business and the purchase of new and outstanding securities involve a similar analysis of financial position and credit standards. In the case of private placements, negotiations between lender and borrower are direct (although investment bankers may frequently serve as intermediaries), and the lender has a greater voice in determining the terms of the loan. The life insurance company is in a position to obtain from loan applicants detailed information concerning their finances and operations on which to base investment decisions; in some instances, this information is more extensive than that which corporations usually submit to commercial banks and greatly in excess of that supplied to the SEC by businesses floating new security issues publicly.

The securities division, however, does not always handle all business loan applications. In many companies the mortgage division appraises mortgage loans to businesses to purchase, construct, and/or carry income-producing real estate. This division of labor appears to be partly the result of custom and usage, because these loans are clearly for business purposes. Nevertheless, a distinction is usually drawn between them and loans extended to business to acquire plant and equipment and to finance the production and distribution of goods and services. But the distinction is not too clear, because loans of the latter type are frequently secured by a mortgage on facilities. On the other hand, the two classes of loans involve essentially different types of credit analysis, and this may be another basis for the inclusion of mortgage loans to business in the mortgage section of the investment department. In general, the real estate loan involves an appraisal of factors such as the value of the land and buildings, shifts in neighborhood population, the income-producing prospects of the property, and the tenants' ability to pay. In the case of loans for general business purposes, the lender usually looks to the borrower's earning power for repayment. Here a general credit or financial, rather than a real estate, analysis is involved. Even when such loans are secured by a mortgage on plant and equipment, the decision to make them is based on the earning power of the borrower, since special purpose property often has a limited resale market should foreclosure become necessary. It is this characteristic of industrial property, furthermore, which reduces the role of the mortgage division when loans secured by mortgages are made for general business purposes. On the whole, life insurance companies seem to be in accord with the practices of other lending institutions, especially the commercial banks, in classifying their real estate loans to certain lines of business (such as real estate companies, hotel corporations, public warehouse and storage companies, etc.) as urban mortgage or real estate loans, and their other mortgage and unsecured loans to industry and commerce as business loans.[13]

In general, negotiations and closings of loans are made by investment officers of life insurance companies. The assignment of managerial responsibility for investments differs considerably among companies; in most institutions a financial vice-president is the key officer, but in other companies the treasurer may be given this duty. But whatever the designation, the operating officers interpret the company's investment policy (as developed by the finance committee) and apply it to individual loan applications. On the other hand, junior personnel tend to specialize in certain fields. Their function is largely one of analysis. They provide investment officers with statistical and other information in the form of balance sheets, income accounts, history of the borrowing company, an appraisal of its management, the company's position in the industry, industrial trends, etc. Junior personnel also keep continuous check on borrowers' finances and operations, watch current developments in their industries, and make certain that borrowers are not breaking the terms of their loan agreements with the life insurance company. Apparently, many members of the investment staffs in some of the larger life insurance companies have been recruited from investment banking firms, particularly from the buying department. Many life insurance investment officers have a Wall Street background, but it seems that few companies have turned to commercial banks to attract personnel with experience in lending to large corporations. Moreover, the companies seldom, if ever, attempt to adopt commercial banks' lending methods as a guide to their own operations and as a means of increasing their ability to compete for the banks' term loan business.

Life insurance companies as a rule do not solicit loans from corporations; instead borrowers usually take the initiative in seeking loans, although they may enlist the assistance of investment bankers. In addition, some loans develop through contacts of directors, trustees, or officers in the business community at large. But the typical case seems to be the one in which corporate borrowers come directly to an insurance company through knowledge that a competitor has secured funds. Frequently, commercial banks guide borrowers interested in loans with maturities in excess of those the bank normally makes to life insurance companies. According to an officer of one New England insurance company, in many cases banks have been able to avoid tying up their funds in revolving short-term loans by referring their customers to life insurance companies. Moreover, banks frequently participate in some of the larger corporate loans by making term loans due in a few years, while life insurance companies take up the long maturities. But whatever the external source of loan applications, the investment staff scrutinizes the relevant supporting data and determines which items should be presented to the finance committee. Thus, to some extent, the lower echelons also participate in the rationing of funds. Because they can anticipate a negative response of the finance committee in some cases, they can prevent many of these proposals from running the full length of the decision-making process.

Life insurance companies acquire real estate mortgages in a variety of ways, but the most frequently used technique is the appointment of exclusive loan correspondents. This method was mentioned by almost one-half of the companies replying in the BBER-MSU Survey of investment practices undertaken in the spring of 1959. (See Table III-5.) Correspondents who also service other companies were mentioned as the second most popular source. In fact, only nine companies reported that they rely on their own field staff. Four of these are among the largest in the United States, and the rest are generally small institutions operating in the area of their home offices. Reliance on the correspondence system appears to be unrelated to the size of company, but there is a slight tendency for correspondents serving several companies to be associated with smaller institutions.

The mortgage correspondence system works somewhat as follows: A real estate broker in a particular community is selected by the life insurance company to solicit loans and take applications. The company usually gives the correspondent an annual commitment of funds to ensure stability in his operations. The applications are checked by the loan correspondent and then submitted to the home office for final selection and approval. When an application is approved, the funds are disbursed by the insurance company, and the correspondent is relied on to service the loan. He must see that interest and principal payments are made when due, that the property is kept in good repair, and that taxes and insurance premiums are kept up to date. If the loan has to be foreclosed, then that too must be handled by the loan correspondent who will frequently rent the property or manage it for the life insurance company and later arrange its sale.

The correspondent is compensated for his services by the sale of the loan instrument to the life insurance company at one or more points above par. For example, a $10,000 loan might be sold at $10,200, the additional $200 covering the costs of handling the loan plus a profit

TABLE III-5

LEADING SOURCES OF RESIDENTIAL MORTGAGES ACQUIRED BY LIFE INSURANCE COMPANIES, BY SIZE GROUP[1]

Source	Total	Size Group I	Size Group II	Size Group III	Size Group IV
Originated by own field staff	9	4	3	1	1
Originated by exclusive correspondents	52	14	11	13	14
Originated by correspondents who also service other companies	14	1	6	3	4
Combination of above sources	33	7	8	10	8
Companies not acquiring residential mortgages	2	2	0	0	0
No reply	1	0	0	1	0
Total	111	28	28	28	27

1. Asset ranges as listed in footnote to Table III-4.

SOURCE: BBER-MSU Survey, Spring 1959.

on the transaction. Moreover, the life insurance company would typically pay its correspondent ½ of 1 percent of the loan balance annually. For instance, if the loan were written at an interest rate of 5 percent, the correspondent would collect this interest charge from the borrower, remit 4½ percent to the life insurance company and keep the remainder as his fee.

But the field organization, whether a branch office or correspondent, comprises only part of the personnel required for mortgage lending. The home office organization is also of vital importance. Economic trends in lending areas must be studied. Relationships with correspondents must be maintained in order to obtain business and to make certain that field and home office appraisals at least follow similar patterns. Loan inspectors or review appraisers must be acquainted with the lending territories, modern construction trends, and construction costs. Personnel must also be available to assist in the management and liquidation of foreclosed real estate. Not only do the details considered by the mortgage staff differ from those reviewed in appraising business loans, but the presentation before the finance committee is also distinct. Typically a decision has to be made on the application of a single firm in the case of business loans. Mortgages against commercial and industrial properties may require the same specialized analysis given to business loans. In contrast correspondents usually combine residential mortgage applications, and the life insurance company approves the package as a whole—or takes a part of the face value without reference to the individual properties.

Footnotes

1. Paul v. Virginia, 75 U.S., 168, 183 (1868).
2. L. A. Griffin, "The N.A.I.C. Committee on Valuation of Securities," *Examination of Insurance Companies* (New York: New York State Insurance Department, 1954), Chapter 15, pp. 517-60.
3. A similar law was enacted in Wisconsin in 1865, but it was repealed in less than a year. See Winston C. Beard, *The Effects of State Investment Requirements for Life Insurance Companies,* University of Arkansas, College of Business Administration, Industrial Research and Extension Center, 1958, Part IV, pp. 56-66.
4. *Ibid.* It is estimated that between 1907 and 1958, bills based on the principle of Texas' Robertson Law were introduced 242 times in 41 states. All of them failed.
5. State of New York, *Testimony, Exhibits and Reports of Legislative Insurance Investigating Committee,* 1905.
6. Houghton Bell and Harold Fraine, "Legal Framework, Trends and Developments in Investment Practices of Life Insurance Companies," *Law and Contemporary Problems,* Winter, 1952, p. 47.
7. Lester W. Zartman, *The Investments of Life Insurance Companies* (New York: Henry Holt & Co., 1906), pp. 138-39.
8. The variable annuity controversy generated a voluminous literature. The following is a sample: Robert M. Duncan, "A Retirement System Granting Unit Annuities and Investing in Equities," *Transactions of the Society of Actuaries,* 1952, pp. 332-37; William A. Berridge, "Economic Facts Bearing on Some 'Variable Annuity' Arguments," *Journal of Insurance,* November, 1957; Robert I. Mehr, "The Variable Annuity: Security or Insurance," *Journal of Finance,* September, 1958, pp. 386-411; Harold D. Kirchner, "The Variable Annuity," *Business Topics,* Autumn, 1959, pp. 49-57.
9. William C. Greenough, *A New Approach to Retirement Income* (New York: TIAA-CREF, 1951).
10. On December 6, 1956, the Equity Annuity Life Insurance Company, also registered in Washington, D.C., on its own motion was permitted to intervene as a defendant. On April 12, 1957, The National Association of Security Dealers was granted its motion to intervene as a plaintiff.
11. *Business Week,* June 30, 1956, p. 71.
12. *Commercial and Financial Chronicle,* December 17, 1954.
13. George W. Coleman, "Lending and Investment Practices of Commercial Banks," *Law and Contemporary Problems,* XVII, 1 (Winter, 1952), 118-20.

CHAPTER IV

Liquidity Requirements, Interest Rates, and Investment Decisions

SECTION I
INTRODUCTION

As a rule, in making investment decisions, life insurance companies generally strive for the highest net yield obtainable consistent with reasonable standards to ensure the safety of policyholders' reserves. Most of them try to remain fully invested while making forward commitments to deliver funds at currently prevailing interest rates; such a policy, it is believed, provides an assured outlet for funds and protection against future declines in market yields. While these institutions have virtually no need for liquidity to meet policyholders' withdrawals, they do require working balances in the management of their portfolios.

Several factors set the framework in which the companies' investment decisions are made:

They have little need for liquidity.

They try to keep fully invested, and to this end they attempt to extend loans on an advance commitment basis.

They do not accumulate funds in anticipation of interest rate increases nor borrow or otherwise overcommit themselves in expectation of rate declines.

They do not trade in securities in the sense of buying and selling issues for capital gains. On the contrary, they are long-term investors who purchase securities to hold for income.

Of course, if these generalizations were literally true, the tasks of portfolio management in these institutions would be purely routine, because they would passively take what the market provides in the way of long-term interest rates. In fact, portfolio managers are extremely interest-rate conscious; they frequently write and speak on the subject and apparently spend a significant amount of time trying to forecast the future course of rate movements. Nevertheless, there are certain characteristics of life insurance companies' investment environment which permit them to reduce idle cash and liquid assets to an appreciably low level; there are other characteristics which compel them to pay major attention to the earning power of their assets consistent with the safety of their investments. Yet, in this conflict of objectives, interest rates do play a strategic role in the companies' investment decisions; this influence is clearly shown in the evidence presented below.

In this chapter, the companies' cash flow and liquidity requirements are discussed in Section II. The influence of interest rates on investment decisions is examined in Section III, and the role of forward commitments in the investment process is outlined in Section IV. Finally, in Section V, an estimate is made of the time lags among movements in interest rates, new commitments, and the acquisition of securities and mortgages by life insurance companies. The framework sketched here is used in subsequent chapters as a guideline in the analysis of their investment behavior in the major sectors of the capital market.

SECTION II
CASH FLOW AND LIQUIDITY REQUIREMENTS

The main factors which enable life insurance companies to minimize their holdings of liquid assets are illustrated in Table IV-1. The net increase in savings resulting from the persistent excess of premiums and investment income over benefit payments and operating expenses has already been examined in Chapter II. What these new statistics show is an entirely different dimension of the investment process in life insurance companies which is only roughly suggested in the size of the net flow of funds into various sections of the capital market. The actual cash flow in recent years has been about double the amount of new savings accumulated by policyholders and approximately 1.8 times the net increase in total assets. To a considerable extent, this enormous inflow of funds arises through contractual payments of outstanding loans and through decisions made outside these institutions. Liquidation of

TABLE IV-1

GROSS FLOW OF INVESTMENT FUNDS (CASH FLOW) THROUGH U. S. LIFE INSURANCE COMPANIES
(In Millions of Dollars)

	1957		1958	
	Amount	Percent of Total Available	Amount	Percent of Total Available
Net Inflow of Funds	5,201	—	5,339	—
Less: adj. for due and uncollected items	233	—	188	—
Net new money (cash basis)	4,968	49.8	5,151	47.0
Repayment of Previous Loans	3,830	38.3	4,470	40.7
Mortgages	2,770	27.7	3,170	28.9
Amortization and partial prepayments	1,960	19.6	2,110	19.2
Other cash repayments in full	810	8.1	1,060	9.7
Securities	1,060	10.6	1,300	11.8
Bond maturities	710	7.1	900	8.2
Contingency sinking funds	120	1.2	100	0.9
Other security calls	230	2.3	300	2.7
Sales of Assets	1,280	12.8	1,570	14.4
Mortgages	30	0.3	10	0.1
Securities	1,130	11.3	1,410	12.9
U.S. government, long-term	430	4.3	620	5.7
Other securities	700	7.0	790	7.2
All other sales	120	1.2	150	1.4
Net Increase (—) in Cash and Short-term Investments	−100	−1.0	−220	−2.0
Total Available for Long-term Investment	9,970	100.0	10,971	100.0

Note: Data on repayments and sales are estimated from reports to the Life Insurance Association of America on the actual cash flow of 39 life insurance companies holding 57 percent of total assets at the end of 1958. Other data are from tabulations of the LIAA and the Institute of Life Insurance.

SOURCE: Kenneth M. Wright, "Gross Flow of Funds Through Life Insurance Companies," **Journal of Finance,** May, 1960, p. 156.

long-term securities by life insurance companies and adjustments in holdings of cash and short-term assets also add to the volume of funds available for lending. On the other hand, while the contractual inflow of cash relieves life insurance companies of the necessity for holding large balances for liquidity purposes, it also presents them with a major reinvestment problem.

The relatively large proportion of investment funds available to life insurance companies through contractual sources is one of the chief factors influencing the management of their portfolios. For example, in 1957 and 1958, repayments of previous loans (including bond maturities, purchases for sinking funds, and mortgage amortizations) accounted for roughly 28 percent of the total funds available for long-term lending. In addition, sources beyond the companies' control (mainly calls of corporate bonds before maturity and terminations and refinancing of mortgages when homes are sold) represented about 10 percent of the total in 1957 and rose to 12 percent in 1958. The substantial rise in cash inflow because of fully paid mortgages in 1958 can be attributed partly to increased activity in the resale market for homes, but refinancing by borrowers on more favorable interest rates probably also had some influence. The decline in cash inflow in 1958 because of the operation of contingency funds may reflect the adverse impact of the recession on corporate profits. When earnings are good, corporations frequently display a greater tendency to retire bonds at a faster rate than required in the contract; declining profits weaken this tendency. Other security calls, at the option of borrowers, rose somewhat in 1958 in relation to total sources of funds; these consisted primarily of refunding operations stimulated by lower interest rates.

Proceeds from sales of assets contributed 13 percent of total investible funds in 1957, and the proportion rose to 14 percent in 1958. However, the type of investments liquidated by life insurance companies is perhaps of greater interest than the actual volume of sales. Virtually all of the cash flow of this type originated in sales of securities; sales of mortgages represented only a negligible amount. Liquidation of long-term United States government securities quickened appreciably in 1958 and was almost 50 percent above the volume of the previous year. The increased sales were probably facilitated by the high bond prices prevailing in the early months of 1958 because sales tapered off in the last half of the year. Sales of other securities, including corporate and state and local government, also rose slightly in 1958.

The decision of life insurance companies to sell securities is influenced by many factors. In the first place, while sales are made purely at the option of the companies, apparently they are seldom planned over a long period of time. Instead, decisions to sell seem to arise from short-run opportunities to raise yields, improve quality, or further diversify the portfolio by changing its composition. But whatever the motives underlying security sales, the decision to proceed depends on the expected gain as measured by the margin between possible capital losses and the higher yield on the new asset acquired. Thus, the willingness of life insurance companies to sell securities would be strengthened by a rise (and weakened by a decline) in bond prices. Sales of other assets (principally real estate and transportation equipment) provided minor sources of funds in both years. These data do not cast serious doubt on the view, held by most life insurance spokesmen, that these institutions are long-term investors and not traders in securities. Yet, they do suggest that substantial liquidation does occur. Furthermore, a considerable proportion of sales centers in corporate and municipal bonds which most companies hold as long-term investments—in addition to United States government issues, although the latter are generally viewed as more liquid. Moreover, the sale of Governments in 1957 and 1958 was exceptionally small compared with previous years. This may have been due to the shrinking ratio of Governments to total assets, but declining bond prices (except in late 1957 and early 1958) may have exerted some influence.

The detailed figures on cash flow for life insurance companies are not made public by the Life Insurance Association of America which collects them, but these figures permit an analysis of cash flow by size of company. This evidence suggests that there is great similarity in the structure of cash flow in life insurance companies of all size groups. Where appreciable differences are observable, they apply mainly to companies of medium size.[1] This tendency is evident in all of the main sources of cash inflow shown in Table IV-1. For example, in 1957 both the large and small companies derived from new savings about 47 percent of the funds supplied to the capital market, while the share obtained from this source by intermediate sized companies was 52 percent. Loans to policyholders (not shown in the table) constituted a slightly heavier drain on the cash of medium sized companies than for either small or large ones where the impact was about the same. The inflow of cash from mortgages and securities displayed virtually the same pattern for companies of each size group, but medium sized companies derived a somewhat larger percentage from the inflow attributable to mortgage terminations related to sales of properties—and a much smaller proportion from securities—than was registered by the other two groups. On the whole, companies in the middle group seem to have less tendency to sell securities before maturity than either small or large institutions. In 1957, those in the intermediate range acquired about 10 percent of their total cash inflow by selling existing assets in contrast to 16 percent and 13 percent, respectively, for large and small units. This is especially evident in the case of sales of United States government securities which provided less than 2 percent of their investible funds compared with 5 percent of those of the largest institutions and 8 percent for the smallest.

In contrast to the relative uniformity in the pattern of cash flow of companies of various sizes, there appears to be an appreciable difference in the structure of their short-term assets. The smallest institutions held over four-fifths of their liquid assets in the form of cash and bank deposits and only 12 percent and 6 percent, respectively, in short-term government obligations and commercial paper in 1957. Cash and deposits accounted for only 55 percent of the total liquid assets held by the largest companies and slightly more than three-fifths of such assets held by companies in the middle group; on the other hand, Governments of short maturity accounted for one-third and one-quarter, respectively, of the liquid assets held by the latter two groups.

The predictable cash inflow and long-term nature of their liabilities reduce life insurance companies' need for liquidity, but they need a certain amount of liquid assets to facilitate portfolio management. According to one observer:

> The primary liquidity requirements have arisen from the desire to shift the portfolio from one area of investment to another. This shift has frequently been made in order to obtain investments which, at that moment, appear to provide the best solution of the investment problem. These liquidity requirements arise in an internal sense, in that investment opportunities are continually changing and the changes occur at irregular intervals. Consequently, the demand for liquidity arises from the desire to remain fully invested, yet at the same time to have the ability to shift the composition of the portfolio at any time without incurring a loss on securities sold.[2]

This source of demand for liquidity has frequently been overlooked by many officers of life insurance companies, and even some astute observers of the industry's investment practices have not always kept it fully in view. For example, James J. O'Leary, Director of Investment Research for the Life Insurance Association of America, has argued that these institutions, unlike the typical investor visualized in most modern theoretical discussions of the demand for money, have no "liquidity preference."[3] He suggests that the pressure to earn income on policy reserves prevents the accumulation of idle balances in anticipation of favorable changes in interest rates. Furthermore, he believes the absence of speculation on interest rate changes is demonstrated by the small ratio of cash, or cash and short-term Governments, to the companies' total assets. This ratio is nearly always less than 2 percent, and changes in it are also small. Thus, O'Leary concludes that the liquidity problem of life insurance companies is insignificant.

This argument, however, still leaves the basic question of their liquidity needs unanswered. One can readily agree that life insurance companies do not hold liquid assets against the possibility of a substantial drain on policyholders' reserves. Even in the depression of the 1930's, when policy loans expanded considerably, companies were able to provide cash simply through accumulating premiums and proceeds from the repayment of loans. In the typical situation, the cash required for operating purposes is related to the payment of life and annuity benefits. These outflows are generally predictable, although the pattern has been slightly disturbed in recent years by the growing tendency of policyholders to withdraw funds previously left with the companies under supplemental contracts. On the whole, the companies can anticipate such needs and can easily meet them from the normal cash inflow. Consequently, one should not associate large variations in the volume of liquid assets they hold with operating activities on the insurance side of their business.

Yet, if one compares life insurance companies' liquid assets with benefit payments, substantial and sometimes sharp variations in the ratio are evident. This suggests that such variations are not associated with the demand for cash for operating purposes but with portfolio activities. This probability is clearly suggested in Chart IV-1. This shows net changes in life insurance companies' holdings of short-term (treasury bills and certificates) and long-term United States government securities, and yields on long-term Governments. The figures plotted for net changes are three-month moving averages designed to bring out the basic trends aside from the sometimes erratic monthly shifts. The series strongly suggest that holdings of short-term Governments, acquired primarily for liquidity purposes, generally rise when sales of long-term Governments are large; the reverse is also true. The explanation appears to be as follows: life insurance companies generally sell long-term Governments in anticipation of the necessity to meet commitments for corporate bonds and real estate mortgages. Rising interest rates in the first instance stimulate an expansion in commitments beyond the inflow of savings, and long-term Governments are subsequently sold to bridge the gap. However, there may be a time lag between sales of long-term Governments and the take-down of commitments by private borrowers. During these short periods, life insurance companies hold short-term Governments to avoid keeping the proceeds of bond sales idle.

While the build-up in the companies' holdings of short-term Governments usually coincided with sales of long-term issues, there were several periods during which the relationship did not hold. For example, from

CHART IV-1

Yields on Long-Term U. S. Government Bonds and Net Change in Holdings of Short-Term and Long-Term U. S. Government Securities by Life Insurance Companies

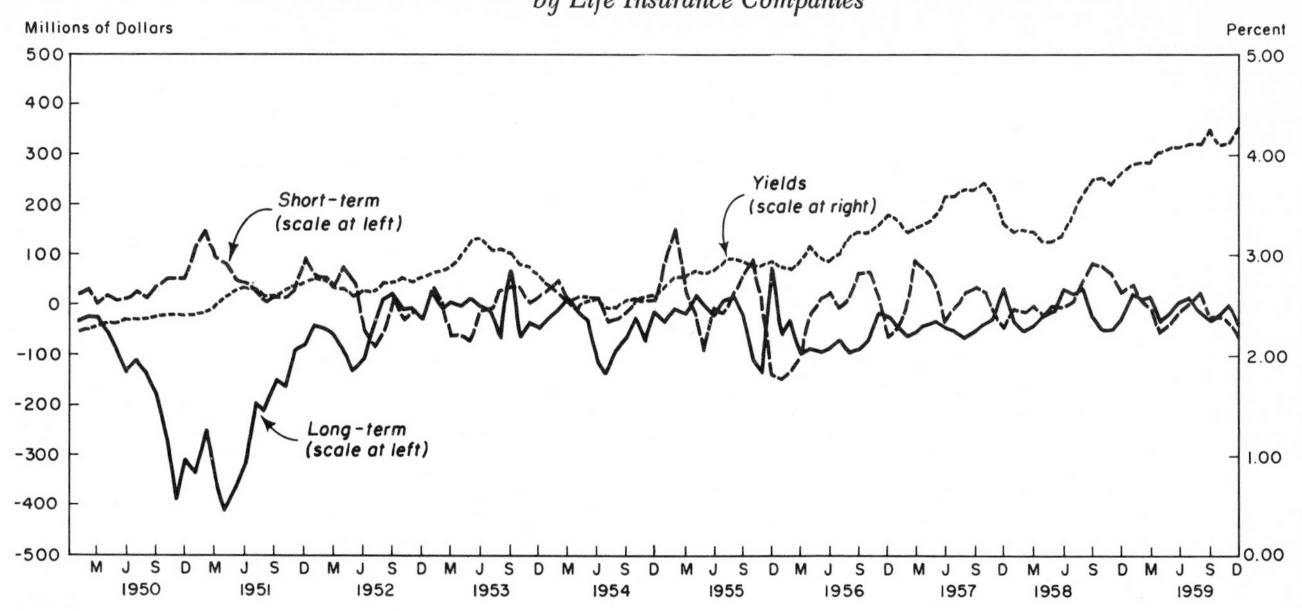

Note: "Short-term" securities are Treasury bills and certificates of indebtedness.
"Long-term" securities are Treasury notes and bonds.
Figures plotted for net changes are three-month moving averages.

SOURCE: *Federal Reserve Bulletin.*

mid-1954 through mid-1955 sales of long-term Governments steadi. shrank, but changes in their portfolio of short-term obligations were mixed. After remaining virtually unchanged during the last half of 1954, these registered a sharp gain in early 1955 and then dropped as abruptly as they had risen. Apparently, life insurance companies were accumulating funds from the normal cash inflow in order to honor a part of the huge backlog of commitments (especially commitments for VA mortgages) accumulated during the 1953-54 recession. In addition, some of the deviation from the expected relation between changes in short- and long-term Governments may be explained by the growing use of short-term commercial paper as a temporary lodging for funds set aside to meet commitments. For this purpose, many life insurance companies find particularly attractive the commercial paper placed directly by five or six of the leading sales finance companies. Moreover, because sales finance companies are also heavy borrowers from life insurance companies through direct placement of bonds, the latter frequently find it convenient to purchase the former's three to six month commercial paper and subsequently roll it over into long-term issues.

These data and the analysis show that life insurance companies do accumulate short-term assets in expectation of the draw-down of commitments. Without the increase in liquidity, the problem of portfolio management would be greatly aggravated, and the companies would be forced to forego many investment opportunities. The question of whether the observed changes in life insurance companies' liquidity are motivated by conscious speculation on interest rate movements cannot be settled either way on the basis of available data. On the other hand, there is no doubt that expectations about the trend of interest rates do influence the companies' willingness to make forward commitments. Since the take-down schedules for these require portfolio managers to accumulate liquid assets to meet them, interest rates do have an indirect effect on life insurance companies' demand for liquidity. Thus, the sequence of responses is clear, and the crucial question is the length of the time lag between each link in the chain. Although it has not been possible to measure these time lags precisely, some rough estimates are given in Section V of this chapter.

Section III
Interest Rates and Investment Decisions

Within the framework set by the cash flow and liquidity requirements discussed above, life insurance companies turn to the capital market in search of investment outlets. The quantity of funds supplied to various sectors of the capital market is primarily a function of the structure of long-term interest rates. A survey of the investment behavior of life insurance companies since World War II arrived at the following conclusion:

> The ebb and flow of investment opportunities in the corporate bond market, as reflected in the rise and decline of corporate bond prices, have mainly determined the availability of life insurance funds to other borrowers. . . . Fluctuations in the total volume of life insurance funds channeled into the private capital market as a whole have . . . reflected changes in the supply and composition of new long-term debt rather than variations in the flow of savings to these institutions. In fact, when the flow of savings to life insurance companies was insufficient to meet the acceptable requests for funds, life insurance companies have sold Government securities and reinvested the proceeds in private obligations—although the pace of selling was, as a rule, dampened during periods of declining bond prices.[4]

The web of relations connecting interest rates and life insurance companies' investment behavior is rather difficult to disentangle, but beneath the skein a definite pattern is discernible. On the other hand, while attention in the following discussion is focused on the influence of interest rates on the companies' investment activities, it should not be supposed that these activities themselves have no impact on the structure of interest rates. On the contrary, the preference of these institutions for particular types of assets plays a major role in price determination in the capital market.[5] They are simultaneously partners in the rate-making process and respondents to interest rates generated elsewhere in the capital market. But for the purpose of this study, their latter role is the more important.

While interest rates determine the investment earnings of the companies, they also serve as capitalization factors establishing the present value of invested assets expected to provide income over a succession of years. Changes in interest rates, then, signify that a favorable or unfavorable investment climate lies ahead. A decline in rates produces an incentive to reach out for higher income, and a rise induces them initially to seek the relative safety of less risky assets. As already mentioned, the flow of new savings to life insurance companies is more or less fixed in the short run and does not adjust quickly to either changes in interest rates or to the demand for investment funds. Consequently, the adjustment of these institutions to interest changes takes place through the volume of funds they are willing to supply to the capital market. As a rule, a rise in interest rates (for example, on corporate bonds) will initially induce life insurance companies to shift a greater proportion of their investible funds to this market. After a time, however, the uptrend in interest rates may result in a narrowing of the spread among yields on government securities, corporate bonds, and mortgages, and will increase both the probability and the size of capital losses. Such a prospect may lead portfolio managers to ration funds to a greater extent than previously, and in the process they will strive to improve the quality of their assets by reducing the margin of acceptable loans.

The greater selectivity in lending by life insurance companies associated with a rise in interest rates does not stem solely from a purely rational appraisal of potential capital losses resulting from lower bond prices. Certain institutional elements also underlie their concern with bond values, and among these the valuations standards prescribed by the National Association of Insurance Commissioners are of major importance. The Association's rules do not apply to real property or to real estate mortgages, and investment officers can carry these assets on their books at their full face value until default occurs in the case of mortgages or until real property is destroyed.[6] The valuation of bonds, however, is subject to rather detailed supervision, although the standards employed are not constant and predictable. As a rule,

> the Commissioners set standards each year for evaluating the quality of bonds. Those bonds which meet whatever may be current standards set by the Commissioners in a given year may be carried at stable values, technically known as amortized values, quite regardless of what the current market prices of such bonds may be. Bonds which fail to meet the current standards set by the Commissioners must be valued at prices set by the Commissioners—at market prices if the bonds are quoted, and at prices assigned by the Commissioners if they are not.[7]

Thus, by the last criterion, all of the bonds acquired by life insurance companies through direct placement (probably over three-fifths of all corporate bonds owned by them) must be reconsidered by the commissioners each year. Of course, only the commissioners are thoroughly familiar with the techniques employed in the valuation of directly placed obligations, but it is generally presumed that they search for a bond with most of the same characteristics as the bond in question, but quoted in the market. Thus, directly placed bonds are indirectly valued on the basis of expected returns capitalized at the appropriate current rate of interest including an allowance for credit and market risk. Given these valuation difficulties, portfolio managers must devote considerable attention to the liquidity and marketability of their total portfolio. While they do not require liquidity to meet policyholders' claims (and certainly do not intend to liquidate a substantial part of their assets on short notice), bond prices are of major importance in portfolio valuation because a charge must be made against surplus to offset the amount of discount on bonds selling below par.

In general then, in a period of rising interest rates, life insurance companies, while first attracted by the higher yields available on assets of greater credit risk, gradually become more restrictive and selective in their investment activities. They become less willing to sell government securities to acquire higher yielding, but more risky, private debt. This is due partly to the fact that discounts on Governments deepen progressively with an uptrend in rates, and they become more hesitant to accept the increasing capital losses. Also, they become more interested in retaining in, or adding to their portfolios, the more liquid types of assets. This motivation springs from concern over the decline in the market value of a substantial share of their investment portfolio as well as from the general uncertainty about the future course of interest rates. Finally, the higher interest rates on government securities in a period of tightening credit approximate more closely the average rate of return which life insurance companies must obtain on their earning assets to meet the interest rates guaranteed in contracts with policyholders.

But the strategic place of Governments in the portfolio management of life insurance companies rests on still other grounds. As previously mentioned, at the end of World War II, nearly one-half of their total assets consisted of these safe but low-yielding obligations, and a continuing objective in subsequent years was to redress the balance by replacing them with private issues paying higher returns. Their freedom to make the switch, however, depended not only on the availability of private investment outlets but also on conditions in the Government securities market itself. This is the only market which has a common frontier with all other financial markets and is thus the one place where the interplay of supply and demand for credit can in general have full sway. Consequently, government securities are the ultimate standard against which the qualities of all other investment opportunities can be judged. A sharp or persistent decline in government bond prices generates widespread uncertainty and before long may lead to deterioration throughout the capital market. Under these circumstances, the willingness of life insurance companies to sell Governments to acquire private assets would be severely dampened.[8]

As mentioned previously, the steady inflow of funds exerts considerable pressure on life insurance companies to find investment outlets. To minimize the size of the investment problem, most of these institutions have adopted the practice of committing their funds in advance to corporate borrowers and mortgage correspondents. For the most part, forward commitments are made at currently prevailing interest rates. But as yields advance, portfolio managers may become increasingly willing to commit funds in an attempt to avoid the necessity of investing at a later date when rates may be declining. After a time, however, commitments may run well ahead of cash inflow, and the companies may have to step up the liquidation of government securities to meet the take-down schedules. Simultaneously, the backwash of declining prices of Governments will dampen the extension of commitments. It follows that well before the uptrend in interest rates is actually reversed the general availability of credit from the insurance companies will probably decline. On the other hand, before interest rates began to climb again, these investors would probably find themselves holding excessive liquidity (reflecting cash inflow from the repayment of previous loans) and would try to broaden their investment outlets. In addition to competing more vigorously for new and outstanding issues, they would become more interested in assuming commitments to lend in the future, although to meet such commitments it might be necessary to sell government obligations. While the incentive for such a decision is stimulated by higher yields on long-term debt, it is also supported by the reduced fear of capital losses (if not by actual capital gains). The result would be an expansion in the availability of life insurance funds even before the market signals a growth in the demand for funds through an increase in interest rates.

Of course, most life insurance companies cannot actually adjust their investment portfolios as rapidly or precisely as the above analysis suggests. Legal restrictions and customary relationships as well as investment objectives peculiar to each company may intervene to produce a substantially different pattern. However, when the industry is taken as a whole, its investment behavior in response to changes in the structure of interest rates is of the general pattern outlined. The strategic factor influencing the level and structure of long-term interest rates has typically been the autonomous demand for funds by corporations. Consequently, developments in the corporate sector of the economy have been the chief indirect determinant of the flow of funds from life insurance companies.

Within the limits of portfolio balance and diversification, life insurance companies as a group seem to prefer corporate bonds to other types of investments. This preference is derived primarily from the high yields on corporate bonds relative to the credit risk the investor assumes. Corporations sell bonds mainly to finance expenditures on plant and equipment—the limit being set by the expected rate of return on such investment. When anticipated earnings exceed the cost of the project, these enterprises seem prepared to make the outlay from internal funds or through equity if possible, but through borrowing if necessary. Aside from the availability of funds, a critical factor affecting corporations' decisions to borrow for new capital purposes is the interest cost of funds. In the postwar period, a large share of their interest cost on borrowed money has been passed on to the federal government because such cost is deductible in determining the firms' taxable income. This means that with an improvement in profit prospects, corporations apparently were willing to offer a rate of interest on bonds high enough to attract the required funds. Through the vehicle of direct placements, a major part of this increase in corporate demand for funds would be registered with life insurance companies. These institutions would in turn expand their forward commitments to acquire corporate securities. Thus, the demands of the corporate sector induce life insurance companies to vary the amount of funds made available to other areas of the capital market through the purchase of mortgages and other types of debt.

To some extent, the relative rigidity of interest rates in the mortgage market is itself a major factor determining the flow of funds to this market. However, while this factor undoubtedly must be given some weight in a complete explanation of the investment behavior of life insurance companies, it seems to be far less significant than the stimuli originating in the corporate sector. Undoubtedly, interest rates on federally-underwritten mortgages are pegged below levels which a free market would produce, and conventional rates are far more sticky than those on corporate obligations. Nevertheless, even if mortgage interest rates were more flexible, their influence on the demand for mortgage funds would probably be outweighed by the effects of changes in personal income, terms of mortgage contracts (such as down payment requirements and maturities), and the rate of household formation. Therefore, no matter from what point the analysis begins, the progress of autonomous investment in the corporate sector remains the key to an understanding of the lending behavior of life insurance companies. While these institutions never withdraw entirely from the mortgage or other sectors of the capital market (and despite the fact that some companies specialize in mortgages), their willingness to channel a larger proportion of their funds into mortgages usually is prompted by a diminished corporate demand for loans.

In summary, variations in the structure of interest rates seem to generate the following response in the investment behavior of life insurance companies:

The expansion (contraction) in corporate demand for funds causes corporate bond yields to advance (decline) relative to other interest rates.

Life insurance companies respond initially by increasing (decreasing) their forward commitments to acquire corporate securities.

If the inflow of new savings lags behind (runs ahead of) the drawdown of forward commitments, life insurance companies will initially sell United States government issues at a faster (slower) pace.

The proportion of life insurance companies' investible funds channeled into the corporate sector of the capital market will increase (decrease).

After a time, however, the rise (fall) in interest rates will generate expectations of capital losses (gains), and the liquidation of Governments will decrease (increase).

With this decrease (increase) in the willingness of life insurance companies to sell Governments, forward commitments and the supply of funds to the corporate securities market will decrease (increase), and the availability of funds for mortgages will increase (decrease).

SECTION IV
FORWARD COMMITMENTS AND THE INVESTMENT PROCESS

As mentioned above, most life insurance companies attempt to keep fully invested and in pursuing this aim commit themselves to lend funds in the future according to a set schedule. These institutions have been employing the forward commitment technique for many years, but it first attracted public attention in connection with the Voluntary Credit Restraint Program designed to curtail lending for nondefense purposes during the Korean War. Because commitments are a crucial link in the lending process, they must be examined more closely.

A forward investment commitment is essentially an agreement by the life insurance company to acquire a borrower's securities in installments. Thus, it is not a line of credit similar to those extended by commercial banks. The commitment is a firm pledge, oral or written, by the lender to supply funds according to a fixed payment schedule and a fixed set of credit terms—the most important of which are the rate of interest and the maturity of the loan. Life insurance companies are not the only institutions which rely on commitments in their lending activities. Commercial banks, in making term loans, follow procedures virtually identical to those used by life insurance companies. Uninsured corporate pension funds also make forward commitments when they acquire securities through direct placement. Furthermore, mutual savings banks and savings and loan associations use the forward commitment technique in mortgage lending.

But it is among life insurance companies that the technique has been most fully developed. Moreover, forward commitments are employed by companies differing greatly in size and are used in both securities acquisition and mortgage lending. In the purchase of corporate bonds, commitments arise through direct placements and are never used when bonds are acquired in the open market. Forward commitments for mortgages vary somewhat depending on whether the loan is secured by business and industrial properties or residential real estate, but the practice is widely used in mortgage lending. Many large-scale builders obtain forward commitments from life insurance companies which serve as the basis of construction loans from commercial banks. Sale-lease-back arrangements may also generate forward commitments, and the device occasionally is relied on in the acquisition of state and local government securities.

As already mentioned, the forward commitment is an agreement by the life insurance company to lend a lump sum, and the company must arrange to have the funds available on specific call dates established in advance. In practice, the timing of withdrawals is frequently imprecise, and to minimize unexpected drains life insurance companies require that borrowers give notice one or two weeks before funds are to be made available. Among the largest companies (for whom forward commitments are a crucial part of the investment process), the forward commitment is usually a written contract which the companies consider as legally binding, and the borrower is expected to stand by it. If this were not the case, the forward commitment technique would lose some of its appeal as a device to ease the investment problem faced by the institutions. On the other hand, many of the smaller life insurance companies view the forward commitment as a less rigorous arrangement and are usually more willing to cancel it if the potential borrower's business prospects deteriorate.

To ensure that the borrower stands by his part of the bargain (and also to compensate the lender for risking the possible loss of more favorable opportunities), most life insurance companies charge a commitment fee. When part of the loan is actually drawn down, the regular interest rate is paid. The typical commitment fee falls between ½ of 1 percent for securities and between 1 and 2 percent for mortgages. A substantial number of institutions (primarily the smaller companies) do not charge a commitment fee. But among the life insurance companies which do require a fee, the rate tends to be lowest at the large institutions. A few of the latter quote rates below ½ of 1 percent; on the other hand, the fee is seldom above 2 percent at any company. This somewhat systematic variation in the size of the commitment fee seems to be related to several factors. The lower fee for securities basically reflects the high credit standing and strong bargaining position of large corporate borrowers who place their obligations directly with the leading life insurance companies. The average forward commitment for securities is well over $500 thousand, and many individual loans exceed $50 million.[9] Thus, a share of the economies obtained by concentrating on transactions of this magnitude can be passed on to the borrower in the form of lower financing cost. In contrast, the cost of mortgage lending is much higher and is due partly to the multiplicity of small loans which must be handled. But to some extent the higher fee also reflects the greater tendency for borrowers to withdraw from the contract.

The commitment process in the acquisition of securities and mortgage lending differs appreciably. Securities commitments are made primarily for funds to be spent on plant and equipment rather than for refunding or working capital. Lump sum loans are generally obtained for the latter two purposes. Because many capital projects involve very long lead times, some corporations prefer to time the draw-down of loan proceeds to coincide with actual expenditures on buildings and equipment. While forward commitments and the subsequent sale of bonds through direct placement cost more than floating issues in the public market, many corporations find the former method more convenient. In the first place, if bonds are sold through public underwriting, the registration requirements of the Securities and Exchange Commission may prove too time-consuming, and when the issue does come out it may encounter an unsettled market. Secondly, all the funds would have to be raised at one time, because the alternative of selling a number of small issues as proceeds were needed would be excessively expensive. Once the lump sum had been raised in the public market, the corporation would probably use the temporarily idle balances to acquire treasury bills or other short-term United States government obligations until the funds were required to finance outlays on plant and equipment. Nevertheless, the yield on the short-term securities would probably fall well below the full interest rates the corporation would be paying on the outstanding bonds. For these reasons, from the viewpoint of the corporation, the forward commitment approach offers a considerable advantage because the availability of funds can be tailored to the borrower's own needs.

From the standpoint of the life insurance companies (particularly the largest ones), the forward commitment is an excellent instrument for planning investment activities. As mentioned above, many life insurance companies must invest (and reinvest) an enormous volume of funds each year, in some cases amounting to twice the net increase in total assets. This inflow of funds creates persistent pressure on portfolio managers to seek expanding capital market outlets.

Forward commitments for securities are highly concentrated among borrowers in manufacturing industries and public utilities. Purely commercial and financial corporations (including sales finance companies which borrow heavily from life insurance companies) make little use of forward commitments. The explanation of this industrial pattern of forward commitments is readily understood. Public utilities and certain manufacturing enterprises (especially chemical and electronic firms) typically plan their capital expenditures in a systematic way and for a considerable period into the future. Consequently, they are among the leading borrowers through forward commitments, and the related takedown schedules are among the longest encountered.

Life insurance companies' forward commitments to acquire mortgages vary somewhat depending on whether loans are made to builders or ultimate purchasers. Since most companies originate residential mortgages through correspondents rather than through their own field staffs, the preferred commitment of this type is for an individual borrower taking out a conventional mortgage. In this arrangement, the lenders generally require that homes be sold to buyers acceptable to the life insurance company. While this preference cannot be pressed to the same extent when commitments are for loans backed by FHA or VA, the companies still try to lend to the home owner. On the other hand, forward commitments are made to builders with high credit ratings. As a rule, however, the mortgage amounts per house are smaller, the maturities are shorter, and the interest rates are higher than those for final purchasers. Moreover, when forward commitments are made to builders of "project" type homes to be financed ultimately through a large number of small loans, many life insurance companies attempt (through their correspondents) to limit the proportion of FHA and VA mortgages in the total. The main objective is to restrict the amount of low-yielding federally-underwritten mortgages in favor of more profitable conventional loans.

To further understand the forward commitment process in life insurance companies, these institutions were questioned about the technique in the BBER-MSU Survey, 1959. The replies (summarized in Table IV-2) show that while virtually all life insurance companies use forward

TABLE IV-2

SELECTED ASPECTS OF LIFE INSURANCE COMPANIES' FORWARD COMMITMENTS[1]

	Total Number of Companies	Size Group I	Size Group II	Size Group III	Size Group IV
Forward Commitments Used					
Securities					
Yes	76	26	23	18	9
No	35	2	5	10	18
Mortgages					
Yes	104	27	28	26	23
No	7	1	0	2	4
Average Length of Commitments (Months)					
Securities: 2-5	27	4	11	7	5
6-11	37	15	10	9	3
12 and over	12	7	2	2	1
Mortgages: 2-5	31	9	7	4	11
6-11	59	13	19	17	10
12 and over	14	5	2	5	2
Response of Average Length of Commitment to a Rise in Interest Rates					
No Change	70	13	22	21	14
Increase	33	14	6	4	9
Decrease	1	0	0	1	0
Maximum Commitment (Months)					
Securities: 2-11	15	0	6	6	3
12-17	23	5	7	7	4
18-23	17	5	7	5	0
24 and over	21	16	3	0	2
Mortgages: 2-11	25	0	6	8	11
12-17	42	9	15	10	8
18-23	25	11	5	5	4
24 and over	12	7	2	3	0
Range of Commitment Fee (Percent)					
Securities					
none	9	2	4	1	2
¼-½	6	4	2	—	—
½-1	35	17	8	8	2
1	12	—	1	6	5
1-2	12	3	7	2	—
2	1	—	—	1	—
over 2	1	—	1	—	—
Total	76	26	23	18	9
Mortgages					
none	29	4	10	7	8
¼-½	2	2	—	—	—
½-1	13	4	4	4	1
1	28	5	5	9	9
1-2	24	10	6	4	4
2	4	2	1	1	—
over 2	2	—	1	1	—
Total	102	27	27	26	22

1. Size groups are those shown in Table III-4.

SOURCE: BBER-MSU Survey, Spring, 1959.

commitments in mortgage lending, the method is employed primarily by the large institutions in connection with the acquisition of securities. For example, only one-third of the companies in the smallest group invest in securities through commitments compared with 93 percent in the largest group. This finding is to be expected when it is recalled that commitments for securities arise chiefly through the direct placement of corporate bonds in which the largest institutions play the dominant role.

There is substantial variation in the average length of forward commitments when these are analyzed by type of loan and size of lender. The weighted average of both security and mortgage commitments outstanding with all life insurance companies in the spring of 1959 was about eight months, and the range was from two months to well over one year. But when the largest and smallest companies are compared, one observes that the average length of commitments made by the largest institutions exceeds that for the smallest by a considerable margin. Among companies at the forefront of the industry, forward commitments for securities averaged about 9.7 months against 6.3 months for companies in the last quartile; the figures for mortgages were 8.1 and 6.7 months, respectively. Moreover, all life insurance companies reported that they were willing to make forward commitments for longer periods than the average length of those outstanding. Taking all groups together, they were prepared to offer forward commitments for a maximum of 17.4 months for securities and 15.3 months for mortgages. In both cases, the maximum is about twice the average length of commitments actually given. The largest life insurance companies reported a willingness to increase the pay-out schedule considerably further. The weighted average of their maximum commitments for securities was 22.8 months, and that for mortgages was 19.8 months; these terms were, respectively, 2.34 and 2.47 times the length of commitments already on their books. In contrast, while the smallest institutions were prepared to increase the length of securities commitments to the same extent as the largest companies (e.g., from an average of 6.3 months to a maximum of 14.5 months, or 2.30 times), they were less ready to stretch the pay-out period for mortgages; here the maximum schedule of 11.6 months was 1.73 times that of outstanding commitments to make real estate loans.

The diversity in the term over which life insurance companies will commit their funds is closely related to the diversity of the investment problems which they face. The actual length of the pay-out schedule they set for particular loans, of course, depends on a number of factors. The important elements are the size of the lender, the size of the borrower, the nature of the borrower's expansion plans, the expected inflow of funds, and the trend of interest rates. Because the largest life insurance companies have the most pressing investment problem, they are usually receptive to exceptionally long commitment propositions. In contrast, the smaller institutions operate with much shorter planning periods and are somewhat reluctant to undertake the detailed synchronization of cash inflow and outflow which is necessary when funds are committed for long periods into the future. Among borrowers, the larger the corporation, the more systematic its planning and capital budgeting and extensive its expansion program, the stronger will be the desire to obtain an advance commitment of the required financing. In turn, only the largest life insurance companies are able to handle such loans.

Life insurance companies' expectations about the trend of interest rates are also determinants of the length of time over which they will pledge to lend funds. In general, one might expect life insurance companies to reduce the commitment period if they anticipated a rise in market yields. The shortening of the commitment schedule (and with it the total volume of commitments outstanding) would enable the companies to take advantage of the prospective advance in rates. On the other hand, when it appeared that interest rates were approaching a peak and that the level thereafter might be either stable or declining, one would normally expect the commitment period to stretch. The self-interest of borrowers would suggest efforts in the opposite direction: they would seek long-term commitments when higher interest rates and reduced availability of funds are anticipated; they would be less concerned over securing commitments when a downtrend in interest rates and easy financial conditions seem in prospect.

In the BBER-MSU Survey, however, about two-thirds of the life insurance companies reported that the trend of interest rates has no influence on the term of forward commitments. Moreover, virtually all of those which vary the length of commitments in response to interest rate changes react just the opposite of the behavior pattern described in the above paragraph. A rise in interest rates induces an increase, rather than the expected decrease, in the average length of commitments. Moreover, about one-half of the largest companies (which presumably are more sharply attuned than are smaller companies to the effects of interest rate changes) reported the same puzzling type of adjustment.

Upon closer analysis, however, this apparent paradox in investment behavior quickly vanishes. To the borrowing corporation, once it has adopted a program of capital expenditure within the framework of a long-range plan, the availability of funds when required is probably more decisive than interest rates in determining the term of the commitment desired. While interest rates constitute an important element of cost in carrying out a project, the adverse effects on the investment program which may result from interrupting the capital plan in the hope of benefiting from a future decline in market yields may be even more costly. As a result, expected changes in interest rates probably have little influence on the scheduling of commitments by corporations.

In the case of the large life insurance companies, as mentioned above, the steady cash inflow and the effort to avoid idle balances forces a search for investment outlets which may be only moderately dampened or stimulated by expectations in the trend of interest rates. For these institutions, the paramount considerations are the attractiveness of alternative investment opportunities and the relationship of current interest rates to their contractual obligations. If the yield obtainable at a given time equals or exceeds the minimum required, most life insurance companies seem fully prepared to accept the current rate of return. Furthermore, aside from compensating the lender for reserving his funds on behalf of the borrowing corporation, the commitment fee also serves as a reward for not waiting for a rise in interest rates. Finally, portfolio managers encounter serious obstacles in attempting to forecast the trend of interest rates, and this too may reduce the influence of changes in interest rates on commitment practices. Nevertheless, once a substantial shift has occurred in the level and structure of interest rates, and if this generates expectations that the new trend will continue, the change will undoubtedly affect the period over which life insurance companies would be willing to commit their funds.

Section V
Interest Rates, Forward Commitments, and the Acquisition of Assets

The interrelations and time lags among interest rate changes, forward commitments, and the actual acquisition of securities and mortgages by life insurance companies are illustrated in Charts IV-2 and IV-3. In Chart IV-2, the interest rate series is the quarterly average of yields on newly sold corporate bonds rated Aa by Moody's Investors Service. Yield indexes are also available for other bond ratings (Aaa, A, and Baa), but the Aa series probably is a closer approximation of the average quality of corporate bonds acquired by life insurance companies. The statistics on forward commitments are collected by the Life Insurance

CHART IV-2

Interest Rates and New Commitments by Life Insurance Companies to Buy Securities and Real Estate Mortgages, 1952-1959

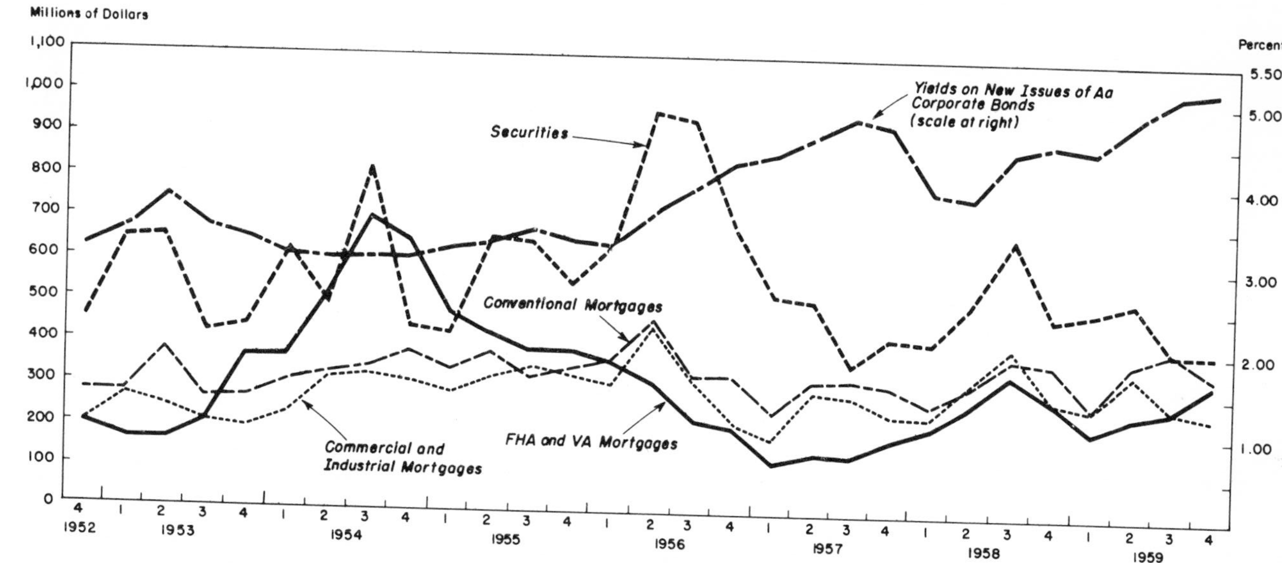

SOURCE: Life Insurance Association of America and Moody's Investors Service.

CHART IV-3

Interrelations Among Interest Rates, New Forward Commitments, and the Acquisitions of Corporate Securities and Real Estate Mortgages by Life Insurance Companies, 1952-1959

(*Ratio Scale*)

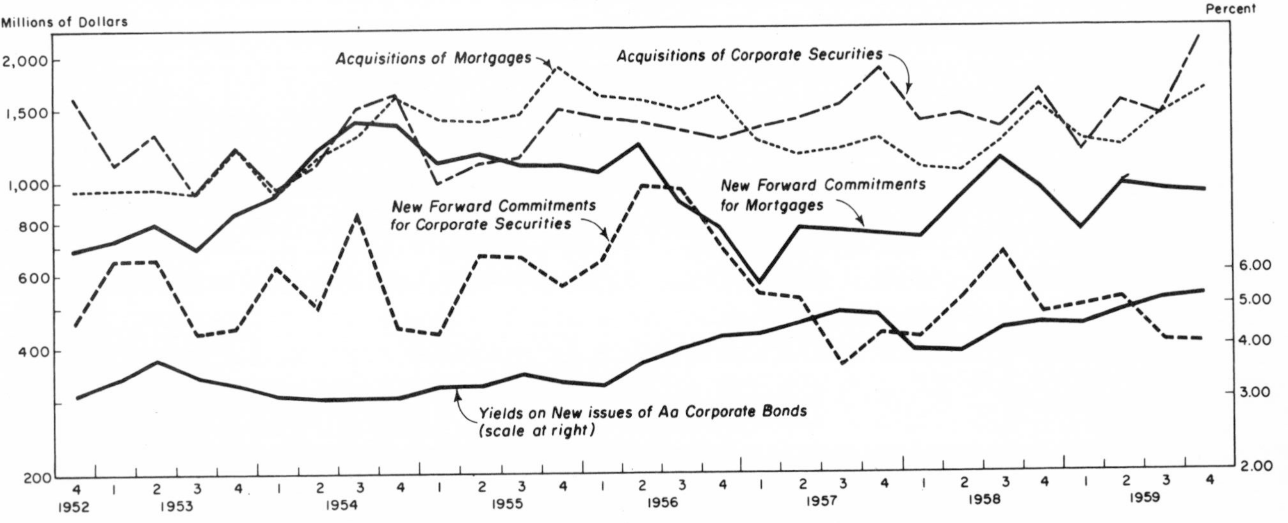

SOURCE: Life Insurance Association of America, Institute of Life Insurance, and Moody's Investors Service.

Association of America (LIAA) in monthly reports from 39 companies with about two-fifths of the industry's total assets. These companies make approximately two-thirds of all forward commitments.[10] These ratios are used by LIAA to inflate the reported figures in order to obtain an estimate of forward commitments for all life insurance companies. The reports include statistics on forward commitments outstanding at the end of the month and new commitments made during the month. Co-operating companies are asked to distinguish between commitments for securities and for real property and mortgages. Securities commitments include those to acquire both public and private obligations; however, at most times the private issues account for virtually the entire amount, and in this discussion forward commitments to buy issues of state and local governments are neglected except in a few instances. Private securities commitments are subdivided into railroad, public utility, and business and industrial bonds; the latter are further broken down into the categories of the Standard Industrial Classification developed by the United States Department of Commerce. Included in real property and mortgage loans are business and industrial mortgages, real property for lease or rental, home office buildings, farm mortgages, and nonfarm residential loans. Residential mortgages are classified as FHA-insured, VA-guaranteed, and conventional loans. In addition, life insurance companies report the amount of forward commitments outstanding in each category expected to be taken down within one, two, and six months; the amounts actually taken down and cancellations are also shown. The forward commitment reports are summarized in a number of statistical series which LIAA distributes to Association members and to a few federal government agencies, but these are not otherwise made available to the public. However, some of the broad categories have been published in congressional documents. Some of this information is shown in Table IV-3.

Chart IV-2 shows new commitments made by life insurance companies during each quarter beginning with the last quarter of 1952 and extending through 1959. In a study of the influence of interest rates on investment decisions in life insurance companies, the new commitment series is more illuminating than the statistics on outstanding commitments. The timing of changes in new commitments seems to support the previous argument that expectations of future interest rate movements have a major influence on the companies' investment behavior. Swings in commitments to buy securities are clearly cyclical, and lead variations in interest rates. For example, in 1953, securities commitments leveled off one quarter before interest rates reached a peak and subsequently

TABLE IV-3

NEW COMMITMENTS OF LIFE INSURANCE COMPANIES FOR FHA AND VA RESIDENTIAL MORTGAGES, CORPORATE BONDS, AND COMMERCIAL AND INDUSTRIAL MORTGAGES, 4TH QUARTER, 1952-4TH QUARTER, 1959

(In Millions of Dollars)

Quarter		FHA and VA Mortgages	Commercial & Industrial Mortgages	Corporate Bonds	Residential Mortgages			
					Total	FHA	VA	Conventional
1952	4	203	205	457	485.8	154.7	48.1	283.0
1953	1	165	275	648	444.0	125.5	39.4	279.1
	2	166	245	650	547.3	118.2	47.5	381.6
	3	210	211	428	478.6	105.5	105.0	268.1
	4	370	199	444	644.6	145.3	225.0	274.3
1954	1	372	236	625	683.2	141.3	230.6	311.3
	2	524	320	498	860.2	142.6	381.8	335.8
	3	705	330	834	1,050.3	124.1	580.8	345.4
	4	654	315	445	1,937.2	176.0	478.0	383.2
1955	1	476	290	430	816.4	161.5	314.0	340.9
	2	427	327	656	820.1	162.7	264.2	393.2
	3	394	350	649	728.4	153.4	240.5	334.5
	4	393	333	556	737.8	174.3	218.7	344.8
1956	1	365	312	643	733.6	120.9	244.1	368.6
	2	312	445	963	774.5	108.1	203.5	462.9
	3	234	322	940	568.8	84.8	149.0	335.0
	4	209	220	693	544.4	68.5	140.1	335.8
1957	1	134	187	529	377.2	80.4	53.5	243.3
	2	152	292	516	470.7	101.4	50.5	318.8
	3	144	286	360	468.2	119.3	24.7	324.2
	4	182	242	426	496.8	166.7	15.1	315.0
1958	1	216	240	416	486.1	195.3	20.3	270.5
	2	266	324	513	584.1	257.0	9.3	317.8
	3	341	407	661	722.3	318.2	22.6	381.5
	4	290	286	479	662.8	264.8	25.7	372.3
1959	1	212	267	498	485.9	192.3	20.1	273.5
	2	250	345	523	627.0	226.6	23.1	377.3
	3	264	265	408	673.0	221.6	42.1	409.3
	4	330	248	405	679.0	250.3	79.4	349.3

SOURCE: Life Insurance Association of America.

Life insurance companies reporting commitments represent about 65 percent of total assets of all United States life insurance companies. New commitments include only those made during a month that were still outstanding at the end of the month. Most of these statistics (through the third quarter of 1958) have been published in **Study of Mortgage Credit, Hearings,** before a Subcommittee of the Committee on Banking and Currency, U.S. Senate, 86th Congress, 1st session, May, 1959, pp. 270 and 272.

declined more abruptly than open market yields. However, while long-term yields were still declining, new securities commitments began to expand, and despite sharp fluctuations, were generally high throughout 1954. This was apparently the one period during the postwar years when commitments for state and local government issues mainly determined the behavior of securities commitments. Late 1953 through early 1955 was the heyday of turnpike financing, and many life insurance companies rushed into the municipal market to take up revenue bonds sold by special authorities. Because of the long construction schedules involved, some authorities arranged forward commitments and withdrew funds as they were required to meet expenditures. Moreover, even in some cases before turnpike issues were sold in the public market, highway managers made short-term arrangements with life insurance companies until long-term obligations could be floated. By the middle of 1955 the crest of the turnpike wave had passed, and life insurance companies' participation in the municipal securities market receded to the normal level.

Also by mid-1955, many corporations were at work planning projects which later generated the plant and equipment boom of 1956-57. Again life insurance companies' forward commitments anticipated the subsequent increase in corporate demand for funds. New securities commitments climbed appreciably in the first quarter and remained high through the next six months, although at a level well below that set in the beginning of the year. The spectacular jump began in the last quarter, and by mid-1956 the companies' new commitments to purchase securities had set a record which still stood at the end of 1959. While long-term interest rates continued to rise for the next year and a half, the extension of new commitments to purchase securities shrank steadily until the last quarter of 1957 when the uptrend in rates was reversed. This pattern of commitment behavior reflects to some extent the ebbing demand for funds as corporations completed capital projects. In addition, increased discounts on United States government bonds (the chief residual source of funds to meet commitments when new savings are insufficient) probably persuaded many life insurance companies to be more cautious in making commitment agreements. It should be observed that both types of developments would have occurred well before the peak was actually reached in market yields.

The behavior of life insurance companies with regard to new securities commitments from late 1957 through 1959 illuminates the modesty of the economy's recovery from the 1957-58 recession. While commitments continued to lead the general recovery, the rise was shorter in duration and of much lesser magnitude than the expansion which preceded the plant and equipment boom of 1956-57. At their highest level in the third quarter of 1958, new securities commitments were only two-thirds of the record volume extended in the second quarter of 1956. Moreover, the turn around in commitments came only one quarter after corporate bond yields began to rise and despite the fact that the uptrend in yields continued through 1959 and into the first half of 1960. Throughout the period of relative prosperity in 1958-59, life insurance companies' new forward commitments for securities averaged about one-third below the level in the comparable phase of the 1956-57 expansion.

Forward commitments for commercial and industrial mortgages display the same contours as those for securities. Life insurance companies typically lend to small businesses by advancing funds against real property secured by mortgages. Certain types of construction, especially shopping centers, are financed in the same manner.[11] Moreover, in the interest of greater balance within the mortgage portfolio, some companies have been concentrating more heavily on commercial and industrial mortgages rather than on residential loans. For these and other reasons, commitments for nonresidential mortgages have essentially the same cyclical pattern as commitments for securities.

Life insurance companies' new commitments to buy nonresidential mortgages show a mixed pattern with respect to business cycles and interest rate trends. Forward commitments for conventional mortgages display a relatively mild contra-cyclical profile. In contrast, commitments to acquire federally-underwritten mortgages have the strongest tendency of all life insurance companies' investment outlets to run against the cycle. Most of this instability derives from the critical role of VA-guaranteed mortgages, but those insured by FHA are also less stable than conventional loans. The pegged interest rates on federally-underwritten mortgages enhance their appeal to life insurance companies and other investors when other open market yields are declining; the reverse is also true. In fact, the inverse movements of corporate bond yields and the companies' new commitments for FHA and VA mortgages are almost perfectly synchronized. With few exceptions, peaks in bond yields coincide with troughs in new commitments for these types of mortgages. However, the amplitude of fluctuation in FHA and VA commitments was dampened appreciably toward the end of the 1950's. In the early years, especially in the 1953-54 recession, VA mortgages were the main alternative investment outlet available to life insurance companies to compensate for the decline in corporate demand for funds. In this period, their new commitments for such mortgages revived within a few months of the downturn in economic activity and interest rates in mid-1953, and for the next year and a half they rose without interruption. At the peak in the third quarter of 1954, the extension of new commitments for FHA and VA mortgages was two and one-half times the volume at the beginning of the upswing. This record was not even closely approximated in the rest of the decade. New commitments for federally-supported mortgages again expanded during the 1957-58 recession and the months of faltering economic activity in 1959. But during the period of heaviest extensions in the third quarter of 1958, new commitments of this type were only slightly more than one-half of the volume in the same quarter of 1954. Furthermore, extensions centered primarily in FHA loans.

Several factors help to explain the smaller role of federally-underwritten mortgages in life insurance companies' investment activity in the last half of the 1950's. In the first place, the reduced rate of growth in new savings after 1955 (as explained in Chapter II) lessened the pressure on them to find investment outlets. On the demand side of the mortgage market, the shrinking number of veterans eligible for VA loans also narrowed the market. But perhaps of more importance was the spread of discounts first against VA mortgages and subsequently against FHA mortgages as well. These discounts not only brought the effective yield on such mortgages more into line with the rate of return a free market would impose, but they also made VA and FHA yields more responsive to capital market trends. As a result, the differentials between yields on federally-supported mortgages and open market obligations widen less during recessions and narrow less during recovery periods than was the case in the early 1950's.

Chart IV-3 gives some idea of the time lags between life insurance companies' new commitments for securities and mortgages and their actual acquisition of these assets. However, the picture sketched is only a rough approximation of the time lag because the series shown do not measure precisely the relationship in question. In the chart, the new commitments for securities are the same as described above, but the mortgage series combines commitments for residential and nonresidential mortgages. This is necessary because life insurance data on acquisitions do not distinguish between residential and business and industrial mortgages. Only corporate securities are included in the acquisitions series. The interest rate series is the same one plotted in Chart IV-2.

Although the pattern is somewhat blurred, one can detect a systematic relationship among movements in interest rates, securities commitments, and securities acquisitions. There is also a suggestion of a definite sequence among the mortgage series, but it appears to be somewhat weaker than that outlined for securities. This is partly explained by the presence of business and industrial mortgages in which variations are attuned to those in corporate securities. New securities commitments seem to lead changes in interest rates by at least one quarter and in some instances as much as six months. Turning points in interest rates and new commitments for mortgages seem to occur simultaneously and to move in opposite directions. With respect to acquisitions, a divergent pattern is also evident. The time lag between securities commitments and acquisitions seems to be at least six months and that for mortgages about three months. These general conclusions are consistent with, and reinforce, the evidence gathered in the BBER-MSU Survey which was discussed above. Moreover, data on the companies' expected pay-out schedules for outstanding commitments point in the same direction. During the years from 1952 to 1956, an average of 75 percent of non-farm residential mortgage commitments were expected to be withdrawn within six months, and the figure was about 57 percent for business and industrial mortgages. In contrast, the companies expected only 44 percent of outstanding commitments for business and industrial bonds to be withdrawn within the same period.[12]

Footnotes

1. The Life Insurance Association of America groups companies by size of assets as follows: small, less than $200 million, medium, $200 million to $1 billion; large, over $1 billion.

2. Willis J. Winn, "Government Securities," *Investment of Life Insurance Funds*, p. 90.

3. James J. O'Leary, "The Institutional Savings-Investment Process and Current Economic Theory," *American Economic Review, Papers and Proceedings*, May, 1954, pp. 461-65.

4. Federal Reserve Bank of New York, "Life Insurance Companies in the Postwar Capital Market," *Monthly Review*, September, 1958, pp. 133-34.

5. Andrew F. Brimmer, "Credit Conditions and Price Determination in the Corporate Bond Market," *Journal of Finance*, September, 1960, pp. 368-69.

6. Sherwin C. Badger, "The Valuation of Assets," *Investment of Life Insurance Funds*, p. 214.

7. *Ibid.*, p. 215.

8. Robert V. Roosa, "Interest Rates and the Central Bank," in *Money, Trade and Economic Growth, Essays in Honor of John Henry Williams* (New York: The Macmillan Company, 1951), pp. 270-95.

9. See Section IV of Chapter VI.

10. James J. O'Leary, "Forward Investment Commitments of Life Insurance Companies," *The Quality and Economic Significance of Anticipations Data*, a study sponsored by the National Bureau of Economic Research (Princeton: Princeton University Press, 1960), p. 326.

11. *Ibid.*, p. 331.

12. *Ibid.*, Chart 11, p. 341.

PART II

Investment Behavior of Life Insurance Companies in the Capital Market

CHAPTER V

Investment Behavior in the Market for United States Government Securities

SECTION I
DEMAND FOR UNITED STATES GOVERNMENT SECURITIES BY LIFE INSURANCE COMPANIES

There are several reasons why the market for United States government securities is the focal point of the following studies of participation by life insurance companies in the capital markets. First, as mentioned in Chapter IV, the yields on federal government obligations are the key interest rates in all maturity sectors of the financial markets. These key rates serve as anchors to yields on private instruments, while the latter generally are higher. The differentials are based on the higher credit risk attached to private or nonfederal issues, their lower marketability, and the higher cost of investigation. By each of these standards, Governments are superior investment outlets for life insurance companies. On the other hand, the lower yields on Governments make it necessary for portfolio managers to search elsewhere for assets whose rates of return are more in line with the rates guaranteed in insurance policies. Nevertheless, most life insurance companies have a basic demand for small amounts of Governments to satisfy liquidity needs and to provide portfolio diversification.

Secondly, government securities in excess of the amounts required for liquidity and diversification also serve as residual investments for life insurance companies. A theme running throughout this study is that these institutions generally prefer higher-yielding mortgages and corporate bonds to holding Governments. It is only if they have long-term funds in excess of the amounts they are able to invest in loans and securities that they will buy government issues on a large scale. When they can find alternative investment opportunities (providing yields more than sufficient to compensate for the additional risk assumed), life insurance companies seem generally willing to sell Governments to acquire the more profitable investments.

This pattern of behavior has been fundamentally a reflection of the legacy of depression and war finance. During the depression of the 1930's life insurance companies turned increasingly to the government bond market to find outlets for their funds as private demand declined. Although it was in that decade that life insurance companies became the leading purchasers (and virtually the only ones) of corporate bonds, they put almost half of the net increase in their assets into government securities. In World War II, these institutions provided 12 percent of the total funds borrowed by the federal government, while their acquisitions of long-term issues accounted for more than one-third of the total offered during the war loan drives. Furthermore, federal obligations as an outlet for life insurance funds served to compensate for the decline in holdings of other types of assets, since the rise in their holdings of Governments represented about 106 percent of the growth in their total assets.

Just as Governments constituted a residual use of life insurance companies' funds during the depression and war years, they were a residual source of funds in the postwar period. Policyholders' saving through net premiums has been the primary source of funds supplied to the capital market by life insurance companies, but these institutions have sold Governments and reinvested the proceeds in private obligations when the volume of savings was insufficient to meet the acceptable requests for loans. As a rule, the rate of liquidation of Governments has dampened during periods of declining bond prices. The postwar investment policies of life insurance companies fall into two easily identifiable phases determined by the Federal Reserve-Treasury accord of March, 1951. Prior to this date, government bond prices were in effect pegged by Federal Reserve action, whereas subsequently, bond prices were freed to respond to ordinary money market forces. In general, the pre-accord period was one of large-scale liquidation of Governments whose pegged prices made them virtually the equivalent of cash; while liquidation continued during the post-accord years, it was undertaken with hesitation. In fact, by the end of the 1950's, life insurance companies had generally brought their government holdings into balance in relation to the rest of their portfolios and they were frequently found on the buying side of the market during the last few years. One can identify three broad divisions among the postwar years within which the investment behavior of life insurance companies can be examined. Within these, of course, there were subperiods in which the flow of life insurance funds experienced radical shifts. This was especially true during alternating periods of credit stringency and ease.

At the end of 1959, life insurance companies owned $6,868 million of United States government securities, representing 6.0 percent of total assets.[1] Since 1946, ownership of Governments by life insurance companies declined in every year except 1958 when a slight increase was induced by the drop in private demand for funds during the 1957-58 recession. From $21,629 million held at the end of 1946, the amount had thus fallen $14.7 billion by December, 1959. While the rate of decline averaged $1,130 million per year, $5.6 billion (38 percent of the total liquidation) occurred in two years—1948 and 1951.

While the liquidation of government securities by life insurance companies in the postwar period is emphasized in this study, the argument should not be interpreted to imply that there is no basic demand for Governments by these institutions. On the contrary, the role of Governments in the portfolios of life insurance companies is so fundamental that these institutions, virtually without exception, would hold some government securities under almost all economic conditions. This fact was clearly borne out in the BBER-MSU Survey of the companies' investment policies. In the survey, portfolio managers were asked to indicate their company's main objective, other than to obtain the interest return, in holding United States government securities. Only one of the 111 officers who replied reported that his company "does not own any Governments and does not want any." The reason why life insurance companies have a basic demand for Governments is easily understood. The increased flexibility in monetary policy after the Treasury-Federal Reserve accord of 1951, prompted portfolio managers to give more attention than ever to the course of interest rates on government issues.[2] Market yields on these obligations are generally considered to be the basic rates in the short-, intermediate-, and long-term markets for funds. Because of the large supply of treasury obligations, their marketability, and the absence of credit risk, life insurance companies use them as the criteria against which to measure all other investments.

In the 1959 survey, individual companies reported a variety of specific objectives motivating their decision to hold a minimum amount of government securities. The major objectives can be summarized under a few broad headings; these are classified in Table V-1 according to size group of companies submitting replies. The leading motives behind the demand for Governments seems to be the provision of (1) portfolio

TABLE V-1

MAJOR OBJECTIVES OF LIFE INSURANCE COMPANIES IN HOLDING U. S. GOVERNMENT SECURITIES, BY SIZE OF COMPANY, MARCH, 1959

Objective	Total	Size Group I	Size Group II	Size Group III	Size Group IV
A. Overall Portfolio Liquidity	32	11	8	5	8
B. Portfolio Diversification	32	4	5	11	12
C. Temporary Investment to Meet Previous Commitments	5	4	1	0	0
D. Contingency Reserve to Take Advantage of Favorable Investment Opportunities	5	1	2	1	1
E. Other Objectives	18	4	5	6	3
"Locked-in," prefer to sell	7	2	1	3	1
To assist U.S. Treasury in debt management	3	0	0	2	1
"Window-dressing"	2	0	1	1	0
Deposit requirement or tax advantage in some states	4	0	3	0	1
Other reasons	2	2	0	0	0
F. Combination of Objectives	18	4	7	5	2
A. and B.	5	2	2	0	1
B. and D.	6	1	1	3	1
Other combinations	7	1	4	2	0
G. No U.S. Governments Owned	1	0	0	0	1
Total Companies	111	28	28	28	27

Size Group	Size Range in Millions of Dollars
Group I	359-13,919
II	121-357
III	52-111
IV	23-52

SOURCE: BBER-MSU Survey, Spring, 1959.

liquidity and (2) diversification without specific reference to liquidity. The frequency of these two reasons was heavy among companies in each size group; these reasons were also given in combination with one or more other objectives. However, the liquidity motive tends to predominate among the larger companies; three-fifths of the institutions assigning top priority to liquidity were in size Groups I and II, where the total assets of individual companies were $111 million or above. On the other hand, more than 70 percent of the companies citing portfolio diversification as the main objective were in Groups III and IV, in which the assets of individual companies ranged between $23 million and $50 million. Before examining other objectives shown in Table V-1, the two most popular aims will be analyzed more closely.

As mentioned in Chapter IV, life insurance companies require liquidity to facilitate portfolio management rather than to meet withdrawals of funds by policyholders. It was shown that these institutions shift funds from one investment area to another when differentials in yields make this action appear desirable. Many investment officers say that this shifting has nothing to do with liquidity.[3] Nevertheless, they would be unable to take advantage of favorable yield spreads unless they held an appropriate amount of liquid assets. A substantial part of their Government holdings meets this requirement. Moreover, as also mentioned above, uncertainty about future interest rate trends may also induce life insurance companies to build up liquidity through holdings of short-term Governments. This behavior has been questioned.[4] However, one observer re-inforced the argument as follows:

> I have never been convinced fully by the explanation given of the rise in liquidity of life insurance companies during the fall and winter of 1950-51. Large residential mortgage commitments were made by lenders in the late summer and early fall of 1950 to "beat the gun" of Regulation X. Then cash and short-term governments increased about 800 million dollars in the portfolios of life companies. But why did these commitments lead to such an extent to the sale of long-term governments and the build-up of liquidity? Why did the companies not count on future sales of long-term governments to cover commitments? Federal policy had made long-terms the equivalent of demand obligations for nearly ten years. Could it not have been the increased uncertainty as to the continuation of par support for long terms? This uncertainty started as early as August 18, 1950, when the Treasury and Federal Reserve issued statements indicating sharp disagreements as to proper policy, and certainly had grown to great proportions by March, 1951. While the selling of long-terms might have been less at this time without the mortgage commitments, I suspect it would have been considerably less without the uncertainty.[5]

The above position is supported by other students of the Government securities market.[6] Numerous portfolio managers, while arguing that the post-Korean increase in liquid assets held by life insurance companies is attributable to increases in forward commitments, also testify to the crucial role of Governments in the provision of liquidity.[7]

The use of Governments to achieve portfolio diversification was cited by several life insurance companies in the BBER-MSU Survey as being superior to the alternative of trying to acquire a variety of assets in numerous industries spread over diverse economic areas. This objective was cited mainly by smaller companies without facilities to perform the security analysis necessary to maintain diversification in the traditional way. For them, the acquisition of Governments is both easy and direct. They can always choose from a variety of issues of different maturities. The ordinary processes of security analysis are unnecessary; the credit rating of the borrower is obviously satisfactory, and no question must be raised concerning technical efficiency or managerial ability. As for safety of principal, government securities can be acquired with absolute confidence, and their marketability in case of need is never in doubt.

A few large companies reported that they hold government securities chiefly as a temporary investment of funds intended to meet previous commitments. While the inflow of funds through premiums and repayment of loans is normally sufficient to meet such commitments, portfolio managers indicated that it is sometimes necessary to accumulate funds in anticipation of exceptionally large or sustained drawings against commitments. None of the smaller companies reported holding Governments mainly for this purpose. A few companies also reported that they hold Governments as a contingency reserve to take advantage of favorable investment opportunities. However, from the context of both of these reasons given by life insurance companies for holding government securities, it is difficult to distinguish between the overall liquidity demand mentioned above and the necessity to meet commitments or maintain a contingency reserve.

A fair number of companies reported that they still hold a sizable amount of government securities because they wish to avoid the capital losses they would suffer if they were to sell such issues—as they would like to do. A few companies said that in the recessions of 1953-54 and 1957-58, they sold government bonds when the rise in prices pared the size of capital losses, and reinvested the proceeds in mortgages or in treasury bills to await the acquisition of mortgages for which forward commitments had been made. It should be observed from Table V-1 that the fear of capital losses as an explanation of the ownership of Governments was given by small as well as large life insurance companies. Undoubtedly a much larger number of companies would have emphasized this motive during the early postwar years; but by the spring of 1959 most companies had probably achieved a desirable balance in their holdings of Governments in relation to the rest of their portfolios.

Three companies replied that they hold Governments simply to aid the United States Treasury in managing the public debt. All of these were small companies. Two other companies said that their Governments are only "window dressing"—held simply because supervisory officials expect to see Governments in life insurance companies' portfolios. Otherwise they would prefer to hold cash for liquidity needs and to acquire assets providing a higher rate of return than that obtainable on Governments. Both of these were medium sized stock companies. Some states require life insurance companies to maintain within the state a certain amount of assets in relation to policy claims of their citizens; a few companies have chosen to meet the requirement by holding government securities. Moreover, several states offer a tax advantage to life insurance companies if they hold a certain amount of assets represented by loans extended to domestic firms. While the objective of this type of provision is to foster economic development within the state, the requirement has been liberally interpreted in some states to mean that it can be satisfied by holding Governments if the companies claim that suitable outlets are not readily available through loans to domestic enterprises.

Several other motives were given by life insurance companies for holding Governments, and the above objectives were mentioned in various combinations. An examination of these in detail would add little to the overall perspective and therefore will not be pursued. Instead, the participation of life insurance companies in the government securities market will be traced. Section II contains a survey of investment experience with Governments prior to World War II; the main focus is on the depression years of the 1930's. The contributions of life insurance companies to the financing of World War II are appraised in Section III. The postwar experience is explored in Section IV, with special emphasis on the impact of monetary and debt management policies on the investment behavior of these institutions.

Section II
Investment in Government Securities Before World War II

A. Early Experience

As indicated earlier, the history of life insurance company investments in obligations of the federal government is primarily the reflection of a lack of private demand for funds. This story is clearly told in Table V-2.

TABLE V-2

NET CHANGES IN HOLDINGS OF U. S. GOVERNMENT SECURITIES BY LIFE INSURANCE COMPANIES IN PERIODS OF PROSPERITY, DEPRESSION, AND WAR
(In Millions of Dollars)

Period	Net Change in U. S. Government Securities	Net Change in Total Assets	Net Change in Governments as Percent of Net Change in Total Assets
Prosperity Periods			
1890-1893	− 1	217	− 0.5
1897-1916	− 13	4,192	− 0.3
1922-1930	− 552	10,228	− 5.1
1945-1959	−13,715	68,853	−19.9
Depression Periods			
1893-1897	10	357	2.8
1920-1922	77	1,332	5.8
1930-1940	5,583	11,922	47.1
War Periods			
1916-1919	778	1,254	62.3
1940-1945	14,816	13,995	105.9

SOURCE: **1960 Life Insurance Fact Book,** p. 64.

But even during the periods for which no detailed statistics on investments are available, one can find evidence to support this conclusion. Until the outbreak of the Civil War, government securities were not generally considered an investment outlet for life insurance funds.[8] After 1861, however, investments quickly shifted into government bonds. During the war years, the government resorted to large issues of paper currency, and the efforts of the public to use the expanded money supply in the face of reduced availability of civilian goods led to highly inflated commodity prices. At the same time, gold went to an unparalleled premium. Interest on government bonds was payable in gold, and many life insurance companies sold their government holdings, realizing a rate of return in paper as high as 10 percent. This rate was so attractive that practically all new insurance funds went into Governments which many companies subsequently sold. With the conclusion of the war, the general level of prices declined sharply and carried the premium on gold down with them. As the yields on Governments dropped appreciably, life insurance companies sold them and invested in other assets. Briefly, after the depression of 1873 and the great decline in real estate values, insurance companies again purchased Governments—even at a lower yield. Nevertheless, Governments decreased from about 10 percent of assets during the Civil War to 8.7 percent in 1880. By 1893, they had declined further to the nominal figure of 0.5 percent.[9]

From 1890, the record of life insurance companies' investments is detailed enough to permit a systematic analysis of their activities in the government securities market. It will be seen in Table V-2 that these institutions made net purchases of $10 million of Governments during the depression of 1893-97, which represented 3 percent of the growth of total assets. While these acquisitions were rather small, they occurred despite the considerable rise in the companies' holdings of railroad bonds, which advanced from 21 percent of total assets in 1890 to 29 percent in 1900.

The next and far more striking example of the use of government securities as a residual outlet for life insurance funds is provided by the World War I experience. At the end of 1916, life insurance companies held only $2 million in federal obligations, an amount much less than 0.1 percent of total assets. By the end of 1919, they owned $780 million of such securities, equal to 12 percent of all assets. Furthermore, during the war, these institutions placed more than three-fifths of their new funds in Governments. While perhaps some part of life insurance companies' investment in Governments during the war years can be attributed to patriotic motives, their behavior in the immediate postwar period was purely economic in character. From the end of 1919 through mid-1920, yields on long-term treasury bonds rose from around 4.5 percent to well over 5.5 percent.[10] As the prices fell, government bonds appeared to be bargains to many portfolio managers, a view reinforced by the shrinkage in alternative investment opportunities. On balance, life insurance companies channeled almost 6 percent of their new funds into Governments during 1920-22. Many companies, no doubt, were greatly impressed by the safety features of these issues which were clearly highlighted by the business difficulties encountered in these depression years.

B. Experience During the Depression of the 1930's

The experience of the early 1920's, however, was only a slight indication of the shift to Governments which was to occur during the next depression. Not only did these securities provide the major outlet for life insurance funds during the 1930's, but it was also in this decade that life insurance companies emerged as dominant factors in the government bond market.[11] Between 1930 and 1940, life insurance companies' investments in federal issues multiplied eighteen times. In other words, the rise in life companies' holdings of government securities in that decade was far more rapid proportionately than either the growth in the public debt or the growth in treasury issues held by any other financial institutions. At the end of 1940, life insurance companies owned $5,767 million of government obligations, representing nearly one-fifth of their total assets. Since 1931, there had been no interruption in their annual purchases of treasury issues. Over the period as a whole, these institutions increased their holdings of Governments by $5,583 million, an amount equal to 47 percent of the rise in total assets. At the bottom of the depression, however, the proportion of new funds invested in Governments was far greater: in 1933, the rise in Governments was almost three times the increase in total assets, while in 1934 the expansion of Governments was 106 percent of the net increase in total assets. (See Table V-3.)

This dramatic transition to the government securities market was noted at the time by the life insurance companies themselves. It was observed that the ". . . sharply accelerating trend toward federal obligations since 1932 . . . has been the most striking reaction of life insurance funds to the abnormal conditions affecting the investment market."[12] This reorientation of life insurance companies' investment activities can be explained on numerous grounds. First, of course, was the persistent growth of savings in the form of policy reserves. Even in 1933, these reserves increased by $238 million, and over the entire decade they rose by an aver-

TABLE V-3

NET CHANGES IN U. S. GOVERNMENT SECURITIES
AND IN TOTAL ASSETS HELD BY LIFE INSURANCE COMPANIES, 1931-1940
(In Millions of Dollars)

Year	Net Change in U. S. Government Securities	Net Change in Total Assets	Net Change in Governments as Percent of Net Change in Total Assets
1931	55	1,280	4.3
1932	75	594	12.6
1933	412	142	290.1
1934	1,008	948	106.3
1935	1,042	1,372	75.9
1936	1,031	1,658	62.2
1937	719	1,375	52.3
1938	321	1,506	21.3
1939	431	1,488	29.0
1940	487	1,559	31.2

SOURCE: **1960 Life Insurance Fact Book,** pp. 62 and 67.

age of $1,100 million per year. Simultaneously, there was a considerable contraction of alternative investment outlets, reflected in the demoralization of the railroad bond and real estate market, and in the decline in new corporate security flotations. Thus, life insurance companies became interested in the government securities market primarily for safety reasons but also because they could find little else to do with their funds. While the growth of the federal debt (considerable in terms of pre-World War II experience) was leading many investors to actively study the government bond market more closely in search of investment opportunities, numerous life insurance companies preferred to hold idle balances for several years and only turned to Governments as the pressure to obtain earning assets forced them to reduce their cash holdings.[13]

When life insurance companies did enter the market for government obligations, the impact was far greater than is indicated by the increase in their holdings of these issues. Their emergence was also reflected in the quickening of competitive bidding. Perhaps of more significance was the reservoir of purchasing power which life insurance companies brought to the market. On numerous occasions after 1935, when commercial banks and other investors withdrew from the market and left it to flounder without leadership, life insurance companies entered large buying orders and—through their activities—stimulated the entire government list. For example, their role was especially evident in the spring of 1937. During those months, a few scattered life insurance companies were virtually the only purchasers in the market except for federal agencies.[14] Over the year 1937 as a whole, these institutions increased their holdings of Governments by $697 million; in the same period, they purchased $750 million of government bonds from commercial banks, and thus provided funds which the banks could use to acquire additional bonds. By the end of the decade, life insurance companies had acquired a wide reputation as leading investors in government securities. In fact, so secure was that reputation that the Treasury developed around these institutions a major part of the program for financing World War II and shaped many of its long-term issues to suit them.

Section III
Investment in Government Securities During World War II

A. General Framework of War Finance

As was to be expected, the investment behavior of life insurance companies during World War II was dominated by the financial policies of the federal government. Congress failed to adopt a fiscal policy with taxes sufficiently high to pay for the bulk of war expenditures; instead, more than one-half of the required funds came from deficit financing, with a sizable share of the debt being acquired by life insurance companies and other nonbank investors, and an even larger share being acquired by commercial banks. To facilitate this borrowing, the Treasury, with the help of the Federal Reserve System, set and maintained maximum rates of interest for its new issues. The structure of rates, mainly based on the low yields prevailing during the depression years of the 1930's, was characterized by a wide spread between the short-term and long-term ends of the yield curve. However, minor changes were made from prewar yields. Treasury bills, which yielded only slightly above zero, were permitted to increase to a yield of ⅜ percent. This rate was solidified by the announcement that the Federal Reserve Banks would purchase all bills offered to them and would permit those who sold bills to the System to repurchase them before maturity at the same yield. The rate on certificates maturing in one year was set at ⅞ percent. The rates adopted on longer-term issues (in which life insurance companies were particularly interested) were 2 percent on 8-10 year bonds and 2½ percent on those of 20-25 year maturity. The latter were to be ineligible for general purchase by commercial banks. Market yields for securities of other terms were kept adjusted to these maximum rates. Within this structure of rates, the Treasury issued virtually identical securities in each of the eight war loan drives, and this more or less guaranteed the appearance of speculative subscriptions.[15]

At first, the pattern of rates was viewed with skepticism by many investors who doubted the government's ability to keep it stable. Numerous investors, on the other hand, were afraid of the consequences which would follow the successful execution of the plan. Despite the misgivings of the market, the Treasury made the first offering of 8-10 year 2 percent bonds in October, 1942. The offering was made with the knowledge that its success depended on the response of commercial banks and insurance companies as well as of other savings institutions, but these investors were disappointed with the terms of the issue. An adequate amount of subscriptions to cover the loan was obtained only as a result of strong requests by Treasury and Federal Reserve officials directed to principal institutions and dealers. It was followed by the Treasury's announcement that 2 percent was the maximum rate that it would pay on securities available for commercial bank holding. After this near failure, the Treasury adopted a new method of preparing the market for its offerings. Instead of coming to the market with frequent offerings on short notice and with little publicity and little time to promote sales campaigns, the Treasury shifted to the procedure of using what were termed war loan drives. In the new approach, considerable advance notice and publicity were given the issues to be included in each drive and the quotas, or sales goals, for the volunteer organizations to reach.

At about the same time, commercial banks, life insurance companies, and other professional investors began to recognize that the pattern of rates provided a virtually unavoidable appreciation in the price of each new issue of longer than one-year term. A 2 percent, 8-year bond that could be purchased at par had to increase steadily in price along a line of yields that ended at ⅞ percent for one year. As the market became more confident that the government would not permit yields to exceed the maximum rates established, subscriptions for new issues increased sharply. Investors had translated the actions of the authorities to mean that the war would, in fact, be financed within the structure of rates adopted; this meant that intermediate and long-term government securities were almost bound to provide yields substantially above the coupon rates as a result of the combination of interest and appreciation. Increasingly, the profits to be obtained encouraged speculative subscriptions for securities and the sale of those acquired in a prior drive in order to subscribe for issues offered in a current one. The practices became known as "free riding" and "playing the pattern of rates."

The conflict between the Treasury's stated policies and its borrowing methods created a situation in which insurance companies, mutual savings banks, and others were able to oversubscribe for bank-restricted bonds, hold them a short time, and then sell them to commercial banks at an assured profit. Since the commercial banks' profit was also assured, they continued to reach out for such obligations; in addition, many individuals subscribed for bank-eligible bonds in the drives for the sole purpose of selling them to the banks. The removal of reserve requirements against war loan deposits provided the commercial banks with the necessary funds to acquire the bonds liquidated by other investors. Since most of the nonbank subscriptions were paid for by crediting war loan accounts, against which commercial banks were not required to hold reserves, the resulting transfer of deposits from private accounts to war loan accounts reduced the reserve requirements of commercial banks. This, too, gave to the banks excess funds that they could invest. The banks, of course, felt perfectly safe in purchasing these securities, because the Federal Reserve System had an unlimited bid for all government securities at the pegs. Whenever the banks ran short of reserves they sold securities, and the latter, in the absence of private demand, were purchased by the

System. Since all taxable government securities consequently were in effect demand obligations at the various points in the yield curve, the banks obviously preferred to sell the lowest yielding securities that they had in their portfolios. They first sold the ⅜ percent bills, and as their holdings of bills became depleted they shifted their sales to ⅞ percent certificates.

The Treasury, in an effort to restrict commercial banks' subscriptions for government securities, used a formula in the first two drives which allowed them to subscribe only specified dollar amounts. In the third war loan, commercial banks were not permitted to subscribe during the drive, but were allowed to subscribe under a formula after the drive. In subsequent drives, subscriptions by these banks were allowed only on the basis of a scheme that permitted small subscriptions relative to only their time deposits. In the seventh war loan, the Treasury eliminated 2 percent bonds and included 1½ percent bonds instead, with a resulting sharp rise in prices of outstanding bank-eligible issues.

For the most part, the Treasury and the Federal Reserve System were successful in financing the war according to the plan adopted in late 1941 and early 1942. In retrospect, the statement made by the System in December, 1941, reads more like a description of later developments than a confident prediction:

> The existing supply of funds and of bank reserves is fully adequate to meet all present and prospective needs of the Government and private activity. The Federal Reserve System has powers to add to these resources to whatever extent may be required in the future. The System is prepared to use its power to assure that an ample supply of funds is available at all times for financing the war effort and to exert its influence toward maintaining conditions in the United States Government security market that are satisfactory from the standpoint of the Government's requirements.[16]

In the last sentence of this statement, one finds the seeds of the difficulties which were to plague the monetary authorities in the postwar period. In this commitment, the System agreed to keep the market in such a condition that interest rates on future security issues could be whatever the Treasury chose to make them. It was also a sharp break with previous responsibilities assumed by the System, which, theretofore, had undertaken only to see that orderly conditions existed in the market. With this commitment, and after the Treasury's choice of a pattern of yields, the Federal Reserve System found it necessary to prevent the development of disorderly conditions in the market. The stage was set not only for war financing but also for the postwar engine of inflation to which life insurance companies were destined to add considerable fuel.

B. Purchases of Governments by Life Insurance Companies

As already mentioned, when the program for financing World War II was being developed, treasury officials gave special attention to the long-term funds accumulating with life insurance companies. In fact, one of the major decisions as to the form which borrowing should take was influenced by the possibility of tapping these funds.[17] With this objective in mind, the Treasury designed a 20-25 year security carrying a coupon of 2½ percent and not available for investment by commercial banks. The first issue of these bonds appeared on May 4, 1942, and an additional amount was offered in the following October. In every one of the eight war loans which followed subsequently, the Treasury included a substantial amount of the long-term bank-restricted bonds. The extent to which life insurance companies participated in the purchase of these and other securities is shown in Tables V-4 and V-5.

In view of the method adopted by the Treasury for establishing quotas for different types of investors, one is not surprised to discover that life insurance companies acquired an average of 12 percent of the total amount of securities issued in the eight war loans. Moreover, in terms of the types of securities acquired, the pattern is consistent with their needs as long-term investors. The 2½ percent bank-restricted bonds represented almost three-fourths of their total acquisitions. Although the proportion of a long-term offering obtained by life insurance companies dropped to just over one-fifth in the eighth war loan, these institutions purchased an

TABLE V-4

PARTICIPATION OF LIFE INSURANCE COMPANIES IN WAR LOANS DURING WORLD WAR II
(In Millions of Dollars)

War Loan	Total Amount Issued	Acquired by Life Insurance Companies: Amount	Acquired by Life Insurance Companies: Percent of Total
I	12,947	1,436	11.1
II	18,543	2,049	11.0
III	18,943	2,315	12.2
IV	16,730	1,803	10.8
V	20,639	2,273	11.0
VI	21,621	2,534	11.7
VII	26,313	3,072	11.7
VIII	21,144	2,569	12.2
Total	156,880	18,051	11.5

SOURCE: **U. S. Treasury Bulletin.**

TABLE V-5

PARTICIPATION OF LIFE INSURANCE COMPANIES IN WAR LOANS BY TYPE OF SECURITIES ACQUIRED

(In Millions of Dollars)

Loan	⅞ Percent Certificates			2 Percent Bank-eligible Bonds			2½ Percent Bank-restricted Bonds		
	Total	Acquired by Life Insurance Companies		Total	Acquired by Life Insurance Companies		Total	Acquired by Life Insurance Companies	
	Issued	Amount	Percent	Issued	Amount	Percent	Issued	Amount	Percent
I	3,800	10	0.3	3,062[1]	184	6.0	2,831	1,242	43.9
II	5,251	37	0.7	4,939	581	11.8	3,762	1,431	38.0
III	4,122	23	0.6	5,257	775	14.7	3,777	1,517	40.2
IV	5,036	93	1.8	3,331[2]	622	18.7	1,920	1,088	56.7
V	4,770	49	1.0	5,229	919	17.6	2,263	1,305	57.7
VI	4,405	42	1.0	6,939	971	14.0	2,711	1,487	54.9
VII	4,784	10	0.2	5,077[2]	421	8.3	7,088	2,641	37.3
VIII	3,737	1	—	3,045[2]	280	9.2	9,819	2,288	23.3
Total	35,905	265	0.7	36,879	4,753	12.9	34,171	12,999	38.0

1. 1¾ percent bond.

2. 2¼ percent bond, bank-restricted.

SOURCE: **U. S. Treasury Bulletin.**

average of 38 percent of total long-term issues sold during the drives. In the fourth and fifth loans, their share of long-term bonds rose as high as 57 percent. As an inducement to life insurance companies to invest in government securities, and as an aid to help them carry their allotments, the Treasury permitted them to defer payment for almost 30 days on their subscriptions to the 2 percent and 2½ percent bonds offered during the third war loan drive.[18] This practice was repeated for all the remaining loan drives and, beginning with the fifth loan, was broadened to include other savings institutions, state and local governments, and public corporations and agencies.

This participation of life insurance companies in war financing was clearly reflected in the transformation of their portfolios. At the end of 1940, they held $5,767 million of government securities, representing about one-fifth of their total assets. By the end of 1945, their government holdings had risen almost four times and amounted to $20,583 million, or about 46 percent of total assets. The impact of the shift to the government securities market is shown in Table V-6. Government issues not only provided an outlet for new funds flowing to life insurance companies but also offset the decline in their holdings of private debt. Over the period as a whole, the growth of the companies' government portfolio was about 6 percent greater than the rise in total assets. However, at the height of war financing in 1944, life insurance companies made net investments of close to $4 billion in Governments while total assets increased by $3.3 billion; in that year the expansion in government securities was more than one-fifth greater than that of total assets.

Many investment officers have emphasized patriotic motives in explain-

TABLE V-6

NET CHANGE IN TOTAL ASSETS AND IN U. S. GOVERNMENT SECURITIES OWNED BY LIFE INSURANCE COMPANIES, 1941-1945
(In Millions of Dollars)

Year	Net Change in Governments	Net Change in Total Assets	Ratio of Net Change in Governments to Net Change in Total Assets (Percent)
1941	1,029	1,929	53.3
1942	2,499	2,200	113.6
1943	3,242	2,835	114.4
1944	3,994	3,288	121.5
1945	4,052	3,743	108.3
Total	14,816	13,995	105.9

SOURCE: **1960 Life Insurance Fact Book,** pp. 62 and 67.

ing the concentration of life insurance companies on Governments during World War II.[19] On close examination, however, one discovers that these institutions had a considerable incentive derived purely from the investment advantages of Governments. These advantages, combined with the virtual absence of alternative outlets for funds, were major stimulants to the flow of life insurance funds to the government securities market. It will be recalled that the war years were marked by a large growth in the supply of investible funds, an improved financial position of business which led to large-scale repayment and refunding of corporate and private debt, and a further narrowing of yield differentials. Although the yields on the new offerings of Governments were below the contractual earnings rate required by many companies, the more or less absolute safety of these issues, compared with the few alternatives available, induced nearly all portfolio managers to turn to Governments.

C. Sales of Governments by Life Insurance Companies

Behind the rapid absorption of government securities by life insurance companies one can detect a countertrend. While their total holdings of these issues advanced by $14.8 billion between 1941 and 1945, they liquidated close to $4.6 billion of low-yielding tax-exempt securities. In other words, as shown in Table V-7, life insurance companies were able to obtain almost one-third of their net investment in Governments during World War II through the sale of issues held at the beginning of the

TABLE V-7

HOLDINGS AND NET CHANGES IN TOTAL AND TAX-EXEMPT
U. S. GOVERNMENT SECURITIES OWNED BY LIFE INSURANCE COMPANIES, 1941-1945
(In Millions of Dollars)

	Holdings of Governments			Net Change in Holdings		
		Tax-exempt[1]			Tax-exempt[1]	
Year	Total	Amount	Percent of Total	Total	Amount	Percent of Total
1941	6,796	4,820	70.9	1,029	—	—
1942	9,295	4,042	43.5	2,499	− 778	−31.1
1943	12,537	2,538	20.2	3,242	−1,504	−46.4
1944	16,531	1,309	7.9	3,994	−1,229	−30.8
1945	20,583	270	1.3	4,052	−1,039	−25.6
Total	—	—	—	14,816	−4,550	−30.7

1. Includes securities both wholly and partially exempt from federal income taxes.

SOURCE: **U. S. Treasury Bulletin** and **1960 Life Insurance Fact Book,** p. 67.

conflict. A considerable part of the securities sold by life insurance companies was purchased by commercial banks, thus offsetting to some extent the efforts of the Treasury to minimize bank financing of the war effort. The revision of the federal income tax regulations early in 1942 provided a major inducement to life insurance institutions to sell tax-exempt bonds. In the spring of that year, the Treasury worked out a procedure with representatives of the life insurance industry which had the practical effect of holding the amount of tax on the companies' investment income to about 3 percent.[20] With this change, it was clearly to the companies' advantage to sell tax-exempt securities and acquire those taxable issues coming onto the market. Even after taxes, long-term Governments carrying a 2½ percent coupon still provided a net yield well over 2.4 percent, considerably more than that obtainable on the tax-exempt issues.

During the greater part of 1942, the uncertainty in the minds of commercial bankers and other investors subject to high tax rates (especially uncertainty relating to the stability of wartime financing yields and tax legislation) reduced the demand for wholly or partially exempt securities which were potentially for sale by both life insurance companies and savings banks. This relative narrowness of the market is reflected in the fact that life insurance companies reduced their holdings of tax-exempt issues by only $778 million in 1942 although they acquired well over $3 billion of taxable Governments. Early in 1943, however, the situation changed drastically.[21] The demand from commercial banks expanded rapidly, and over the course of the year life insurance companies liquidated $1.5 billion of wholly and partially tax-exempt issues. This rate of reduction was almost twice as fast as that of the previous year. Moreover, the amount sold was 46 percent of the increase in total Governments held by these institutions.

However, issues possessing a tax advantage for commercial banks were not the only type of government obligations sold by life insurance companies during the war years. As shown in Table V-8, these institutions liquidated a substantial part of the taxable bank-eligible intermediate bonds acquired in the various war loan drives. Of the $3,187 million of bank-eligible issues of intermediate term which life insurance companies purchased in the eight war loans, they sold $1,056 million (or 33 percent) by March 31, 1946. On the other hand, by March, 1946, they had sold virtually none of those securities with similar maturity but not eligible for investment by commercial banks. The heaviest selling of intermediate securities centered in those acquired during the first and second loans. Almost three-quarters of the $190 million of the issue obtained in the first loan was subsequently sold, while 44 percent ($256 million) of the

TABLE V-8

INTERMEDIATE SECURITIES ACQUIRED BY LIFE INSURANCE COMPANIES DURING WAR LOANS AND SUBSEQUENTLY SOLD BEFORE MARCH 31, 1946

(In Millions of Dollars)

	Amount Acquired		Sales by March 31, 1946			
					Percent of Acquisition	
War Loan	Bank-eligible	Bank-restricted	Bank-eligible	Bank-restricted	Bank-eligible	Bank-restricted
I	190	—	141	—	74.2	—
II	582	—	256	—	44.0	—
III	775	—	147	—	19.0	—
IV[1]	—	757	—	75	—	9.9
V	669	—	191	—	28.6	—
VI	971	—	321	—	33.1	—
VII[1]	—	421	—	−139[2]	−33.0	−33.0
VIII[1]	—	280	—	—	—	—
Total	3,187	1,458	1,056	− 64[2]	33.0	− 4.4[2]

1. Bank-restricted issues were sold.

2. Represents an increase.

SOURCE: **U. S. Treasury Bulletin.**

$582 million acquired in the second was liquidated. The intermediate issues sold by life insurance companies traded at substantial premiums during the period March 31, 1943 through March 31, 1946 and afforded sizable capital gains. Although the pattern of sales was mixed, the pace of liquidation quickened considerably as the premium rose, and bank-eligible issues tended to carry larger premiums than those restricted to nonbank investors.

D. Speculation in Government Securities

As indicated above, one of the most serious problems to arise in connection with the financing of World War II was posed by the practice of free riding. This phrase covers numerous types of speculation in government bonds, but the essential feature as applied to activities during the war loans was the purchase of securities with the aim of obtaining a riskless profit by rapid resale of issues allotted by the Treasury.[22] While free riding acquired the proportion of a major financing industry after the first two loans were over, it has been generally held that life insurance companies did not participate in the practice to any significant extent.[23] The objective in this section is to present an estimate of the part which these institutions actually played in free riding. First, however, the nature and origins of free riding during World War II will be sketched.

Free riding sprang directly from underpricing of securities by the Treasury. Since issues were sold at par and rationed among subscribers, the latter could count on reselling all or a major part of their allotments at a premium. The exclusion of commercial banks from direct participation in war loans (after the first two had passed) and the maintenance by the Federal Reserve System of a fixed structure of interest rates more or less guaranteed enormous profits from free riding. The prospect of the market being flooded within a few months by the issuance of new bonds of the type outstanding served only to reduce premiums on existing issues and not to eliminate free riding.

Actually, speculation in the government bond market was a practice widely engaged in long before World War II.[24] The crucial difference was that in earlier years speculators took considerable risk, while during the period of war financing no such risk was involved. On the eve of the United States' entry into World War II, the Treasury for the first time took definite steps to insure a minimum of free riding.[25] For the two offerings of bonds on December 4, 1941, potential subscribers were grouped into four classes and specific conditions of allotments were established. Subscriptions were limited as follows:[26]

> Insurance companies, mutual savings and cooperative banks, federal savings and loan associations, trust accounts and investment corporations, pension funds, and similar institutions and funds—not to exceed 10 percent of total resources.
>
> Banks and trust companies for their own account—not to exceed 50 percent of capital and surplus.
>
> Corporations organized for profit, and dealers and brokers—not to exceed 50 percent of net worth.
>
> Individuals—not to exceed 50 percent of net worth or 100 percent of cash deposited with subscription, but no preferred allotment was made on such fully-paid subscription.

Soon after the beginning of hostilities, the Treasury made another effort to remedy the situation created by speculative subscriptions. On May 4, 1942, in connection with an offering of 2½ percent bonds of 1962-67, the Treasury specified that all subscriptions other than those submitted by banking institutions must be accompanied by payment in full; it was announced also that all subscriptions other than those of commercial banks would be allotted in full. As war financing developed, the Federal

Open Market Committee virtually required dealers to shape their operations according to the committee's direction, a further effort to eliminate free riding. For the fourth and fifth war loan drives, an understanding along similar lines was reached between the Treasury and government bond dealers. These restrictions on subscriptions by dealers and others, however, were only partially effective. The allotment in full of all subscriptions to nonbank investors and the restriction of such allocations to commercial banks for the investment of their time deposits went quite far in establishing the conditions for the re-emergence of free riding. The limitation on purchases by commercial banks imparted a scarcity value to bank-eligible issues and made these institutions excellent markets for the subscriptions of free riders. At the same time, the policy of fully allotting the nonbank subscriptions made it possible for free riders to profit on the whole amount of their applications. Previously, the speculative subscriber assumed a risk on the entire application since he did not know what proportion would be allotted; on the other hand, he stood to gain only on the amount actually allotted. The new policy removed the risk basis and equated the profit basis to the whole amount of securities applied for.

The scope of free riding was only partially curbed by the periodic flooding of the market with securities of substantially the same description. Through the first five war loans, the potential gains from free riding were relatively small. In Table V-9 are shown the premiums on selected securities offered in the war loans on the first day of trading following the close of the loan and two months thereafter. In terms of closing over-the-counter bid prices, first trading day premiums on certificates never exceeded $0.07 per $100 through the middle of 1944, and those on 2½ percent bank-restricted bonds were never greater than $0.12 per $100. In contrast, premiums on bank-eligible 2 percent bonds on the first day of trading rose to $0.25 per $100 during the fifth war loan. These higher premiums were a reflection of the wider market provided by commercial banks as well as their scarcity value, derived from the frequent changes in the types of intermediate securities offered and from the elimination of such issues in the fourth and eighth loans. During the first five war loans, premiums obtained two months after the close of the loan were usually (but not consistently) higher than on the first day of trading. But even after two months of trading, the premiums on bank-eligible issues were never as high as one point; in the case of bank-restricted securities the premium was even smaller. The situation changed rapidly with the sixth war loan, however. In the previous loans, the potential profit through free riding aggregated about $62 million—more than one-third of which

TABLE V-9

PREMIUMS ON SELECTED SECURITIES OFFERED IN THE WAR LOANS ON THE FIRST DAY OF TRADING FOLLOWING THE CLOSE OF THE LOANS AND TWO MONTHS THEREAFTER

(Premiums in Dollars and Cents Per $100 Based on Over-the-Counter Bid Prices)

		⅞ Percent Certificates		2 Percent Bank-eligible Bonds		2½ Percent Bank-restricted Bonds	
Loan	First Day of Trading	First Day	Two Months Later	First Day	Two Months Later	First Day	Two Months Later
I	December 24, 1942	0.00	0.12	0.03[1]	0.44[1]	0.00	0.38
II	May 3, 1943	0.04	0.14	0.22	0.94	0.12	0.47
III	October 11, 1943	0.03	0.08	0.19	0.19	0.09	0.00
IV	February 16, 1944	0.06	0.08	n.o.	—	0.00	0.12
V	July 10, 1944	0.07	0.08	0.25	0.50	0.03	0.38
VI	December 18, 1944	0.04	0.10	0.28	1.62	0.16	1.60
VII	July 2, 1945	0.07	0.03	1.31[2]	1.19[2]	1.41	2.88
VIII	December 10, 1945	0.05	0.10	n.o.	—	0.81	4.44

1. 1¾ percent bond.

2. 1½ percent bond.

n.o.: none offered.

SOURCE: Henry C. Murphy, **The National Debt in War and Transition** (New York: McGraw-Hill Book Company, Inc., 1950), p. 181.

accrued during the fifth war loan. On the first day of trading during the sixth loan (December 18, 1944), the premium on the 2 percent bank-eligible bond rose to $0.28 per $100. This represented an aggregate premium of $23 million on total sales of the particular issues amounting to $8.5 billion. Simultaneously, the premium on the 2½ percent bank-restricted bonds went to $0.16 per $100 for an aggregate potential gain of $4 million. These were the highest initial premiums at which newly offered war loan securities had sold up to that time. Two months later these premiums had risen to $1.62 and $1.60 per $100, respectively; this was also a new high for premiums after that lapse of time.

By the time the seventh war loan got under way, speculators were numerous and enthusiastic. In fact, in this drive and the final one which followed, premiums obtained from speculative subscriptions greatly exceeded anything known up to that time. Windfall gains had become predictable, and speculative purchases of securities were widely engaged in. On the first day of trading, the medium-term, bank-eligible securities (1½ percent bonds) offered in the seventh war loan closed at a premium of $1.31 per $100, and the potential gain aggregated $22 million. To avoid a repetition of this situation, no bank-eligible securities (other than certificates) were offered in the eighth loan. The initial premiums on the 2½ percent bank-restricted bonds offered in the seventh war loan and in the final loan were $1.41 and $0.81 per $100, respectively. Thus, the aggregate premiums on these issues on the first day of trading after the loans closed amounted to $268 million, or 70 percent of the aggregate premiums obtainable on the first day of trading on all issues offered during each of the eight war loans. Furthermore, the last two war loans were followed by waves of speculation which sent premiums on the bank-restricted securities offered up to $2.88 and $4.44 per $100 respectively, two months after the beginning of trading following the close of the loans.

From the above discussion, it is evident that free riding aggravated the problem of war financing. From Table V-10, one can obtain an appreciation of the magnitude of the potential profits which were to be made. As indicated in the table, life insurance companies, on the basis of the proportion of different types of securities purchased in relation to the total amount issued, were in a position to obtain about 8 percent of the aggregate premiums at the close of the first day of trading on all the marketable issues included in each of the eight war loans. The issues which life insurance companies bought most heavily (the 2½ percent bank-restricted bonds) afforded aggregate premiums of $284 million, an amount almost three times as large as the aggregate premiums on bank-eligible bonds—although the total sales of the latter were two-thirds as large as sales of bank-restricted bonds. While over three-quarters (or $295 million) of the aggregate potential gain of $385 million was concentrated in the seventh and eighth war loans, only two-thirds of the potential windfall profits of life insurance companies accrued during these drives. In fact, approximately $7.7 million (one-quarter) out of the $29.5 million of profits which these institutions could have reaped emerged during the fifth and sixth war loans. How much of these potential profits were actually taken by life insurance companies, or any other investors, cannot be readily determined.

Other evidence, however, suggests that life insurance companies were influenced to a considerable extent by the possibility of capital gains through large subscriptions to war loans. These institutions borrowed heavily from commercial banks on a temporary basis to acquire bonds during the war loan drives. This was in sharp contrast to the companies' traditional behavior since they ordinarily do not borrow in order to acquire investments. Moreover, investors in general made relatively small use of bank loans to purchase securities offered in the war loan drives.

TABLE V-10

POTENTIAL SHARE OF LIFE INSURANCE COMPANIES IN AGGREGATE PREMIUMS ON MARKETABLE SECURITIES (EXCLUDING TREASURY BILLS) SOLD IN THE WAR LOANS ON THE FIRST DAY OF TRADING FOLLOWING THE CLOSE OF THE LOAN[1]

					Life Insurance Companies		
Loan	Type of Issue	Total Sales ($ Billions)	Premium (Cents Per $100)	Aggregate Premium ($ Millions)	Total Purchases ($ Millions)	Percent of Total Sales	Share of Potential Gains ($ Thousands) (5) x (7)
(1)	(2)	(3)	(4)	(5)	(6)	(7)	(8)
I							
	Certificates	3.8	none	none	10	0.3	—
	Other bank-eligible securities	3.1	0.03	1	184	6.0	60
	Bank-restricted bonds	2.8	none	none	1,242	43.9	—
		9.7	0.01	1	1,436	14.8	60
II							
	Certificates	5.3	0.04	2	37	0.7	14
	Other bank-eligible securities	4.9	0.22	11	581	11.8	130
	Bank-restricted bonds	3.8	0.12	5	1,431	38.0	190
		14.0	0.13	18	2,049	14.6	334
III							
	Certificates	4.1	0.03	1	23	0.6	6
	Other bank-eligible securities	5.3	0.19	10	775	14.7	147
	Bank-restricted bonds	3.8	0.09	3	1,517	40.2	1,206
		13.2	0.11	15	2,315	17.5	1,359
IV							
	Certificates	5.0	0.06	3	93	1.8	54
	Bank-restricted bonds	5.3	0.06	3	1,710	32.4	972
		10.3	0.06	6	1,803	17.5	1,026
V							
	Certificates	4.8	0.07	3	49	1.0	30
	Other bank-eligible securities	7.2	0.26	18	919	12.8	2,304
	Bank-restricted bonds	2.3	0.03	1	1,305	57.7	577
		14.3	0.16	22	2,273	16.0	2,911
VI							
	Certificates	4.4	0.04	2	42	1.0	20
	Other bank-eligible securities	8.5	0.27	23	971	11.4	2,622
	Bank-restricted bonds	2.7	0.16	4	1,487	54.9	2,196
		15.6	0.19	29	2,500	16.2	4,838
VII							
	Certificates	4.8	0.07	3	10	0.2	6
	Other bank-eligible securities	1.7	1.31	22	—	—	—
	Bank-restricted bonds	12.2	1.42	173	3,062	25.1	43
		18.6	1.06	198	3,072	16.5	49

TABLE V-10 (cont.)

POTENTIAL SHARE OF LIFE INSURANCE COMPANIES IN AGGREGATE PREMIUMS ON MARKETABLE SECURITIES (EXCLUDING TREASURY BILLS) SOLD IN THE WAR LOANS ON THE FIRST DAY OF TRADING FOLLOWING THE CLOSE OF THE LOAN[1]

					Life Insurance Companies		
Loan	Type of Issue	Total Sales ($ Billions)	Premium (Cents Per $100)	Aggregate Premium ($ Millions)	Total Purchases ($ Millions)	Percent of Total Sales	Share of Potential Gains ($ Thousands) (5) x (7)
VIII							
	Certificates	3.7	0.05	2	1	—	—
	Bank-restricted bonds	12.9	0.74	95	2,568	19.9	18,905
		16.6	0.58	97	2,569	15.5	18,905
All Loans	Certificates	35.9	0.05	17	265	7.4	130
	Other bank-eligible securities	30.6	0.28	85	3,430	11.2	5,263
	Bank-restricted bonds	45.6	0.62	284	14,322	31.4	24,089
		112.1	0.34	385	18,017	16.1	29,482

1. Based on closing over-the-counter prices.

SOURCE: Data on sales and premiums are from Murphy, **op. cit.**, pp. 184-85. Data on life insurance purchases are from the **U. S. Treasury Bulletin.**

While the statistics in Table V-11 are only rough indices, they suggest that more than one-third of the total securities obtained by life insurance companies during the war loan drives was financed temporarily by commercial bank funds. The statistics in the table show the increase in loans by weekly reporting member banks of the Federal Reserve System for the purpose of purchasing or carrying securities associated with each of the war loans. Borrowings by life insurance companies have been derived on the basis of the following description given by Murphy:

> The loan figures [in Table V-11] are, of course, not all-inclusive. They include only loans made by weekly reporting member banks, and some loans actually made by these banks for the *purpose* of purchasing or carrying United States securities were probably not so classified. But they probably include the great bulk—say three quarters—of all loans actually made for the purpose of subscribing to war loan securities. Furthermore, a substantial proportion—probably the greater part—of the borrowing in connection with the war loans was done by bona fide investors—particularly insurance companies. . . .[27]

Accepting Murphy's assumption that his estimate of total borrowings for the purpose of carrying securities was a low one, and since life insurance companies did practically all of the borrowing by insurance companies, 50 percent of total borrowings has been attributed to life insurance companies. This proportion seems reasonable, for life insurance companies were the only leading purchasers of securities during the war loan drives to enter into special and continuing arrangements with commercial banks to obtain loans with which to acquire issues as they were offered. According to Murphy:

> the banks considered (and reported) these arrangements as loans for the purpose of purchasing securities; the insurance companies considered them as purchases of government securities for future delivery and did not report them as loans. All such arrangements entered into in connection with any given war loan were normally liquidated before the beginning of the next loan.[28]

In the case of both total borrowings and those by life insurance companies, the increase shown in Table V-11 is from the low point immediately preceding the war loan to the high point immediately following it. For the first three war loans, the figures include loans for purchasing or carrying all securities; beginning with the fourth loan, they include only loans for purchasing or carrying United States government securities.

The increase in loans attributable to life insurance companies varied from about $350 million in the first loan to around $1,400 million in the seventh loan. The estimated total of such borrowings by life insurance companies amounted to about 38 percent of the average volume of securities purchased in the eight war loans. The smallest ratio was for

TABLE V-11

ESTIMATED BANK BORROWINGS BY LIFE INSURANCE COMPANIES FOR THE PURCHASE OF U. S. GOVERNMENT SECURITIES[1]
(In Billions of Dollars)

					Life Insurance Companies		
Loan	Period of Increase	Total Increase in Bank Loans	Total Marketable Securities Sold in Loan[2]	Ratio of Bank Loans to Securities Sold	**Estimated** Borrowings	Purchase of Securities	Ratio of Borrowings to Purchase of Securities
		Loans for purchasing or carrying all securities					
I	Nov. 25, 1942-Dec. 23, 1942	0.7	9.7	7.2	0.35	1.44	24.3
II	March 10, 1943-April 28, 1943	1.3	14.0	9.3	0.65	2.05	31.7
III	Aug. 11, 1943-Oct. 6, 1943	1.9	13.2	14.4	0.95	2.32	40.9
		Loans for purchasing or carrying U. S. Government securities					
IV	Jan. 5, 1944-Feb. 16, 1944	1.0	10.3	9.7	0.50	1.80	27.8
V	May 31, 1944-July 5, 1944	1.8	14.2	12.7	0.90	2.27	39.6
VI	Nov. 8, 1944-Dec. 20, 1944	1.7	15.6	10.9	0.85	2.25	37.8
VII	April 4, 1945-July 3, 1945	2.8	18.6	15.1	1.40	3.07	45.6
VIII	Nov. 7, 1945-Dec. 12, 1945	2.6	16.6	15.7	1.30	2.57	50.5
	Average of All Eight Loans	1.7	14.0	12.1	0.85	2.26	37.6

1. Increases in loans by weekly reporting member banks for the purpose of purchasing or carrying securities associated with each war loan.

2. Excluding treasury bills.

SOURCE: Murphy, **op. cit.**, p. 188. Life insurance data on purchases of securities are from the **U. S. Treasury Bulletin**; loan estimates represent 50 percent of borrowings from member banks to obtain or carry securities.

the first loan when it was only one-quarter; the highest was for the last loan when it rose to more than one-half. Life insurance companies had a compelling motive to borrow from commercial banks for the purpose of buying securities. By investing their funds in the 2½ percent bank-restricted bonds, they immediately began earning the higher rate; the alternative was to allow their funds to accumulate in money market issues (in ⅞ percent certificates, for example) until they were able to pay for subsequent subscriptions in full. On the other hand, through loans from the commercial banks (secured by notes which life insurance companies viewed as "premium anticipation certificates"), these institutions were able to turn the term structure of interest rates in their favor rather than against themselves. These borrowings also set the pattern for the "warehousing" arrangements which were to become familiar in connection with mortgage lending by life insurance companies in the postwar period.

Section IV

Investment Behavior Since World War II

The participation of life insurance companies in the government securities market since the end of World War II has passed through four broad phases: the early postwar period, 1946-49, brought a dramatic shift from acquisition to liquidation of Governments on a large scale which was only interrupted by the first postwar recession. The second phase covered the first year of the Korean war during which massive sales of Governments by life insurance companies and other investors led to the unpegging of the market and to the accord between the Treasury Department and the Federal Reserve System. In the new environment, risk of capital losses again became a major consideration for life insurance companies contemplating switching from Governments into private obligations; and although sales of Governments continued, the timing was influenced to a much greater extent by the structure of interest rates as well as by the availability of alternative outlets. The recession of 1957-58 seems to have opened a new phase of life insurance companies' participation in the government securities market. No longer did many portfolio managers consider their holdings of Governments excessive. Moreover, as yields on Governments rose in tandem with other open market rates through the recovery of 1958 and the return to prosperity in 1959, life insurance companies again began to view Governments as competitive with alternative investment outlets.

A. EARLY POSTWAR PERIOD, 1946-49

1. *Beginning of Liquidation*

In carrying out their investment decisions, life insurance companies first shifted from Governments into corporate obligations and subsequently into mortgages. The year 1947 marked the beginning of these movements, since at the end of 1946 the companies' total holdings of Governments were $1,046 million higher than at the end of 1945. As business activity quickened and industry expanded in 1947, life insurance companies sold on balance $1,678 million of Governments; two-thirds of these sales occurred during the last half of the year, with the final quarter alone accounting for $662 million or almost two-fifths of the total. This year marked the first significant reappearance of life insurance companies in the corporate bond market, which absorbed more than one-half of the total funds made available by these institutions to the capital market. Here also the flow of funds into the market was heavily concentrated in the last quarter of the year. While life insurance companies were not the only investors to switch from Governments on a large scale, they were the leaders among the nonbank holders. Their behavior during late 1947 and early 1948 provides an excellent opportunity to appraise the impact of changes in the structure of interest rates on the availability of life insurance funds in the capital market; the case is studied more closely below.

In the late fall and early winter of 1947, the United States economy was operating at a level close to full capacity, and the capital markets were experiencing a severe strain. The response of life insurance companies and other investors to the rising demand for funds and the resulting consequences have been described succinctly by Allen Sproul, then president of the Federal Reserve Bank of New York:

> The insurance companies, and other institutional investors were finding increased opportunities to employ their funds at higher rates than they were receiving on large holdings of Government securities purchased during the war. In order to meet this demand for funds, which was in excess of their currently accumulating cash resources, in order to improve their earnings, and in order to protect paper profits in Government securities which were selling at a premium, they began to sell long-term Government bonds.
>
> The Federal Reserve Banks, in their role as guardian of an orderly market in Government securities, were the unwilling buyers of the bonds. Nearly $5 billion of bonds were bought by the Federal Reserve Banks during the most acute phase of this development (November 19, 1947 to the end of February, 1948).
>
> Even though there were offsetting sales of short-term Government securities by the Reserve Banks, so that there was a net reduction of more than $1 billion of total Government security holdings of the System, this episode created another wave of discussion of the adequacy of the System's power of credit control to cope with

current problems. For a time it looked as if initiative with respect to the expansion of reserve funds had been surrendered not only to the commercial banks, but also to the insurance companies and other institutional investors, who had no apparent responsibility to the supervised banking system.[29]

In the pages immediately following, a brief summary is given of the major steps taken by the monetary authorities to stabilize the government securities market in the execution of the policy outlined by Mr. Sproul. The role played by life insurance companies is then appraised, and some of the consequences and implications of their actions are indicated.

The government securities market began to weaken as early as October, 1947. A general slide in prices had developed by December which reached avalanche proportions in January and February, 1948. Underlying the pessimistic view of future capital values was the uncertainty generated by (1) the unpegging of interest rates on treasury bills and certificates the previous summer, (2) the steady selling of long-term bonds by institutional investors, and (3) a widespread expectation of higher long-term rates.

Before further examination of the developments in the market and the specific actions taken by the Federal Reserve System, it is perhaps desirable to outline briefly the framework of thinking within which the moves were made. When the market began to break, there apparently was no question whether it would be supported. Rather, attention seems to have centered on two issues: should bank-eligible as well as bank-ineligible issues be supported and at what price levels? The decision was made to sustain prices of both types of bonds at levels set in the market during mid-November.[30] Since many holders of the public debt had chosen to monetize it, the System had to absorb, by some means, the additional reserves provided to the banking system. If these reserves were not offset, the inflationary potentials of market support would be enormous. Although at the end of the process of debt monetization commercial banks would hold the reserves thus created, the primary danger did not rest here, for the added liquidity of the banks could be wiped out through special sales by the System of short-term securities. To a large extent this was actually done.

Rather a more dismal prospect was that presented by the large-scale shifting of long-term bonds to the Federal Reserve System by life insurance companies and other savings institutions. Ordinarily these institutions are not holders of large amounts of short-term government securities; if they sold the longer maturities, they very likely would reinvest the funds in private obligations. In addition, widening spreads between yields on treasury and private obligations (sparked, of course, by the uncertainty surrounding the trend of prices on Governments) would act as greater inducement for insurance companies and others to speed up the rate of liquidation of Governments. In fact, the worst of these expectations were fulfilled. Life insurance companies dropped more than $1 billion of bonds on the market during the support period and continued to liquidate Governments after the initial flood of selling by other investors was over. Against its will, the Federal Reserve System became a mechanism whereby any holder of marketable bonds could add to bank reserves at will.

In an attempt to dam the flood of reserves, the System and the Treasury operated in common harness. They agreed to a systematic reduction in the holdings of government securities by the Federal Reserve System. When surplus funds and the exigencies of the market permitted, the System was to exchange its holdings of maturing obligations for cash. In the six-week period, November 6-December 11, 1947, treasury bills were retired at the weekly rate of $100 million; practically all of these retirements came from the portfolios of Federal Reserve Banks. Over the period of most active support, System holdings of bills, certificates, and notes declined by more than $6 billion.[31] Aside from the market support which these steps made possible, the System began to purchase bonds in the open market just after the middle of November. The structure of rates the System chose to defend was anchored at two points. Long-term bond prices (15 years and over) were held at 101⅞ for a yield of 2.37 percent; prices of intermediate bonds (7-9 years) were pegged at a yield of 1.77 percent—24 basis points above the September average.

During November, Federal Reserve open market operations resulted in net purchases of over $260 million; Treasury trust accounts made net acquisitions of an additional $200 million. These purchases by the System were about offset by debt retirement, and total holdings of government securities remained approximately constant. But this mild support was short-lived. It became evident in the first three weeks of December that the System had established a line of defense which it was determined to hold despite the progressive worsening of the market. Here was a situation in which windfall profits could be had simply for the cost of the transaction. Led by insurance companies, commercial and mutual savings banks as well as others rushed to sell and realize their gains. The System bought more than $400 million of government bonds in the first two weeks of December, but in the third week the average rate exceeded $300 million. Beneath the weight of this liquidation, the original System aim of ready but hesitating support was forced to give way to a more determined effort to stay the tide. It became clear to System officials that a full-scale movement was underway in which private investors were attempting simultaneously to shed vast quantities of Governments.[32] But the System had to move with caution if a paralyzing shock to the market was to be avoided. Nevertheless, it was necessary to introduce some uncertainty with respect to bond support prices, and on December 9, 1947, the Federal Open Market Committee decided to change its instructions to the executive committee to accomplish this end. The background of the Committee's thinking was described as follows:

> It was understood that, in carrying out the direction, the executive committee would continue the existing prices at which Government securities were being supported until after the Treasury January refunding had been completed at which time prices of bonds should be permitted to decline rapidly, if the market did not support itself, to a level not more than 100½ and not less than par on the longest restricted 2½ percent issue and to not less than par on 1⅛ percent one-year certificates. It was also understood that if, before the completion of the January refunding, market selling should increase substantially, the executive committee would be authorized to permit prices to decline to the level stated above as rapidly as was consistent with the maintenance of orderly market conditions.[33]

The standby authority to act before the completion of the Treasury's refunding was used on December 24, 1947; the potential selling visualized on December 9 materialized, and the System stood firm in its determination to support the market. While Federal Reserve holdings of bonds increased by $421 million in the four-week period November 19-December 10, the System made net acquisitions of bonds of approximately $498 million in the two weeks ending December 24. In an attempt to stem this selling wave, the System acted drastically. The action taken was summarized subsequently as follows:

> Effective December 24 the Federal Open Market Committee reduced the prices at which purchases of United States Treasury bonds would be made in the market for the Federal Open Market Account. During the preceding period of five weeks there had been a large volume of selling of Government bonds in the market, but Federal Reserve and Treasury purchases maintained prices of these securities substantially unchanged at levels previously established in the market. The price reductions on December 24 were larger in the case of bonds selling at substantial premiums than for others. No bond was permitted to decline below par. . . .[34]

When the market opened on December 26, the selling wave reached new proportions. In fact, a situation approaching panic was created by the stampeding sellers, led mainly by bankers and life insurance officials. Between Christmas and New Year's Day, the Open Market Account bought on balance $1,143 million of bonds. These purchases were made at average yields of 2.45 percent for the longest issues and 1.99 percent for those of intermediate maturity. The drive of investors to sell continued through February. Over $1,700 million of bonds was purchased by the System in January and $1,100 million in the following month. Toward the end of February, the general contours of a market reappeared; there was once again some confidence in the ability and willingness of the Open Market Committee to maintain orderly conditions in the market and protect capital values.

During the support operations, the Treasury aided to a considerable extent. In November, 1947, Treasury investment accounts made net market purchases of federal securities amounting to $221 million; this was followed by net acquisitions of $696 million in December, and $177 million in February. The Treasury also retired on balance $4,355 million of debt. Actually, $5,888 million of certificates and $1,294 million in bills were redeemed while $702 million of 2 percent bonds were converted into 1⅛ percent notes on December 1, 1947. Consequently the net expansion of $3,535 million in notes outstanding offset to some extent the debt reduction in other areas.[35]

Some indication of the source of securities purchased by the Federal Reserve System is given in Table V-12. Between the end of October, 1947, and the end of February, 1948, the Federal Reserve System increased its bond holdings by $4,980 million, while its treasury notes rose by $923 million. The sum of these acquisitions was more than offset by reductions of $4,352 million and $2,696 million in treasury bills and certificates, respectively. As a result of these transactions, the System's total holdings in government securities declined by $1,145 million. The heaviest sellers of treasury obligations during the support period were commercial banks, who decreased their bond holdings by $3,257 million; despite an increase of $1,763 million in bills and $493 million in notes, their total portfolio of Governments fell by $2,381 million. Life insurance companies sold net $1,410 million of bonds and raised their bill holdings by only $262 million. Thus, they accounted for one-quarter of the total volume of Governments sold by private investors, but unlike commercial banks, who took up nearly $2 billion of the bills sold by the Federal Reserve, and the group of unspecified investors (mainly individuals), who acquired on balance about $2 billion in notes, life insurance companies shifted the bulk of the proceeds from government bond sales to private borrowers.

2. *Slackening in the Pace of Selling*

The shifts in the volume and direction of life insurance companies' investments which began in late 1947 continued in the following year. However, the consequences for monetary policy were not nearly as serious as those which developed during the support operations of 1947-48. The total quantity of life insurance funds reaching the market rose by approximately one-third, from $5,625 million to $7,289 million. (See Table V-13.) Practically all of the increase in the rate of investment

TABLE V-12

NET CHANGE IN AMOUNT OUTSTANDING AND IN OWNERSHIP OF MARKETABLE U. S. GOVERNMENT SECURITIES, OCTOBER 31, 1947-FEBRUARY 29, 1948

(In Millions of Dollars)

Holder	Total	Bills	Certificates	Notes	Bonds	Panama Canal Bonds	Guaranteed Issues
U. S. Government Trust Accounts	+1,148	+ 61	− 6	+ 1	+1,092	—	—
Federal Reserve Banks	−1,145	−4,352	−2,696	+ 923	+4,980	—	—
Commercial Banks	−2,381	+1,763	−1,381	+ 493	−3,257	+1	+1
Life Insurance Companies	−1,147	+ 263	− 16	+ 18	−1,410	—	−1
Other Insurance Companies	+ 151	+ 53	+ 82	+ 79	− 64	1	—
Mutual Savings Banks	− 179	+ 53	+ 95	+ 53	− 378	—	−2
Other Investors	− 803	+ 865	−1,967	+1,968	−1,664	−2	−3
Total Outstanding	−4,355	−1,294	−5,888	+3,535	− 702	−1	−5

SOURCE: **U. S. Treasury Bulletin,** December, 1947 and April, 1948.

TABLE V-13

SOURCES AND USES OF LIFE INSURANCE FUNDS, BY QUARTERS, 1947-49

(In Millions of Dollars)

Year	1947				1948				1949				1947-49
Quarter	I	II	III	IV	I	II	III	IV	I	II	III	IV	Period as a Whole
Sources of Funds													
New savings[1]	866	831	765	1,091	1,207	838	740	984	975	987	914	1,243	11,439
Cash	—	285	—	—	140	—	—	92	7	46	—	—	—
U. S. government securities	400	171	445	662	546	713	1,042	974	261	647	460	88	6,339
State and local securities	5	—	3	—	—	—	—	—	—	—	—	—	—
Railroad bonds	—	—	30	28	—	—	—	—	7	—	3	—	—
FHA mortgages	43	—	—	—	—	—	—	—	—	—	—	—	—
All other sources	—	—	—	—	—	—	—	13	—	—	—	—	—
Total sources	1,314	1,287	1,243	1,781	1,893	1,551	1,782	2,063	1,250	1,680	1,377	1,331	17,778
Uses of Funds													
Cash	486	—	88	104	—	5	116	—	—	—	22	30	281
State and local securities	—	2	—	1	22	37	131	73	33	23	37	87	438
Corporate bonds	436	812	640	1,125	1,077	901	755	400	518	1,009	600	445	9,650
Railroad	6	22	—	—	12	45	40	61	—	15	—	10	142
Public utility	77	427	400	450	382	442	389	587	196	489	196	142	4,177
Industrial and misc.	353	363	240	675	683	414	326	752	322	505	404	293	5,331
Nonfarm mortgages	312	300	392	469	445	500	528	590	463	471	388	528	5,418
Conventional	169	132	178	183	173	221	215	209	165	191	179	199	2,214
FHA	—	25	71	117	177	211	254	341	256	256	184	302	2,226
VA	143	143	143	169	95	68	59	40	42	24	25	27	978
All other uses	80	173	123	83	349	108	252	—	236	177	330	241	1,991
Total uses	1,314	1,287	1,243	1,781	1,893	1,551	1,782	2,063	1,250	1,680	1,377	1,331	17,778

1. Net increase in total assets.

SOURCE: Institute of Life Insurance; special tabulations made for the author.

was financed through net sales of Governments; these amounted to $3,275 million or nearly 90 percent more than in the previous year, and provided 96 percent of the net expansion in the supply of funds from life insurance companies. For the most part, these institutions continued to move into corporate bonds, in which their holdings rose by $4,133 million, representing almost three-fifths of the total uses of funds and accounting for over two-thirds of the growth in total uses compared with the year before. This pattern was consistent with rational behavior in response to changes in the structure of interest rates, for during 1948 the yield spread between corporate bonds and Governments widened appreciably. Moreover, mortgage yields also became increasingly attractive, and life insurance companies made net investments of $2,063 million in nonfarm mortgage debt in 1948, accounting for more than one-third of the net increase in the flow of funds from these investors.

The interruption in economic activity during the recession of 1949 was reflected in several ways in the investment behavior of life insurance companies in the government securities market. In the first place, since the total demand for funds declined, these institutions were able to obtain through the normal growth of assets, a much larger proportion of the resources required to meet commitments. This is shown by the fact that, while the total volume of life insurance funds reaching the capital markets declined by $1,651 million compared with 1948, the rate of liquidation of Governments fell by $1,819 million. Absolute sales of federal obligations continued, of course, but only $1,456 million were sold in 1949, an amount less than one-half of the volume in the previous year. The decline in the demand for life insurance funds resulted from the slackening in business capital outlays. New plant and equipment expenditures declined from an annual rate of $22.1 billion in 1948 to $19.3 billion in 1949;[36] total corporate bonds and notes outstanding rose by $3.3 billion in contrast to $4.7 billion in the year before.[37] The extent to which life insurance companies participated in the financing of the business investment which did occur was less both relatively and absolutely than in the year earlier. The net increase in 1949 in their holdings of corporate obligations was $2,572 million, a reduction of $1,561 million from the $4,133 million gain registered in 1948. The actual rise in these securities absorbed almost one-half of total funds made available compared with around three-fifths in 1948. Moreover, in 1949 life insurance companies supplied only three-fourths of the increased corporate demand for funds reflected in the growth of debt, although their share, in 1948, was 97 percent.

TABLE V-14

SOURCES AND USES OF LIFE INSURANCE FUNDS, BY QUARTERS, 1950 AND 1951
(In Millions of Dollars)

Year	1950				1951			
Quarter	I	II	III	IV	I	II	III	IV
Sources of Funds								
New savings[1]	912	1,049	1,091	1,338	1,165	899	1,049	1,200
Cash	29	—	—	—	—	150	11	—
U. S. government securities	79	446	440	862	742	853	430	419
State and local securities	—	—	—	—	—	13	—	22
Total Sources	1,020	1,495	1,531	2,200	1,907	1,915	1,490	1,641
Uses of Funds								
Cash	—	104	—	99	108	—	—	148
State and local securities	41	21	30	8	35	—	19	—
Corporate bonds	351	420	397	674	461	840	570	780
Railroad	23	81	33	33	13	8	32	69
Public utility	163	217	204	239	136	151	139	227
Industrial and misc.	165	122	160	402	312	681	399	484
Nonfarm mortgages	499	656	791	1,061	967	862	633	557
Conventional	177	216	311	382	404	345	245	233
FHA	293	284	244	298	204	182	143	157
VA	29	156	236	381	359	335	245	167
All other uses	129	294	313	358	336	213	268	156
Total Uses	1,020	1,495	1,531	2,200	1,907	1,915	1,490	1,641

1. Net increase in total assets.
SOURCE: **Life Insurance Fact Book** and **Tally of Life Insurance Statistics.**

B. Investment Behavior During the Treasury-Federal Reserve Accord Period

1. *Revival of Liquidation*

The revival of business in 1950 and the outbreak of hostilities in Korea in June of that year combined to generate considerable demand for life insurance funds. Again the government securities market offered a residual source of funds to meet the needs of private investors. Although the net amounts of Governments sold over the year as a whole was only 12 percent higher than in the previous year ($1,827 million compared with $1,456 million) nearly three-fourths of the liquidation ($1,300 million) centered in the last half of the year. (See Table V-14.) In the fourth quarter alone, life insurance companies disposed of $862 million of federal obligations. This time, however, the chief motivation inducing sales of Governments was the desire of portfolio managers to acquire real estate mortgages before expected restrictions on residential construction reduced the demand for mortgage loans.[38]

In the second half of 1950, nonfarm mortgage debt outstanding rose by $5.7 billion, an advance of 16 percent compared with the last six months of 1949. The expansion in mortgage ownership by life insurance companies was far more spectacular. Between June and December, 1950, their holding of urban mortgages advanced by $1,852 million, a rate of growth more than double the gain of $916 million achieved in 1949. As a consequence of this relative shift in the flow of funds, life insurance companies acquired nearly one-third of the net increase in nonfarm real estate mortgages and put into these loans almost one-half of the total funds they made available to the capital market. The rate of acquisition of urban mortgages was $1,157 million higher than in 1949; actual net acquisitions of $3,007 million in 1950 was the largest amount purchased in any year up to that time.

The considerable increase in sales of Governments, the proceeds of which went mainly into mortgages, was one of the major factors leading to the unpegging of the government securities market during the spring of 1951. The participation of life insurance companies in this market during these critical months is discussed more fully below.

2. *Investment Behavior and the Treasury-Federal Reserve Accord*

On March 4, 1951, the Federal Reserve System, in cooperation with the Treasury, made an attempt to reconcile the conflicting objectives of debt management and credit control. This step, made possible through the accord between the two agencies, was the first move in a long journey back to flexibility in monetary policy. The change in policy meant a decisive shift away from the System's commitment to support the market for government obligations. As demonstrated by developments in late 1947 and early 1948, the choice of when to create bank reserves rested solely with holders of government securities—so long as the Federal Reserve System found it necessary to support the market. Under the impact of rising private demands for credit, life insurance companies and other investors did not hesitate to liquidate their Governments in order to obtain the higher yielding assets then becoming available. The resulting monetization of the government debt at the same time provided commercial banks with new reserves for further possible multiple credit expansion. Through its open market operations since the end of World War II, the Federal Reserve System had sustained the market for treasury issues whenever it was under pressure. In order to remove some of the bank reserves thus created, the System developed a compensatory method of operating in the market. By sales and redemptions in the short sector of the market, it was able to absorb the reserves released through its purchases in the long-term sector. Nevertheless, it could not offset fully the addition to bank reserves from gold inflows and other factors.

After the outbreak of the war in Korea, a rapid acceleration occurred in the demand for credit. Under this pressure, many institutions shifted from Governments to private securities, and the System lost virtually all power to restrain the creation of bank reserves. The most serious challenge came in the area of long-term bonds. While it soon became obvious that the System would have to cease making possible the automatic transfer of all funds from bonds into money, there were major obstacles to such a change in policy. Over the preceding decade, investors in government securities had become conditioned to markets in which prices were maintained at par or above. While maintenance of par prices on securities issued at the low rates prevailing during World War II was an anomaly in a period of intense credit demand, there was also need for caution. If the System were to draw back from further purchases, the prices of the longer-term government securities would fall rapidly below par. The shock to the market which this action might produce could have led to a panic among investors. In the face of this prospect, the transition to a more flexible monetary policy required caution as well as courage.

In a statement released March 4, 1951, the Secretary of the Treasury and the Chairman of the Board of Governors of the Federal Reserve System made the following announcement:

> The Treasury and the Federal Reserve System have reached full accord with respect to debt-management and monetary policies to be pursued in furthering their common purpose to assure the successful financing of the Government's requirements and, at the same time, to minimize monetization of the public debt.[39]

On the same day, the Treasury announced that it would offer holders of the two longest outstanding bank-restricted bonds (2½ percent bonds of June and December, 1967-72) an opportunity to convert at par into a new offering of nonmarketable bonds at a higher yield (2¾ percent bonds of April, 1975-80). Although these bonds could not be traded, they could be converted at the holders' option on the first of April and October each year into five-year marketable notes carrying a coupon of 1½ percent. In making this offering, the Treasury sought to encourage long-term investors to retain their holdings of government securities. Aside from the issuance of the nonmarketable bond, the Treasury (through its investment accounts) joined with the Federal Open Market Account and made substantial purchases to facilitate the market's adjustment to the unpegging of yields. For a period of six weeks, purchases were made of outstanding bonds at declining prices. By April 12, the initial price adjustments were completed, and the market subsequently settled at a level sustained primarily by the interaction of private forces.

As indicated earlier, the role of life insurance companies in the government securities market during this time was critical. Over the eight months preceding the accord, these institutions had reduced their holdings of Governments by $1,586 million. Simultaneously, their total assets rose by $3,277 million, $500 million less than the increase in their holdings of corporate bonds and real estate mortgages combined. Since other uses of funds were also expanding, life insurance companies found themselves under growing pressure to sell Governments. Because these sales were concentrated in the bank-restricted bonds of 1967-72, the two measures which grew out of the accord bore special implications for life insurance companies. With respect to the exchange offering of nonmarketable 2¾ percent bonds, these institutions responded as the Treasury hoped they would. They exchanged virtually all of their holdings of the two bank-restricted issues. In the April-June period, their ownership of the obligations maturing 1967-72 declined by $2,944 million while they acquired $2,921 million of the nonmarketable investment issue. Thus they made further net sales of only $23 million of these bonds in which liquidation had centered. This immediate and full response of life insurance companies to the exchange offering is a clear reflection of the tailoring of the issue to fit their requirements.

The effect of the exchange offering was to remove from the market, at least temporarily, a large block of government securities, part of which might otherwise have been sold by life insurance companies and other investors in order to go forward with investment in private sectors of the economy. However, since the 2¾ percent nonmarketable bonds received in exchange could be converted into five-year marketable notes, there was still the possibility that holders would shift some part of these funds into the private economy. As it actually developed, these institutions held the nonmarketable issue rather firmly through the first six years. Of the $2.9 billion which they acquired, they still owned $2.5 billion at the end of 1957; but in the next two years, they liquidated over $600 million and at the end of 1959 held $1.8 billion of the nonmarketable bonds.

Along with the exchange offering, the unpegging of government securities prices and the subsequent decline in these prices had a strong effect on life insurance companies' investment behavior. The realization that Governments were no longer the equivalent of cash and could not be sold in the future at known fixed prices had the effect, in most cases, of causing life insurance companies to restrict current investment commitments more nearly to the flow of funds which would develop from sources other than further disposals of Governments.[40] As prices of government securities declined, the potential loss on sales became an important factor deterring further sales. This follows from the fact that sales of Governments at declining market prices would probably result in sizable capital losses for life insurance companies; such losses would have to be charged against surplus, and life insurance companies are reluctant to show large fluctuations in surplus.

Although the unpegging of the government bond market was clearly a major shock and created much uncertainty, the rate of liquidation of Governments by life insurance companies actually increased during the second quarter of 1951, advancing from $742 million to $853 million. The continued sales were apparently necessary to meet commitments made during the last few months before the cessation of market support. Liquidation of Governments did not mean, however, that life insurance companies simply withdrew abruptly from the government securities market. Instead, funds were shifted temporarily into shorter-term issues to await more permanent investment in corporate bonds and mortgages. During the 12 months ending in June, 1951, these institutions made net purchases of $872 million of treasury bills and notes, an amount equal to more than one-third of the proceeds of net sales of long-term bonds. Beginning in the third quarter of 1951, the reluctance to sell bonds at a loss began to have a deterrent effect. As shown in Table V-15, total sales in the June-September period were only $430 million and, in the final quarter of the year, totaled only $419 million. Moreover, sales in the last half of the year were concentrated in the short-term issues, with treasury bills

TABLE V-15

CHANGES IN LIFE INSURANCE COMPANIES' HOLDINGS OF U. S. GOVERNMENT SECURITIES, BY TYPE AND BY QUARTERS, 1950 AND 1951

(In Millions of Dollars)

Year	1950				1951			
Quarter	I	II	III	IV	I	II	III	IV
Type of Securities								
Bills	15	−16	178	187	261	104	−134	−194
Certificates	−17	−13	−74	−32	−1	113	65	39
Notes	17	11	82	17	130	−87	−86	−121
Bonds	−94	−428	−626	−1,034	−1,132	−983	−275	−143
Total	−79	−446	−440	−862	−742	−853	−430	−419

SOURCE: **U. S. Treasury Bulletin.**

and notes accounting for more than three-fifths of net sales of Governments which in turn were only two-thirds the volume registered in the last half of 1950.

As one would expect, the reduced rate of liquidation of Governments led to a corresponding decline in the total availability of funds from life insurance companies. This decline centered primarily in real estate mortgages, the net expansion of which was only $1,190 million during the last six months of 1951 compared with $1,829 million in the first half. On the other hand, net acquisitions of corporate obligations actually rose—from $1,301 million to $1,350 million. On an overall basis, life insurance companies supplied $610 million more to the capital markets in 1951 than they did in the previous year. It is somewhat surprising, in view of the reluctance of these institutions to take capital losses, to discover that the increased rate of liquidation of Governments provided an additional $602 million of funds compared with 1950. This represented almost the only source of the increased rate of flow of funds from life insurance companies to the capital market.

C. Investment Behavior Since the Accord

Since most of 1951 was required for life insurance companies and other investors to adjust to the relatively free capital market created by the accord, 1952 marks the real beginning of the return to more orthodox investment behavior. In the few years preceding the accord, numerous observers had argued that even small decreases in the yield spread between Governments and private obligations would induce financial intermediaries to buy Governments or reduce the rate at which they were being liquidated; a small increase in the yield spread was held to set off or accelerate sales of Governments. This view was generally referred to as the "credit availability doctrine" the seeds of which were planted in the moneary experience of the 1930's.[41] The renewed interest in this argument, however, sprang from the desire of the monetary authorities to increase the effectiveness of general credit controls while continuing to support the government securities market.[42]

It was argued above that life insurance companies increase their sales of long-term government securities during a period of falling interest rates and reduce the pace of liquidation as interest rates rise. Their actual behavior in the government securities market between 1952 and 1959 confirms this general pattern of response. The statistics in Tables V-16 and V-17 support this conclusion; the relationship between yields on long-term government bonds and sales of these issues by life insurance companies is shown in Chart V-1.

CHART V-1
U. S. Government Bond Yields and Net Changes in Life Insurance Companies' Holdings of U. S. Government Bonds and Other Securities, by Quarters, 1952-59

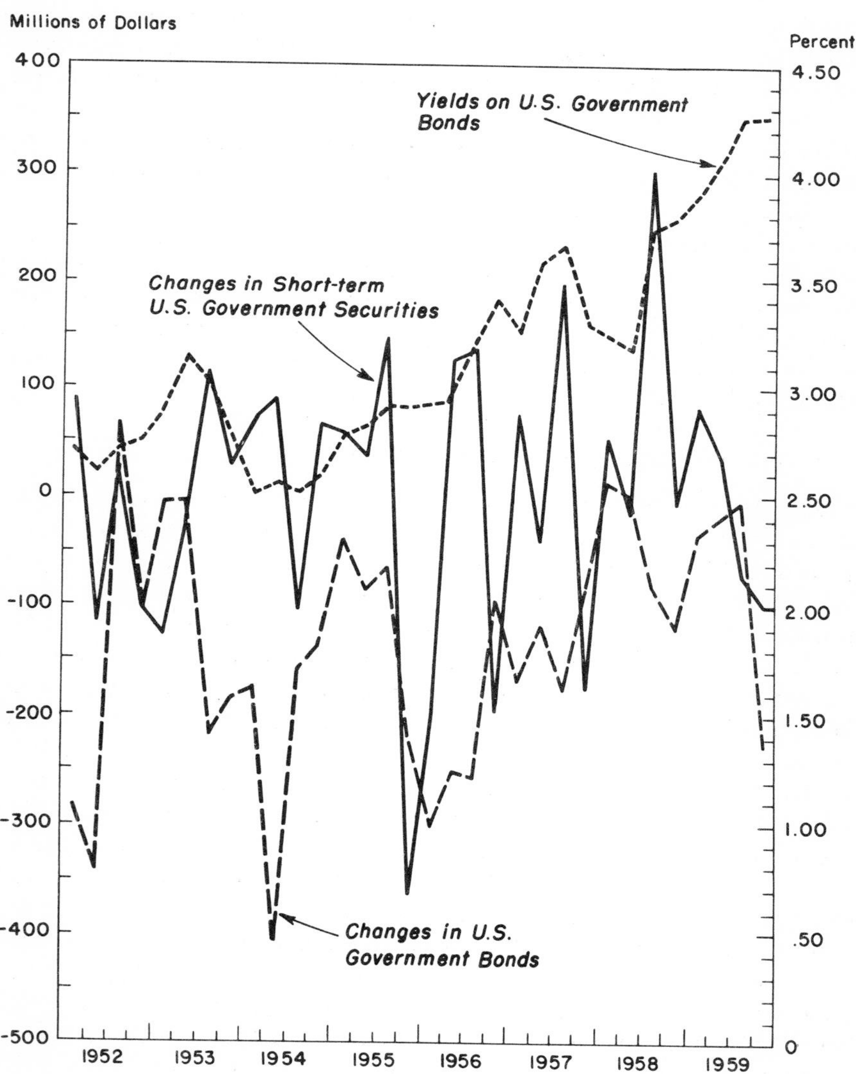

SOURCE: *Federal Reserve Bulletin* and *The Tally of Life Insurance Statistics.*

TABLE V-16

SOURCES AND USES OF LIFE INSURANCE FUNDS, BY QUARTERS, 1952-55
(In Millions of Dollars)

Year	1952				1953				1954				1955			
Quarter	I	II	III	IV	I	II	III	IV	I	II	III	IV	I	II	III	IV
Sources of Funds																
New savings[1]	1,264	1,096	1,255	1,468	1,260	1,105	1,230	1,563	1,451	1,339	1,435	1,736	1,146	1,335	1,562	1,690
Cash	82	—	12	—	156	42	—	—	155	—	—	—	211	—	—	—
U. S. government securities	193	455	—	203	132	30	103	158	109	321	261	68	—	45	—	583
State and local government securities	37	10	—	10	—	—	—	—	—	—	—	—	—	7	—	—
Railroad bonds	—	—	—	—	—	—	—	—	—	—	26	—	—	—	—	—
All other assets, n.e.c.[2]	—	—	46	—	—	29	—	—	—	—	—	—	—	—	—	—
Total Sources	1,576	1,561	1,313	1,681	1,548	1,206	1,333	1,721	1,715	1,660	1,722	1,804	1,357	1,387	1,562	2,273
Uses of Funds																
Cash	—	62	—	81	—	—	82	185	—	41	10	129	—	35	78	112
U. S. government securities	—	—	92	—	—	—	—	—	—	—	—	—	21	—	83	—
State and local government	—	—	40	—	50	15	40	40	165	194	134	55	118	—	26	15
Bonds of business and Industry	792	731	757	894	771	742	555	728	571	543	618	623	255	399	405	679
Railroad	63	65	49	59	29	4	11	54	17	76	—	47	6	53	16	60
Public utility	151	174	175	215	153	185	227	309	233	184	212	55	109	49	129	161
Industrial	578	492	533	620	589	553	317	365	321	283	406	521	140	297	260	458
Nonfarm mortgages	526	402	424	405	444	449	444	553	446	561	619	866	701	681	715	1,141
Conventional	281	252	293	292	307	337	332	370	269	333	311	392	314	328	381	489
FHA	125	94	111	93	115	83	59	74	48	26	6	24	45	41	58	150
VA	120	56	20	20	22	29	53	109	129	202	302	450	342	312	276	502
All other assets, n.e.c.[2]	258	366	—	301	283	—	212	215	533	321	341	131	262	272	255	326
Total Uses	1,576	1,561	1,313	1,681	1,548	1,206	1,333	1,721	1,715	1,660	1,722	1,804	1,357	1,387	1,562	2,273

1. Net increase in total assets.

2. Not elsewhere classified.

SOURCE: Compiled from data in **Life Insurance Fact Book.**

In the first half of 1952, credit conditions were relatively easy compared with the immediately preceding six months, and all types of interest rates declined slightly. For example, average yields on government bonds receded from 2.70 percent to 2.61 percent, while corporate yields (as measured by Moody's Aaa series) declined from 3.01 to 2.49 percent. Under these conditions, net sales of Governments by life insurance companies totaled $648 million, or nearly $1.3 billion at an annual rate. This reduction in Governments accounted for approximately one-fifth of the total volume of funds which these institutions supplied to the capital market. Beginning in mid-1952, interest rates rose steeply for almost a full year; in June, 1953, the average yield on long-term Governments had climbed to 3.13 percent, a gain of more than half a point. In the face of this advance, net sales of Governments by life insurance companies declined to $273 million; in fact, during the third quarter of 1952 these

TABLE V-17

SOURCES AND USES OF LIFE INSURANCE FUNDS, BY QUARTERS, 1956-59
(In Millions of Dollars)

Year	1956				1957			
Quarter	I	II	III	IV	I	II	III	IV
Sources of Funds								
New savings	1,276	1,340	1,536	1,425	1,230	1,165	1,778	1,292
Cash	215	—	2	—	217	—	—	—
U. S. government securities	500	125	121	280	92	157	—	260
State and local government securities	—	—	—	—	—	—	—	—
Railroad bonds	—	19	4	9	—	—	—	—
All other assets	—	—	—	—	—	—	—	—
Total Sources	1,991	1,484	1,663	1,714	1,539	1,322	1,778	1,552
Uses of Funds								
Cash	—	37	—	198	—	62	33	143
U. S. government securities	—	—	—	—	—	—	18	—
State and local government	182	11	86	37	34	49	72	37
Bonds of business and industry	662	426	558	522	581	552	809	738
Railroad	26	—	—	—	8	1	10	5
Public utility	106	147	180	111	130	195	234	190
Industrial and misc.	530	279	378	411	443	356	565	543
Nonfarm mortgages	894	829	771	869	655	411	542	524
Conventional	250	457	445	536	397	312	451	443
FHA	265	76	44	50	29	8	32	71
VA	379	296	282	283	229	121	59	10
All other assets	253	181	248	88	269	297	304	110
Total Uses	1,991	1,484	1,663	1,714	1,539	1,322	1,778	1,552

TABLE V-17 (cont.)

SOURCES AND USES OF LIFE INSURANCE FUNDS, BY QUARTERS, 1956-59

(In Millions of Dollars)

Year	1958				1959			
Quarter	I	II	III	IV	I	II	III	IV
Sources of Funds								
New savings	1,402	1,297	1,485	2,087	1,365	1,479	1,422	1,780
Cash	124	—	—	—	—	11	27	—
U. S. government securities	—	12	—	125	—	—	77	321
State and local government securities	—	—	—	—	—	—	—	—
Railroad	5	8	—	7	23	24	9	—
VA mortgages	23	46	116	110	104	89	105	38
All other sources	—	—	—					
Total Sources	1,554	1,363	1,601	2,329	1,492	1,603	1,640	2,139
Uses of Funds								
Cash	—	37	2	154	152	—	—	154
U. S. government securities	67	—	224	—	47	17	—	—
State and local government	92	93	84	86	179	163	153	85
Bonds of business and industry	556	548	552	681	588	650	347	558
Railroad	—	—	1	—	—	—	—	2
Public utility	141	140	233	173	179	112	31	211
Industrial and misc.	415	408	318	508	409	538	316	345
Nonfarm mortgages	454	338	519	723	432	430	709	815
Conventional	306	206	351	462	184	242	499	573
FHA	148	132	168	261	248	188	210	242
VA	—	—	—	—	—	—	—	—
All other assets	385	347	220	685	94	343	431	527
Total Uses	1,554	1,363	1,601	2,329	1,492	1,603	1,640	2,139

SOURCE: **1960 Life Insurance Fact Book** and **The Tally of Life Insurance Statistics.**

institutions made net purchases of $92 million of Governments, consisting primarily of treasury bills and bonds approaching the date when they would be eligible for ownership by commercial banks. Sales of Governments during early 1952 had centered in those World War II issues with roughly 15 years to maturity. The substantial rise in yields and the drastic fall in prices of bonds in these categories severely dampened life insurance companies' incentives to sell. The magnitude of the losses they would have absorbed is clearly shown in the following example. At the end of June, 1952, a 15-year, 2½ percent obligation yielding 2.60 percent was priced around 98.76, necessitating, if sold, a loss of approximately $12.40 per $1,000 of face value if the bond had been acquired at par. A year later, however, sale of a similar bond would have entailed a loss of $71.50 on each $1,000 of face value; over the same period yields moved to the neighborhood of 3.10 percent and prices plunged to around 92.85. To compensate for such a potential loss (nearly six times that at the end of the previous year), life insurance companies would have had to obtain a yield well over 4.30 percent on a 15-year corporate bond carrying a coupon in line with those prevailing in the spring of 1953—if the bond could have been purchased at par. Since corporate bonds rated Aaa by Moody's provided an average yield of only 3.40 percent in June, 1953, many life insurance companies were less prepared to switch from Governments into corporate issues. Thus, they relied almost exclusively on the growth of new savings as the source of funds supplied to the capital market.

As the rate of growth in national income and employment slackened and then declined from the peaks reached in the second quarter of 1953, the Federal Reserve System acted to ease the credit situation. Yields on treasury bills fell drastically, declining by more than 70 percent between June, 1953 and June, 1954. In the long-term sector, the decline in both government and corporate bond yields was even sharper than the previous rise. Over these twelve months, net sales of Governments by life insurance companies revived and totaled $691 million. Actually, sales of long-term Governments totaled $860 million, but this amount was partly offset by an increase of $169 million in their holdings of treasury bills. This spurt in sales of Governments can be attributed partly to the fact that a large proportion of long-term bonds held by life insurance companies had become eligible for commercial bank ownership. As the demand for bank loans slackened after mid-1953, commercial banks reached out for Governments which life insurance companies and other investors eagerly sold. For example, at the end of June, 1953, life insurance companies owned $2,301 million in five series of previously bank-restricted bonds; over the next twelve months their holdings in the same series declined by $577 million and accounted for two-thirds of the $860 million of total sales of long-term Governments during the period. At the same time, commercial bank holdings of these newly eligible issues rose by $1,666 million.

As interest rates rose from the middle of 1954 and reached record heights by the end of September, 1955, there was an appreciable decline in sales of Governments by life insurance companies. The net reduction amounted to only $374 million, as sales of $411 million of long-term obligations were partly offset by an increase of $37 million of short-term issues—especially treasury bills. The annual rate of liquidation of Governments during this period was less than half that for the preceding year of credit ease, and such sales were only about two-fifths as important as a source of funds as they had been during the period of declining interest rates. However, this situation did not persist very long. Over the next six months, covering the fall of 1955 and the winter of 1956, a pause occurred in the uptrend of bond yields. The demand for long-term funds increased sharply as the annual rate of growth in corporate bonds outstanding rose by 56 percent (in contrast to a decline of 22 percent in the previous period), while the demand for mortgage funds remained vigorous. To take advantage of these alternative investment opportunities, life insurance companies reduced their holdings of Governments by $1,083 million; this was the fastest pace of liquidation since the first half of 1952.

From the spring of 1956, business firms began increasingly to announce optimistic investment plans which forecast a renewed expansion in the demand for funds. Reflecting these expectations as well as the actual demands currently registered in the market, long-term interest rates advanced virtually without a pause through the rest of 1956, and by the year end even the highest grade corporate bonds required yields of between 4 and 4½ percent to insure successful distribution. Yields on long-term government issues also participated in the uptrend and averaged 3.40 percent in the last quarter compared with 2.93 percent in the first half of the year. Responding to the mounting yields, life insurance companies drastically reduced the pace at which they liquidated government securities; in the last half of the year, net sales of Governments totaled $400 million, or less than two-thirds the volume of the first half of the year. As interest rates rose further to historic peaks in the summer of 1957, the lessened rate of liquidation continued through the second quarter of that year. Moreover, life insurance companies made small net additions to their holdings of Governments in the third quarter of 1957, which was the first such net increase in two years. Although sales of Governments tended to revive on a modest scale in 1958 and 1959 as the companies found it necessary to meet commitments in excess of the inflow of funds, the massive liquidations evident in the earlier years did not reappear. In fact, in half of the ten quarters between the middle of 1957 and the end of 1959, these institutions were net purchasers of Governments, and on balance their holdings fell by only $62 million. This was the smallest decline in a comparable length of time during the entire postwar period. Thus, by the end of the decade, it seemed that the era was over when life insurance companies viewed government securities as a readily available source of funds to be tapped whenever private demands rose.

D. Characteristics of Companies Which Expanded Their Government Securities Holdings, 1945-57

So far in this section, the discussion has emphasized the liquidation of United States government securities by life insurance companies under varying credit conditions and the reinvestment of the proceeds in the private sector of the economy. From the point of view of the entire industry, this emphasis is appropriate because net liquidation rather than net acquisition of Governments has been the dominant characteristic of these institutions' investment behavior in the government securities market since World War II. As mentioned above, life insurance companies disposed of $13,715 million of such issues between 1945 and 1959, an amount representing two-thirds of their holdings at the end of the earlier year. Nevertheless, some institutions have been net purchasers of Governments during the postwar period. In general, the life insurance com-

TABLE V-18

DISTRIBUTION OF THE 150 LARGEST LIFE INSURANCE COMPANIES BY ASSET SIZE, ANNUAL RATES OF GROWTH OF TOTAL ASSETS AND ANNUAL RATES OF CHANGE IN HOLDINGS OF U. S. GOVERNMENT SECURITIES, 1945-57

Group	Asset Range of Companies, 1957 (In Millions of Dollars)	Number of Companies by Type of Change in Holdings in U.S. Government Securities		Annual Rates of Change (Percent): Companies Experiencing an Increase in Holdings of U.S. Government Securities		Annual Rates of Change (Percent): Companies Experiencing a Decrease in Holdings of U.S. Government Securities	
		Increase	Decrease	Total Assets	U. S. Governments	Total Assets	U.S. Governments
I	1,329-15,536	1	14	+11.0	+0.4	+6.3	−7.8
II	514- 1,273	1	14	+17.4	+0.7	+7.7	−6.9
III	236- 497	4	11	+16.1	+5.3	+7.6	−6.9
IV	142- 234	2	13	+15.2	+6.3	+9.1	−6.5
V	100- 141	2	13	+12.4	+5.8	+8.8	−6.4
VI	82- 97	3	12	+16.1	+3.7	+8.6	−6.0
VII	59- 81	1	14	+12.1	+0.9	+7.7	−7.1
VIII	41- 57	5	10	+12.8	+3.8	+9.3	−6.5
IX	34- 41	6	9	+13.6	+3.3	+9.2	−6.6
X	25- 33	10	5	+19.6	+6.4	+11.9	−5.9
All Companies		35	115	+13.7	+3.0	+6.7	−7.6

SOURCE: Compiled from **Best's Life Insurance Reports,** 1958.

panies which expanded their ownership of Governments were among the smaller firms in the industry. But, given the size of the institution, those companies which built up their government portfolios also generally experienced rates of growth in total assets far exceeding both the industry average and the average for those firms which were net sellers of Governments.

These tendencies are clearly evident in Table V-18; the table shows the distribution of the 150 largest life insurance companies by asset size at the end of 1957, annual rates of growth of total assets, and annual rates of change in holdings of United States government securities between 1945 and 1957. The companies have been arranged into 10 groups, each containing 15 companies. Between 1945 and 1957, 35 of the life insurance companies expanded their holdings of Governments, and about three-fifths of these were in the three smallest groups. Moreover, in the smallest group, two-thirds of the companies added to their government portfolios in the period under review. Within each size group, companies have been separated according to whether they experienced an increase or decrease in their holdings of Governments, and the annual rates of change in their total assets and government securities are compared. It should be noted that the annual growth rate was 13.7 percent for the institutions which were net purchasers of Governments, or more than twice the rate for the companies which were net sellers of these securities; the same tendency prevails within each size group. Furthermore, among the life insurance companies which expanded their Governments, there is a close association between the rate of growth in total assets and the rate of growth of Governments, although the degree of association is somewhat weaker than that already noted.

Several related factors seem to explain the investment behavior of life insurance companies with respect to government securities shown in Table V-18. In the first place, the smaller companies generally do not have the sophisticated investment managers necessary to participate in the variety of opportunities open to the large institutions. Secondly, the rapid growth of the small companies (partly reflecting the lower base from which they began but also reflecting sizable absolute gains) suggests that in some cases local investment opportunities in mortgages and other outlets probably did not keep pace with the inflow of funds. Thus, these smaller institutions may well have been induced to buy Governments to avoid accumulating idle resources. In contrast, the larger companies, because of their wider participation in different sectors of the national capital market, were generally able to discover numerous ways to invest their funds. Moreover, their relatively slow rates of growth implied that the inflow of savings was insufficient to meet the demand for loans originating in the private sector. Faced with this pressure, the large companies liquidated Governments on an enormous scale.

Reflecting these diverse patterns, a substantial shift occurred in the distribution of Governments among life insurance companies during the postwar period. In 1957, the 35 companies which expanded their holdings over the preceding 12 years owned about 7.0 percent of the total government securities held by the 150 companies shown in Table V-18; in 1945 their proportion was only 1.6 percent. Moreover, at the end of World War II, the ratio of Governments to total assets among the above 35 companies was well below the industry average—although this was not the case for the one company in Group VII. While the ratio of Governments to total assets for the remaining 115 companies was about the same as for the industry as a whole in 1945, the proportion for the larger companies greatly exceeded the average, and the ratio declined with size of company. By the end of 1957, government securities accounted for about 10 percent of total assets among the 35 companies which were net purchasers of Governments compared with 6.6 percent for the remaining 115 institutions. Thus, an expanding market for Governments still exists among some life insurance companies, but it is limited in scope because only the smaller institutions generally find such securities attractive.

Section V
Conclusions

The main conclusions of this chapter have been given in each section, and they can be summarized here. It was shown that, while life insurance companies' demand for United States government securities arises primarily from the need for liquidity and portfolio diversification, these securities also serve as a residual source or use of investment funds, depending on the availability of investment opportunities in the private sector of the economy. It was argued that the companies' demand for liquidity is related to portfolio management rather than to any expectation of a sudden or large-scale withdrawal of reserves by policyholders. Furthermore, it was shown that fluctuations in the institutions' liquid assets (composed mainly of short-term government securities) are rather closely associated with expectations regarding the future course of long-term interest rates and related variations in the volume and maturity of the companies' forward commitments to purchase corporate securities and real estate mortgages. Many life insurance companies have discovered that United States government securities offer a convenient way to diversify their portfolios and no longer strive to acquire as wide a selection of assets in terms of the geographical and industrial distribution of borrowers to provide diversification. This trend appears to be especially marked among smaller institutions which lack the personnel and facilities to undertake the security analysis required to achieve diversification in the traditional way.

The actual investment behavior of life insurance companies in the government securities market was examined under rather diverse economic conditions. The pre-World War II experience demonstrated the extent to which life insurance companies looked upon Governments as a residual use of funds. Even in the last part of the 19th century, these institutions turned to Governments during wars and depressions when the private demand for funds shrank. In later years, this tendency was intensified, and during World War I life insurance companies placed more than three-fifths of their new resources in Governments. However, the Great Depression induced these lenders to enter the government securities market on an unprecedented scale. Over the decade of the 1930's, their investment in federal issues multiplied eighteen times; they became the dominant participants in the market toward the end of the decade and at times were virtually the only sizable bidders in the market.

So secure was the place of life insurance companies in the government securities market in the early 1940's that, when methods of financing World War II were being considered, the Treasury decided to offer in each war loan long-term bonds designed especially for these institutions. While life insurance companies acquired an average of 12 percent of the total amount of securities issued in the eight war loans, they purchased an average of 38 percent of long-term bonds, and in the fourth and fifth loans their share of long-term obligations rose to almost three-fifths of the total. Reflecting this participation in the government securities market during World War II, their Governments portfolio rose almost four times between 1940 and 1945 and at the end of the latter year accounted for almost one-half of their total assets. Moreover, government issues not only provided an outlet for new funds flowing to life insurance companies but also offset the decline in their holdings of private debt. Over the period as a whole, the growth in the companies' government securities was about 6 percent greater than the rise in total assets.

Behind the rapid absorption of Governments by life insurance companies during World War II, however, one can detect a countertrend. While their ownership of Governments advanced by $14.8 billion between 1941 and 1945, the companies liquidated close to $4.6 billion of low-yielding tax-exempt federal government issues; this amount was equal to almost one-third of the net increase in their holdings of Governments during the war. A considerable part of the tax-exempt issues sold by life insurance companies was absorbed by commercial banks. These institutions also sold—again primarily to commercial banks—a sizable part of taxable bank-eligible intermediate bonds which they acquired in the various war loan drives. Thus, life insurance companies to some extent partly offset the efforts of the Treasury to minimize bank financing of the war effort.

Furthermore, life insurance companies borrowed heavily from commercial banks to acquire government securities in the war loan drives. This behavior was in sharp contrast to the companies' traditional practice, since they ordinarily do not borrow in order to acquire investments. Although the estimates are rough, it seems that more than one-third of the total securities obtained by life insurance companies during the war loans was financed temporarily by commercial bank funds. While the bulk of such loans was undoubtedly obtained without reference to the possibility of capital gains through large subscriptions to war loans, there is considerable evidence suggesting that some life insurance companies were active participants in the practice known as free riding. The foundation of free riding was the underpricing of securities by the Treasury. Since issues were sold at par and rationed among subscribers, the latter could count on reselling all or a major part of their allotment at a premium. The exclusion of commercial banks from direct subscription in war loans (after the first two had passed) and the maintenance by the Federal Reserve System of a fixed structure of interest rates more or less guaranteed enormous profits from free riding. A rough estimate indicates that, given the pattern of subscriptions and price changes immediately following each war loan, life insurance companies were *potential* beneficiaries of perhaps 8 percent of the capital gains which could have been realized from free riding. How much of these potential gains were actually realized, of course, cannot be determined.

After World War II, life insurance companies generally viewed the government securities market as a residual source of funds. Through the disposal of Governments, they acquired $13.7 billion between 1945 and 1959, an amount equivalent to one-sixth of the total volume of funds they made available to the capital market in that period. The participation of life insurance companies in the government securities market in the postwar years passed through four broad phases. The early postwar period, 1946-49, brought a dramatic shift from acquisition to liquidation of Governments on a large scale which was only interrupted by the first postwar recession. The second phase covered the first year of the Korean War, during which the massive sales of Governments by life insurance companies and other institutions led to the unpegging of the market and the accord between the Treasury and the Federal Reserve System. Until this agreement released the Federal Reserve from its commitment to support the market at the wartime structure of interest rates, United States government securities were virtually the same as *money*, and the vast majority of life insurance companies seldom hesitated to sell even long-term bonds when the proceeds could be re-employed at higher yields in corporate bonds and real estate mortgages. The strength of this willingness to liquidate Governments was clearly demonstrated during the period from November, 1947 to February, 1948; over these few months they disposed of more than $1.4 billion of United States government bonds. Other investors, especially commercial banks, also liquidated Governments on a huge scale at this time. Given the pegged market for Governments, the Federal Reserve System had to absorb the $5 billion of long-term bonds and $1 billion of notes which were thrown on the market. Although the System was able actually to reduce its holdings of Governments through net sales of treasury bills, the release of long-term funds greatly expanded the availability of credit for corporations and borrowers against real estate mortgages. This in turn gave a sizable boost to inflationary pressures.

The revival of business in 1950 and the outbreak of hostilities in Korea in June of that year combined to generate a considerable demand for life insurance funds. Again the government securities market offered a residual source of funds to meet the needs of private investors. Although the net amount of Governments sold by life insurance companies over the year as a whole was only 12 percent higher than in the previous year, nearly three-fourths of the liquidation centered in the last half of the year. During the first half of 1951, the rate of sales was even heavier. The proceeds of these sales went mainly into mortgages. As already mentioned, the increased sale of Governments by life insurance companies and other investors was a major factor leading to the unpegging of the government securities market during the spring of 1951.

This event opened the third phase of life insurance companies' investment experience in the government securities market since World War II. Since most of 1951 was required for the institutions to adjust to the relatively free capital market resulting from the Treasury-Federal Reserve accord, 1952 marks the real beginning of the return to more orthodox investment behavior. In the new environment, one can observe changes in the flow of funds from life insurance companies in response to variations in the structure of long-term interest rates. Prior to the accord, numerous observers had argued that even a small increase in the yield spread between government and private obligations would induce life insurance companies and other financial institutions to sell Governments or reduce the rate at which they were buying them; a small decrease in the yield spread was said to produce the opposite results. This view was generally referred to as the "credit availability doctrine." While the seeds of the doctrine were planted in the monetary experience of the 1930's, the renewed interest in the argument sprang from the desire of the monetary authorities to increase the efficiency of general credit controls while continuing to support the government securities market.

The actual investment behavior of life insurance companies in the government securities market between 1952 and 1959 seems to confirm the pattern of response suggested by the credit availability doctrine. During periods of steady or declining yields on Governments (when the yield spread between these and corporate bonds tended to widen), these institutions greatly stepped up the pace at which they sold government bonds. On the other hand, rising interest rates and narrowing yield spreads seem to have retarded the pace of selling. Moreover, through the period 1952-59, there was a clear tendency for life insurance companies to build up their holdings of short-term government securities (especially treasury bills) in tandem with sales of bonds. This pattern apparently reflects the use of short-term issues as a liquidity reserve to await the drawing of funds previously committed to corporations and mortgage borrowers.

The final phase of life insurance companies' participation in the government securities market began with the recession of 1957-58. With the decline in the private demand for funds, these institutions again turned to Governments as an investment outlet. Although net sales of Governments revived on a modest scale in late 1958 and early 1959, as the companies found it necessary to meet commitments in excess of the inflow of funds, the massive liquidations of earlier years did not reappear. In fact, by the end of the decade of the 1950's, it seemed that the era was over when life insurance companies viewed government securities as a readily available source of funds to be tapped whenever private demand expanded. Moreover, it was shown that some companies actually increased their holdings of Governments over the entire postwar period; however, these were predominantly small institutions and thus did not offer much of a market for Governments. Nevertheless, it seems evident that even the largest life insurance companies would again provide a sizable market for Governments if a substantial decline occurred in the overall demand of private borrowers for long-term loans.

Footnotes

1. Institute of Life Insurance, *1960 Life Insurance Fact Book*, p. 64.

2. James J. O'Leary, "Life Insurance Investments and the Mortgage Market," *Commercial and Financial Chronicle*, June 28, 1956, p. 32.

3. See replies of life insurance company officials in *Monetary Policy and the Management of the Public Debt*, materials submitted to the Subcommittee on General Credit Control and Debt Management, Joint Committee on the Economic Report, 82nd Congress, 2nd Session (Washington: U.S. Government Printing Office, 1952), pp. 1227-48. These documents are referred to below as Patman Materials (after Representative Wright Patman, Texas, Chairman of the Subcommittee).

4. James J. O'Leary, "The Institutional Savings-Investment Process and Current Economic Theory," *American Economic Review*, May, 1954, p. 461.

5. Burton C. Hollowell, Professor of Economics, Wesleyan University, Middletown, Conn., in discussing the article by O'Leary, *op. cit.*, pp. 483-84.

6. Leroy M. Piser, *U.S. Government Bond Market Analysis* (New York: New York Institute of Finance, 1952), p. 14.

7. See Patman Materials, pp. 1227-33.

8. George T. Conklin, Jr., "A Century of Life Insurance Portfolio Management," *Investment of Life Insurance Funds*, pp. 271-72.

9. *Ibid.*

10. C. F. Childs, *Concerning U. S. Government Securities* (Chicago: C. F. Childs and Co., 1947), pp. 139-44.

11. Sylvia F. Porter, *How to Make Money in Government Bonds* (New York: Harper and Bros., 1939), p. 149.

12. Michael J. Cleary, "The Response of Life Insurance Funds to American Needs," address to the Association of Life Insurance Presidents, December 2, 1937.

13. Porter, *op. cit.*, p. 153.

14. *Ibid.*, p. 152.

15. Henry C. Murphy, *The National Debt in War and Transition* (New York: McGraw-Hill Book Company, 1950), pp. 119-28.

16. *Federal Reserve Bulletin*, January 1942, p. 2.

17. Murphy, *op. cit.*, pp. 110-12.

18. Childs, *op. cit.*, pp. 526-28.

19. Replies of life insurance officials to Patman Committee. See Patman Materials, pp. 1227-33.

20. First Boston Corporation, *Securities of the United States Government and its Instrumentalities* (New York: The Corporation, 1943), p. 51.

21. Childs, *op. cit.*, p. 301.

22. Murphy, *op. cit.*, p. 177.

23. Marriner S. Eccles, *Beckoning Frontiers* (New York: Alfred A. Knopf, 1951), p. 362.

24. Childs, *op. cit.*, pp. 93-94 and 389 ff.

25. Murphy, *op. cit.*, p. 177 ff.

26. Childs, *op. cit.*, p. 391.

27. Murphy, *op. cit.*, p. 189.

28. *Ibid.*

29. Allen Sproul, "Changing Concepts of Central Banking," *Money, Trade and Economic Growth, Essays in Honor of John Henry Williams* (New York: The Macmillan Company, 1951), p. 310.

30. Board of Governors of the Federal Reserve System, *Annual Report*, 1947, pp. 96-97.

31. *Federal Reserve Bulletin.*

32. Sproul, *op. cit.*, p. 310.

33. Board of Governors of the Federal Reserve System, *Annual Report*, 1947, p. 97.
34. *Federal Reserve Bulletin*, January, 1948, p. 11.
35. *U. S. Treasury Bulletin*, December, 1947, and April, 1948.
36. U. S. Department of Commerce, *U. S. Income and Output*, 1958, p. 193.
37. Securities and Exchange Commission, *Statistical Bulletin*, 1955, p. 12.
38. James J. O'Leary, "The Effects of Recent Credit and Debt Management Policies upon Life Insurance Company Investments," *Journal of Finance*, May, 1952, p. 313.
39. *Federal Reserve Bulletin*, March, 1951, p. 267.
40. Testimony of various life insurance executives before the Patman Committee. See Patman Materials, p. 1228 ff.
41. John H. Williams, "The Implications of Fiscal Policy for Monetary Policy and the Banking System," *American Economic Review*, XXXII, No. 1, March, 1942.
42. Robert V. Roosa, "Interest Rates and the Central Bank," in *Money, Trade and Economic Growth* (New York: The Macmillan Co., 1951), pp. 270-96.

CHAPTER VI

Investment Behavior in the Corporate Bond Market

SECTION I
INTRODUCTION

The problem of investing the steadily growing pool of savings has forced life insurance companies to search continuously for new investment opportunities. One of the areas to which they have turned increasingly during the last decade and a half is the market for corporate bonds, although the rate of acquisition has varied under different economic and financial conditions. The participation of life insurance companies in the corporate section of the capital market had already resulted in several major changes in the structure and functioning of the market before World War II, but there have been further shifts since the end of the war. An outstanding example of the change is the continued decline in the traditional role of investment banking houses in financing corporate expansion. Moreover, the shrinkage of market transactions in outstanding corporate bonds has continued. This transformation of the capital market is a result, as well as a reflection, of the technique of placing corporate securities directly with long-term lenders, and among the latter life insurance companies occupy the dominant position—although corporate pension funds also began to play a significant part during the last decade.

This chapter appraises the general impact made by life insurance companies on the structure and operation of the corporate bond market since the end of World War II. Initially, trends in the participation of these companies in the market are summarized. Subsequently, the nature and advantages of direct placements are considered, an analysis is made of the competition for securities among life insurance companies and between them and other investors, and, finally, the effects of this competition on the investment banking machinery of the capital market are appraised.

A. Demand for Corporate Bonds

In view of the long-term nature of the obligations of life insurance companies, long-term corporate debt is especially attractive to these institutions. There are several reasons for this. First, long-term corporate obligations are issued for definite periods of time and usually carry fixed interest rates. The known maturity and predictable income, plus the fact that debt represents a prior claim on the assets of the issuer, strongly recommend corporate debt to life insurance company portfolio managers. This prior claim on assets does not ordinarily depend solely on the existence of specific assets.[1] Indeed, a considerable proportion of industrial debt financing commonly takes the form of debentures or promissory notes. This means that the basis of the prior claim lies in the protective covenants drawn by the lender. While these are used in a few cases when corporate debt is floated in the public market, the bulk of covered issues acquired by life insurance companies is obtained through direct or private placements. Typically, covenants include the following provisions: (a) the assets of the borrower cannot be pledged or mortgaged without at least equally securing the outstanding debentures or notes, (b) additional long-term debt can only be incurred in limited amounts, and (c) dividends and other distributions to common stock holders can only be made from income.

Corporate debt as an outlet for life insurance funds is, of course, quite competitive with other types of eligible long-term investments. In making a comparison of the various fields from the point of view of relative safety and net income prospects, portfolio managers see the following attributes afforded by corporate debt: (a) the highly impersonal nature of corporate bond investment, (b) the greater ability to recognize in terms of yield the various degrees of credit standing, (c) the superior marketability of corporate bonds (although this aspect may be seriously compromised if the issue has been directly placed), and (d) the flexibility of the instrument. Within the broad field of corporate bonds, investment managers have shown different preferences at different times for obligations of railroads, public utilities, and industrial and commercial enterprises. Railroad bonds, however, have been unattractive as investment outlets since the 1930's, but the other types of issues have held their appeal continuously. Public utility bonds absorbed a substantial share of the funds which went into corporate bonds during the early postwar years, but obligations of industrial and commercial firms were the leading investment media during the 1950's.

B. Supply of Long-Term Corporate Bonds

The extent to which life insurance companies' demand for corporate bonds can be satisfied is limited by the overall availability of such debt. This availability is itself influenced by the trend and pace of economic growth: while the trend has been rising during the postwar years, it has also fluctuated appreciably from year to year depending on the cyclical pattern of corporate expenditures on plant and equipment. In years when these outlays were large, the growth of corporate debt was substantial; the reverse was also the case.

This observation is supported by the statistics in Table VI-1. These

TABLE VI-1

CORPORATE BONDS OUTSTANDING AND LIFE INSURANCE COMPANIES' OWNERSHIP OF CORPORATE BONDS, BY TYPE, 1940 AND 1945-59

		Held by Life Insurance Companies		Type of Corporate Bonds Held by Life Insurance Companies ($ Millions)		
Year	Total Outstanding ($ Billions)	Amount ($ Millions)	Percent of Total Outstanding	Railroad	Public Utility	Industrial and Miscellaneous
1940	39.6	8,645	21.7	2,830	4,273	1,542
1945	23.5	10,060	43.0	2,948	5,212	1,900
1946	24.4	11,775	48.4	2,872	5,587	3,316
1947	27.2	14,754	54.4	2,844	6,941	4,969
1948	31.5	18,894	60.0	3,002	8,741	7,151
1949	34.2	21,461	62.9	3,017	9,764	8,680
1950	35.7	23,300	65.3	3,187	10,587	9,526
1951	39.1	25,983	66.5	3,307	11,235	11,441
1952	43.7	29,200	66.8	3,545	11,953	13,702
1953	47.1	31,997	67.9	3,643	12,827	15,527
1954	50.5	34,194	67.7	3,757	13,511	16,926
1955	53.4	36,059	67.6	3,912	13,968	18,179
1956	57.0	38,184	67.0	3,877	14,520	19,787
1957	63.4	40,832	64.4	3,863	15,252	21,717
1958	69.2	43,220	62.4	3,843	15,938	23,439
1959	73.5	45,334	61.5	3,774	16,455	25,105

SOURCE: Outstanding Corporate Bonds: Board of Governors of the Federal Reserve System. Ownership by Life Insurance Companies: **1960 Life Insurance Fact Book** and **Tally of Life Insurance Statistics.**

data show total corporate bonds outstanding for the years 1940 and 1945-59; also shown are corporate bonds held by life insurance companies, by type and the ratio of their holdings to the total outstanding.[2] As one would expect, the unprecedented expansion of corporate investment since World War II produced a twofold increase in the volume of corporate bond indebtedness. In fact, the annual rate of growth of corporate debt averaged 15 percent during the last decade and a half, the highest rate in history. This pattern stands in sharp relief against the experience of the prewar years. During the 1920's the rate of growth of long-term corporate debt, reflecting the vigorous expansion of investment, averaged almost 6 percent per year, rising from $33.8 billion at the end of 1921 to $51.1 billion at the end of 1930. In the subsequent depression decade, outstanding corporate debt declined to $42.5 billion at the end of 1936 and remained at approximately this level until the limitations on corporate borrowing during World War II induced a further decline. By the close of the war, the total outstanding was $38.3 billion. Immediately after the war, corporations financed a large share of their additions to capacity from the sizable holdings of liquid assets accumulated during the conflict, and made only small claims on the capital market. Beginning in 1947, however, they turned to outside sources on a large scale and except for 1950, have borrowed at least $2.7 billion each year through net sales of corporate bonds. In years of rapid expansion in plant and equipment expenditures, the increase in bond indebtedness was much larger and amounted to a record $6.4 billion in 1957.

Aside from the general limitations imposed by the rate of capital formation, the level of long-term corporate debt outstanding at any given time will depend on the decisions of corporate managements regarding the place of debt in the capital structure compared with the financing of new capacity through the use of retained earnings and preferred and common stock. Similarly, management will decide whether long-term or short-term debt can best be employed at a given time, and if long-term debt is to be relied upon, whether it will be sold publicly through an investment banking syndicate or sold directly to investors by the private placement method. Clearly, corporate managements will have to consider the availability of funds from the various alternative external and internal sources and then seek an appropriate balance. In some cases, serious limitations on management's freedom in arranging the terms and methods of corporate financing are found in the public utility and railroad fields, where some regulation of the nature and method of financing is exercised by state public service commissions, the Securities and Exchange Commission, and the Interstate Commerce Commission.

During the last decade and a half, when corporations have turned to external financing they have relied to a substantial degree on the supply of funds emanating from life insurance companies. An indication of the importance of these institutions as sources of long-term funds is provided by the statistics shown in Table VI-2, which summarize the sources and uses of corporate funds since World War II. It will be noted that internal funds (retained earnings and depreciation and depletion allowances) accounted for almost three-fifths of the total funds expended by corporations for working capital and plant and equipment. Only slightly more than two-fifths of their total funds came from external sources. Furthermore, retained profits and depreciation represented almost 90 percent of

TABLE VI-2

SOURCES AND USES OF CORPORATE FUNDS,[1] 1946-59

(In Billions of Dollars)

	Amount	Percent of Total
Uses of Funds		
Plant and equipment expenditures	312.2	65.7
Increase in working capital	163.2	34.3
Total Uses	475.4	100.0
Sources of Funds		
Internal		
Retained profits	129.8	27.2
Depreciation and depletion allowances	144.8	30.4
Total Internal Sources	274.6	57.6
External		
Stocks	35.1	7.4
Bonds	50.0	10.5
Other sources	117.1	24.6
Total External Sources	202.2	42.5
Total Sources	476.8	100.0
Discrepancy (uses less sources)	−1.4	—
Memorandum:		
Net increase in corporate bonds held by life insurance companies		
Amount (billions of dollars)	35.0	
Ratio to net increase in total corporate bonds outstanding (percent)	70.0	

1. All U. S. corporations excluding banks, insurance companies, and investment companies.

SOURCE: Securities and Exchange Commission.

gross expenditures on plant and equipment during the period. As far as the external sources are concerned, corporate bonds represented about one-quarter and stocks just over one-sixth; other sources (mainly trade debt, bank loans, and mortgages) accounted for the remaining proportion. From these figures, it should be evident that new money bond sales, relatively speaking, were of secondary importance as a source of funds and represented only about 10 percent of capital formation by corporations during this period. Again it is emphasized that the leading source was retained earnings of $275 billion, a source of capital about five and one-half times as important as bond sales. This fact, of course, underscores the extremely significant role which corporate savings play in the functioning of the economy today. In summary, then, it should be stressed that during the postwar period corporate managements have relied on long-term debt financing as a secondary source.

Nevertheless, when corporations did resort to outside bond financing, they depended quite heavily on life insurance companies. Taking the period as a whole, these institutions purchased $35 billion (net) of the $50 billion increase in corporate bonds outstanding, an amount representing about 70 percent of the total. The reasons why life insurance companies have become increasingly important as holders of corporate long-term debt are found in the fundamental changes that have taken place in the economic, financial, and tax structure in the last three decades. The general nature of these changes will now be discussed.

SECTION II
INVESTMENT IN CORPORATE BONDS: PREWAR HERITAGE

Many of the principal trends in life insurance companies' investment activities in the corporate bond market since the end of World War II actually represent the continued unfolding of tendencies already evident during the two decades preceding the war. Consequently, this background should be reviewed briefly, because otherwise one may ascribe too much weight to developments since 1945.

A. INVESTMENT BEHAVIOR DURING A DECADE OF PROSPERITY, 1921-30

For the corporate sector of the economy, the 1920's was a decade of almost uninterrupted prosperity. Private demand for capital funds far exceeded that of federal, state and local governments combined. The outstanding features of the decade were a persistent rise in industrial production and a moderate but steady decline in long-term interest rates as the supply of savings edged ahead of available outlets. Output of industry rose by 20 percent[3] between 1921 and 1930, while high-grade railroad bond yields receded from about 4.50 percent to 4.25 percent.[4] Another notable characteristic of the decade was the substantial dependence of corporations on the sale of securities to finance the high level of capital formation. For the period as a whole, the total amount of new money raised from external sources was $47.7 billion, of which one-third came from stock sales, almost two-fifths from the rise in long-term bonds and the remainder from retained earnings. Because of the extensive public interest in stock ownership, corporations were able to sell stocks at prices substantially in excess of the underlying net worth of the enterprises. This opportunity, plus the inducement offered by relatively low corporate income taxes, encouraged many firms to rely on equity financing for a significant portion of capital requirements.

Even so, the supply of corporate debt available for purchase by life insurance companies was more than adequate. While outstanding corporate debt rose from $33.8 billion in 1921 to $51.1 billion at the end of 1930, life insurance companies' holdings expanded by only $3 billion. Thus, the companies acquired 17 percent of the increase in outstanding long-term corporate obligations, and these purchases accounted for around one-third of the growth in the companies' total assets. At the end of the period, they owned about 11 percent of the total corporate debt outstanding, as contrasted with around 6 percent at the end of 1921. Nevertheless, while the companies' total assets increased from $7.9 billion in 1921 to $18.9 billion in 1929, an increase of over 140 percent, their corporate bond holdings did not advance appreciably, rising from 24 to 26 percent of total assets.

The dominant principle guiding life insurance companies' investment in corporate debt during the 1920's seems to have been that real property, rather than the current or prospective earning power of industry, represented the best security for loans.[5] Thus, railroad mortgage bonds, backed by property, dominated the corporate bond portfolio during these years. At the end of 1921, railroad bond holdings of $1.7 billion represented about 90 percent of the corporate bond portfolio. Moreover, despite the increasing importance of the public utility industry during the decade, railroad obligations still constituted three-fifths of the companies' corporate bond portfolio at the close of 1930. Public utility bonds of $1.6 billion at the end of that year accounted for one-third of their corporate bonds, and industrial and miscellaneous bonds for the remaining 8 percent.

B. Investment Behavior During a Decade of Depression, 1931-40

In this depression decade, the corporate bond market, like that for other financial instruments, shrank to a shadow of what it had been during the previous ten years. The demand for capital by private business was almost wholly absent. The federal government initiated numerous large-scale public works and relief programs in an attempt first to stimulate expanded employment opportunities, and subsequently to provide them directly. Thus the federal demand for funds was the dominant factor in the capital market throughout the period. In this environment, a substantial wave of bankruptcies occurred producing a considerable reduction in the supply of long-term corporate debt. There was also a precipitous drop in long-term interest rates as high-grade bond yields fell by almost one-third. In fact, for the entire decade, bond yields remained well below those on stocks. Nevertheless, corporate management, except for the years 1937-38, sought little new outside capital—despite the fall in the cost of long-term funds to the lowest levels in history up to that time. Furthermore, American businessmen actually consumed a sizable portion of their fixed capital stock. In financial terms, capital invested in industry fell by $17.8 billion during the decade, of which $5.8 billion centered in outstanding corporate bonds.

In contrast to the general stagnation described above, the life insurance industry continued its vigorous growth. Total assets rose by $12 billion, registering an annual average gain of over 6 percent. By the end of 1940, assets owned by life insurance companies stood at $30.8 billion. This persistent increase in assets in the face of declining investment opportunities created a difficult problem for portfolio managers. Most companies sought a solution in the United States government securities market, but a small number apparently preferred to build up liquid assets rather than accept the prevailing low interest rates.[6] Yet, taken as a group, life insurance companies continued to find outlets for their funds in the corporate bond market, an achievement of the first magnitude since this market was waning throughout the period. While long-term corporate bonds outstanding fell from $45.4 billion to $39.6 billion between 1930 and 1940, the holdings of these institutions rose by $3.7 billion, or from $4.9 billion to $8.6 billion. Thus their relative share of the corporate bond market doubled during the decade.

On the other hand, corporate obligations relative to total assets remained virtually unchanged and represented about 28 percent of total investments in both 1930 and 1940. Still it should be noted that it was during this decade (in 1936, in fact) that corporate bonds first became the most important category of assets owned by life insurance companies. This type of investment retained its premier position until 1943 when United States government issues moved to the forefront. It was also during the 1930's that public utility bonds replaced railroad issues as the leading type of asset in the companies' corporate portfolios. At the end of 1940, public utility bond holdings of $4.3 billion represented one-half of all corporate obligations, railroad bonds of $2.8 billion constituted one-third, and industrial and miscellaneous bonds of $1.5 billion made up 18 percent.

The rise of life insurance companies to a position of dominance is partly due to the transformation of the economic and financial environment during the decade of the 1930's. As already mentioned, corporate demand for outside funds was practically nonexistent, and, in fact, corporate debt was being retired out of internal savings.[7] Perhaps of more significance was the transfer of outstanding debt induced by the downtrend in long-term interest rates. As bond yields fell to exceptionally low levels, many individuals (previously leading purchasers of corporate obligations) began to liquidate their holdings, and accumulated large amounts of idle cash or bought state and local and United States government securities. Simultaneously, corporations undertook large-scale redemptions of debt issues (floated at the relatively high interest rates of the 1920's) to refinance their requirements at the considerable interest savings currently obtainable.[8] Since the funds of life insurance companies were increasing steadily, they were able to acquire bonds sold by individuals as well as to take up corporate refunding issues. Also during the 1930's it became the practice to place new corporate issues directly with institutional investors, thus by-passing the public market. The nature and consequences of this development, which was to attain major significance in subsequent years, are discussed below.

C. Investment Behavior During World War II, 1941-45

In this period, the capital market was again dominated by the financial requirements of the federal government. To finance the war effort, the national debt rose by $208 billion between 1940 and 1945 (from $45 billion to $253 billion). A significant proportion of the funds obtained by the government was used directly to finance the construction of plant and equipment to produce munitions, or in prepayment on contracts let to private business.[9] One result was the almost complete cessation of corporate demand for long-term external funds. Indeed, long-term corporate bonds outstanding fell by $5.3 billion, from $39.6 billion at the end of

1940 to $34.3 billion at the end of 1945. Associated with this situation was the considerable expansion of corporate savings. During the years 1941-45, net corporate income after taxes amounted to $4.8 billion; after paying 46 percent of this sum as dividends, corporations retained about $26 billion. While part of this saving was used to carry the larger inventories required for war production, a major share was set aside to finance plant reconstruction and expansion during the postwar period.

Under these conditions, life insurance companies' investment activity in the corporate bond market was predictable. Their holdings declined relatively during the second World War, from 28 percent of total assets in 1940 to 23 percent at the end of 1945. Although there was a moderate increase in absolute corporate bond holdings from $8.6 billion to $10 billion, this was primarily a prolongation of the shift in ownership which began in the 1930's. Almost the entire increase in corporate bond obligations was accounted for by the rise in public utility issues, which advanced by almost $1 billion—from $4.3 billion to $5.2 billion and constituted just over one-half of the corporate bond portfolio. Railroad bonds of $2.9 billion accounted for three-tenths, and industrial and miscellaneous bonds of $1.9 billion for two-fifths. The further reduction in outstanding corporate bonds resulted in life insurance companies' raising their share of the total from 22 percent in 1940 to 29 percent at the end of 1945.

Section III
Investment Behavior Since World War II

United States life insurance companies have played a major role in supplying the capital requirements of business in the postwar years. Their corporate bond investments of $45.3 billion at the end of 1959 were two-fifths of their total assets, and the $35 billion increase in such holdings over the last decade and a half represented a slightly larger proportion (42 percent) of the total funds supplied to the capital market in the same period. A more striking measure of the part played by life insurance companies in postwar corporate finance is the comparison of the increase in their holdings with the rise in total corporate bonds outstanding. Between 1945 and 1959, this aggregate amount rose by $50 billion. Thus, the portfolio of life insurance companies absorbed 70 percent of the increase; this expanded their share of corporate bonds to three-fifths of the total outstanding in 1959 compared with slightly more than two-fifths at the end of World War II. In other words, the relative position of life insurance companies in the corporate bond market was almost half again as strong as it was immediately after the close of the war.

Toward the end of the last decade, however, life insurance companies began to encounter severe competition for the available corporate bonds. Their strongest competitors are corporate pension funds. These relatively new institutions have been growing at a phenomenal rate since 1950, and they have even more freedom in investment management than do life insurance companies. Their long-term liabilities enable them also to follow investment policies similar to those of life insurance companies, and they have acquired a sizable proportion of the new corporate bonds sold in the last decade. In 1951, they owned just under 8 percent of the corporate bonds outstanding, but this ratio had doubled by 1959.[10] Thus, the impact of the pension funds on life insurance companies' investment opportunities in the corporate bond market has been considerable. And although the latter's much greater resources still make them the primary lenders to corporations, the pension funds are rapidly gaining a respectable proportion of new loans.

Within the various segments of the corporate bond market, the strides made by life insurance companies in the industrial and commercial sector are the most dramatic. By the end of 1959, these issues accounted for one-fifth of their total assets and for more than one-half of their corporate bond portfolio. In 1951, industrial and miscellaneous bonds, at 17 percent of total assets, became the single most important type of investment owned by life insurance companies. Since then these obligations have been the principal focus of the companies' investment activity, although the degree of concentration on them has varied greatly depending on the corporate demand for outside funds. Their holdings of railroad and public utility bonds (reflecting the other main parts of the corporate bond market) have grown far less rapidly—although public utilities were especially attractive during the early postwar years. The investment behavior of life insurance companies in each of these major subsectors of the corporate bond market during the last decade and a half will now be discussed more fully.

A. Railroad Bonds

Since World War II, the railroad industry has been only a minor outlet for the investment funds of life insurance companies, although these institutions continue to be important creditors of the railroads. In terms of dollar volume, railroad bonds held by life insurance companies reached a peak of $3.9 billion in 1955 and have been sliding off each year since then (see Table VI-1 and Chart VI-1). By the end of 1959, their holdings had receded to $3.8 billion and accounted for only 3.4 percent of their total assets—the smallest proportion since the 1870's. However, in relation to total assets, railroad bonds have been declining since 1917, which is as far back as the continuous record extends. Railroad bonds, however, were not always such unattractive investments for life insurance companies. These institutions played a significant role in financing railroad development in the pioneering years of the 1870's and 1880's. In the early part of the twentieth century, railroad bonds were about one-third of the

CHART VI-1
Corporate Bonds as a Percentage of Total Assets of Life Insurance Companies
1946-1959

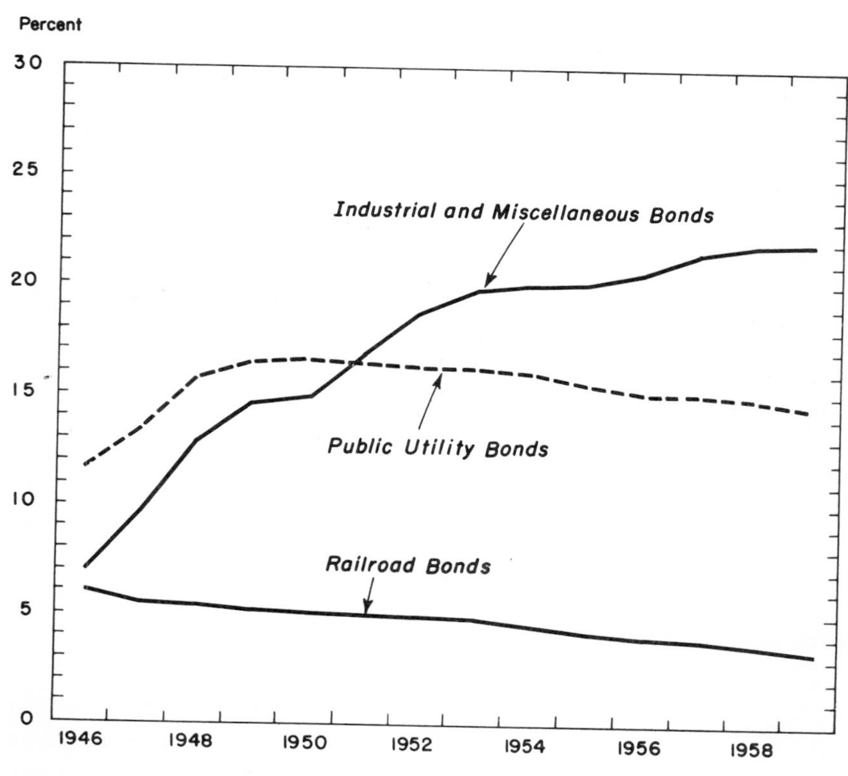

SOURCE: *Life Insurance Fact Book.*

total assets of life insurance companies, and the companies held about the same proportion of railroad debt outstanding. During the 1920's the companies' dollar volume of railroad bonds mounted at a brisk pace, but their total assets moved ahead even faster; consequently, such issues dropped from just over one-quarter of total assets in 1919 to about one-sixth by the end of the next decade.

With the coming of the depression and the subsequent bankruptcies of the 1930's, the flight from railroad bonds was greatly accelerated, aided partly by the sizable refundings which occurred. Nevertheless, while the confidence of most life insurance companies in railroad bonds was destroyed in this period, the actual record of losses and liquidation of such bonds is quite different from that implied by the incidence of railroad failures. In fact, a large part of the frequently mentioned capital losses were paper depreciations rather than realized losses, because many companies retained the railroad bonds in their portfolios. For example, the railroad bond investment experience of the 18 largest life insurance companies over the years 1929 to 1950 shows that losses were surprisingly small.[11] These institutions held about $2,700 million of railroad bonds in both years. Their aggregate losses were about $146 million, or approximately 5½ percent of the 1929 portfolio. In the same period, however, these 18 companies received $2,363 million in interest earnings. Thus, losses were hardly noticeable when set against the size of the principal involved and the aggregate income received.

Since World War II, the railroad industry has continued to decline relative to the rest of the economy, and life insurance companies, like other investors, have found little attraction in railroad issues. Consequently, only a few lines find it possible to raise funds for new capital on their general credit. Fewer still are able to do so through the sale of preferred stock, and virtually none could sell additional common stock. In most instances, the only salable financial instruments are equipment trust certificates, which are secured by the issuer's rolling stock. Under these circumstances, the potential losses on general railroad bonds (most of whose prices seldom advance above 80) and the continued attenuation in the relative place of railroads in the nation's transportation system have induced investment officers in life insurance companies to approach the industry with much apprehension—if not to avoid it completely. Life insurance companies nevertheless remain an important source of funds for the railroads; they held about two-fifths of total railroad long-term debt at the end of 1959 compared with one-fifth in the 1930's.

B. PUBLIC UTILITY BONDS

At the end of 1959, life insurance companies held $16.5 billion of public utility bonds, representing 14.5 percent of their total assets and about two-fifths of the bonded indebtedness of the nation's public utility enterprises. Since the end of the second World War, these institutions have supplied about two-fifths of the new capital raised by public utilities through sales of long-term debt. The participation by life insurance companies in this part of the capital market has fluctuated greatly from year to year, but two main phases stand out. During the early postwar years, life insurance companies purchased public utility bonds faster than new issues appeared, so they were also active bidders in the secondary market. After 1950 their investment activities in both the primary and secondary sectors of the market slackened appreciably.

As shown in Chart VI-2, life insurance companies have played a consistently smaller role in the market for public utility bonds than in the market for industrial and miscellaneous issues. Since 1951, the proportion of new long-term funds supplied by these investors to the public utility industry has declined steadily. In fact, the only main interruptions in the downtrend in the proportion of such funds originating in life insurance companies occurred during recessions. Three primary factors seem to lie behind this pattern and help to explain it. While life insurance companies find public utility issues a reliable outlet for the savings mobilized by them, the lower yield on public utility bonds makes them somewhat less attractive than the obligations of industrial, commercial, and other enterprises. The lower yields, of course, reflect the smaller risk of capital losses which such issues entail as well as the broad market stimulated by the safety feature. In addition, because most public utility bonds are sold through public bidding, many life insurance company investment officers (who look for opportunities to make large individual loans) find it difficult to satisfy their requirements in this area of the capital market. Moreover, since public utility bidding also entails lower yields and fewer chances to tailor the provisions in bond covenants than directly placed issues, many life insurance companies prefer the latter. The place of direct placements is discussed more fully below. Finally, during recessions, with the concomitant drop in long-term interest rates, many public utility enterprises rush to float loans postponed because of previously high interest rates. Still other firms hasten to the market to refund at lower interest cost outstanding issues with high coupons. On balance, the supply of public utility bonds expands (or shrinks only moderately) while the volume of industrial and miscellaneous bonds reaching the market declines. Because recessions make little, if any, difference regarding the inflow of life insurance company funds which must be invested, these institutions direct more of their investment activity to public utility bonds.

CHART VI-2

Participation by Life Insurance Companies and Corporate Pension Funds in the Corporate Bond Market, 1946-1959

(Percentage of Net Flows)

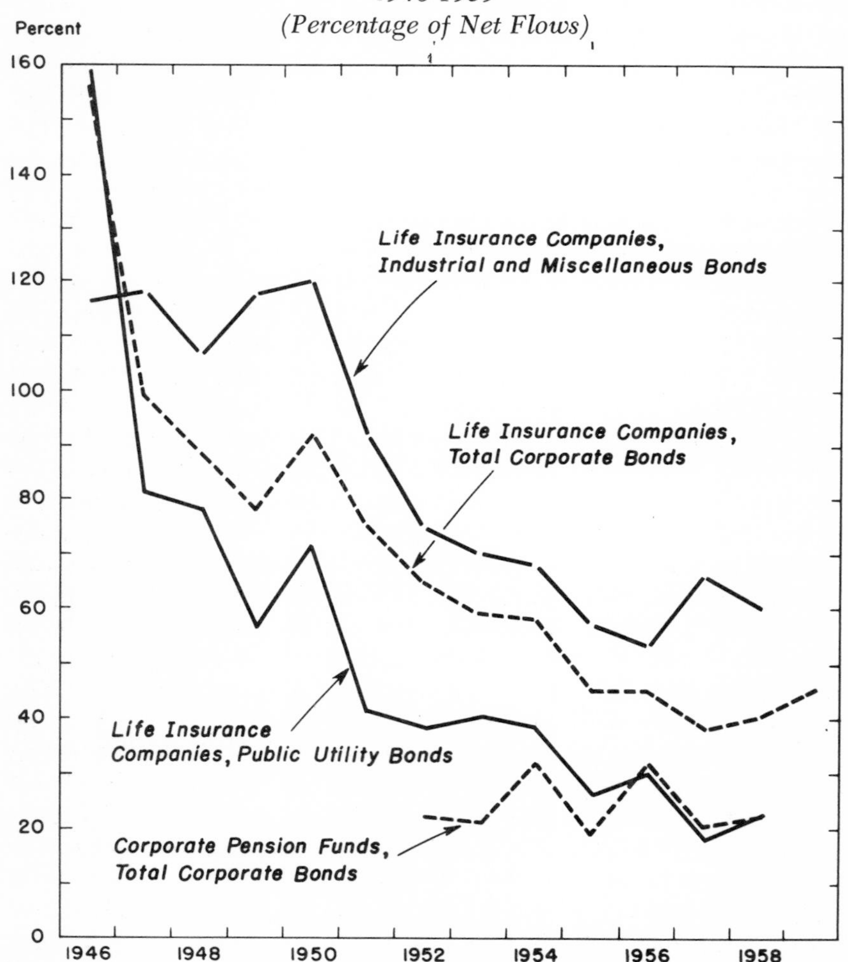

SOURCE: Based on data from the Securities and Exchange Commission and *Life Insurance Fact Book.*

This tendency is shown in Chart VI-2, where the shifts during the 1953-54 and 1957-58 recessions stand out clearly.

The move of life insurance companies into the market for public utility bonds on a large scale during the years immediately following World War II was actually the third time these institutions had channeled a major share of their increased resources into public utility issues. The previous periods were the decade of the 1920's and the last half of the 1930's. The most recent shift, however, reflected a much greater willingness on the part of life insurance companies, than they have traditionally had, to bear the risk of technological change in the public utility industry.

Initially, the interest of life insurance companies in public utility bonds centered in the obligations of water and gaslight companies, to which they had made loans as early as the middle of the last century. But as these institutions began to acquire gaslight issues in sizable amounts, the future prospects of the firms manufacturing gas were virtually erased by the successful launching of the electric light industry in the early 1880's. The new industry expanded rapidly, inducing a few life insurance companies to extend long-term loans to the pioneering enterprises. Yet the uncharted course was too risky for most life insurance portfolio managers, who saw the many small firms, competing in limited market areas, primarily as speculative ventures. This apprehension naturally led to only insignificant acquisitions of electric light company bonds.

Life insurance companies were next drawn to telephone and telegraph issues whose investment performance was generally satisfactory. They were much less fortunate in their excursion into street railway issues in the late 1880's and early 1890's. As municipalities sought ways to transport their growing urban populations, the new industry expanded rapidly, and life insurance companies provided vigorous financial support. By 1906, these investors owned about $160 million of street railway bonds issued by a sizable number of the leading cities, and these issues represented over one-half of the companies' total holdings of public utility obligations. The prosperity phase of the industry's growth, however, was rather short-lived. By 1919, approximately one-sixth of the nation's street railways were in receivership, struggling desperately (and almost universally failing) even to meet interest payments on their debts. Capital losses suffered by investors were enormous, and life insurance companies were among the heaviest losers.[12]

During the 1920's and 1930's, life insurance companies shifted into electric light company bonds on a large scale, but they were responding to different stimuli in each period. Their purchases in the earlier period were induced by the infectious wave of optimism about the future of electricity and the enthusiastic promotions of public utility holding companies. In this spirited atmosphere, life insurance companies increased their public utility holdings tenfold to $1.4 billion and raised their utility portfolios from 1.7 percent to 8.7 percent of their total assets. After the stock market crash of 1929, their investment activity in this part of the capital market was greatly abated. The next upsurge began in 1934 as a growing number of life insurance companies sought a haven from the storm of bankruptcies and liquidations which swept the depressed economy. Between 1933 and 1941, these investors expanded their public utility portfolios from $1.8 billion to $4.9 billion, more than two and one-half times the amount held at the trough of the depression.

During the second World War, the companies' ownership of public utility bonds declined only slightly in amount, but in relation to their total assets the decrease was substantial. The reduced rate of investment in utility issues is primarily attributable to the suspension of new issues by utility enterprises unable to obtain material to expand their capacity. However, an immense volume of refundings and maturities also resulted in considerable erosion of life insurance companies' public utility holdings. For example, in 1945 alone, $1,278 million of such issues in their portfolios were redeemed; this was about one-quarter of the total owned by them at the beginning of the year.[13]

Partly because of such depletions in their public utility holdings and partly because the massive accumulation of liquid assets enabled many well-established manufacturing and commercial enterprises to expand without coming to the capital market during the early postwar years, life insurance companies turned again to public utility bonds with renewed interest. This time, they concentrated on financing thousands of miles of pipelines carrying natural gas from Texas and other southwestern producing fields to populous consuming centers, including New York and Chicago. During 1946 to 1950, these institutions invested more than $1 billion in natural gas pipelines, an amount representing nearly three-quarters of the average bonded indebtedness of pipeline companies in these years. These net acquisitions also accounted for one-fifth of the rise in life insurance companies' total public utility holdings.

Some indication of the relative position of each major type of public utility issue in the companies' portfolios is provided by a survey conducted in 1955 by the Institute of Life Insurance.[14] Bonds of electric light and power companies headed the list; these totaled $7.7 billion or 55 percent of the utility investments. Obligations of gas utilities ($1.3 billion) and natural gas pipelines ($1.9 billion) together represented 23 percent. Investments in communications industries, consisting primarily of the bonds sold by telephone and telegraph companies, amounted to $2.6 billion and equaled 18 percent of all utility holdings. The balance of life insurance companies' investments in public utilities was in the bonds of private water supply companies, local transportation companies, and other miscellaneous utilities, amounting to $500 million and 4 percent of the public utility bond portfolio. While these proportions may have changed somewhat during the last five years, the overall structure of life insurance companies' public utility portfolio is probably about the same.

C. Industrial and Miscellaneous Bonds

Perhaps the most striking feature of the investment activity of life insurance companies since World War II is their intensive concentration on industrial and commercial financing. At the end of 1959, these institutions owned $25.1 billion of industrial and miscellaneous bonds, representing 22 percent of their total assets and well over one-half of their corporate bonds. At the end of 1945 their portfolio of these issues amounted to only $1.9 billion and 4 percent of their total assets. During the fourteen years ending in 1959, industrial and commercial enterprises (other than railroads and public utilities) received more than one-quarter of all long-term loans made by life insurance companies. This was the largest single share of funds supplied to the capital market by these investors and was almost one and one-half times as large as the next largest share, which went into conventional mortgages.

The immense expansion of life insurance companies' investments in this area is, of course, a mirror of the enormous growth of the nation's industrial and commercial facilities in the last decade and a half. However, it is also the harvest of seeds sown well before World War II in the capital markets at large, and in life insurance companies' investment policies in particular. In the capital market at large, the unfavorable experience with railroad bonds during the depression of the 1930's induced life insurance companies to search for alternative outlets for their funds. Industrial and commercial bonds presented a wide range of promising opportunities, and some of the larger insurance companies had already begun to acquire sizable amounts of such issues before the war began. Moreover, the relatively high income tax rates made corporations more willing to finance capital formation through floating long-term debt because nearly one-half of the interest cost could be deducted from profits before taxes and thus passed along to the federal government. This attitude toward debt was reinforced by the public's strong aversion to buying equity securities until the striking revival of confidence in stocks in the 1950's. Within the life insurance industry, several major developments in prewar years prepared the way for the companies' entry into the industrial sector of the capital market once hostilities had ceased. In 1928, the New York State investment law (which controls the investment of over 90 percent of life insurance funds) was amended to allow companies to purchase debentures, a form of financing used extensively in the industrial field. The intervention of the depression and the war postponed the full impact of this amendment which began to be felt in the mid-1940's. The emergence of direct placements in the 1930's as a method of financing also gave life insurance companies a special incentive to make industrial loans. The direct placement technique, affording wide opportunities to tailor agreements to fit lenders' terms, appealed to many investment managers in life insurance companies and as explained more fully below, they increasingly used this method of acquiring bonds in the postwar period.

Trends in life insurance companies' participation in the industrial and commercial sectors of the capital market are shown in Table VI-1 and Chart VI-2. While their portfolio of industrial and miscellaneous bonds was multiplied thirteen times between 1945 and 1959, four broad phases stand out in the overall trend. In the early postwar years, the insurance companies were a major source of funds for reconversion of industry to civilian purposes. While numerous corporations had accumulated liquid resources during the war which were sufficient to finance their own projects, many other firms had to rely on outside funds. This was especially true of new firms established to acquire government-owned war plants as they were sold to private groups. Life insurance companies extended a considerable share of loans raised by firms in industries such as aluminum, rubber, and steel. As a result, their industrial bond holdings rose by three-quarters in 1946. The decisive efforts of industry to eliminate the deficit in capacity also generated a vigorous demand for long-term loans in the next two years. To partly meet this demand and to reap the higher yields offered by corporate borrowers, life insurance companies liquidated $1.7 billion of United States government securities in 1947 and $3.3 billion in 1948. These sales accounted for approximately one-third and one-half, respectively, of the total funds supplied by life insurance companies to the capital market in these two years. In each year, industrial and miscellaneous bonds represented about one-third of the total amount of loans extended. The companies' holdings of these issues rose by one-half in 1947 and by one-quarter in 1948.

The recession of 1949 checked the rate of life insurance companies' investment in industrial and commercial obligations. During the Korean War, however, the companies returned to this sector of the capital market with renewed vitality. Unlike the policy followed in World War II, the United States government did not itself build the additional industrial capacity required to support mobilization but left this task to private industry. Consequently, life insurance companies and other lenders were called upon to finance a substantial part of the defense plants and defense-supporting facilities built by corporations during the Korean conflict. Thus, in 1951 and 1952, they purchased $4.1 billion of industrial and miscellaneous bonds, almost twice the amount acquired in the previous two years. These institutions also participated in the Voluntary Credit Restraint Program which sought to divert funds to the most essential uses. For example, in 1951 they made about $1.5 billion of long-term loans to concerns engaged in defense activities, an amount which accounted for about one-half of the companies' total defense financing in that year.[15]

The recession of 1953-54 again dampened life insurance companies' investment opportunities in the industrial and commercial field, and to compensate they turned to the mortgage market on a large scale. However, as the rate of capital formation revived in 1955 and increased further in the next two years, corporations floated new securities at a record rate. Life insurance companies again responded to the more favorable lending prospects and for the first time in history acquired over $4 billion of industrial and miscellaneous bonds in a single year. Their actual purchases were $4.0 billion in 1956 and $4.8 billion in 1957. In the latter year, industrial and miscellaneous bonds accounted for over two-fifths of the total funds supplied by life insurance companies to all parts of the capital market, the highest proportion since the peak year of Korean War financing. In 1958 their acquisitions eased off somewhat as the recession weakened corporate demand for long-term credit, and the moderate downtrend continued in 1959.

As evident from Chart VI-2, the portion of the market for industrial and miscellaneous bonds centering in life insurance companies has been declining sharply with only scant interruptions since 1950. Several factors cast some light on the possible causes of the shrinkage in their share of the market relative to other lenders. In the first place, a considerable proportion of industrial and miscellaneous bonds acquired by life insurance companies is distributed through direct placements, and only the largest companies use this method to any appreciable extent. The proportion of industrial and miscellaneous obligations obtained through direct placements has been climbing consistently. As recently as 1956 about 81 percent of such bonds held by insurance companies had been acquired through direct negotiation; the ratio rose to 83 percent in 1957, to 87 percent in 1958, and to 88 percent in 1959. On the other hand, while life insurance companies as a group are heavily committed to investing in industrial and miscellaneous bonds, many small companies do not make such loans at all or extend them only occasionally and to firms close to home. For example, of the 106 United States life insurance companies replying in the author's survey conducted in the spring of 1959, 16 reported that they do not make such loans. All of these were small institutions having assets of $100 million or less at the end of 1957. Several of the investment officers of these small companies observed that the more complex task of appraising industrial bonds (compared with public utilities) makes them unwilling to venture into this segment of the capital market.

This attitude and the investment policies which grow from it are also clearly traceable in the distribution of assets when companies are grouped by size. At the end of 1957, industrial and miscellaneous bonds accounted for 22 percent of the combined assets of the 150 largest companies in the United States. However, among the top 15 companies (with assets ranging from $1.3 billion to $15.5 billion), such obligations were 26 percent of assets. Below the first tier, the proportion dropped abruptly to 12 percent of assets among the second group of 15 companies and declined steadily to only 4 percent of assets among the sixth group. On the other hand, the incidence of ownership of industrial and miscellaneous bonds increased to 7 percent of assets among the remaining four groups of smaller companies. This appears to be another reflection of the tendency of small companies to rely on the advice of outside investment advisory services. Thus, the above analysis suggests that as the total supply of industrial and miscellaneous bonds advances, life insurance companies' share of the market would be expected to decline because only the larger companies are the most active purchasers. Because these institutions also attempt to maintain diversification in their investment portfolios, their demand for industrial and commercial bonds would probably not keep pace with the growth in the supply reaching the market.

As explained above, the growing competition of corporate pension funds is also a major factor which helps to explain the relative reduction in life insurance companies' role in the acquisition of industrial and miscellaneous bonds. Corporate pension funds acquire a sizable proportion of direct placements as well as of issues sold through public distribution. In both cases, they tend to concentrate on long-term loans to industrial and commercial concerns for the same reasons which make the latters' debt attractive to life insurance companies.

As one would expect, industrial and miscellaneous bonds held by life insurance companies are concentrated in those industries experiencing the most rapid rates of growth in the postwar period. While the bulk of these are manufacturing fields, a few nonmanufacturing industries also fall in the same category. Statistics in Table VI-3 clearly show these tendencies. In 1957, petroleum, refining, and related industries accounted for 12 percent of the total, the largest single share of any group. Obligations of chemicals, rubber, and plastic products firms represented 10

TABLE VI-3

INDUSTRIAL AND MISCELLANEOUS BOND HOLDINGS OF U. S. LIFE INSURANCE COMPANIES, BY TYPE OF INDUSTRY, 1957
(In Millions of Dollars)

	Total		United States Industries		Canadian Industries	
Type of Industry	Amount	Percent	Amount	Percent	Amount	Percent
Manufacturing Industries						
Aircraft	33	0.1	33	0.1	—	—
Automobile	701	3.2	699	3.4	2	0.2
Chemicals, rubber and plastic products	2,180	10.0	2,155	10.4	25	2.6
Food, tobacco and kindred products	1,447	6.7	1,430	6.9	17	1.8
Iron and steel	1,326	6.1	1,281	6.2	45	4.7
Machinery, equipment and supplies	2,118	9.8	2,065	9.9	53	5.5
Nonferrous metals	938	4.3	794	3.8	144	14.9
Paper, printing, publishing and allied products	979	4.5	910	4.4	69	7.2
Petroleum, refining and related industries	2,657	12.3	2,448	11.8	209	21.7
Textiles, apparel and leather	678	3.1	677	3.3	1	0.1
Other manufacturing	1,564	7.2	1,542	7.4	22	2.3
Total	14,621	67.3	14,034	67.6	587	60.9
Nonmanufacturing Industries						
Finance and credit	3,433	15.8	3,259	15.7	174	18.0
Retail trade	1,149	5.3	1,119	5.4	30	3.1
Services	406	1.9	406	12.0	—	—
Transportation and communications	1,365	6.3	1,220	5.9	145	15.0
Wholesale trade	36	0.1	33	0.1	3	0.3
Other nonmanufacturing	707	3.3	682	3.3	25	2.6
Total	7,096	32.7	6,719	32.4	377	39.0
Total Industrial and Miscellaneous Bonds	21,717	100.0	20,753	100.0	964[1]	100.0

1. Includes $8 million of bonds issued by industries in other countries.

SOURCE: **1960 Life Insurance Fact Book,** p. 78.

percent. Both of these industry groups have been vastly transformed by technological innovations and the introduction of an extensive array of new products. Life insurance companies have thus contributed in a significant way to their development and have benefited from their highly favorable financial experience. Loans to machinery firms also represented about 10 percent of total industrial and miscellaneous bonds. Machinery-producing firms have also made great technical strides in the last decade—especially those engaged in electronics and other new branches. The long-established capital goods industries (iron and steel and nonferrous metals) and consumer goods industries (food, tobacco, textiles, apparel, and leather) which have achieved only modest rates of growth, have attracted a much smaller ration of industrial finance supplied by life insurance companies.

A similar theme is observable in the distribution of life insurance companies' loans to nonmanufacturing enterprises. Bonds of finance and credit institutions represented 16 percent of the total in 1957 and almost one-half of the loans extended to commercial firms. The chief borrowers in the finance group have been sales finance companies active in the extension of consumer credit. As the demand for installment credit has grown in tandem with the demand for consumer durable goods, sales finance companies have turned to life insurance companies to raise long-term capital, and they occasionally obtain short-term funds as well. Firms engaged in transportation and communication had received over 6 percent of the commercial loans outstanding with life insurance companies in 1957. Included in this group were airlines, trucking concerns, petroleum pipelines, radio and television systems and related enterprises which have registered such impressive gains since World War II. Table VI-3 also shows that the distribution of bonds of Canadian enterprises held by United States life insurance companies is about the same as that for American industries.

Section IV
Development and Use of Private Placements

A. Origin and Development of Private Placements

As mentioned above, the hegemony which life insurance companies hold in the corporate bond market dates from the depression of the 1930's and is partly attributable to their direct lending to corporations. As the demand for external funds declined and as numerous corporations took advantage of the prevailing low interest rates to reduce their indebtedness, life insurance companies had a difficult time finding outlets for their increasing volume of savings. They were forced to turn increasingly to investment bankers for aid in placing their funds. The latter, in turn, were anxious to find markets for the new security issues which did appear. Thus, investment bankers began to rely heavily on life insurance companies to move their inventories. As the strategic position of life insurance companies became more evident, it was a short step to the drastic reduction of the role of investment bankers; large corporate borrowers soon found themselves negotiating directly with these savings institutions over the terms of new issues.[16] Meanwhile, as long-term interest rates fell appreciably, individual investors, personal trust funds, and financial corporations sought the more advantageous investment opportunities provided by tax-exempt obligations. This shift in investors' preferences left the corporate bond market to life insurance companies.

Private negotiations between life insurance companies and corporate borrowers is apparently a practice of long standing. However, it was stimulated by the passage of the Securities Act of 1933. Among other provisions of the Act was one requiring corporations planning to issue securities to file registration statements with the SEC, giving considerable data on business operations as well as a detailed description of the proposed new issue. The Act also fixed legal liabilities of officers, directors, and others for the accuracy of such statements. Perhaps the most important provision of the new law in terms of the present discussion was that for the exemption from registration of new issues offered to a limited number of investors. Thus, through private placement, it was possible to avoid the delays and expense involved in the registration process required for publicly-sold obligations.[17]

Beginning in 1934, the volume of direct placements climbed steadily; this climb was interrupted by the second World War. Statistics in Table VI-4 show the trend of direct placements since 1946. The strong advance of direct placements as a proportion of total corporate bonds sold extended through 1951, and the actual amount of direct placements reached a peak of about $4.0 billion in 1952. A marked cyclical pattern is also observable in the flotation of direct placements. In both the 1953-54 and 1957-58 recessions, securities sold through private channels fell more sharply than total flotations. This is easily understandable when one recalls that the direct placement technique is employed primarily in marketing industrial bonds which decline as corporate outlays on plant and equipment recede. On the other hand, the total volume of flotations is considerably influenced by sales of public utility issues which tend to expand (or fall only slightly) during recessions as utilities refund obliga-

TABLE VI-4

PUBLIC SALE AND PRIVATE PLACEMENT OF CORPORATE BONDS, 1946-59

(In Millions of Dollars)

Year	Total Issues	Public Offerings	Direct Placements	Direct Placements as Percent of Total Issues
1946	4,882	3,019	1,863	38.2
1947	5,036	2,889	2,147	42.6
1948	5,973	2,965	3,008	50.4
1949	4,890	2,437	2,453	50.2
1950	4,920	2,360	2,560	52.0
1951	5,691	2,364	3,326	58.4
1952	7,601	3,645	3,957	52.1
1953	7,083	3,856	3,228	45.6
1954	7,488	4,003	3,484	46.5
1955	7,420	4,119	3,301	44.5
1956	8,002	4,225	3,777	47.2
1957	9,957	6,118	3,839	38.6
1958	9,653	6,332	3,320	34.5
1959	7,253	3,556	3,697	51.0

SOURCE: Securities and Exchange Commission, **16th Annual Report** (1950), p. 182; **23rd Annual Report** (1957), p. 212; **Federal Reserve Bulletin,** May, 1960, p. 532.

tions to reduce interest costs or sell issues previously postponed because of high rates.

Private placements consist primarily of bonds, and life insurance companies customarily absorb approximately 90 percent of the total. Because federal regulatory agencies and those of most states require that most public utility and railroad security offerings be made through competitive bidding, the largest part of the privately placed issues consists of securities of industrial and financial corporations, including manufacturing, mining, trade, sales, and personal finance companies.[18] It is through the vehicle of private placements, therefore, that industrial and miscellaneous bonds have become a significant portion of life insurance companies' investments. As already mentioned, at the end of 1959 about 88 percent of the companies' total holdings of these issues had been acquired through direct placements.[19]

Life insurance companies enjoy a considerable advantage over other investors in the competition for private placements; this edge rests mainly on the ability of these institutions to take large blocks of corporate securities and thus avoid the problems and expense of distribution. Despite the moderately higher cost of private placements compared with public issues,[20] corporate borrowers seem to prefer this method of obtaining funds. Apparently the flexibility of private loan agreements and the ease with which additional funds may be secured once relationships between borrowers and lenders have been established, the ability to secure firm commitments in advance, to defer drawing down funds until they are needed, and to obtain funds regardless of prevailing conditions in the market, are factors held in high regard by corporate financial management. The fact that life insurance companies are generally willing to make commitments to supply a definite amount of funds to the borrower at a specified time convenient to the latter is a leading advantage of the private placement technique. As compensation for assuming this obligation, life insurance companies typically receive a commitment fee of ½ of 1 to 1 percent until the funds are drawn, at which time the regular interest rate (as determined during the negotiations) applies.[21] Since most commitments to lend to corporate borrowers are connected with the expansion of industrial facilities, the actual flow of such funds from the life insurance companies is related to the difference in the timing of negotiations for credit (a one-time procedure or one of relatively short duration) and the use of funds (which may extend over a period of six to eighteen months as plant construction and equipping progress).

Life insurance companies, too, see considerable advantage in negotiating directly for securities. The chance to allocate funds in advance of their actual receipt makes the investment problem much easier. In making direct loans, these institutions establish contacts which frequently lead to additional business with the borrowing corporations and many times to opportunities to lend to other firms known to existing customers. Through direct placements life insurance companies are able to write covenants which impose protective conditions, many of which would not be suitable or possible in the case of a publicly offered bond issue. These include provisions for sinking fund and pay-out clauses, and various restrictions on borrowers' financial operations (such as the maintenance of working capital at a specified level, or limitations on the pledge or sale of assets). And more important, these terms can be tailored to the individual transaction, including both the borrower's and lender's requirements, to provide better security for the loan.[22] As indicated above, life insurance companies usually earn a higher rate of interest on private placements than they could obtain by purchasing securities in the open market. While some part of the gain represents the lender's share of the savings effected by avoiding SEC regulations, it must also include the coverage of additional risk which the investor assumes by taking the entire issue. For example, the underwriting firm which managed the distribution of $125 million of Aluminum Corporation of America bonds in early 1952 reported that the 12-year issue could have been placed privately at an interest cost of 3½ percent compared with the actual cost of 3⅛ percent established in the public sale. He attributed part of the differential rate for private placement to the potential lender's desire for a higher return if he were to take the whole amount.[23]

From the above discussion it is evident that the private placement method of corporate financing has both advantages and disadvantages. Despite the protective features which life insurance companies write into loan contracts, the lack of ready marketability of the issue may result in serious losses if the obligation must be sold. In acquiring direct placements, however, the portfolio manager of a life insurance company is probably influenced to some extent by the fact that many bond issues (even of the most prominent corporations) have a limited marketability when a bondholder tries to dispose of a sizable block of bonds over a short period of time. As for the borrowing corporation, it usually must pay a higher interest rate on a directly placed issue than on one offered in the public market. It also loses the privilege of repurchasing its securities at a discount for sinking fund or other purpose should interest rates subsequently rise (sinking funds in direct placements usually provide for payments at par), a disadvantage which may become very real in a flexible bond market. The managements of borrowing corporations may also find some objection to the limitations placed on financial operations by the terms of direct placement agreements. On the whole, however, the advantages of the direct placement technique to the private parties involved obviously outweigh considerably the disadvantages because the technique has not only held its own with public sales but has grown enormously in the postwar period.

B. Use of Private Placements

The investment policies of life insurance companies regarding private placements were illuminated in the survey conducted by the author in the spring of 1959. Portfolio managers were asked to indicate whether the company regularly acquires corporate bonds by direct placement and the percentage of each type of bonds (railroad, public utility, industrial and miscellaneous) obtained by this method in 1958. The results are summarized in Tables VI-5, VI-6 and VI-7. The question about direct placements was answered by 106 companies; 73 reported that they do make direct placements and 33 that they do not use this method to ac-

TABLE VI-5

DISTRIBUTION OF LIFE INSURANCE COMPANIES BY SIZE GROUP AND NUMBER ACQUIRING CORPORATE BONDS THROUGH DIRECT PLACEMENT

Size Group of Companies (Assets as of December 31, 1957 In Millions of Dollars)	Total Number of Companies	Companies Acquiring Bonds Through Direct Placement	Companies Not Making Direct Placements
I (376-14,732)	26	26	0
II (121-357)	26	18	8
III (53-111)	26	18	8
IV (25-52)	28	11	17
All Companies	106	73	33

SOURCE: BBER-MSU Survey, Spring, 1959.

TABLE VI-6

DISTRIBUTION OF LIFE INSURANCE COMPANIES BY TYPE OF CORPORATE BONDS ACQUIRED THROUGH DIRECT PLACEMENT

Type of Bonds	Number of Companies
Railroad only	0
Public utility only	6
Industrial and misc. only	11
Railroad and public utility	0
Railroad and industrial and misc.	1
Public utility and industrial and misc.	39
Railroad, public utility, and industrial and misc.	16
All Companies	73

SOURCE: BBER-MSU Survey, Spring, 1959.

quire corporate bonds. To highlight the variations among companies, the respondents were arranged into four roughly equal groups according to asset size as shown in Table VI-5. These data show that direct placements appeal primarily to the largest companies. All institutions in the first group purchase corporate bonds through direct placements, while only two-thirds of the companies in the second and third groups employ this method. Among the smallest companies in group four, the proportion making direct placements drops to only two-fifths. Further understanding of direct placements in the investment practices of life insurance companies can be gained from Table VI-6, which shows the distribution by the type of bonds acquired by life insurance companies making direct placements. A few companies make direct placements in only one area, over one-half restrict themselves to purchasing public utility and indus-

TABLE VI-7

DISTRIBUTION OF LIFE INSURANCE COMPANIES BY SIZE GROUP AND PERCENTAGE OF EACH TYPE OF CORPORATE BONDS ACQUIRED THROUGH DIRECT PLACEMENT IN 1958

Percent of Bonds Acquired Through Direct Placement	Size Group(1) I	Size Group II	Size Group III	Size Group IV	Total
Railroad					
None acquired(2)	5	4	1	—	10
Zero(3)	13	19	25	26	83
1-25	7	—	1	—	8
26-50	1	—	—	—	1
51-75	—	—	—	—	0
76-100	2	5	1	1	9
Total	28	28	28	27	111
Public Utility					
None acquired	—	—	—	—	0
Zero	3	14	11	20	48
1-25	4	2	10	4	20
26-50	6	6	5	1	18
51-75	7	4	2	—	13
76-100	8	2	—	2	12
Total	28	28	28	27	111
Industrial and Misc.					
None acquired	—	—	—	—	0
Zero	—	11	13	17	41
1-25	3	5	6	6	20
26-50	2	4	4	1	11
51-75	7	3	1	2	13
76-100	16	5	4	1	26
Total	28	28	28	27	111

1. Size groups are the same as in Table VI-5.

2. "None acquired" means that companies in this category did not purchase bonds of the particular type in 1958.

3. A "zero" percent means that companies in this category in 1958 acquired through direct placement zero percent of the bonds of the particular type (or 100 percent through the public market).

SOURCE: BBER-MSU Survey, Spring, 1959.

trial and miscellaneous bonds through private negotiation. Just over two-fifths acquire all three types of obligations on a private basis. The predominant role of industrial and miscellaneous bonds in direct placements is also clear, however, for 11 companies reported that they purchase only these issues and 56 companies that they combine them with other types of bonds. In contrast, only six companies reported acquiring only public utility issues, although 39 reported public utilities in combination with industrial and miscellaneous bonds.

The concentration of direct placements among the largest companies with special emphasis on the debt of industrial and commercial firms is documented even more strongly in Table VI-7, which shows the distribution of life insurance companies by size group and the percentage of each type of corporate bonds acquired through direct placements in 1958. An overwhelming proportion of the largest companies acquire the bulk of their investments in industrial and miscellaneous bonds through direct placement; 15 of the 26 institutions in the first group obtained three-quarters or more of their portfolio by this technique. Of the same group, less than one-third of the companies acquired a similar proportion of their public utility holdings by direct placement. As one proceeds through the medium sized and smaller companies, the degree of reliance on direct placements diminishes rapidly. Not only does a smaller number of companies use the direct placement method but they also generally obtain a decreasing proportion of corporate bonds of all types by private negotiation with borrowers or with investment bankers representing borrowers.

The strategic role of the largest life insurance companies in the direct placement of corporate securities is further illustrated in comparative studies of direct placements in 1946-49 and 1955. As part of a more comprehensive study, Robert M. Soldofsky examined all direct placements made in 1955 and reported in *Investment Dealers' Digest.* Part of his findings were published in the spring of 1960[24] and compared with E. Raymond Corey's data on the use of direct placements by the 18 largest United States life insurance companies in 1946-49.[25] The relevant statistics from these two studies are summarized in Tables VI-8 and VI-9.

The most striking feature of Table VI-8 is the large proportion of direct placement loans which went to large firms, a fact implied by the relatively large average size of loans. Soldofsky found that in 1955, about $3.8 billion of direct placements were made, perhaps 90 percent of which were made by life insurance companies. However, more than 97 percent of the total amount and about three-quarters of the total number were

TABLE VI-8

COMPARISON OF PRINCIPAL AMOUNT
AND NUMBER OF DIRECT PLACEMENTS FOR 1946-49 AND 1955
(In Thousands of Dollars)

Principal Amount of Loan	Percentage of Total Amount		Percentage of Total Number of Loans	
	Corey 1946-49	Soldofsky 1955	Corey 1946	Soldofsky 1955
Under $50	0.0	0.004	0.6	0.6
50-100	0.0	0.01	1.6	1.2
100-200	0.1	0.2	4.2	6.8
200-500	1.0	1.0	14.4	17.1
500-1,000	2.7	2.1	18.7	16.2
1,000-2,000	6.5	5.0	22.6	19.3
2,000-5,000	12.4	10.9	19.1	17.8
5,000-10,000	12.6	11.9	8.8	9.0
10,000-25,000	14.3	16.6	4.9	6.4
25,000-50,000	23.9	15.2	3.7	2.6
50,000-100,000	14.6	21.1	1.0	1.7
Over 100,000	11.9	16.0	0.4	0.7
	100.0	100.0	100.0	100.0
Total Direct Placements	$8,956,000	$3,801,000	2,002	760

SOURCE: Robert M. Soldofsky, "The Size and Maturity of Direct-Placement Loans," **The Journal of Finance**, March, 1960, p. 34. Soldofsky reproduced 1946-49 data from E. Raymond Corey, **Direct Placement of Corporate Securities** (Boston: Harvard University Press, 1951), pp. 10-11.

supplied in loans of $500 thousand or more.[26] Compared with the early postwar period, lenders were concentrating much more heavily on larger loans by the mid-1950's. For example, Corey estimated that loans of $50 million and above represented about 27 percent of the total in 1946-49; by 1955 loans above this figure accounted for 37 percent of the amount of direct placements. The same shift was also evident in terms of the number of loans. Although one cannot determine on the basis of data available whether the shift simply reflected an increase in the size of borrowers because of normal growth, the fact remains that only the very largest industrial and commercial corporations can absorb a $50 million loan. This is even more true regarding the five direct placements made in 1955 each of which was for $100 million.

In line with the large size of average loans, the longer maturities involved in direct placements also make them attractive to life insurance companies. Both Corey and Soldofsky found that less than one-sixth of the amount and about one-third of the number of loans were for 12 years

TABLE VI-9

COMPARISON OF NUMBER OF YEARS TO FINAL MATURITY
OF DIRECT PLACEMENTS FOR 1946-49 AND 1955

Number of Years to Final Maturity	Percentage of Total Amount		Percentage of Total Number of Loans	
	Corey 1946-49	Soldofsky 1955	Corey 1946-49	Soldofsky 1955
1-2	0.1	0.7	0.2	1.5
3-7	3.3	1.8	6.6	4.1
8-12	11.4	12.4	23.9	29.5
13-17	26.9	19.5	30.2	25.0
18-22	36.3	24.6	17.6	19.2
23-27	11.9	26.0	10.5	12.7
28-32	8.2	4.0	10.2	6.8
33-37	1.4	1.3	0.5	0.1
38-40	0.5	3.0	0.3	0.5
41-49	—	2.7	—	0.3
50-99	—	—	—	—
100	—	4.0	—	0.3
	100.0	100.0	100.0	100.0
Total Direct Placements	$8,797,000,000	$3,785,000,000	1,914	749

SOURCE: Robert M. Soldofsky, "The Size and Maturity of Direct-Placement Loans," **The Journal of Finance,** March, 1960, p. 36. Soldofsky reproduced 1946-49 data from E. Raymond Corey, **Direct Placement of Corporate Securities** (Boston: Harvard University Press, 1951), pp. 10-11.

or less. (See Table VI-9). On the other hand, there has been a substantial shift toward the longest maturities. While Corey's data show no loans with maturities in excess of 40 years, Soldofsky discovered that 7 percent of the dollar amount and about 1 percent of the number of direct placements carried repayment periods of more than 40 years. The four very long-term direct placements reported for 1955 also illustrate the extent to which the larger life insurance companies are willing to commit themselves in terms of both size of loans and maturities.[27] The largest loan to International Business Machines ($110 million, 3¾ percent convertible notes due in 2055) was made by the Prudential Insurance Company. Metropolitan Life advanced $75 million for American Airlines' 4 percent notes due in 1996 and $25 million for Monsanto Chemical represented by 3¾ percent income debentures due in 2002. Mutual of New York, Prudential, and Metropolitan teamed up to acquire $50 million of Goodyear Tire and Rubber's 3¾ percent notes due in 2055.

Section V
Competition and the Transformation of the Corporate Bond Market

A. Competitive Position of Life Insurance Companies in the Corporate Bond Market

The superior competitive position commanded by the largest life insurance companies in the private placement sector of the corporate bond market has resulted in a substantial decline in the availability of corporate debt to smaller life insurance companies and other investors. Competition among investors for publicly offered high grade corporate bonds has become especially intense, and in this segment of the market, the larger life insurance companies are also important competitors. The bulk of public offerings originate with public utility concerns, and to a lesser extent, with railroads. The attempt of insurance companies to diversify their portfolios by acquiring bonds of gas, water, electric, and communication enterprises has meant that other investors have found it difficult to satisfy their investment needs. One study shows that a group of major insurance companies acquired 36 percent of all publicly offered corporate bonds in 1948 and that purchases of the 22 largest companies amounted to 38 percent of total new corporate debt publicly offered in that year.[28]

Still other evidence for more recent years supports the view that investors other than the larger life insurance companies may be unable to achieve the degree of portfolio diversification required for balance. A study of the corporate bond portfolios of the 150 largest life insurance companies in the United States at the end of 1957 is summarized in Table VI-10. The 15 largest companies held 83 percent of the corporate bonds owned by the 150 companies although they held only three-quarters of the total assets. In contrast, the second group of 15 companies held 11 percent of the total assets and 9 percent of the corporate bonds. This same pattern is traceable throughout as one descends the array of companies ranked by size of assets. Moreover, the heavy concentration of corporate bonds in the portfolios of the largest companies is even more evident in the case of industrial and miscellaneous bonds; the largest 15 companies held 89 percent of these obligations, while the next group held only 6 percent, and the smallest group held only 0.2 percent—or one-half its share of total assets. Furthermore, while not shown in Table VI-10, the largest 15 companies were able to maintain their position in the market for industrial and miscellaneous bonds during the postwar period, although their share of total assets and of the aggregate amount of corporate bonds declined moderately between 1945 and 1957. Immediately

TABLE VI-10

DISTRIBUTION OF TOTAL ASSETS AND CORPORATE BONDS, BY SIZE GROUP OF 150 LARGEST LIFE INSURANCE COMPANIES IN THE UNITED STATES, BY TYPE OF CORPORATE BONDS, 1957

(In Millions of Dollars)

Asset Range of 15 Companies in Each Group	Assets of Group		Corporate Bonds Held: Total		Railroad		Public Utility		Industrial and Misc.	
	Amount	Percent of Total	Amount	Percent of Total	Amount	Percent of Total	Amount	Percent of Total	Amount	Percent of Total
I (1,329-15,536)	72,891	74.7	32,991	82.7	3,133	82.7	10,975	73.9	18,891	88.8
II (514-1,273)	10,898	11.2	3,410	8.5	305	8.1	1,818	12.3	1,291	6.1
III (236-497)	5,213	5.3	1,344	3.4	92	2.4	744	5.0	508	2.3
IV (143-234)	2,704	2.8	672	1.7	74	2.0	408	2.7	190	0.9
V (100-141)	1,774	1.8	494	1.2	76	2.0	289	1.9	129	0.6
VI (82-99)	1,348	1.4	262	0.7	21	0.6	181	1.2	60	0.3
VII (59-81)	1,023	1.0	272	0.7	38	1.0	161	1.1	73	0.3
VIII (42-58)	736	0.8	189	0.5	17	0.4	116	0.8	56	0.3
IX (34-41)	563	0.6	136	0.3	19	0.5	77	0.5	40	0.2
X (25-33)	437	0.4	129	0.3	11	0.3	85	0.6	33	0.2
Total	97,587	100.0	39,911	100.0	3,786	100.0	14,854	100.0	21,271	100.0

SOURCE: Compiled by author from balance sheets of individual companies presented in **Best's Life Insurance Reports,** 1958. The list of companies by size was published in **Best's Insurance News, Life Edition,** July, 1958.

after the second World War, the 15 largest companies held about 80 percent of the total assets owned by the 150 companies studied, but the proportion had fallen to 75 percent by 1957. Yet, their share of industrial and miscellaneous bonds remained unchanged at 89 percent while their share of railroad and public utility issues decreased in line with their proportion of total assets.

Further understanding of the competitive position of life insurance companies in the market for public issues can be provided by an analysis of data on the industrial composition and method of sale of new corporate debt issued during the six years, 1950-55.[29] Public issues were about one-half of total offerings, but the ratio of public issues to the total varied widely. Thus, those offered in the open market represented less than one-fifth of total offerings for manufacturing, real estate, financial, commercial and miscellaneous, and transportation (other than railroad) enterprises. On the other hand, about two-thirds of the new bond issues of electric, gas, and water companies, and approximately 90 percent of those of communications corporations were floated in the public market. The latter situation, of course, reflects the fact that a considerable part of all public utility and railroad obligations must be offered through competitive bidding in the open market. But in the public sector also the largest life insurance companies have been aggressive bidders and have acquired a significant share of public utility and other issues coming into the public market. For example, in 1948 over two-fifths of publicly floated utility obligations were purchased by a group of major insurance institutions;[30] this same group also absorbed one-fifth of railroad and almost one-third of industrial bonds reaching the public market. Corresponding proportions for the 1948 public acquisitions of the 22 largest life insurance companies came to two-fifths, one-fifth, and over three-fifths, respectively, of new publicly offered utility, railroad, and industrial and miscellaneous debt flotations.

From this analysis the following conclusions appear warranted: the larger life insurance companies have come to acquire a very large part of the direct placements of corporate bond issues, and a sizable proportion of those offered in the public market as well. The volume of new corporate debt securities taken by the smaller life insurance companies and other institutional investors has been relatively small and has to some extent lacked as balanced a representation of borrowing industries.

B. Changing Structure of the Corporate Bond Market

Aside from the relative displacement of other investors in the market for corporate debt, the investment activities of life insurance companies have stimulated a major transformation of the structure and operation of the entire mechanism of corporate bond trading. Under the impact of these institutions, the breadth of the market has been progressively narrowed. Some share of the decline in bond trading must be attributed to the virtual disappearance of high income individuals (who apparently sought refuge from high taxation through the purchase of tax-exempt state and local government securities) and trust funds from the market; the main explanation, however, is probably the growing volume of private placements which initially by-pass the market completely and are seldom, if ever, traded. The declining trend is shown in the volume of corporate bonds traded on the New York Stock Exchange.[31] From a pre-war peak of around $3.7 billion in 1934, such transactions dropped to a trough of $773 million in 1952 and totaled approximately $980 million in 1955; by 1959, the figure stood at slightly more than $1 billion. These data seem to be indicative of the shrinkage of the bond market even though considerably more corporate bonds are traded in over-the-counter markets than on all registered exchanges.

The declining dollar volume of trading has been accompanied by a decrease in the number of transactions, and amounts bid for or offered have usually been small. Since the 1920's the actual number of buyers and sellers participating in the market has dropped appreciably, and sizable blocks of bonds have often had to be exchanged at prices substantially below quoted prices in order to effect transfers of ownership.[32] This thinness of the market has been only partially countered by the rise of pension funds and the renewed interest in the bond market recently shown by commercial and mutual savings banks. The techniques traditionally employed to handle corporate long-term bond financing have borne the brunt of the pressures generated by the rise of life insurance companies to their position of dominance in the capital market.[33] This appears to be the case despite the profound shock suffered by the investment banking industry as a result of the 1929 stock market crash and the subsequent sharp break in all phases of the securities business. Support for this view is found in the fact that while revival of security prices and the volume of trading began in 1932-33, the recovery in corporate long-term financing through investment bankers and security dealers (principally for refunding purposes) was retarded by the growth of direct placement of new issues between industrial corporations and life insurance companies.[34] As the scope of the public market for corporate bonds shrank, many investment bankers and security dealers were forced to expand their other operations because of declining income from underwriting corporate bonds. Many of these emphasized more heavily their inventories of United States government securities, tax-exempt issues, common stocks, and mutual fund shares as well as branching out as investment counselors.[35]

Furthermore, the appearance of life insurance companies as direct purchasers of corporate obligations circumvented the underwriting process and eliminated the need for an organization to handle wide distribution of issues. Thus, there followed a considerable reduction in the number of investment underwriting firms and the consolidation of others. The role of the investment banker has not completely disappeared, however. Frequently, he is employed by life insurance companies to find suitable borrowers, and he also acts as an intermediary in transactions. Moreover, investment bankers serve as consultants to borrowing firms concerning the latter's general financial problems as well as the terms and conditions of proposed loans. In this last capacity, the bankers resume some part of their previous roles, for in providing information on prevailing conditions in the public and private markets they aid in the maintenance of balance between the two segments.

It is reported that investment bankers in many instances have enabled borrowing corporations to obtain more favorable terms from direct lenders than the borrowers otherwise would have been able to secure.[36] In performing their functions as corporate agents in private placement negotiations, investment bankers have often been instrumental in closing the gap between a borrower's needs and the investment requirements of life insurance companies (as determined by legal and policy considerations). In other words, much of the tailoring of individual direct placement transactions to borrower's and lender's needs is facilitated if not effected by investment bankers. Fees earned by bankers for these services are frequently considerably below those earned on publicly offered issues which underwriters usually purchase outright from issuers. However, all the fees earned on a direct placement typically accrue to one firm instead of being shared with the many firms participating in the larger aggregate commission of a public issue. Furthermore, operating expenses and overhead are considerably lower.

Another consequence of the extensive participation of life insurance companies in the market for directly placed corporate obligations has been to the advantage of firms offering issues through public distribution. This advantage is the considerable narrowing of the investment banking "spread"—the difference between the price at which bankers acquire an issue and the offering price to the public. This result appears to be derived partly from the intensive competition for the limited supply of public issues and partly from the pressure which life insurance companies exert directly on the price spread. The decline in the banker's margin, of course, has been an additional factor in the contraction of the security distribution machinery. In fact, investment bankers retain the full range of their former function only in such areas as the marketing of state and local bonds where individual investors remain important purchasers of securities.[37]

SECTION VI
SUMMARY AND CONCLUSION

Throughout this chapter, it has been emphasized that long-term corporate debt is an extremely attractive outlet for life insurance funds. These obligations possess characteristics which recommend them to most portfolio managers, while the long-term nature of life insurance companies' liabilities and the steady rise in assets make these institutions prime sources of capital to finance the fixed investment of private business. The interaction between demand and supply forces in the long-term capital market has resulted in life insurance companies holding an increasing proportion of total corporate bonds outstanding, although the rise of corporate pension funds in recent years has challenged their hegemony in an appreciable way. This expansion in the role of life insurance companies in the corporate bond sector of the capital market is the outcome of several factors. Primarily, of course, it is a reflection of the pace of growth of the life insurance industry itself and of the special qualifications of corporate long-term debt for life insurance company investment. In addition, however, it is the result of fundamental changes in the economic environment induced by the monetary and fiscal policies followed by the federal government at different times. Thus, declining interest rates and the rising tax burden, both the result of federal policy, seem to have induced many individuals and certain types of financial institutions to leave the corporate bond market during the 1930's.

It has been shown that, although internal funds have come to satisfy a major proportion of corporate capital requirements, an appreciable share of total funds is still obtained from the capital market. The bulk of these external funds is raised through debt issues, and life insurance companies have been the leading purchasers of these obligations. During the postwar period, life insurance companies were able to expand their holdings of corporate bonds by the sale of United States government securities as well as by the use of new savings. The substitution of private for government debt was stimulated partly by the increasing attractiveness of higher yielding corporate bonds in relation to the latter and partly by the desire of portfolio managers to correct the imbalance of their holdings resulting from the dearth of corporate bond financing during the 1930's and the World War II period. In switching from Governments into corporate issues, the institutions exhibited a clearly defined pattern which was virtually a retracing of the corporate demand for funds.

With respect to the growth of direct placement of corporate securities with life insurance companies, it is evident that the practice offers considerable advantages to both parties. Since life insurance companies negotiate loans directly with corporate management, these can be tailored to meet the needs of the borrower and lender. Conditions under which loans are granted are quite flexible in the sense that mutually desirable changes in the agreement can be executed more readily than in the case of a security offered publicly. The borrower gets an almost immediate commitment, thus avoiding the risk that the market will change before a public offering can be made. Because of more economical handling of loans through direct placements, the insurance companies are frequently able to obtain higher returns and the borrowers in some cases receive lower interest costs on such loans through sharing the savings resulting from the elimination of the cost of entering the public market.

The existence of these advantages does not reveal the full story of the impact of private placements on the capital market, however. Perhaps the most serious shortcoming of the direct placement technique is that it discriminates against small enterprises and small lenders. Small life insurance companies are not equipped to make direct loans and do not have the opportunity to participate in the larger loans. Thus, these institutions are cut off from a large portion of the modern capital market. This situation cannot be alleviated by turning to the public sector of the capital market because here also the larger life insurance companies have a much stronger competitive position. A similar obstacle must be faced by small enterprises seeking funds. For the most part, they do not have access to the private placement market because their requirements are generally not large enough to induce life insurance company officials to expend the resources necessary for a credit analysis and appraisal. When small companies do obtain funds directly from life insurance companies, the cost to them is necessarily high in relation to the amount borrowed since the cost of administering loans does not vary appreciably with the size of the loan.

Nevertheless, despite these disadvantages to smaller enterprises, the direct placement technique appears to make it possible for life insurance companies as a group to participate more fully in the financing of industrial and commercial facilities and, as a consequence, in the creation of greater employment opportunities. The relative losses initially suffered by the investment bankers have probably been fully compensated because many of the firms involved have been able to shift to other activities. On the whole, then, the investment activities of life insurance companies in the corporate bond market appear to have been beneficial to the country at large.

Footnotes

1. Houghton Bell and Harold G. Fraine, "Legal Framework, Trends and Developments in Investment Practices of Life Insurance Companies," *Law and Contemporary Problems*, Winter, 1952, pp. 57-58.

2. Life insurance companies also lend money to corporations through taking up mortgages; however, these are lumped together with mortgages against properties of noncorporate businesses and are discussed in Chapter IX.

3. *Federal Reserve Bulletin*, December, 1951.

4. Frederick R. Macaulay, *Some Theoretical Problems Suggested by the Movements of Interest Rates, Bond Yields and Stock Prices in the United States Since 1865* (New York: National Bureau of Economic Research, 1938), pp. A127-29.

5. Arnold R. LaForce, "Corporate Debt," *Investment of Life Insurance Funds*, p. 140.

6. Homer Jones, "The Optimum Rate of Investment, Savings Institutions and the Banks," *American Economic Review*, May, 1948, pp. 333-36.

7. George T. Conklin, Jr., "A Century of Portfolio Management," *Investment of Life Insurance Funds*, p. 276.

8. *Ibid.*

9. Henry C. Murphy, *National Debt in War and Transition* (New York: McGraw-Hill, 1950), Ch. 5.

10. Securities and Exchange Commission, "Corporate Pension Funds, 1959," Statistical Series, Release Number 1680, May 31, 1960.

11. Sherwin C. Badger, "The Restoration of Railroad Credit," address before the Annual Meeting of the Treasury Division of the Association of American Railroads, September 11, 1952.

12. George T. Conklin, Jr., "A Century of Life Insurance Portfolio Management," *Investment of Life Insurance Funds*, pp. 279-81.

13. *1947 Life Insurance Fact Book*, p. 59.

14. *1960 Life Insurance Fact Book*, p. 75.

15. *1952 Life Insurance Fact Book*, p. 77.

16. George Conklin, "Direct Placements," *Journal of Finance*, June, 1951, pp. 160-61.

17. Frazer B. Wilde, "The Pros and Cons of Direct Placements," an address read before the American Life Convention, October 6, 1950.

18. Bell and Fraine, *op. cit.*, p. 57.

19. *1960 Life Insurance Fact Book*, p. 77.

20. In a special study in 1955, the SEC found that, for bond flotations of about the same size and maturity, private placements cost about one-quarter more than issues sold publicly. cf., *Cost of Flotation of Directly Placed Corporate Securities*, Washington, D.C., 1955.

21. A more extensive discussion of the commitment process is presented in Chapter IV.

22. Houghton Bell, "Does Direct Placement of Securities Lead to Corporation Control?" *The Commercial and Financial Chronicle*, December, 1949, p. 9.

23. *The New York Times*, January 30, 1952, p. 39.

24. Robert M. Soldofsky, "The Size and Maturity of Direct-Placement Loans," *Journal of Finance*, March, 1960, pp. 32-44.

25. E. Raymond Corey, *Direct Placement of Corporate Securities* (Boston: Harvard University Press, 1951).

26. The feasibility of only large loans in direct placements is explicitly stated by an investment banking firm in material prepared for potential clients: "Although each company is judged on its own merits, there is a minimum standard that experience has taught us to observe. If your company is not in a position to issue $500,000 to $1,000,000 of debt or equity securities, then the private placement fee is seldom justified." Kidder, Peabody and Company, Inc., *An Executive's Guide to Private Placements*, 1959, p. 7.

27. Soldofsky, *op. cit.*, pp. 36-37.

28. Joint Committee on The Economic Report, *Hearings on Volume and Stability of Private Investment*, 81st Congress, 1st Session, 1949, p. 206 ff. (Hereafter referred to as JCER, *Private Investment Hearings.*)

29. SEC statistics.

30. JCER, *Private Investment Hearings*, p. 255.

31. Stock Exchange *Year Book*.

32. La Force, *op. cit.*, p. 166.

33. Sullivan and Cromwell, *Corrected Opinion of Harold R. Medina in United States* v. *Morgan Stanley and Co.* (*Investment Bankers Case*) (New York: 1955), pp. 15-57.

34. Corey, *op. cit.*, pp. 146-48.

35. *Investment Bankers Case*, p. 48.

36. *Ibid.*

37. Roland I. Robinson, *Postwar Market for State and Local Government Securities*, a study sponsored by the National Bureau of Economic Research (Princeton: Princeton University Press, 1960), Chapter 4.

CHAPTER VII

Investment Behavior in the Mortgage Market

SECTION I
DEMAND FOR MORTGAGES

A. INVESTMENT ADVANTAGES AND DISADVANTAGES OF REAL ESTATE MORTGAGES

Life insurance companies have always found real estate mortgages an attractive investment outlet. The main attraction is the net yield on mortgages, which compares favorably with that on other types of assets of similar maturity and riskiness. For example, the rate of return on mortgage loans held by the 150 largest companies in 1957 averaged about one percentage point above that on bonds and approximately one-half percentage point more than the investment portfolio as a whole. In many cases, mortgages afforded returns only slightly below those achieved on common stocks. However, because of the pegged interest rates on federally-underwritten mortgages, the substantial fluctuations and general uptrend in other types of interest rates during the postwar years at times made FHA and VA mortgages somewhat less attractive. Thus, while rising yields induced an enormous increase in the companies' total mortgage holdings, the interest rate ceilings on FHA and VA loans imparted considerable instability to the flow of funds into these sectors of the market.

Mortgages also provide considerable security for investment funds. In appraising the property, life insurance companies or their correspondents typically allow a sizable safety margin by estimating its value well below what the market would probably set. The percentage they can lend against this hedged value is generally limited by law to around two-thirds. In fact, for about one-half of the companies, the ratio is only 60 percent for conventional loans. Much higher ratios are permitted on FHA and VA loans because of the federal government insurance or guarantee. On conventional loans, however, the maximum loan-to-value ratios set for life insurance companies are among the lowest allowed financial institutions.[1] Finally, the mortgage gives the investor a lien on the property which is the ultimate security behind the loan. But investment officers almost without exception have come to look to the income and debt-paying capacity of the borrower as the real index of security for mortgages. The high incomes and large stock of liquid assets held by borrowers, reflecting the increased stability in employment, have assured mortgage lenders that the prospect of large-scale losses through mortgage loans (as occurred in the 1920's and 1930's) has seriously diminished.

Maturities on mortgages in the postwar years have steadily lengthened to the point where 25-year mortgages are typical, compared with 15 years or less before World War II. And while such loans are usually erased before final maturity by prepayments, the longer period enables life insurance companies to invest a good share of their funds without experiencing an almost immediate return flow to further aggravate their already serious problem of finding outlets.

Diversification of the mortgage portfolio on the basis of geography enables life insurance companies to concentrate on areas enjoying the most rapid rates of growth, and this also adds to the portfolio's strength. The results of this general tendency are clearly shown in the regional distribution of mortgages compared with the volume of life insurance in force. The Northeast and North Central states, the areas of general surplus in savings, have acted as vast pumping stations, mobilizing funds and channeling them to the South and West, the sections of the country with the greatest deficits. For example, in 1949-50 the Northeast region had 35 percent of the life insurance in force but only 21 percent of the mortgages outstanding; by 1958-59 its share of life insurance had declined to 31 percent and its share of mortgages to only 14 percent. The experience of the North Central section was mixed; while its relative proportion of insurance in force decreased two percentage points to 30 percent, its share of mortgage debt remained about the same, reflecting a rate of economic growth somewhat above that of the Northeast but below that for the South and West. The latter regions registered large gains in both life insurance in force and in their percentage of total mortgages. In the South, the face value of life insurance policies rose from 22 percent to 25 percent of the total, and its share of mortgages increased from 35 percent to 37 percent. The largest advance in both categories occurred in the

West; the insurance proportion increased from 11 percent to 15 percent and mortgages from 17 to 21 percent.[2] Thus, the pumping system in the mortgage market became immensely more efficient in the last decade and greatly improved the possibilities open to life insurance companies to diversify their mortgage portfolios on the basis of geography.

A mortgage portfolio owned by a life insurance company also gains strength through the diversity of family incomes and credit backing the properties against which the loans have been made. The several million residential mortgages owned by life insurance companies have been taken out by families and individuals representing a wide range of occupations, businesses, and professions. While some borrowers may encounter adverse economic circumstances, it is most unlikely that—in the absence of a prolonged and generalized depression—all of them will be struck simultaneously.

From the point of view of life insurance companies several unattractive features partly offset the advantages of mortgages. In the first place, the cost of originating mortgages is relatively high. No matter what organization is used to acquire mortgages (loan correspondents, the companies' own branch offices, or some combination of these), a sizable burden still rests with the home office because of the necessity of supervising the field activities. While the correspondence system apparently is less costly than maintaining branches, the fees paid mortgage bankers and correspondents are still substantial. The task of servicing mortgages is also a disadvantage which is not fully overcome through the use of local agents. In addition, a problem is posed for the lender through the prepayment of mortgages as properties are sold. Although this increases the portfolio's liquidity, it also makes it necessary to search constantly for opportunities for reinvestment. Finally, some borrowers do default their mortgages, and the disposition of the property can be troublesome. Most state laws severely limit the amount of property life insurance companies can own beyond the amount required as offices, so the property acquired can be held for only a relatively short time. While the number of foreclosures in the postwar period has not come anywhere close to that recorded in the 1930's there is a definite tendency for the incidence to increase during recessions. In spite of these adverse aspects of mortgages as investment outlets, life insurance companies still find them highly favored assets.

B. Structural Changes and the Demand for Mortgages

Mortgage lending by life insurance companies has displayed considerable flexibility, but it has also demonstrated a large degree of specialization. This specialization is revealed rather clearly by the types of property by which loans are secured. The National Bureau of Economic Research, through special sample surveys of the portfolios of institutional lenders as of 1946-47 and by combining these data with statistics from the 1950 census survey of residential financing, was able to present the only detailed description available of the characteristics of mortgages held by life insurance companies and other financial institutions.[3] Measured by the number of loans held, about 90 percent of the mortgages owned by life insurance companies were secured by one to four family structures in 1946-47. This represents a sharp break from prewar years. In 1921, farm mortgages accounted for 18 percent of life insurance assets, and as this proportion declined during the farm depression of the 1920's, mortgages on urban real estate rose rapidly, reflecting the great expansion of construction activities. However, the bulk of these loans financed large scale residential and commercial properties.

This pattern has changed appreciably during the postwar period when viewed in terms of the dollar volume of loans held. While only 44 percent of the mortgage portfolios of insurance companies were backed, as of 1946-47, by one to four family structures, the proportion had risen to 65 percent by 1958. Nevertheless, these institutions continued to extend a substantial amount of their mortgage credit outside the small home field. In fact, life insurance companies supply a relatively large proportion of total mortgage funds employed in the financing of large residential and commercial properties. At the end of 1956, they held about one-third of the mortgages outstanding on both types of properties, while their share of the amount held by financial institutions was also one-third for multi-family dwellings, and one-half for commercial structures.[4]

The spread of fully amortized mortgages has greatly increased the liquidity of the mortgage portfolio—which in turn has exerted considerable influence on life insurance companies' demand for mortgages. During the 1920's, only about 10 percent of life insurance mortgage loans involved amortized repayment schedules.[5] While savings and loan associations had employed the principle for a number of years, life insurance companies adopted it only after this feature became mandatory in the mid-1930's for FHA insured loans.[6] The most notable development, however, is the spread of the practice to the conventional loan field. Of life insurance companies' conventional loans secured by one to four family properties in 1946-47, only about one-tenth was nonamortized, about 25 percent was partially amortized, and the remainder provided for full amortization by maturity.[7] Straight loans providing for no amortization are also infrequent in life insurance company lending on income properties, but in this case contracts calling for only partial amortization by maturity are fairly common, especially on the larger loans. Even so, about one-half of the number of loans on commercial and multifamily structures called for repayment by maturity.

While many life insurance companies were apparently reluctant to adopt the amortization principle in the 1930's, the opinion is currently almost universal that the practice has made the urban mortgage a favored investment instrument.[8] On the other hand, some portfolio managers decry the extension of maturities and the substantial rise in loan-to-value ratios which have accompanied amortized mortgages. The basis of this concern is revealed by data from the National Bureau study and by developments during the last decade. The National Bureau's statistics show that of the amount of conventional credit on one to four family dwellings outstanding with life insurance companies at the time the survey was taken, 68 percent had an original contract maturity of 15 years or longer, a gain of more than one-third compared with 1920. Undoubtedly a large proportion of loans have even longer maturities as a result of the steady lengthening during the postwar years. With respect to the loan-to-value ratio,[9] nearly 80 percent of home mortgages outstanding with life insurance companies in 1946-47 involved borrower equities of less than 40 percent at the time of the loan, and the ratio of equity to the purchase price has fallen drastically since the second World War.

C. Mortgage Preferences of Life Insurance Companies

In making mortgage loans, the vast majority of life insurance companies prefer conventional mortgages to those underwritten by the federal government. This preference was clearly demonstrated in the replies to the question on mortgages included in the BBER-MSU Survey, 1959, of life insurance companies' investment policies. Over two-fifths of the companies replied that they prefer conventional mortgages to FHA or VA loans, while another one-fifth reported that they do not invest in federally-underwritten loans at all. The basis of the preference for conventional mortgages is easily understood: the yield on such loans is usually substantially higher than on FHA and VA mortgages; down payments are considerably higher, and maturities are much shorter. Moreover, institutions have had a much longer period of experience in lending against property secured by conventional mortgages, and the red tape involved is less entangling than that associated with insured or guaranteed loans. On the other hand, almost one-sixth of the life insurance companies reported that they actually prefer federally-underwritten mortgages to conventional loans, and almost one-fifth replied that they choose between the two types purely on the basis of relative yields. Those companies which emphasize relative yields, of course, do not exhibit any unusual features of investment behavior. But the preference for FHA and VA mortgages does appear to be exceptional and requires further examination.

The most frequently cited explanation of the preference for federally-underwritten mortgages focused on the reduced risk combined with a relatively high yield. The companies expressing a preference for FHA and VA loans were among the larger institutions; the scope of their activities allows them to obtain wide geographical diversification in their holdings—a diversification which smaller institutions cannot readily achieve. Moreover, several of the investment officers replied that, even with the relatively low ceilings on interest rates permitted on federally-underwritten loans, they were able to acquire such mortgages at substantial discounts which render their yields competitive with those on conventional loans. For example, a large company replied:

> We have 97 percent of our mortgages in FHA and VA loans. We think FHA and VA loans are relatively very attractive when compared to yields available on the quality of conventional loans we would be willing to purchase. Currently, 5½ percent FHA loans are being purchased at 95½ to 97.

A few companies reported that they make conventional mortgage loans only against commercial and industrial properties and require federal underwriting for all residential mortgages. They generally felt that, while functioning business concerns afford ample security for conventional loans, no such guarantee exists with respect to residential property. On the other hand, 20 of the 111 life insurance companies replying indicated that they do not buy FHA or VA mortgages. Over one-half of these are in the smallest group of institutions. Several of these said they were not equipped in terms of staff to handle such loans; a few others reported that, given the relatively small geographical area in which they operate, the negligible volume and poor quality of such loans precluded development of sizable lending operations.

In interpreting the replies, of course, one must remember that many of the companies which reported a preference for conventional mortgages acquire a certain amount of federally-underwritten real estate loans on a continuous basis. This proportion tends to vary inversely with the overall demand for credit, and during recessions the institutions are more or less forced to acquire FHA or VA loans to maintain the volume of business required to keep their staffs employed. Moreover, during recessions, the return on federally-underwritten mortgages becomes increasingly attractive as market yields decline.

Section II
Investment Behavior in the Mortgage Market, 1920-1945

A. Prewar Experience

At the end of 1959, life insurance companies held about 22 percent of the nonfarm mortgage debt outstanding in the United States. With slight interruptions, the proportion of such debt held by life insurance companies climbed annually between 1920 and 1955 and remained around one-fifth during the last half of the 1950's. The investment behavior of life insurance companies in the mortgage market, however, has been quite different from that of other institutional investors. These differences in behavior have reflected both secular changes and the way life insurance companies have adjusted to cyclical disturbances. From the standpoint of long-run changes, the growth of life insurance companies' portfolios has been remarkable. Between 1920 and 1959, their nonfarm mortgage portfolios expanded by thirty-one times, nearly double the increase registered by all financial institutions taken together. The cyclical variation of the companies' portfolios is more evident during the 1930's than in the previous decade; the vigorous appearance of these investors in the mortgage market shortly after World War I was probably more a structural than a cyclical phenomenon.

The pattern of change in life insurance companies' mortgage investments is shown in Chart VII-1. Their portfolios rose swiftly during the decade of the 1920's and reached a peak in 1931, a year after total institutional holdings began to decline. Furthermore, although mortgage holdings of commercial banks and savings and loan associations began to rise during the middle 1930's while those of mutual savings banks declined more slowly, the portfolios of life insurance companies registered further losses. In fact, the latter were large enough to offset the increased mortgage acquisitions of other institutions so that total institutionally held real estate loans continued to decline until 1936. On the whole the fluctuation of mortgage portfolios of life insurance companies was less drastic than that experienced by commercial banks and savings and loan associations though greater than that shown by mutual savings banks. Between 1931 and 1936, mortgage holdings of life insurance companies fell by 28 percent. In a comparable period (1929-34) those of commercial banks declined by 45 percent, while in seven years (1929-36) mortgage loans

CHART VII-1

Nonfarm Mortgages Held By Life Insurance Companies and Financial Institutions, 1920-1959

(Ratio Scale)

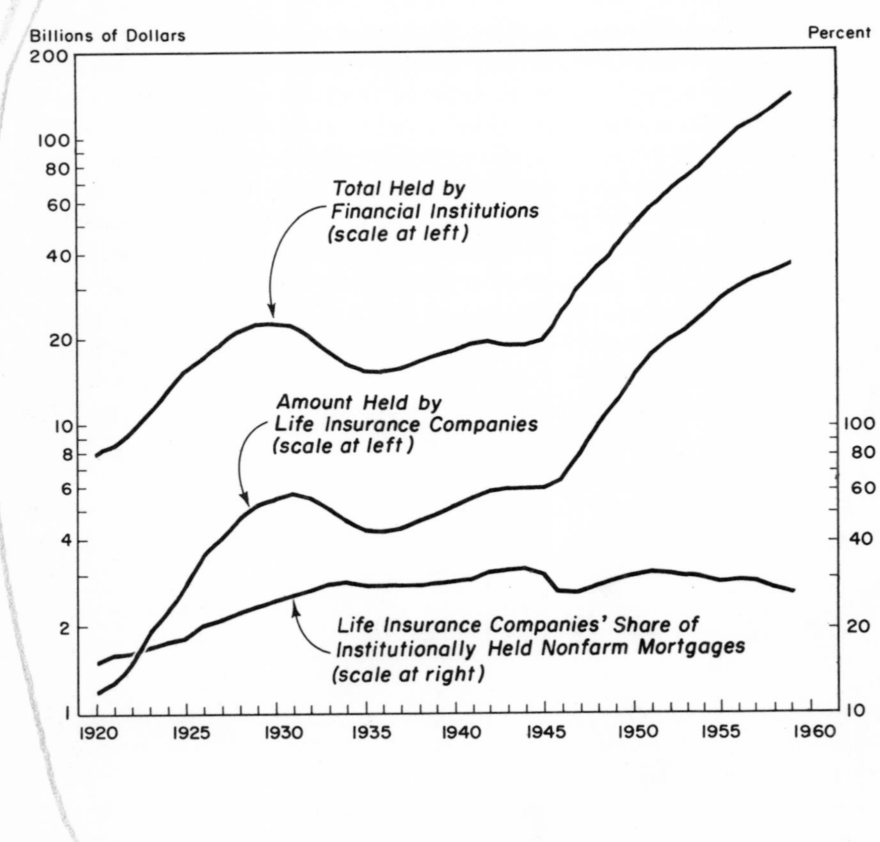

SOURCE: J. E. Morton, *Urban Mortgage Lending: Comparative Markets and Experience* (New York: National Bureau of Economic Research, 1956), p. 169. (Data for 1920-1955); Saul B. Klaman, *The Volume of Mortgage Debt in the Postwar Decade.* Technical Paper 13. (New York: National Bureau of Economic Research, 1958), p. 54.

of savings and loan associations were cut nearly in half. In contrast, real estate loans of mutual savings banks fell by only one-fifth between 1931 and 1938. The factors explaining the different cyclical pattern for life insurance companies include a more flexible lending policy and greater availability of funds, as well as the relatively larger proportion of mortgage loans backed by commercial properties.

Differences in the behavior of urban mortgage portfolios held by life insurance companies become even more apparent, as compared with those held by other institutional lenders, if one examines changes in their relative share of total institutional holdings. Because of their increased interest in mortgages and on the basis of their strong competitive position, life insurance companies were able to expand their share of the market. By World War II, these companies had attained the leading role among institutional investors and continued to hold it until the immediate postwar years. The trend of other institutional mortgage holdings showed a different pattern. For example, the share of commercial banks and savings and loan associations in the combined institutional mortgage portfolio tended to move in conformity with cyclical variations in output and employment. Mutual savings banks held their largest shares during periods of greatest mortgage and real estate distress and their smallest proportions in times of highest activity in the mortgage market. The relative losses of the latter apparently were registered as relative gains of life insurance companies.

Although life insurance companies are currently the most important lenders on income property, they have not always occupied this position of hegemony. The path of their emergence stands out clearly in the record. Commercial banks and mutual savings banks had comparable shares in this market in 1925, and both exceeded by about one-third the proportion held by life insurance companies. By 1929, insurance companies' holdings had expanded greatly as their total assets grew rapidly and as they made further switches from farm mortgages. Only slight declines occurred in the dollar value of their nonresidential urban real estate loans during the 1930's while the amount held by all other investors decreased appreciably. Beginning about 1935, both the absolute amount as well as the relative share of life insurance companies' loans in this market began to rise. Since then they have occupied a dominant position in this area.

The varying importance of nonfarm real estate mortgages as outlets for life insurance companies' investment funds is shown in the ratio of mortgages to total assets. This proportion reached 43 percent in 1926-27, the highest ratio recorded in the last 40 years. From 1928 through 1935, the ratio fell sharply and was rather steady until the rapid repayment of loans during World War II pulled it down to only 15 percent of total assets in 1945-46. During the postwar years the trend has been generally upward, and at the end of 1959 the proportion exceeded one-third. An even more striking indication of the shifting importance of mortgages to life insurance companies is net investment in these loans compared with annual changes in the companies' total assets. Net mortgage investment relative to the growth of total assets has been characterized by considerable fluctuations. The proportion of new assets represented by real estate mortgages began to decline in 1923, about two years before the peak was attained in residential construction. Although the rate of decrease varied slightly, after 1928 the drop became precipitous. By the end of 1931, life insurance companies were liquidating mortgages in the face of a continued rise in total assets, and in 1934 disinvestment in real estate amounted to nearly 90 percent of new assets. For almost five years mortgage liquidation continued, but in 1935 a fairly rapid increase in lending activity began. Within three years, the dollar amount of credit extended had reached the previous record set in 1924. However, because of the steady growth of total assets, net mortgage investment was only 25 percent of new assets in 1941.

These trends in life insurance companies' participation in the mortgage market during the 1920's can be summarized as follows: The high level of their mortgage lending activity that extended from 1926 through 1929 was primarily a reflection of high levels of construction activity. However, the interesting feature of the record is that the companies continued to expand real estate credit through 1929, even though the construction of single family dwellings declined after 1925. This was partly due to the rise of private nonresidential building to unusually high levels in 1928. Because insurance companies were heavy lenders in both fields, they did not experience a slackening in their rate of new lending activity until 1930. While lending on single family dwellings was reduced after 1926, demand for such funds continued to be significant in maintaining the new loan volume of insurance companies after the construction boom had ended. Statistics show clearly that the decline in new loan volume after 1928 was due mainly to a slowing down of credit extensions on large apartment houses and nonresidential buildings. Loans on single family structures continued to be made until 1931, with only a slight downward drift from the peak level of 1926. The wide swings after 1920 in life insurance companies' mortgage lending activity were, in other words, due mainly to economic conditions outside the market for single family homes.

B. DEPRESSION AND WAR YEARS

Over the decade of the 1930's as a whole, life insurance companies reduced their mortgage holdings by $1.6 billion, or by more than one-fifth of the total owned at the end of 1930. Three-quarters of the decline centered in farm mortgages, although such loans accounted for only slightly more than one-quarter of the companies' portfolio at the beginning of the decade. In fact, life insurance companies experienced, during the ten years ending in 1940, a reduction of almost three-fifths in the amount of farm mortgages held. The drastic decline partly reflected the greater impact of the depression on farm income and real estate values than on urban income and property values. By 1940, the companies owned $6.0 billion of real estate mortgages, representing 19 percent of their total assets, a proportion less than one-half of the 40 percent registered in 1930.

The sharp decline in the companies' mortgage holdings concealed, to some extent, the size of their outstanding commitment in the real estate market, because a considerable share of the reduction in their mortgage portfolio was actually offset by real estate acquired through mortgage foreclosures. Between 1930 and 1940, real estate owned outright rose by $1.5 billion (an increase of almost 300 percent) to a total of $2.1 billion. Moreover, the peak in real estate ownership was reached in 1937 when the amount was about $127 million above the 1940 figure.

During the World War II years, life insurance companies were not only able to stop the erosion in their mortgage holdings but also made considerable progress in improving the quality of their loans. They made net additions of more than $800 million to their urban mortgages, but their farm loans continued to shrink. By the end of 1945, their total holdings had climbed to $6.6 billion. Yet, because their total assets grew at an accelerated pace, the ratio of mortgages to the total fell further, to 15 percent. The war brought record prosperity to agriculture as well as industry, and the high incomes, combined with a strong expectation of postwar inflation, created a strong demand for real estate. In this expanding market, life insurance companies were able to dispose of almost three-fifths of the backlog of real estate brought forward from the depression. The reduction was even greater for farm properties where the drop came to about three-quarters of the amount held in 1940. Thus, at the end of World War II, life insurance companies generally felt that their mortgage holdings were grossly out of balance with their total investment portfolios. Given this strong desire to raise the ratio, although not necessarily to the historical level, it was to be expected that life insurance companies would be vigorous competitors in the mortgage market in the postwar period. As described below, this was, in fact, the case.

SECTION III
HOUSING AND THE MORTGAGE MARKET SINCE WORLD WAR II

A. DEMAND FOR HOUSING

Three main influences have been instrumental in shaping the demand for housing since the end of World War II. These are (1) demographic factors, (2) family income, and (3) the availability and terms of mortgage credit. The impact of each of these variables on the demand for housing is discussed in turn.

Among the demographic influences, net new family formation, the birth rate, and the shift in the composition of households have played mixed roles. The outstanding feature of the growth of new families was the continued echo of the depressed birth rates of the 1930's. Most new households are launched shortly after marriage, and over four-fifths of the women who get married do so before their twenty-fifth birthday. In fact, during the last decade and a half, the number of net new marriages (total marriages performed less divorces) varied rather closely with the average number of women entering the 20-24 year age class, although in individual years sizable divergences occurred. Chart VII-2 shows that the downtrend in net family formation was not reversed until 1955; when the trough was reached in 1954, the net number of households started was slightly more than 500,000, or only one-third that registered five years earlier before the shadow of the 1930's began to creep upon the scene. Moreover, the adverse impact of both the 1953-54 and 1957-58 recessions is visible in the chart. The rate of decline in household formation had begun to slow in the two years prior to the earlier slump in economic activity, and the subsequent recovery in the following two years was cut short by the last slump. Although the pace quickened again toward the close of the 1950's, the annual number of net household formations in the last part of the decade averaged about one-fifth less than in the first half. Another feature of household formation which has exerted considerable influence on the demand for housing is the notable rise in the number of households not involving married couples. As evident from Chart VII-2, such units, many of them headed by women, contributed an appreciable proportion of the net increase in the number of households in the postwar years. In fact, during the 1950's, separate households accounted for approximately one-half of the expansion in the number of units—

CHART VII-2

Net New Households, by Types,
1948-1959

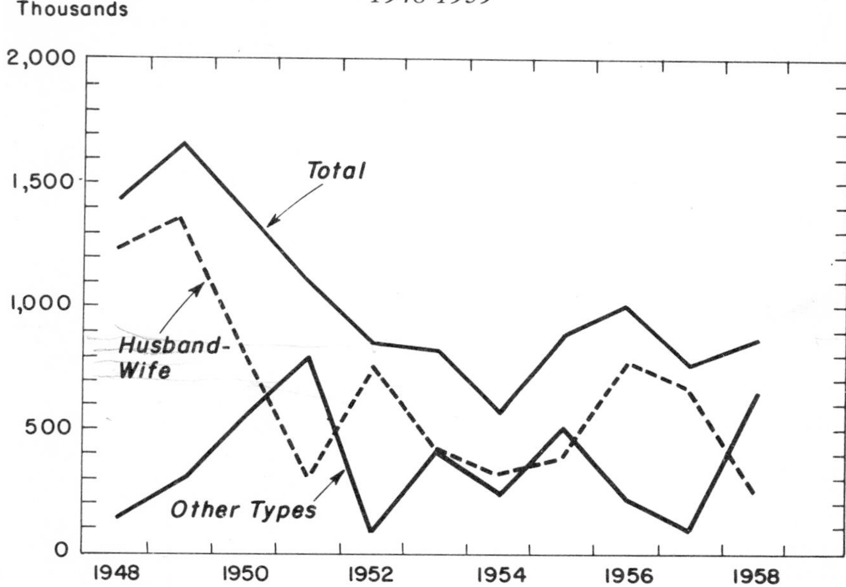

SOURCE: U. S. Bureau of the Census, *Current Population Survey.*

although they constituted only one-fifth of the total at the beginning of the decade. This pattern of household expansion can be attributed to several factors—the most important of which seem to be the increasing numbers surviving in each of the middle and upper age groups and a strong preference on the part of young couples for a separate home. On balance, the increased tendency for new families to establish their own households has meant a remarkable growth in the number of units other than the traditional husband-wife combination. Both trends have added to the demand for housing and mortgage credit.

The continued increase in birth rates during the postwar period provided some stimulus to housing demand, but the strength of the contribution was probably less than one might have expected from the size of the recovery in the number of births per 1,000 females in the childbearing age range (15-44 years). Birth rates, which had declined drastically, underwent a sharp revival during World War II, and the increase continued through 1957. By then the rate was 123 per 1,000 females of childbearing age, a gain of 15 percent from 1950. During 1958 and 1959, the birth rate moved along a high plateau 50 percent above the 1940 level. It is somewhat difficult to disentangle the direct effects of rising birth rates and income on the demand for housing; it is clear that a high birth rate generates a demand for larger houses, but studies seem to indicate that the effect of birth rates on housing demand is swamped by the influence of income. While families with children are more likely to own a home than are childless couples, the value of the house and the current outlays on housing seem to be primarily a function of income. When families within the same income group are compared, the number of children appears to make no difference with respect to either of these general tendencies. Of course, the absolute level of income does make a difference—for the higher the level of income, the higher is the price paid for the house and the greater is the expenditure on housing.

The purchase of a house tends to lag the formation of a new household by a number of years. The length of this delay is approximated by the divergence between the age of marriage and of home ownership of urban families. Whereas more than 75 percent of the men who marry (and an even higher percentage of women) do so before the age of 25, only 16 percent of the nonfarm families whose head was below this age owned homes in 1959. (See Table VII-1.) Moreover, the percentage of home ownership declined steadily from the one-fifth registered in 1949. Home ownership is concentrated in the age group 25-44, with a sharp rise in the proportion after age 35. About 42 percent of the families in the age range 25-35 were home owners in 1959, but the ratio jumped to 64 percent among the age group 35-44. There was little further rise in the proportion owning homes for older heads of households up to age 65—and a slight decrease thereafter. While all age groups showed gains in the percentage of home owners during the last decade, the largest increase occurred in the 35-44 age range. This is partly explained by the boost to home ownership provided by the increased availability of mortgage funds attributable in part to the veterans housing program which is discussed more fully below.

The growth and redistribution of personal income have greatly influenced the demand for housing in the postwar period. In 1958, the median income of nonfarm families was about $5,000, a gain of over 50 percent since 1948; the increase amounted to about 28 percent after allowing for the rise in the cost of living. This uptrend in incomes has induced a much larger proportion of families to become home owners than was the case in the early part of the period. While only one-half of all nonfarm families were home owners in 1949, the percentage had in-

TABLE VII-1

HOME OWNERSHIP AMONG URBAN FAMILIES, BY AGE AND INCOME GROUP

	Percentage Owning Homes		
	1949	1954	1959
All Families	51	56	58
Age of Head of Family			
18-24	21	17	16
25-34	35	42	42
35-44	53	57	63
45-54	59	63	64
55-64	62	66	69
65 and over	59	63	66
Family Income Quintiles			
Lowest	40	45	46
Second	43	46	42
Third	47	51	59
Fourth	55	65	63
Highest	69	71	79

SOURCE: Board of Governors of the Federal Reserve System, "1959 Survey of Consumer Finance: Housing of Nonfarm Families," **Federal Reserve Bulletin,** September, 1959, p. 1107.

creased to almost three-fifths by 1959. (See Table VII-1.) Moreover, the greater incidence of home ownership has been broadly diffused, but the largest gains have taken place among the middle and upper income groups. In 1959, less than one-half of the families in the lowest of the income groups owned their homes, compared with three-fifths in the third and fourth quintiles and 80 percent in the highest income class.

The influence of income on home ownership is also shown in the pattern of home purchases in relation to income. As incomes rise, the value of houses purchased also rises. This tendency is clearly shown in the transactions data for FHA-insured single family homes. Between 1946 and 1959, the median income of families purchasing such homes more than doubled, advancing from $3,300 to $6,900; over the same period, the median value of the property increased from $6,600 to $14,300. Thus, the value of homes purchased rose in step with income, and the value-income ratio remained quite stable at slightly more than 2 to 1. Furthermore, the improvement in incomes has set off a marked trend toward the purchase of more expensive houses. Units costing $20,000 or more accounted for about 8 percent of all houses bought in 1951-53 and for 16 percent in

1956-58. Because such houses are purchased primarily by high income groups, the latter's share of total house sales advanced from about one-quarter in both 1947-49 and 1951-53 to more than one-third in 1956-58.

As incomes have risen, families have also purchased larger homes initially and have also shifted into homes of higher quality. For example, there has been a substantial increase in the average size of house, from about 900 sq. ft. in the early postwar years to 1,100 sq. ft. toward the end of the 1950's. Over the same period, houses with three or more bedrooms rose from less than one-third to four-fifths of the total purchased. The same trend toward better quality homes is evident in the fact that in 1955-57 almost one-half of the houses purchased were acquired by families which previously owned their own home; previous owners accounted for approximately one-third of all purchases in 1949-50.

The availability of funds has been a major factor determining the demand for housing. In the years immediately following the end of the war, the liquid assets accumulated during the conflict enabled many families to make the relatively high down payments required without seriously reducing their resources. Subsequently the accumulated equity in houses (reflecting the steady rise in housing prices) provided sizable capital gains, which many people used to switch into higher priced houses. However, as shown in Table VII-2 total equity in houses increased by about 75 percent while mortgage debt rose three times between 1949 and 1959.

Thus, the main financial factor shaping housing demand has been the availability of mortgage credit. As explained more fully below, the flow of funds into the mortgage market has mainly reflected variations in the rate of capital formation in the corporate sector of the economy. But taking the postwar period as a whole, mortgage funds have played a marked role in the demand for housing. Mortgage debt outstanding on one to four family houses rose from an estimated $23 billion in 1946 to about $118 billion in 1958. Perhaps a better picture of the relation of mortgage credit to home financing is given by statistics in Table VII-2. Between 1949 and 1959, mortgage debt outstanding against owner-occupied homes increased threefold to $106 billion. This reflected a rise in the number of homes mortgaged as well as in the average size of mortgage. While 45 percent of the 20 million homes occupied by their owners were mortgaged in 1949, approximately 56 percent of the 29 million properties were encumbered in 1959. Furthermore, the size of the average mortgage outstanding increased twice as fast as the value of mortgaged properties—rising from $3,700 to $6,650 over the ten-year period. Consequently, the average ratio of mortgage debt to house value rose from 37 percent to 47 percent. This growth in indebtedness, however, appears

TABLE VII-2

MORTGAGE STATUS OF NONFARM OWNER-OCCUPIED HOUSES

Status	1949	1954	1959
Number			
In Millions of Dollars			
Total	20.0	24.9	28.8
Mortgaged	9.0	12.6	16.0
Nonmortgaged	11.0	12.3	12.8
Percentage Distribution			
Total	100	100	100
Mortgaged	45	50	56
Nonmortgaged	55	50	44
Value			
In Billions of Dollars			
Total	183	265	372
Mortgaged-total	90	146	224
Debt	33	60	106
Equity	57	86	118
Nonmortgaged	93	119	148
Total equity	150	205	266
Percentage Distribution			
Mortgaged-total	100	100	100
Debt	37	41	47
Equity	63	59	53

SOURCE: **Federal Reserve Bulletin**, September, 1959, p. 1104.

not to have increased the burden on home owners, because in both 1948 and 1958 mortgagors spent about 12 percent of their income to meet their monthly mortgage payments.

Changes in the terms of mortgage financing have also played a key role in expanding the demand for houses in the last decade and a half. The main elements in mortgage terms are the size of initial down payment required, the maturity of the loan, and the rate of interest. These components of mortgage terms are important because they determine the monthly payment required to sustain the mortgage on an amortized basis. Of these, only the rate of interest has tended to dampen the demand for mortgage credit and for houses.

Down payment requirements have shown three distinct types of movements since the end of World War II. The first of these is cyclical; each of the three postwar recessions generated an appreciable easing in the amount of the down payment required, which lasted for about one year before tighter conditions returned. Nevertheless, the postrecession requirements in each case were below those prevailing before the slackening in economic activity. Underlying this cyclical behavior was a steady downtrend in the initial payment. While this secular decline began with VA-guaranteed mortgages in the early years of the period, it soon spread to FHA-insured and conventional mortgages. This tendency is clearly shown in the record of FHA mortgages: in the late 1940's the down payment on houses financed with such mortgages average 20 percent; by 1959 the average down payment was less than 10 percent. Moreover, because incomes registered such a sizable advance during this period (even after allowing for price increases), the real burden of down payments actually declined much more than indicated by the drop of one-half in the size of the typical down payment. Finally, the substantial shift from VA-guaranteed to conventional financing toward the end of the period partly offset the stimulus to housing demand provided by the cyclical and secular easing in down payments. However, the higher down payments required by conventional loans were softened to some extent by the possibility of borrowers taking out second mortgages, an option which is prohibited in VA and FHA regulations. While the second mortgages would raise the monthly payments, the obstacle to home buyers posed by the initial outlay would be more easily overcome.

The trend to lower down payments, of course, necessarily implies higher monthly payments. To counter this, loan maturities were stretched considerably during the last fifteen years, with 30-year mortgages being fairly common. While the march to longer maturities began with VA mortgages during the late 1940's, an increasing proportion of all types of loans was made in the longer ranges which were permitted as the years progressed. Moreover, because of accelerated amortization and prepayment as houses are sold, the effective maturities of mortgages were actually between twelve and fifteen years. The impact of longer maturities on monthly payments and the stimulus to housing demand are illustrated in Chart VII-3. Assuming that the rate of interest is 6 percent, the monthly payment per $1,000 of loan is $8.44 with a fifteen year maturity. If the maturity is stretched to twenty years, the monthly payment drops to $7.16, or a decline of one-sixth. Successive five year stretches in maturities reduce costs further by 10 percent at twenty-five years and 7 percent at thirty years. It should be noted, however, that the stimulus becomes progressively weaker, and the additional gains would be quite small beyond thirty years. On the other hand, in the middle maturities shown, the reduction in the monthly payment of an increase in maturity from

CHART VII-3

Relation Among Interest Rate, Maturities, and Monthly Mortgage Payments

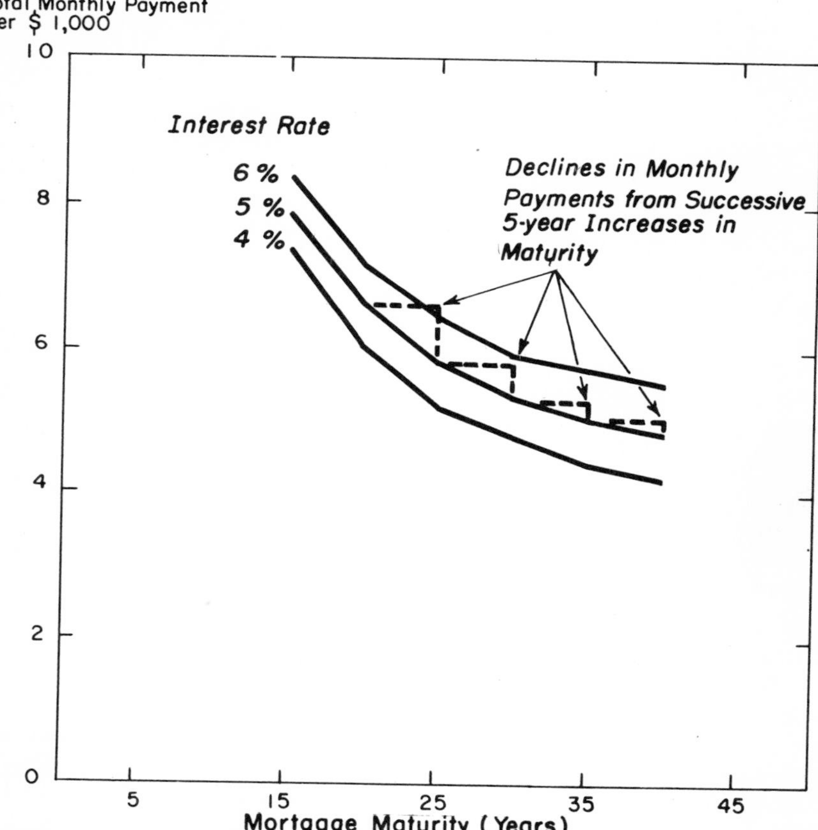

SOURCE: U. S. Department of Commerce, *Survey of Current Business*, April, 1960, p. 21.

fifteen to twenty years for a 6 percent loan is almost as large as that produced by a drop in the interest rate to 4½ percent. Thus, the tendency toward longer maturities also helped to offset the steady rise in interest rates during the postwar period.

B. Supply of Housing

The attempt to satisfy the strong demand for housing has been one of the outstanding features of the economic scene in the United States since the end of World War II. While the rate of capital formation through residential construction has fluctuated considerably from year to year, the net additions to the housing stock have gone a long way toward making up the deficit in dwelling units inherited from the Great Depression and World War II. Moreover, the ebb and flow of residential construction have been important determinants of the pace of output as a whole.

In the one and one-half decades ending in 1959, over 15 million private nonfarm dwelling units were started. This was an average of 1.1 million starts per year, a rate substantially greater than that achieved during the housing boom of the 1920's. While the total economy has also expanded appreciably since the predepression years, the housing sector has played a relatively more important role. A steady rise in the number of new housing starts began immediately after the close of World War II and reached an all-time record in 1950. (See Table VII-3.) Subsequently, housing starts declined by one-quarter in 1951, and advanced by 13 percent from 1953 to 1954, registered a further gain of 9 percent from 1954 to 1955 and dropped by 17 percent from 1955 to 1956. There was another

TABLE VII-3

NEW NONFARM HOUSING STARTS, PRIVATE NONFARM RESIDENTIAL CONSTRUCTION, AND ITS RELATION TO GROSS NATIONAL PRODUCT, 1946-1959

Year	Privately Owned Nonfarm Dwelling Units Started (Thousands)	Residential Nonfarm Construction (Millions of 1954 Dollars)	Residential Nonfarm Construction as Percent of GNP
1946	663	7.3	2.6
1947	846	9.6	3.4
1948	914	11.4	3.9
1949	989	11.2	3.8
1950	1,352	15.5	4.9
1951	1,020	12.9	3.8
1952	1,069	12.8	3.6
1953	1,068	13.6	3.7
1954	1,202	15.4	4.2
1955	1,310	18.2	4.6
1956	1,094	16.2	4.0
1957	993	15.4	3.8
1958	1,142	16.2	4.1
1959	1,342	19.4	4.6

SOURCE: U. S. Department of Commerce, **Survey of Current Business.**

easing off in 1957 followed by a vigorous recovery of 15 percent in 1958 and 17 percent in 1959. The dollar value of residential construction has displayed a pattern similar to that for housing starts, but the fluctuations have been somewhat less severe.

Residential construction has varied from about 2.5 percent to 5 percent of gross national product since World War II with the average around 4 percent. The ratio generally exceeded the average in postrecession years and fell below during periods of credit stringency. In fact, residential construction reached a peak before total output in each of the three postwar recessions. While residential construction led total economic activity by a slight margin in the 1948-49 recession, in both 1953-54 and 1957-58 it moved vigorously ahead, and within about a year of the recession troughs, new peaks were set. Subsequently, the residential construction sector registered sharp declines while output as a whole continued to expand.

Other evidence also demonstrated the extent to which the demand for housing has been met during the postwar period. Table VII-4 shows the growth in the country's housing stock during the last two decades as well as the substantial upgrading in quality which has occurred.

Compared with the prewar period, it is estimated that housing stock expanded by three-fifths and probably totalled close to 60 million units by the end of the 1950's. Moreover, about half of the improvement was achieved during the last decade. The actual improvement was even more striking than the growth in number implies because over 5 million substandard units were eliminated. Although the Census Bureau's definition of substandard units has changed slightly from time to time, the sub-

TABLE VII-4

TOTAL U. S. HOUSING STOCK AND SUBSTANDARD INVENTORY, SELECTED YEARS

(Thousands of Units)

Year	Total Housing Stock	Substandard Inventory	Substandard Inventory as Percent of Total
1940	37,325	18,364	49.2
1950	45,983	16,944	36.8
1956	55,431	13,092	23.7
1960 (estimated)	60,000	11,501	19.2

SOURCE: Renhold P. Walff, "Substandard Dwelling Units and Their Replacement, 1961-70," **Study of Mortgage Credit,** Subcommittee on Housing, Committee on Banking and Currency, United States Senate, 85th Congress, 2nd Session, 1958, p. 45.

standard housing inventory generally includes all dilapidated units plus other units without sanitary facilities, private bath, or hot running water. Housing units in this category declined from about one-half of the total in 1940 to about one-fifth in the most recent years. Moreover, virtually all of the elimination of substandard units occurred after 1950.

Data in Table VII-5 also demonstrate that the demand for and supply of housing were brought more closely into balance during the last decade. The vacancy rate rose by nearly one-half between 1950 and 1959, suggesting a substantial easing in the pressure to find adequate housing. Perhaps of more importance is the shift in the types of vacancies. Houses which were empty because of seasonal factors declined slightly in relation to the total, while year round vacancies gained. In the earlier year, dilapidated units accounted for one-quarter of the total year round vacancies but had declined to only one-fifth by 1959, which implies that a much larger proportion of empty houses reflected an easing in the housing shortage.

C. Growth and Transformation of the Mortgage Market

The mortgage market has been the focus of major shifts in the structure and functioning of the long-term capital market since the end of World War II. Perhaps the outstanding feature of the period is the revival of the market as an instrument through which private demands for funds can be satisfied. During the Great Depression and the second World War, the flow of funds into private uses was substantially reduced, and loanable funds were channeled to meet public needs—especially the enormous

TABLE VII-5

VACANT DWELLING UNITS BY CONDITION AND STATUS, FOR THE UNITED STATES, 1950 AND 1959

(Percentage Distribution)

Condition and Status	1950	1959
All units	100.0	100.0
Occupied	93.1	89.9
Vacant	6.9	10.1
Seasonal vacant	2.5	3.2
Year-round vacant	4.4	6.9
Not dilapidated	3.3	5.6
Dilapidated	1.1	1.3

SOURCE: U. S. Bureau of the Census, **Study of Mortgage Credit, Hearings**: Subcommittee of the Committee on Banking and Currency, United States Senate, 86th Congress, 1st Session, May, 1959, p. 42.

requirements of the federal government. In the fourteen years ending in 1959, the pattern changed completely: private financing absorbed virtually all of the net increase in long-term funds reaching the capital market, as the reduced borrowing by the federal government approximately offset the increased indebtedness of state and local governments.

Behind these general trends, several developments have significantly changed the interrelations among the major sectors of the market, and among the latter the market for mortgages has borne a sizable share of the transformation. Between 1945 and 1959, the total amount of real estate mortgages outstanding in the United States rose threefold to $191 billion, while the total amount of long-term securities increased by only two-thirds. This growth lifted the ratio of mortgages to the total from less than 10 percent to almost three-tenths. Simultaneously, the proportion of mortgage debt secured by one to four family structures rose from around one-half to two-thirds of the total.

The net flow of funds into mortgages and other long-term securities since the end of World War II is shown in Table VII-6. Over the period as a whole, mortgages absorbed $156 billion, which was close to three-

TABLE VII-6

SELECTED LONG-TERM SECURITIES OUTSTANDING IN THE UNITED STATES, 1945 AND 1959

(In Billions of Dollars)

Type of Securities	Outstanding				Change, 1945-59		
	1945		1959				
	Amount	Percent of Total	Amount	Percent of Total	Amount	Percent	Distribution of Change
Mortgages: Total	35.5	8.7	191.0	28.0	155.5	338.0	56.6
Residential	18.6	4.6	131.0	19.2	112.4	604.3	40.9
Nonresidential	16.9	4.1	60.0	8.8	43.1	255.0	15.7
Corporate Securities:							
Total	142.5	35.0	230.1	33.8	87.6	61.5	31.9
Bonds	23.5	5.8	73.5	10.8	50.0	212.8	18.2
Stocks	119.0	29.2	156.6	23.0	37.6	31.6	13.7
State and Local Government Sec.	19.5	4.8	63.3	9.3	43.8	224.6	15.9
U. S. Government Securities	209.1	51.5	197.1	28.9	−12.0	−5.7	−4.4
Total	406.6	100.0	681.5	100.0	274.9	67.6	100.0

SOURCE: U. S. Department of Commerce, **Survey of Current Business,** and **Federal Reserve Bulletin.**

fifths of the total increase in long-term securities. Of this amount, residential mortgages on one to four family dwellings accounted for 70 percent of the rise in mortgage indebtedness, and the rest was accounted for by multifamily dwellings, commercial, and farm properties. About $88 billion went into corporate securities, with corporate bonds representing well over half of the funds raised by these businesses. State and local governments, reflecting the greatly expanded demand for services, borrowed $44 billion net of retirements. On the other hand, the federal government reduced by $12 billion its long-term indebtedness represented by marketable securities. Thus, private borrowers raised about 88 percent of the net flow of funds in the capital market during the last decade and a half, and mortgages absorbed nearly two-thirds of this total.

On the supply side of the mortgage market, the most significant change has been the rise of institutional lenders to positions of undisputed hegemony. In 1945, these investors (mainly life insurance companies, commercial banks, mutual savings banks, and savings and loan associations) held just under three-fifths of total mortgage debt outstanding. (See Table VII-7.) By 1959, the proportion owned by them had expanded to three-quarters. This position of dominance has been achieved despite the fact that institutions as a group have not drastically altered the share of their resources devoted to mortgages. Rather, their increased role in the mortgage market is due primarily to the public's increasing tendency to save through institutions; this has given the latter a constantly rising proportion of total savings.

TABLE VII-7

OWNERSHIP OF MORTGAGES BY FINANCIAL INSTITUTIONS, 1945 AND 1959

(In Billions of Dollars)

Type of Property	1945			1959		
	Total Outstanding	Held by Financial Institutions		Total Outstanding	Held by Financial Institutions	
		Amount	Percent of Total		Amount	Percent of Total
Nonfarm: Total	30.8	19.6	63.6	178.7	140.9	78.8
1 to 4 family houses	18.6	12.2	65.6	131.0	109.3	83.4
Multifamily and commercial properties	12.2	7.4	60.7	47.7	31.6	66.2
Farm	4.8	1.3	27.1	12.3	4.5	36.6
All Properties	35.5	21.0	59.2	191.0	145.4	76.1

SOURCE: **Federal Reserve Bulletin.**

The expansion of mortgage debt, of course, is a reflection of the vast home-building and general construction boom which followed the second World War. However, the most recent construction boom differs appreciably from that of the 1920's, and the growth of the mortgage market mirrors these differences. For example, in the 1920's, the percentage of total owner-occupied homes financed with mortgages rose considerably while the loan-to-value ratio also advanced to new records. Nevertheless, the frequency of home ownership was practically unchanged. The trend was somewhat mixed during the years 1945-59; while the frequency of mortgage debt rose, the loan-to-value ratio was virtually unchanged, and the incidence of home ownership advanced sharply.

Finally, the assumption of risk by the federal government for nearly two-fifths of residential mortgage loans has been one of the outstanding factors influencing the growth of the mortgage market since World War II. In fact, even before the war started, government underwriting was beginning to exert a marked influence on the market. Although there was a considerable lag in the response of most financial institutions to federal inducements to lending provided by the insurance features of the Federal Housing Administration program launched in 1935, interest in insured loans began to appear in the late 1930's. During the war years, FHA mortgages were the mainstay of real estate loan investments. In 1944, the Veterans Administration guarantee program was started, although it did not begin to operate on any scale until 1946. While the details of the two programs differ, the essential purposes are similar. Through them, the risks of mortgage lending are pooled, and a major share of the contingent liability involved is shifted from private lenders to the federal government. As a result of pooling risks, the number of lenders has increased, and the market has become much broader and more fluid. On the other hand, while the maximum interest rates[10] allowed on federally-underwritten mortgages have tended to keep down the cost to eligible borrowers, they have also induced wide swings in the availability of funds in this part of the capital market.

The impact of government underwriting on the mortgage market is partly shown in the proportion of such loans to total nonfarm residential mortgages outstanding and in their distribution among the major financial institutions. As shown in Table VII-8, government-underwritten mortgages accounted for twice the proportion of loans against urban houses in 1958 as they did at the end of World War II. Moreover, within the government-secured total, most of the growth has centered in VA mortgages. Among financial institutions, mutual savings banks made the most drastic shift into the protected sector of the market; they held two-thirds

TABLE VII-8

FEDERAL GOVERNMENT UNDERWRITING OF NONFARM RESIDENTIAL MORTGAGES, 1945 AND 1958

	Total	Government Underwritten			Conventional
	(Billions of Dollars)	(Percent of Total Held) Total	FHA	VA	(Percent of Total Held)
1958					
Total Outstanding	130.7	40	17	23	60
Financial Institutions	108.2	42	18	24	58
Life insurance companies	26.1	52	24	28	48
Savings and loan associations	42.6	21	5	16	79
Mutual savings banks	20.9	66	26	40	34
Commercial banks	18.6	47	29	18	53
All Other	22.5				
Government agencies	4.8	96	29	67	4
Individuals and other	17.7	12	6	6	88
1945					
Total Outstanding	23.3	19	18	1	81
Financial Institutions	15.8	25	23	2	75
Life insurance companies	3.7	38	38	—	62
Savings and loan associations	5.3	11	9	2	89
Mutual savings banks	3.4	12	12	—	88
Commercial banks	3.4	47	44	3	53
All Other	7.5	8	8	—	92
Government agencies	0.9	—	—	—	100
Individuals and other	6.6	9	9	—	91

SOURCE: Figures for 1958 are from **Business Conditions,** Federal Reserve Bank of Chicago, December, 1959, p. 13; 1945 figures are from Saul B. Klaman, **The Volume of Mortgage Debt in the Postwar Decade.** Technical Paper 13. (New York: National Bureau of Economic Research, 1958.)

of their nonfarm residential loans in this form at the end of 1958, compared with only 12 percent in 1945. Savings and loan associations continue to rely on underwritten mortgages to a far lesser extent than all other lenders except individuals. Life insurance companies and commercial banks were already more heavily committed in protected mortgages at the end of World War II. The banks, however, did not increase their holdings of such mortgages in relation to conventional loans, although they did shift into VA mortgages on a large scale. Life insurance companies, on the other hand, greatly expanded their ownership of federally-guaranteed mortgages as a proportion of their total holdings, and VA loans had outstripped those insured by FHA by the end of 1958.

The full extent of federal government underwriting in the mortgage market is not shown by growth of FHA and VA mortgages. In addition to the agencies administering these programs, two others are also instrumental in providing support to the market. The Federal National Mortgage Association (FNMA), through its trading activities, renders valuable service in making the market much broader and more liquid. Although in the reorganization of 1954 FNMA was charged with maintaining three separate programs (secondary market, special assistance, and management and liquidation of the mortgage portfolio inherited from its previous operations), the secondary market functions are the most important. It attempts to provide liquidity to FHA and VA residential mortgages through buying such obligations when and where funds are scarce and selling them when and where there is a demand for mortgage investments. Because its secondary market activities are based primarily on borrowed funds, the ceiling on its indebtedness imposed by Congress effectively limits the extent of its operations.[11] The FNMA also attempts to discourage excessive use of its facilities by tailoring the prices at which it buys and sells to prevailing market conditions. At the end of 1959, FNMA held $5.5 billion of mortgages, of which 55 percent represented VA loans and the rest FHA mortgages. During the year, it purchased $1.9 billion of mortgages and sold only $5 million. This pattern of transactions reflected the fact that while the demand for mortgages by financial institutions was strong, the availability of funds was somewhat less than it had been in 1958 when sales amounted to three-quarters of the amount of mortgages purchased.

The Federal Home Loan Banks attempt to facilitate the flow of funds into home mortgages by advancing credit to their member institutions. Originally established in 1932 to help rescue distressed home financing institutions by providing a central reservoir of credit, the banks have become an integral part of the mortgage scene. Currently, the membership in the system consists almost entirely of savings and loan associations, although other institutions are eligible. Unlike FNMA, the FHLB do not trade in mortgages. Instead, by making loans to member banks whose funds are invested primarily in mortgages, they enable their members to invest correspondingly more in real estate loans. When the FHLB reduce their advances, the opposite trend develops. Thus, the system is a part of the mechanism which determines the ebb and flow of funds to the mortgage market.

SECTION IV
BUSINESS CYCLES AND PARTICIPATION IN THE POSTWAR MORTGAGE MARKET

As already mentioned, the growing tightness in the capital markets toward the top of each postwar boom had an adverse impact on the mortgage market. In all three cases, the vigorous demand for funds by the business sector generated severe stringency through the capital market, and the brunt of the shortage fell on the mortgage market. The impact was especially hard on the government-underwritten sector where relatively inflexible interest rates hampered the price adjustments necessary if such loans were to compete with other uses of funds. On the other hand, the easy money policies during each of the postwar recessions stimulated an increased flow of funds into mortgages and generated a boom of major proportions in residential construction.

The pattern of credit flows in the mortgage market since the second World War is shown in Charts VII-4 and VII-5. It should be noted that variations in total mortgage flows have centered in residential mortgages on one to four family dwellings. Other types of real estate loans (secured by multifamily dwellings, commercial properties, and farms) have fluctuated only moderately. Within the residential mortgage subsector, the availability of VA loans has been the most volatile. However, a more striking cyclical pattern is that exhibited in the relationship between the net flow of funds into mortgages and corporate securities. Every year in which corporate demand for funds expanded was also a year in which the availability of mortgage funds was sharply reduced. The reverse was also true. Thus, the rate of growth of corporate long-term debt is a strategic factor determining the flow of funds into the mortgage market. When such obligations are available, some lenders (especially life insurance companies) seem, on balance, to prefer them to other types of debt instruments—a preference based mainly on the relatively high yields corporate bonds provide compared with the credit risk which they entail.

As shown in Table VII-9, there were three periods between 1949 and 1959 during which home-building activity registered substantial increases which were sustained for 14 months or more. These periods were 1949-50, 1953-55, and 1958-59.

CHART VII-4

Net Flow of Funds in Selected Sectors of the Capital Market, 1946-1959

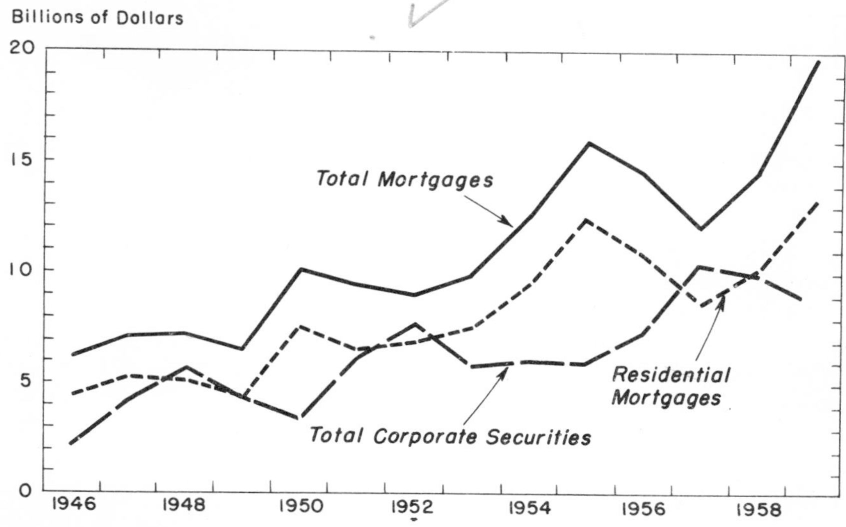

SOURCE: *Federal Reserve Bulletin.*

CHART VII-5

Net Flow of Funds into Residential Mortgages, 1946-1959

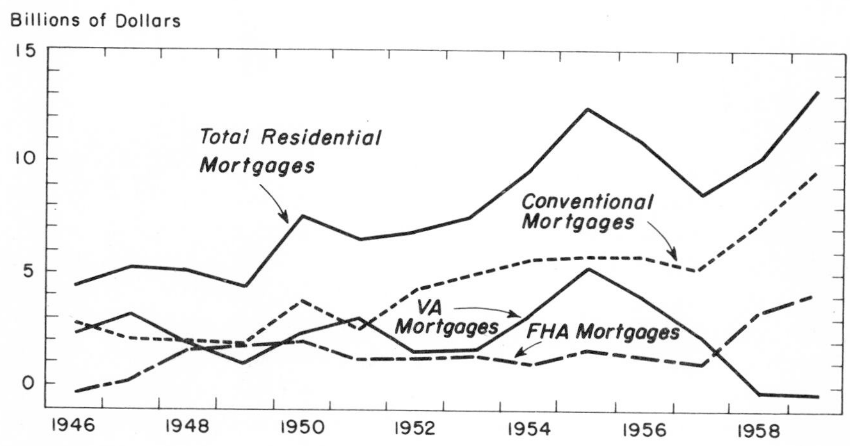

SOURCE: *Federal Reserve Bulletin.*

TABLE VII-9

HOUSING BOOMS IN THE UNITED STATES SINCE WORLD WAR II

Selected Time Periods	Duration in Months	Percentage Increase
New Private Permanent Dwelling Units Started		
I February, 1949-August, 1950	18	90.8
II August, 1953-December, 1954	16	43.3
III February, 1958-April, 1959	14	56.7
Private Residential Construction Expenditures		
I April, 1949-September, 1950	17	79.0
II September, 1953-June, 1955	21	39.7
III April, 1958-May, 1959	14	41.8

SOURCE: U. S. Department of Commerce, **Survey of Current Business.**

A. Investment Behavior During the 1949-50 Housing Boom

A lull in home-building developed in 1947-48 after some of the most urgent housing needs had been met. It was also about this time that Congress realized the potentialities of the VA program and took steps to liberalize terms. This action, combined with the general easing of credit during the first postwar recession, contributed to an upsurge of construction activity which began in the spring of 1949 and reached a climax in September, 1950. In this period, home-building almost doubled; for 1950 as a whole, new housing starts totaled 1,352,000 units—which remains the record for a single year. In both years, single-family dwellings dominated building activity. The boom was facilitated by a vigorous expansion in mortgages; over the two years 1947-48 nonfarm mortgage debt outstanding rose by $15.8 billion and accounted for almost 30 percent of the net increase in total private debt.

The first postwar housing boom was sustained by the interplay of several factors. The backlog of unsatisfied demand for housing (much of it inherited from the Great Depression and World War II) was still large, and this was steadily strengthened by the high rate of household formation. As the recession deepened in early 1949, the monetary authorities further increased bank reserves which, when registered in the capital markets, expanded the availability of funds and reduced the structure of interest rates. For example, high grade corporate bonds receded from the peak of 2.84 percent in November, 1948, to around 2.60 percent a year later and drifted along this floor until mid-1950. In the year ending in November, 1949, yields on long-term United States government bonds were allowed (despite the pegged market) to decline from 2.45 percent to 2.20 percent. This downtrend in yields on corporate and government bonds greatly altered the structure of interest rates, because rates on FHA mortgages were fixed at 4½ percent while those on VA loans were pegged at 4 percent. (See Chart VII-6.) Thus, the differential between mortgage and bond yields widened appreciably, inducing a large-scale swing of lenders into the federally-underwritten sector of the mortgage market. In fact, over 70 percent of the advance in housing starts during 1949-50 were financed by FHA or VA mortgages; the respective shares of these loans were 44 percent and 27 percent and conventional loans accounted for the remaining 29 percent. The willingness of lenders to par-

CHART VII-6

Bond Yields and Mortgage Interest Rates

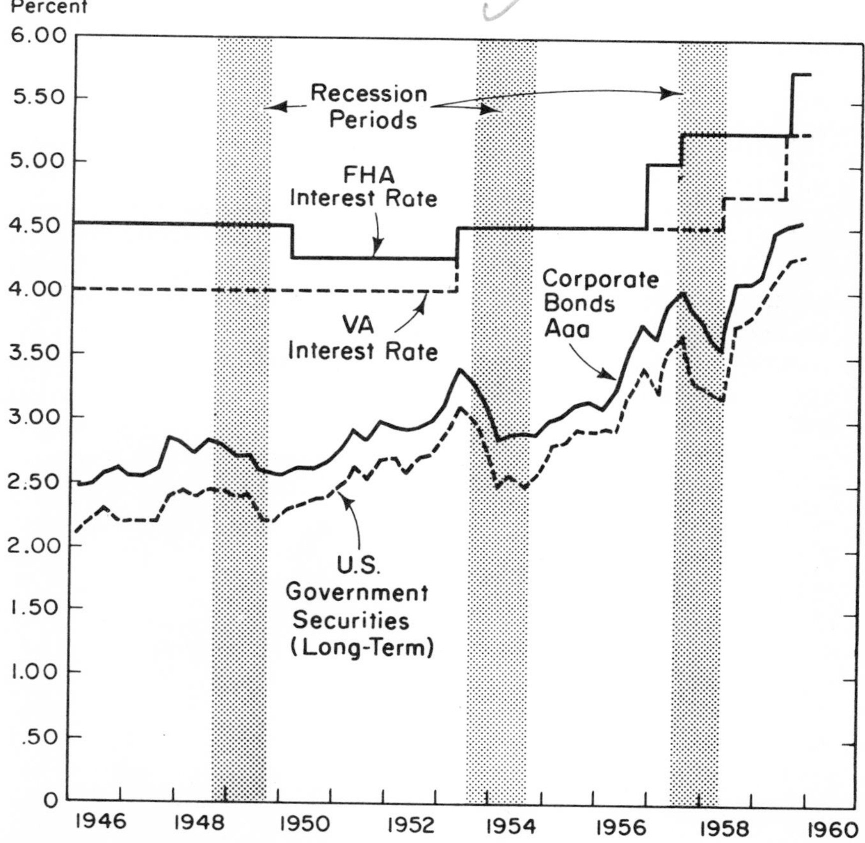

SOURCE: *Federal Reserve Bulletin.*

ticipate more actively in the government-backed part of the market in 1949-50 was enhanced by the expanded role of the FNMA. In July, 1948, Congress enlarged FNMA's authority to purchase VA loans at par and also granted the agency a substantial increase in appropriations. FNMA vigorously entered the market and raised its portfolio of VA mortgages from $11 million in December, 1948, to $1,177 million by the end of 1950. This growth was equivalent to more than one-third of the rise in VA mortgage debt outstanding during the period.

Life insurance companies played a larger role in financing the first postwar housing boom than they have in any other period since World War II. As shown in Table VII-10, they absorbed almost one-third of the net increase in nonfarm mortgages over the two years 1949-50. The rise of $4.9 billion in their ownership of such mortgages was also nearly two-

TABLE VII-10

CHANGES IN NONFARM MORTGAGE DEBT OUTSTANDING, BY TYPES OF HOLDERS, SELECTED PERIODS, 1948-59

(In Millions of Dollars)

Selected Time Periods	Total Outstanding	Held by Financial Institutions: Total	Life Insurance Companies	Savings & Loan Assoc.	Mutual Savings Banks	Commercial Banks	All Other Holders
Postwar Housing Booms							
I December, 1948-December, 1950	15,836	13,326	4,857	3,352	2,445	2,672	2,510
Percent of total	100	84.2	30.8	21.2	15.4	16.8	15.8
II September, 1953-June, 1955	22,025	19,165	4,427	7,947	3,664	3,127	2,860
Percent of total	100	87.0	20.1	36.1	16.6	14.2	13.0
III March, 1958-June, 1959	21,000	16,999	2,442	8,523	2,549	3,485	4,001
Percent of total	100	81.0	11.7	40.6	12.1	16.6	19.0
Other Periods							
I September, 1950-September, 1953	24,529	29,659	6,113	7,459	4,232	2,855	3,870
Percent of total	100	85.0	24.8	30.4	17.2	11.6	15.0
II June, 1955-March, 1958	35,200	28,288	7,805	11,762	5,393	3,328	6,912
Percent of total	100	80.4	22.2	33.4	15.3	9.5	19.6

SOURCE: Saul B. Klaman, **The Volume of Mortgage Debt in the Postwar Decade.** Technical Paper 13. (New York: National Bureau of Economic Research, 1958), pp. 104-5; and **Federal Reserve Bulletin.**

fifths of the gain registered by the leading financial institutions. Moreover, their relative share of the total increase was about twice that for commercial and mutual savings banks and almost 50 percent greater than the proportion accounted for by savings and loan associations. Life insurance companies, however, lagged behind other institutions in their entry into the mortgage market on a large scale during 1949-50. While the total volume of nonfarm mortgages outstanding began to expand rapidly in early 1949, it was only after midyear that these companies began to increase the rate at which they extended real estate loans. While part of the observed lag can be attributed to the delayed acquisition of mortgages for which commitments had been made earlier, it also reflects the demand for funds by the corporate sector which remained relatively strong throughout the first half of 1949. In fact, life insurance companies were actually reducing the rate of acquisition of mortgages over the twelve months beginning with July, 1949, and this apparently was partly attributable to the diversion of funds to the corporate sector. But when life insurance companies did re-enter the mortgage market in the last half of 1950, they expanded their holdings by more than twice the increase during the same months of the previous year.

This shift to mortgages greatly altered the pattern of new investments for these institutions. While nonfarm mortgages represented only one-quarter of the funds they supplied to the capital market in 1947-48, such loans accounted for more than two-fifths of the total in 1949-50. (See Table VII-11.) Furthermore, over three-fifths of the gain centered in federally-underwritten mortgages which had previously been of only minor importance as investment outlets.

The imposition of controls (Regulation X) in the fall of 1950 and the scarcity of building materials during the Korean War dampened activity in the mortgage market in 1951. However, the introduction of Regulation X is reported to have made little difference to life insurance companies.[12] This absence of restraint was due primarily to the heavy backlog of previous commitments which the companies had made in anticipation of government restrictions. The acquisition of FHA and VA mortgages was curtailed in 1951, but the slackening was mainly the result of lessened availability of credit after prices of government securities were unpegged in March of that year. With the abandonment of Regulation X in the spring of 1952, small gains were made in residential construction, and mortgage credit (primarily of the conventional type) advanced moderately. Growing credit stringency after mid-1952 again checked the availability of mortgage funds—despite the increase in the

TABLE VII-11

SELECTED USES OF LIFE INSURANCE FUNDS
DURING THREE POSTWAR HOUSING BOOMS
(In Millions of Dollars)

Selected Time Periods	Total Uses of Funds	Corporate Bonds	Nonfarm Mortgages Total	FHA	VA	Conventional	All Other Uses of Funds
Postwar Housing Booms							
I December, 1948-December, 1950	11,844	4,414	4,857	2,117	920	1,820	2,573
Percent of total	100	37.3	41.0	17.9	7.7	15.4	21.7
II September, 1953-June, 1955	11,366	3,737	4,427	264	1,846	2,317	3,202
Percent of total	100	32.9	38.9	2.3	16.2	20.4	28.2
III March, 1958-June, 1959	8,388	3,019	2,442	997	—	1,445	2,927
Percent of total	100	36.0	29.1	11.9	—	17.2	34.9
Other Periods							
I December, 1950-September, 1953	17,171	7,893	6,113	1,366	1,426	3,321	3,165
Percent of total	100	46.0	35.6	8.0	8.3	19.3	18.4
II June, 1955-March, 1958	18,432	6,488	7,805	931	2,407	4,467	4,139
Percent of total	100	35.2	42.3	5.0	13.1	24.2	22.5

SOURCE: **1951, 1956, 1959, 1960 Life Insurance Fact Book.**

maximum interest rates on FHA and VA loans. Because other long-term rates advanced to record levels in 1952 and early 1953, the appeal of the federally-underwritten real estate loans to life insurance companies and other investors was greatly weakened. Responding to the changing structure of interest rates, life insurance companies channeled almost one-half of their new investments into corporate bonds over the 33 months ending in September, 1953. Although the proportion of their total loan expansion represented by mortgages held up rather well, there was a drastic reduction in the extension of FHA loans. This type of debt accounted for only 8 percent of their total credit outflow or less than one-half of the proportion in the 1949-50 period. On the other hand, the share of funds placed in VA mortgages rose slightly, and the relative share of conventional loans advanced by one-third.

B. Investment Behavior During the 1953-55 Housing Boom

The second postwar recession provided the soil from which sprang the housing boom of 1953-55. The decline in economic activity which began in the summer of 1953 produced a substantial increase in the availability of credit; this was augmented by the Federal Reserve System's easy money policy. Under the combined impact of declining corporate demand for funds and the enlarged supply of bank reserves, interest rates receded at a rapid pace. For example, Aaa corporate bond yields fell from 3.35 percent in June of 1953 to 2.90 percent by March, 1954, and lingered in this neighborhood through the rest of the year. Over the same period, yields on long-term government securities dropped by 50 basis points to 2.50 percent. Because FHA and VA mortgage rates were pegged at 4.50 percent during the entire period, the yield differential between these mortgages and high-grade corporate obligations widened by approximately two-fifths. The response of investors to the increased yield spread was the sharpest registered in the postwar years. Between September, 1953, and June, 1955, nonfarm mortgage debt outstanding rose by $22 billion, and 87 percent of the rise was accounted for by financial institutions.

Late in 1953, the greater availability of finance became evident in the expansion of home-building. During the 16 months, August, 1953–December, 1954, new housing starts rose by 43 percent. Expenditures on residential construction began to rise rapidly in September, 1953, and the advance persisted until June, 1955, by which time the total was 40 percent above the earlier month.

While the annual rate of new housing starts in 1953-55 was the same as in 1949-50, the two housing booms were quite dissimilar. In the expansion of 1949-50, both single and multiple dwelling units rose sharply and relied substantially on FHA, VA, and conventional mortgage financing. In contrast, the 1953-55 boom rested almost entirely on single-family homes, and VA mortgages financed virtually all of the new starts. Several factors help explain the heavy reliance on VA loans. The fact that lenders could obtain cash payments rather than government bonds, in the event of default, created a preference among investors for VA mortgages. However, the liberalization of VA terms seems to have played a larger role. In April, 1953, the VA-guarantee program began to allow no-down payment, 30-year maturity loans; the no-down payment loan also became rather common as veterans were even relieved of closing costs. In contrast, Congress raised maximum maturities on FHA mortgages in August, 1954, and stipulated a down payment of at least 5 percent.

Thus, it is evident that the housing boom of 1953-55 was sustained by roots which extended a considerable distance down the income scale. In fact, the expansion was primarily the result of congressional action to ease the way for poor people to obtain better housing. All of the leading factors which sparked the 1949-50 boom had weakened substantially by 1953. Net household formations had dropped by three-fifths since 1950; the number of married couples without their own household had shrunk by more than three-quarters, and marriages had declined by almost 10 percent. Nevertheless, the potential demand for housing remained strong. Many families had been excluded from the market because down payments were too high and the stringent mortgage terms made it impossible for them to sustain the required monthly payments on the basis of their relatively low incomes. When Congressional action and administrative measures removed the restrictions imposed during the Korean War and further liberalized credit terms on FHA and VA mortgages, these low income families finally had access to the housing market. But this demand remained potential until investors were induced to lend on the more liberal terms. As other interest rates fell steadily until the summer of 1954, the pegged rates on federally-underwritten mortgages became increasingly attractive, and lenders entered the market on a massive scale.

Life insurance companies lingered behind other financial institutions in the expansion of mortgage credit in 1953-55, but the lag was shorter than in the 1949-50 housing boom. By the end of September, 1953, life insurance companies' forward commitments to buy all types of mortgages began to climb. However, commitments for VA mortgages led in a spectacular advance, multiplying nearly twelve times as the total rose from $48 million in the second quarter of 1953 to a peak of $581 million in the third quarter of 1954. In contrast, commitments for FHA mortgages gained only 50 percent between June, 1953, and December, 1954, when the peak of $176 million was reached. (See Charts VII-7 and VII-8 and Table IV-3.) Commitments to buy conventional mortgages fell sharply during the last half of 1953 to $274 million at the year end, a decline of more than one-quarter; a modest rise over the next year barely restored the previous reduction. Life insurance companies' actual acquisition of mortgages did not register an appreciable gain until the spring of 1954, suggesting an average lag of five or six months between commitments and the extension of loans. Once the pace quickened, the companies absorbed mortgages at a rapid rate, and the monthly average of $445 million in 1954 was almost one-quarter above that for the previous year. Moreover, as the heavy commitments made in 1954 were paid off in 1955, the

CHART VII-7

New Commitments of Life Insurance Companies For Residential, Commercial, and Industrial Mortgages, and Corporate Bonds, 4th Quarter, 1952–4th Quarter, 1959

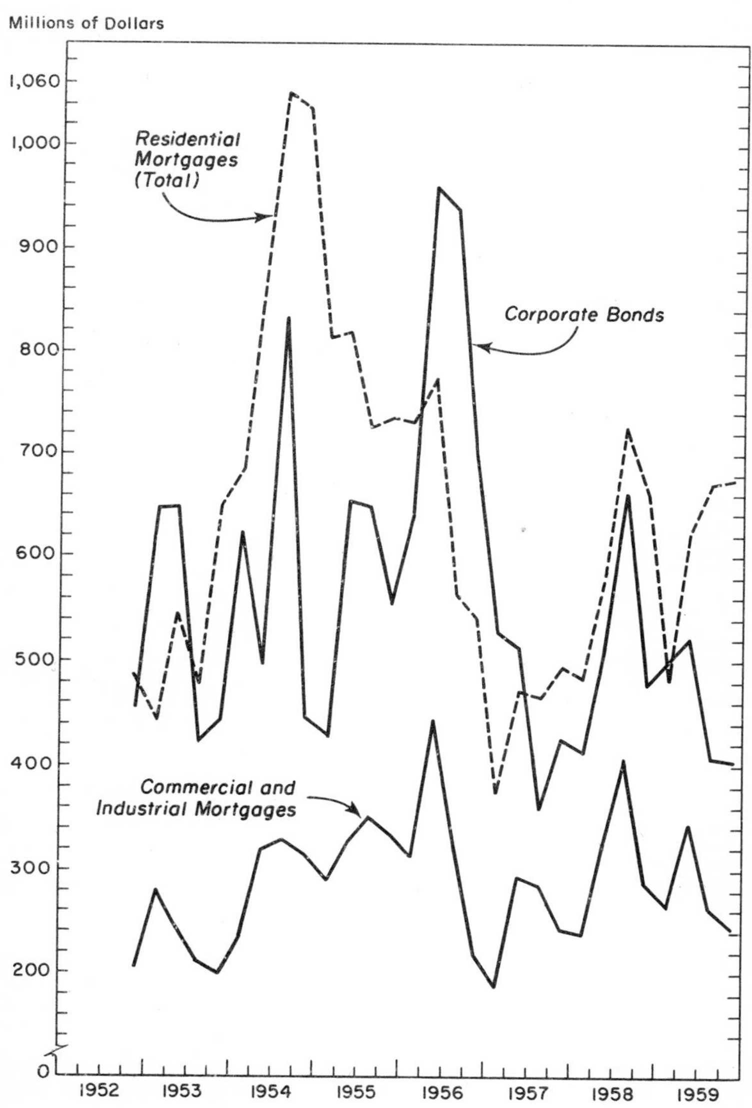

SOURCE: Life Insurance Association of America.

CHART VII-8

New Commitments of Life Insurance Companies for Residential Mortgages, 4th Quarter, 1952–4th Quarter, 1959

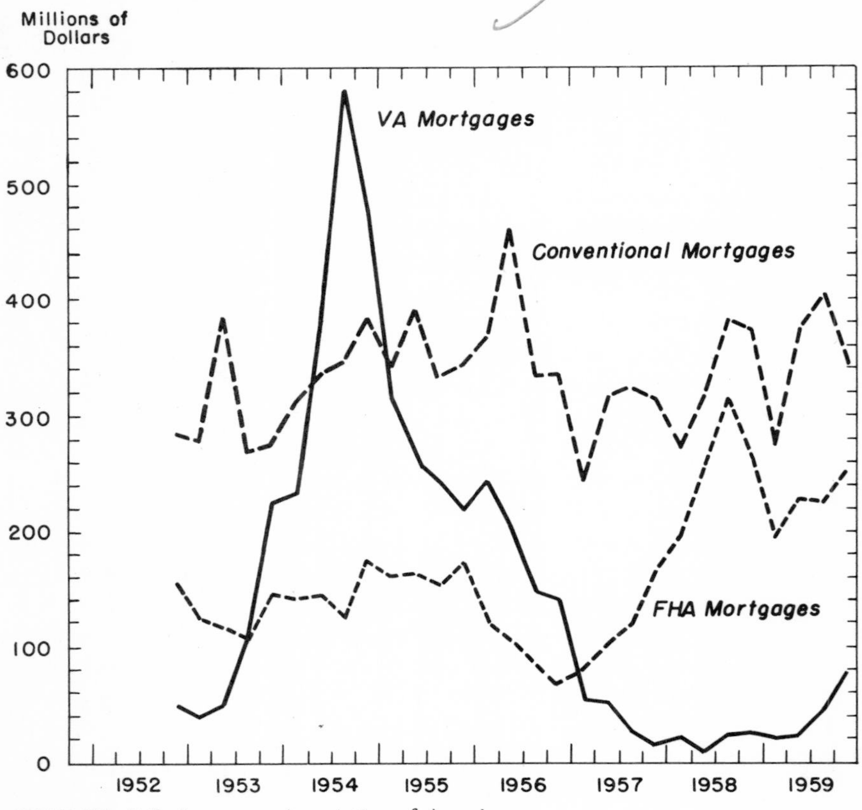

SOURCE: Life Insurance Association of America.

monthly rate of acquisition again rose by one-quarter to an average of $550 million.

Despite the time lag in the expansion of life insurance companies' mortgage lending, they substantially increased their relative share of the market for VA loans during the second postwar housing boom. At the end of 1952, these institutions held $3.3 billion of VA-guaranteed mortgages, representing slightly more than one-fifth of the total outstanding; by December, 1955, their holdings had climbed to $6.1 billion. This gain of $2.8 billion meant that life insurance companies absorbed 28 percent of the net increase in outstanding VA mortgages between 1952 and 1955.

On the other hand, they accounted for a somewhat smaller proportion of the growth in total mortgage debt, and their share in the amount outstanding slipped from 23.3 percent to 21.6 percent. All of the relative loss centered in FHA-insured loans.

Over the more restricted time horizon of September, 1953 to June, 1955, encompassing the main wave of the housing boom, life insurance companies provided about one-fifth of the net increase in mortgage funds, compared with 30 percent in the 1949-50 expansion. The experience of savings and loan associations was almost exactly reversed; they lifted their share of the market from one-fifth to well over one-third. Not all of the gain, however, was at the expense of life insurance companies, because the share of commercial banks also suffered slightly. The role of mutual savings banks was somewhat enhanced.

The vigorous participation of life insurance companies in the mortgage market during this period is clearly evident in the composition of their new investments. (See Table VII-11.) Between September, 1953, and June, 1955, the flow of funds from these institutions amounted to $11.4 billion, and about two-fifths of the total was channeled into the mortgage market. This was approximately the same proportion invested in this fashion during the first postwar housing boom. Nevertheless, behind this total are substantial differences in the types of mortgages acquired. VA-guaranteed loans accounted for over two-fifths of the total in 1953-55, or more than twice the proportion in 1949-50. In the earlier period, FHA represented about two-fifths of the increase in the mortgage portfolio, but in the later boom this dropped sharply to less than 6 percent. The proportion placed in conventional mortgages advanced from around one-third to over one-half of the total. To some extent, the latter growth reflected the fact that interest rates on conventional mortgages, while competitively determined, declined only slightly during the 1953-54 recession and were never subject to the extremely liberal terms offered by the federally-underwritten loans. Consequently, many life insurance companies continued to find conventional mortgages an attractive investment outlet. On the other hand, they relied on conventional loans to a much smaller extent than did savings and loan associations and commercial banks; over three-fourths of the rise in the formers' mortgage holdings centered in conventional loans, while the proportion for the latter institutions was three-fifths. Mutual savings banks, which have concentrated more heavily on FHA and VA mortgages than have other institutions in the postwar years, made virtually all of their new loans in the federally-supported sector of the market.

On balance, life insurance companies remained a major source of mortgage funds in the 1953-55 housing boom, although their participation in the market as a whole was less extensive than in 1949-50. Within the FHA and VA sectors, and especially in the latter, they responded in a vigorous way to the liberal terms designed to improve housing opportunities among the low income groups.

Life insurance companies and other lenders also sought to increase their investment outlets by building up a huge backlog of forward commitments for VA mortgages, which, when fulfilled, caused mortgage flows and construction expenditures to spill over into 1955 and 1956 well after the main phase of the boom had passed. Partly as a result of the housing boom, the composition of aggregate demand shifted drastically. Business investment revived on a substantial scale while consumption remained at high levels. Another period of credit stringency was launched. Open market yields rose at an accelerated rate, and the spread between mortgage returns (especially VA) and other investments narrowed as public utilities and other corporations increased their demands for funds. The earlier patterns in the mortgage market were reproduced: new mortgage commitments of financial institutions declined, terms on mortgage contracts tightened, and the overall availability of funds dropped sharply. Within the market, borrowers able to meet the more rigorous terms of conventional mortgages received a much larger share of credit, while VA loans outstanding began a relative decline which soon became absolute.

C. Investment Behavior During the 1958-59 Housing Boom

The recession which began in the summer of 1957 produced a familiar pattern in the mortgage market. In fact, well before the monetary authorities adopted a policy of easier credit in November, business demand for funds had been receding, and the decline continued well into 1958. Long-term interest rates dropped sharply until February, 1958, when the heavy volume of new flotations (centering in United States government bonds) reversed the trend for a few months. This uncertainty in the government securities market tended to dampen the flow of funds into mortgages during the first quarter of 1958. But with the cessation of sizable Treasury claims on the capital market, lenders turned increasingly to mortgages. The market was further strengthened as a result of the Housing Act of 1958 which increased the resources of the FNMA by $1 billion to be used in buying FHA and VA mortgages at par; moreover, repayment terms were also further liberalized.

These developments, beginning in the spring of 1958, set off a sustained climb in the availability of loanable funds which lasted for about fifteen months. Between March, 1958, and June, 1959, total nonfarm mortgage debt outstanding rose by $21 billion and represented almost one-third of the growth in total private debt. New housing starts, by the time the peak was attained in April, 1959, climbed by 57 percent and closely approached the record set in 1950. Expenditures on new private residential structures, by the time the crest passed in May, 1959, had advanced by 42 percent. This gain was slightly more than that registered in the 1953-55 boom but was somewhat short of that for 1949-50.

Compared with the previous boom, there was a sharp change in the types of mortgages used to finance home construction in 1958-59. In the more recent period, conventional loans supported almost two-fifths of the increase in new housing starts, whereas they made virtually no contribution to the net expansion in 1953-55. The reasons for this heavy reliance on conventional mortgages are rather obscure, but several factors help illuminate the situation. First, savings and loan associations made major gains in resources, and a substantial proportion of these loanable funds was probably channeled into this type of mortgage on which these institutions have traditionally concentrated. Moreover, other lenders also increasingly found conventional mortgages preferable—conventional mortgages afford greater control over terms and typically mature in a shorter period, thus reducing the number of years during which funds are committed. Perhaps of more importance was the effort of many middle- and high-income families to upgrade their housing facilities. While many of these families probably would not have encountered difficulty in making the down payment or sustaining the monthly charges for lower priced homes, a substantial number of them evidently experienced this problem in shifting to more expensive dwellings. This is suggested by the fact that secondary mortgages, land contracts, and other forms of supplemental financing rose sharply in 1958-59. Normally, conventional loans of this type are used by "individuals and others" who are the main sources for such funds. In 1958-59 their mortgage holdings increased by approximately 50 percent over 1957-58, and the gain was more than twice that in the two previous booms.[13]

VA mortgages, which had been the mainstay of the 1953-55 boom, contributed only slightly to the 1958-59 expansion. Exceptionally liberal terms, which greatly stimulated the demand for VA-backed loans in the earlier period, still prevailed, but their overall impact was weakened by a pegged interest rate ceiling considered noncompetitive by lenders. Just before the monetary authorities adopted an easy money policy in November, 1957, the yield spread between Aaa corporate bonds and the 4.50 percent rate on VA mortgages was only 40 basis points, and the latter type of loans were virtually unattainable. Although the decline in the Aaa yield as the recession progressed widened the spread to 1.15 percentage points by June, 1958, many lenders considered the differential as insufficient to warrant investing sizable amounts in VA mortgages. Moreover, despite the fact that VA mortgages could be acquired at large discounts, many of the leading financial institutions chose to stand aside from this sector of the market. Part of their reluctance to employ the discount device to raise the pegged interest rate to a competitive level apparently was due to the desire to avoid congressional criticism and adverse public reaction to a practice generally considered unethical. Builders too were hesitant about accepting large discounts on VA mortgages. The net effect was the virtual disappearance of funds available for investment in VA mortgages.

On the other hand, FHA loans became much more popular and accounted for over two-fifths of the mortgage loans used to finance new housing starts in 1958-59. This increased popularity rested on several factors. As already mentioned, the 1958-59 housing boom, far more than that of 1953-55, reflected the acquisition of relatively high priced single-family homes. Purchasers of these properties have traditionally relied on FHA or conventional financing. In addition, since home buyers under FHA regulations were not legally prohibited from paying more than the FHA appraised price, lenders who wished to engage in discounting found it easier to exact such discounts on FHA loans than on VA mortgages. Finally, throughout 1958 and 1959, FNMA was active in creating a secondary market for mortgages. In these two years, it increased its holdings by almost $1.6 billion, over 80 percent of which represented FHA mortgages.

By the middle of 1959, the third postwar housing boom had passed its crest, and home-building declined during the remainder of the year. Long-term interest rates began to rise again toward the end of 1958, and advanced sharply during most of the following year. As yields climbed to the highest levels experienced since the 1920's, the entire mortgage market began to weaken rapidly. Funds for VA loans were extremely scarce, despite the increase in the maximum interest rate to 5.25 percent in July, 1959. Discounts on 5.25 percent FHA mortgages, which were almost erased in mid-1958, had begun to deepen toward the end of 1958 and became even larger after the VA rate was increased. In an attempt to check the deterioration of FHA loans, the maximum rate was raised to 5.75 percent in September, 1959, but discounts remained substantial until the closing months of that year. With the run-off of much of the backlog of commitments made during the recession, the flow of funds into the government-underwritten sector of the mortgage market began to decline. Reflecting the reduced availability of funds, overall housing activity also eased considerably.

Life insurance companies were a relatively minor source of funds during the 1958-59 housing boom. In fact, the proportion of the new mortgage market garnered by them was little more than one-half that acquired in the 1953-55 boom which in turn was only two-thirds of their share in 1949-50. During the third postwar housing boom, life insurance companies' nonfarm mortgage holdings rose by $2.4 billion and amounted to less than 12 percent of the advance in this type of debt outstanding. Their participation was surpassed (both relatively and absolutely) by all other leading financial institutions.

Several reasons account for this sharply reduced role of life insurance. In the first place, the annual rate of growth in their total assets had been easing since the mid-1950's and this was reflected in the slower increase in their total resources. Part of the lessened rate of growth in their total assets can be attributed to an increase in sales of term insurance and other types of policies involving only slight accumulation of reserves. The pace of growth was also depressed by the increasing tendency of beneficiaries to withdraw policy proceeds for investment in stocks and other types of assets; traditionally a substantial proportion of such funds had been left with insurance companies which added to their loanable resources. Moreover, as their holdings of United States government securities shrank, many life insurance companies became increasingly reluctant to sell these issues to make mortgage loans. In addition, vigorous competition for mortgages by other financial institutions severely limited the amount obtainable by life insurance companies. Among these other lenders, savings and loan associations led the field, accounting for 40 percent of the net expansion in nonfarm mortgage debt. A substantial part of this performance reflected the competitive edge the associations held in the mobilization of savings. For example, in 1958-59, their savings inflow rose by almost one-third compared with 1956-57. Moreover, they were able to supplement their resources by heavy borrowing from the Federal Home Loan Banks.

Reflecting these diverse factors, real estate loans made during the most recent housing boom accounted for a smaller proportion of total lending by life insurance companies than they did in either of the two previous expansions. Such loans represented 29 percent of their total uses of funds in 1958-59, compared with 41 percent and 39 percent, respectively, in 1949-50 and 1953-55. (See Table VII-11.) Furthermore, while they channeled slightly more funds per month into the capital market as a whole in 1958-59 than they did in 1953-55, the rate of investment in mortgages fell by more than two-fifths. On the other hand, corporate bonds were acquired at a monthly rate about 10 percent higher than in the earlier period. The companies' holdings of VA mortgages actually declined moderately as the rising stream of repayments swamped the small volume of new acquisitions. The latter virtually ceased because life insurance companies, perhaps more than any other lenders, were reluctant to engage in the practice of discounting such mortgages to raise their effective yield. Conventional loans accounted for a somewhat larger share of the companies' mortgage acquisitions during 1958-59, advancing by 10 percentage points to almost three-fifths of the total compared with 1953-55. The most striking rise, however, centered in FHA loans. This type of debt represented only 6 percent of the net increase in the companies' mortgage portfolio during the second postwar housing boom but increased to over two-fifths in the third expansion. The shift of life insurance companies to FHA-insured mortgages seems to mirror the special character of the most recent housing upsurge (which was described above) rather than any fundamental change in the institutions' preference for different types of mortgages.

Aside from the slower pace of actual mortgage acquisition by life insurance companies in 1958-59, the companies made a much smaller volume of new commitments, which also indicates a less vigorous response to the growth in demand for real estate loans. (See Charts VII-7 and VII-8 and Table IV-3 above.) Total new commitments of these institutions for residential mortgages amounted to $486 million in the first quarter of 1958 and rose by almost 50 percent to a peak of $722 million in the third quarter of that year. However, over the next six months, new residential commitments declined to the same level from which the advance began. Although a sharp rebound occurred during the remainder of 1959, the year-end level was still well below the peak.

This pattern of new commitments for residential mortgages was quite unlike that for the 1953-55 housing boom. In the earlier period, new commitments for home mortgages rose steadily for a full year and in the third quarter of 1954 amounted to $1,050 million; this increase represented a gain of 110 percent, more than twice that registered in 1958-59. The divergent pattern was primarily due to the diverse behavior of commitments for VA and FHA mortgages during the two housing booms. As already mentioned, the most recent expansion was financed almost wholly by funds secured through FHA and conventional loans, and this fact is clearly reflected in the trend of life insurance companies' new commitments. There was no repetition in 1958-59 of the upsweep in VA commitments recorded in 1953-54. In fact, the decline in VA commitments which began in the last quarter of 1954 continued (with only one interruption) through the second quarter of 1959. At the trough, new commitments to buy VA mortgages amounted to only $9 million compared with $581 million in the third quarter of 1954. During the last half of 1958 and the first half of 1959, new VA commitments lingered between $20 million and $26 million and climbed to $79 million in the closing months of 1959.

In contrast, FHA new commitments, which had been advancing since the fourth quarter of 1956, continued to increase through the third quarter of 1958. In fact, the pace was accelerated between March and September of that year. At the peak such commitments were more than four and one-half times the level from which the rise began. During 1953-55, new FHA commitments fluctuated in the relatively narrow range of $100 million–$176 million. Over the nine months closing with the first quarter of 1959, however, new commitments to lend against FHA mortgages dropped sharply and recovered only moderately during the rest of the year. While new commitments for conventional mortgages displayed a similar V-shaped profile during 1958-59, the amplitude of fluctuation was less than for new FHA commitments. Moreover, the overall pattern was not appreciably different from that sketched in 1953-55. The much greater stability of new conventional commitments, of course, is a reflection of the competitive interest rates on this type of loan compared with the pegged rates on VA and FHA loans.

Another factor which probably had considerable influence on life insurance companies' new mortgage commitments of all types in 1958-59 was the growth of lending opportunities among corporations. New commitments for corporate bonds, which declined sharply from mid-1956 through the third quarter of 1957, increased at approximately the same rate as new commitments for residential mortgages during the first nine months of 1958. In the previous housing boom, the relative decrease in corporate demand for funds was more marked, and the more drastic decline in corporate bond yields made mortgages more attractive as investment outlets. On the other hand, the easing of monetary conditions in late 1957 and early 1958, which helped to generate the 1958-59 housing boom, also induced many corporations (especially public utility firms) to float bond issues which had been postponed during the previous few years of rising interest rates. As some of these borrowers rely heavily on life insurance companies, the latter were increasingly pressed for funds; thus, in many cases the rate of increase in new mortgage commitments in 1958 was held down. This tendency was especially marked during the last quarter of 1958; the new commitments for corporate bonds slackened appreciably after mid-1959, while those for mortgages registered a sharp gain.

Section V
Participation in Mortgage Warehousing

A. Nature of Mortgage Warehousing

In December, 1954, Prudential Insurance Company of America entered into an agreement with Irving Trust Company, New York, (acting as managing agent for a group of commercial banks) which enabled the insurance company to sell up to $350 million of insured and guaranteed mortgages; the agreement contained a provision requiring Prudential to repurchase the mortgages by June 30, 1956.[14] This transaction aroused considerable interest in financial circles and focused attention on a practice which, although at variance with customary views of life insurance companies' investment policies, had been followed for at least a decade. This is the set of financial arrangements known as mortgage warehousing, which is essentially the extension of credit by commercial banks to mortgage lenders. As shown below, life insurance companies are the major nonbank financial institutions participating in these transactions which traditionally had been restricted primarily to mortgage companies. Before examining the statistics, however, a brief discussion of the nature and types of mortgage warehousing will provide an appreciation of the reason why Federal Reserve System officials and certain state banking authorities were critical of some aspects of the practice during 1955.

As in other types of lending, mortgage warehousing arrangements have assumed a variety of forms which make it difficult to discover uniformities in the practice. Despite the complexities of particular mortgage warehousing contracts, it is possible to identify two basic types of commercial bank loans backed by real estate mortgages as collateral: These are essentially production loans, on the one hand, and inventory loans on the other. The basis of this distinction will be clear from the following analysis.

A critical point to keep in mind is that virtually all mortgages involved in warehousing arrangements are FHA-insured and VA-guaranteed, both of which have acquired a collateral status with respect to commercial bank loans which conventional mortgages do not enjoy.[15] Secondly, in a housing development project, no insured or guaranteed mortgage is available until the construction has actually been completed and approved by FHA or VA. Thus, a considerable financial outlay must be undertaken before the mortgage is written and must be borne by someone for a period ranging from nine to twelve months. It is clear, then, that the demand for funds in this instance derives primarily from the production process. To provide the required credit, commercial banks developed a type of lending known as uncommitted mortgage warehousing.

Essentially, this practice consists of a commercial bank extending a loan to a builder with a real estate mortgage as collateral. In making the loan, the bank does not commit itself to purchase the mortgage; however, the bank does set a price on it well below that prevailing in the market. For example, it was reported that over a period of approximately five years, the Chase Manhattan Bank of New York made mortgage loans of this type in amounts ranging from 90 to 97.5 percent of the principal, and which also entailed transaction fees varying from three-quarters of 1 percent to 1.5 percent.[16]

In general, uncommitted mortgage warehousing operates as follows: A builder approaches a mortgage originator (also called mortgage banker or correspondent), submits to him an overall plan for the construction of a group of houses, and arranges the financing of the project with the originator. Several intermediate steps are involved in the process. First, the construction financing is usually undertaken by a bank or other lender near the location of the project. In each instance, the local supplier of funds requires assurance that, once the construction is completed, the loan will be liquidated. The originator takes steps to see that an ultimate market will exist for the mortgage once the house has been completed and sold. This final market rests with life insurance companies and other long-term investors, and it is to these institutions that originators must turn as outlets for their mortgages. While sale to long-term investors is being arranged, the mortgage lies temporarily in a warehouse—the commercial bank.

Another type of mortgage warehousing also related to the purely technical requirements of real estate financing is known as a committed line. This is perhaps the earliest form of mortgage warehousing and operates as follows. A mortgage originator may have obtained from a long-term investor a definite commitment to purchase at a future date a determined dollar amount of mortgages. Before the final investor can obtain the actual mortgages, numerous legal and technical details must be settled with respect to each piece of property. Most life insurance companies and a large number of other investors prefer to reduce the volume of work required by having mortgage correspondents retain the mortgages until a sufficiently large stock has been accumulated. The time required to complete this process may take from one to five or six months, depending on the activity in the particular area.

Few mortgage-originating companies have funds that they can tie up for several months in carrying these mortgages until the package is accepted and paid for by the ultimate investor. Therefore, the original committed mortgage warehouse loan was devised. Under this plan the mortgage originator pledged to a commercial bank the documents securing a particular loan, against which a commitment to purchase the mortgage at a future date had been obtained from a life insurance company or other investor. Thus, the commercial bank carried the loan until final delivery and payment were made. Loans of this type are usually made in an amount determined by the commitment of the permanent investor. For example, if the commitment is at par, the bank loan will be at par or with only a slight margin; if the commitment is less than par, the loan in turn will be made at that figure or again with a slight margin.

From the above discussion, it should be clear that mortgage warehousing arrangements arising from the legal and technical requirements of construction financing are nothing more than special types of short-term business loans of the kind usually extended by commercial banks. The role of the life insurance companies and other long-term investors is only incidental to the process, even though in both the committed and uncommitted contracts the actual mortgage price established by the bank for the purpose of the loan depends partly upon the strength of the pledge given by the final mortgage holder.

It was not this financing procedure, however, which evoked the concern of the monetary authorities. Their opinion of technical warehousing or real estate production loans was stated by Allen Sproul, former President of the Federal Reserve Bank of New York:

> My cautionary talks with some of the commercial banks in this community . . . related to possible abuses in the use of bank credit . . . not to the appropriate and customary uses of bank credit in financing the home building industry. . . . So far as individual situations are concerned, the banks to which I talked presumably know the difference between the customary and proper short-term uses of commercial bank credit in helping to finance the home building industry and the possible abuses of such financing which some of them had reported to me. . . .[17]

The possible abuses which Mr. Sproul had in mind sprang from a type of commercial bank mortgage financing involving long-term lenders directly. The agreement between Prudential Insurance Company and Irving Trust mentioned at the beginning of this section is a typical example of the point at issue. The best description of the motivations behind this arrangement is provided by the following excerpt from a statement by an official of Prudential:

> The money available to the Prudential for investment each year (arises) as a result of the receipts from premiums on policies and contracts, and amortizations and interest payments on existing investments. Each year, there is allocated a certain percentage of this income to the mortgage loan department for new loans. An allocation is also made to our bond investment department.
>
> In the early part of 1954, mortgage-loan authorizations and mortgage-loan disbursements were well within the amount of money available and allocated for new mortgage loans. This was because the demand for mortgage funds during that period was somewhat limited and our mortgage-loan commitments and disbursements were running at a rate considerably below the amount necessary in order to take care of investible funds.
>
> However, shortly after the middle of the year, mortgage-loan commitments mounted rapidly and in the latter part of September we advised our field force that it would be necessary to curtail the volume of new business. Once new business starts to flow in rapidly, and there is a great demand for mortgage money, it takes some time to slow it down and, as a result, new loan approvals which during the first 6 months of 1954 amounted to only $480 million, as of December 1, 1954, had reached $1,234 million. Average approvals during the first 6 months of 1954 were $80 million a month. During the next 5 months they averaged $151 million a month, and the forecasts for the month of December were another $125 million.
>
> In as much as most of the loans approved in the latter part of any year are not disbursed until the following year, it appeared that we would have on our books commitments for approximately $700 million of mortgage loans for disbursement after January 1, 1955, and incidentally, that is about twice what we consider normal. We have been running about $350 million a year, and that amount increases a little each year as our funds available for investment increase, and that is as compared with an allocation of $700 million for new mortgages for the entire year of 1955. It could be seen, therefore, that because of the money for which we were committed, it would not be possible during 1955 to commit any further loans for 1955 disbursement. This would mean partial withdrawal from our normal mortgage-lending activities.
>
> One of the considerations affecting our decision to enter into this agreement was a projection of Prudential investible income for the next several years which indicated that we could absorb the $700 million of commitments outstanding in a period of approximately two years, without materially affecting our normal future commitments for new mortgages during that period. For example, during the year 1955 there was allocated for new mortgage investments in the United States $700 million, whereas in 1956 there has been allocated for the same purpose $900 million.[18]

From the above quotation, it is evident that the type of arrangement into which Prudential entered results in commercial bank financing of mortgage inventories owned by a life insurance company. The case is clearly one in which a long-term investor concluded that in the future the supply of mortgages would be relatively smaller than at the time the decision was made and that, in the face of the continued increase in the supply of investment funds, mortgage prices were likely to rise, causing interest rates to fall. The immediate result of the Prudential arrangement was an increase in the availability of funds to finance FHA and VA mortgages; this served to support the prices of these mortgages to some extent but it also tended to hold down interest rates on conventional loans. At the same time, there apparently was an increase in the share of total mortgages obtained by the life insurance companies in general—and by Prudential in particular.

Fundamentally, there is no practical difference between this situation and speculation in commodity inventories, and the consequences are also similar. This type of mortgage warehousing tends to create a temporary expansion in the supply of mortgage funds which contributes to an unsustainable bulge in residential construction. As with other types of inventory accumulations, when the rate of growth of the stock slows down (in this case the stock is the volume of bank-financed mortgages), a depressive effect is exerted on spending. There is some indication that the rapid expansion of residential construction during 1955 in excess of the growth of long-term savings was partly made possible through the use of commercial bank credit obtained by the latter's acquisition of mortgages on the basis of repurchase agreements with life insurance companies and other investors. As construction costs rose, the Federal Reserve System, along with federal housing officials, took steps to curtail the mortgage expansion. It was reported that many building ventures backed only by standby commitments were caught in this credit squeeze. Subsequently, numerous standby prices, which had looked like bargains twelve months earlier, were only accepted by builders and correspondents because no other permanent investors could be found. Furthermore, many long-term investors had to take loans from their warehouse inventory that could have been bought more cheaply currently.[19]

B. Significance of Life Insurance Companies' Participation

Some indication of the quantitative significance of life insurance companies in mortgage warehousing is given by statistics on credit extended by banks to real estate mortgage lenders. These data, shown in Table VII-12, are obtained through periodic surveys by the Federal Reserve System of weekly-reporting member banks. The surveys were initiated in 1955 when mortgage warehousing practices were causing much concern. According to these data, life insurance companies were major beneficiaries of mortgage warehousing arrangements during the 1953-55 housing boom but since then their participation has become insignificant.

TABLE VII-12

CREDIT EXTENDED BY BANKS[1] TO REAL ESTATE MORTGAGE LENDERS

(In Millions of Dollars)

Item	Outstanding				Increase or Decrease (-)		
	Feb. 11, 1959	Aug. 13, 1958	Aug. 10, 1955	Aug. 11, 1954	Aug. 13, 1958 to Feb. 11, 1959	Aug. 10, 1955 to Aug. 13, 1958	Aug. 11, 1954 to Aug. 10, 1955
Real Estate Mortgage Loans Purchased Under Resale Agreement From:							
Insurance companies	28	22	235	4	6	−213	231
Mortgage companies	129	92	90	44	37	2	50
Other lenders[2]	62	63	12	4	−1	51	8
Total	219	177	338	52	42	−161	286
Other Loans to Real Estate Mortgage Lenders							
Insurance companies	20	17	15	14	3	2	1
Mortgage companies	1,176	905	935	489	271	−30	446
Other lenders[2]	136	110	119	51	26	−9	68
Total	1,332	1,032	1,069	554	300	−37	515
Total Loans to Real Estate Mortgage Lenders							
Insurance companies	48	39	250	18	9	−211	232
Mortgage companies	1,305	997	1,025	533	308	−28	492
Other lenders[2]	198	173	131	55	25	42	76
Total	1,551	1,209	1,406	606	342	−197	800
Unused Portions of Firm Mortgage Commitments							
Insurance companies	31	22	183	n.a.	9	−161	—
Mortgage companies	543	499	894	n.a.	44	−395	—
Other lenders[2]	205	152	219	n.a.	53	− 67	—
Total	779	673	1,296	n.a.	106	−623	—

1. Weekly reporting member banks of the Federal Reserve System.

2. Savings and loan associations, mutual savings banks, builders, and other organizations (other than banks) that make or hold substantial amounts of real estate loans.

n.a. = not available.

SOURCE: **Federal Reserve Bulletin,** December, 1955, p. 1323; March, 1959, p. 255.

During the twelve months August, 1954 to August, 1955, total bank loans to real estate mortgage lenders rose by $800 million, of which $232 million (or 29 percent) represented the expansion of loans to life insurance companies. Three-fifths of the growth was accounted for by mortgage companies, the traditional users of such credit; however, this proportion seems relatively small because these borrowers had received almost 90 percent of the loans to real estate mortgage lenders which were outstanding in August, 1954. The passing of the housing boom in 1955 also induced a decline in loans to real estate mortgage lenders. The spurt in housing in 1958-59 stimulated renewed expansion in such loans, but the advance fell far short of the more than twofold growth which had occurred in 1953-55.

Perhaps of more interest from the point of view of the present discussion is the share of life insurance companies in the expansion of commercial bank loans to real estate lenders under repurchase agreements. During the year ending August, 1955, these loans rose by $286 million although only $52 million had been outstanding a year earlier. About four-fifths of the increase, or $231 million, centered in loans to life insurance companies which in August, 1954, had borrowed only $4 million against mortgages under repurchase agreements. Over the ensuing three years, most of these loans were repaid as life insurance companies withdrew mortgages as required by the repurchase contracts, and by August, 1958, the amount outstanding had dwindled to $22 million. Although the 1958-59 housing boom undoubtedly brought pressure on some life insurance companies to scout for additional loans to meet commitments in excess of the normal inflow of funds, as a group they resorted to commercial banks on only a modest scale. Nevertheless, these institutions continue to participate in mortgage warehousing through repurchase agreements to a greater extent than any other group of nonbank financial intermediaries.

While the emphasis in this discussion has been placed on the possibility of temporary over-expansion in residential construction because of commercial banks' warehousing of mortgage loans, the practice, on balance, is probably a beneficial development. Such a credit device can even out the flow of funds into the mortgage market while at the same time permitting savings institutions to plan their mortgage investments systematically. The flow of funds into the mortgage market and the supply of available mortgages are imperfectly synchronized. In contrast with the general regularity of incoming mortgage payments available for reinvestment by life insurance companies and other long-term lenders, new savings respond to seasonal variations as well as to unpredictable influences. On the mortgage supply side, residential building has a seasonal pattern of its own, besides exhibiting long and pronounced cyclical fluctuations. The demand for mortgages may temporarily slacken when life insurance companies and other institutions, in order to meet their forward commitments, are under pressure to sell securities at a discount in an unfavorable market. Under such circumstances, many companies prefer to wait out the market for a better opportunity to sell, rather than to take immediate losses. Clearly then, there is a need for a balancing mechanism to coordinate the demand with the supply of mortgages. Mortgage warehousing, when conducted within limits set by judicious portfolio management, can serve this function.

SECTION VI
INVESTMENT ACTIVITIES IN THE FARM MORTGAGE MARKET

Life insurance companies provided the largest institutional market for farm mortgages in the postwar period. They moved far ahead of commercial banks, which are their traditional institutional rivals in this part of the mortgage market, and won a sizable piece of the market share relinquished by federal lending agencies. At the end of 1959, life insurance companies held $2.8 billion of farm mortgages, representing over one-fifth of the amount outstanding. (See Table VII-13.) Moreover, their farm mortgage holdings rose by $2.0 billion (or by 175 percent) during the fourteen years ending in 1959. This expansion lifted their farm mort-

TABLE VII-13

FARM MORTGAGE DEBT OUTSTANDING, BY TYPE OF HOLDER, SELECTED YEARS, 1920-59

(In Millions of Dollars)

Holder	1920	1930	1940	1945	1950	1955	1959
Federal Agencies	294	1,202	2,755	1,502	1,211	1,759	2,772
Federal Land Banks	294	1,202	2,010	1,079	947	1,481	2,335
Federal Farm Mortgage Corporation	—	—	713	239	44	—	—
Farmers Home Adm.	—	—	32	184	220	278	437
Private Lenders	8,095	7,729	3,746	3,258	4,860	7,307	9,519
Life insurance companies	975	2,057	899	776	1,327	2,273	2,844
Commercial banks	1,204	997	534	521	968	1,297	1,588
Individuals and misc.	5,916	4,675	2,313	1,961	2,565	3,737	5,087
Total	8,389	8,931	6,501	4,760	6,071	9,066	12,291

SOURCE: U. S. Department of Agriculture, **Agricultural Finance Review**, XX, Supplement, December, 1958, p. 4.
"The Balance Sheet of Agriculture," **Federal Reserve Bulletin**, August, 1960, p. 855.

gage portfolio from 1.8 percent to 2.5 percent of their total assets. While the gain amounted to only 6.2 percent of the rise in the value of mortgages owned by these institutions, it accounted for 28 percent of the increase in total loans outstanding against farm real estate. Life insurance companies also made two-thirds of the net extensions of farm mortgage loans advanced by the leading financial intermediaries between 1945 and 1959, although they held less than three-fifths of the farm real estate debt held by these institutions at the end of World War II. Yet the revival of farm mortgage lending on a large scale by life insurance companies during the postwar period simply restored them to the relative position they had occupied in this sector of the capital market in 1930.

A. Participation in the Farm Mortgage Market Before World War II

Over the decade of the 1920's, life insurance companies and the Federal Land Banks were virtually the only expanding sources of farm mortgage credit. The collapse of agricultural prices and land values in mid-1920 launched a malady destined to linger throughout the interwar period. As the disease crept over the land, the structure of mortgage debt was progressively weakened. Fighting to avoid liquidation, many farmers borrowed against their dwindling real estate equity to pay maturing short-term loans, and such refunding was the primary cause in the rise of farm mortgage debt to a peak of $10.8 billion in 1923. By 1930, farm mortgage debt had shrunk to $8.9 billion, and most of the decline reflected foreclosures with numerous lenders absorbing losses.[20] While the total farm mortgage debt rose by $542 million (about 6 percent) over the decade of the 1920's, both commercial banks and individuals reduced their holdings by approximately one-fifth. In fact, the heavy commitment in defaulted farm mortgages was undoubtedly a major factor underlying the failure of almost 5,000 state and national banks in villages and cities of less than 10,000 population between 1921 and 1929. Farm foreclosures would have been much greater in number if the Federal Land Banks had not substantially increased their mortgage lending. By 1930, their holdings had climbed to $1.2 billion; this amount was more than four times that held in 1920 and raised their share of the total farm real estate debt to 14 percent compared with 4 percent at the beginning of the decade.

But, as already mentioned, life insurance companies supplied the bulk of the funds advanced against farm mortgages in the 1920's. The increase of $1.1 billion in their farm mortgage portfolio was about twice the net expansion in the total outstanding. Thus, a sizable proportion of the farm mortgage debt was shifted from individuals and commercial banks to life insurance companies. However, because of the general deterioration in the farm economy, a large part of the expansion in the companies' farm mortgage holdings actually consisted of poor quality loans. This conclusion can be inferred from changes in farm mortgage debt in relation to supporting factors such as farm income and real estate values. For example, in 1920 mortgage interest payments were 4 percent of gross income from farm production, but the ratio had climbed to 5.8 percent by 1930. (See Chart VII-9.) During the same period, the ratio of mortgage debt to the value of all farms rose from 11.8 percent to 20.9 percent. The advance in the ratio reflected both an increase of 6.5 percent in total farm mortgage debt outstanding and a decrease of 28 percent in the total value of farm lands and buildings.[21]

The lingering sickness which sapped the strength of the agricultural sector in the 1920's became epidemic in the next decade and swept through the entire economy. The index of farm prices fell from 139 in 1928 to 57 in 1932. Net income realized by farmers, which had averaged $5.7 billion during the years 1923-29, shrank to $1.9 billion in 1932. While mortgage interest payments declined slightly after 1929, the sharp reduction in farm income raised the ratio to 27 percent in 1932. In these circumstances, many farmers could no longer survive while others survived with the utmost difficulty. Foreclosures and assignments to lenders rose from 15.7 per thousand farms in 1929 to 38.8 per thousand in 1932.[22] The incidence would have been even greater except for large-scale refinancing by private and government lending agencies.

In the federal government's campaign against the Great Depression, numerous battles were fought in the farm sector. A major effort was devoted to bolstering the financial structure in agriculture. New government capital was poured into the Federal Land Banks; regional agricultural credit corporations were launched, and emergency funds were made available through crop and feed loans. Moreover, the Farm Credit Act of 1933 provided for direct government mortgage loans to farmers unable to meet the standards of the Federal Land Banks. These financial measures, combined with direct controls on farm production and marketing, price controls, parity payments, etc., contributed to increased stability in agriculture during the last half of the 1930's. Net farm income averaged between $4 and $5 billion, but even the highest annual income in this period was only one-half the peak of $9.3 billion registered in 1919.

By 1940, farm mortgage debt amounted to $6.5 billion, a decrease of

CHART VII-9

Farm Real Estate Debt and Its Relation to the Value of Farm Real Estate, 1940-1959

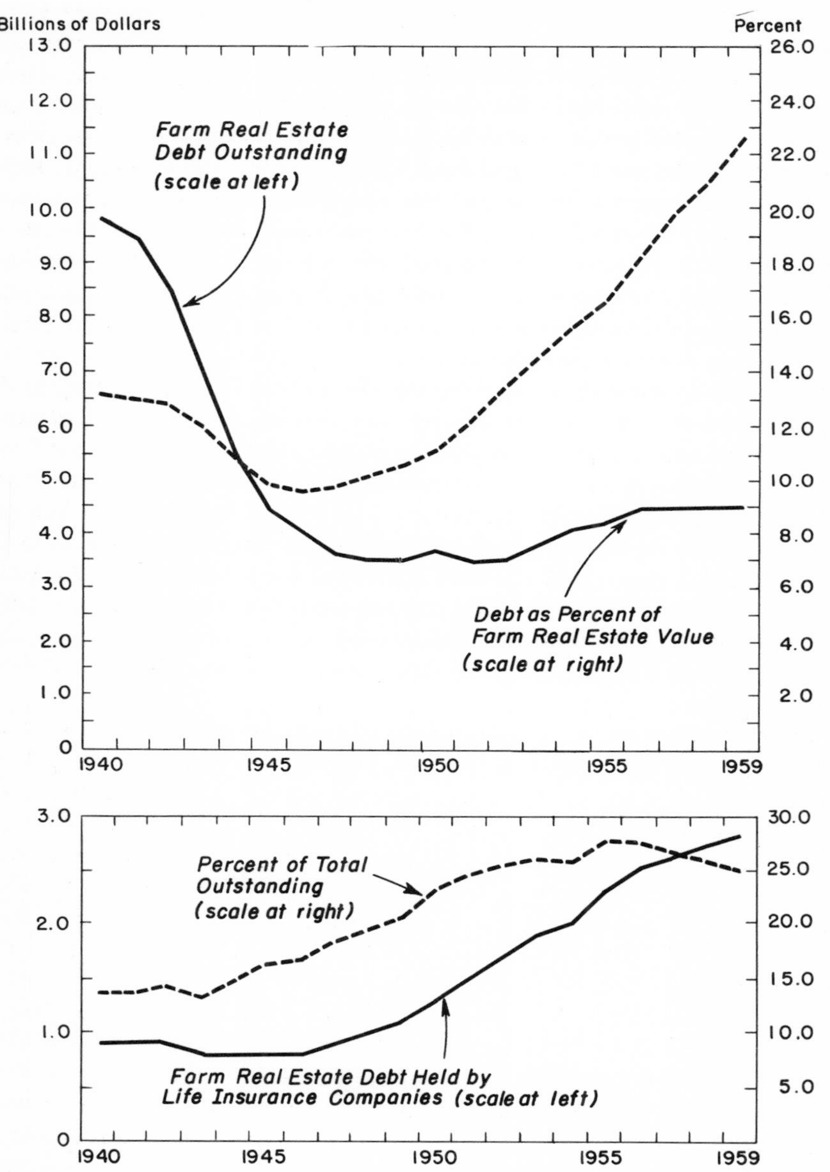

SOURCE: U. S. Department of Agriculture, Bureau of Agricultural Economics, *Impact of the War on the Financial Structure of Agriculture,* 1945; *Federal Reserve Bulletin; 1960 Life Insurance Fact Book.*

more than one-quarter over the previous ten years. Nevertheless, almost the same proportion (39 percent) of all farms in the country were mortgaged in 1940 as in 1930 (42 percent), and most of the percentage decrease probably reflected foreclosures rather than mortgage repayments. However, the distribution of the mortgage debt among holders had changed drastically in favor of federal agencies. These agencies held over two-fifths of the total in 1940; about three times the proportion in 1930. This sharp change was the result of the gigantic rescue operations undertaken during the depression. The Federal Land Banks expanded their mortgage loans by two-thirds, and in 1940, two new agencies, the Federal Farm Mortgage Corporation and the Farmers' Home Administration, had farm mortgages outstanding amounting to $713 million and $32 million, respectively. In fact, because federal farm mortgage credit expanded against the downtrend in the total volume of such loans, the impact of federal lenders on the market as a whole was even greater than indicated by these statistics. All types of private lenders reduced by $4.0 billion the amount of funds supplied to the farm mortgage sector of the capital market during the 1930's. Among these, the decrease was heaviest for individuals who liquidated about one-half of the mortgages they held in 1930. The reduction of $2.4 billion accounted for three-fifths of the total cutback—although they held only slightly more than one-half of the farm debt in 1930. Farm mortgages outstanding at commercial banks at the end of 1940 were $463 million less than ten years earlier. This was equivalent to a drop of 46 percent.

Life insurance companies liquidated almost three-fifths of their farm mortgages during the Great Depression. At the end of 1940 they had $899 million of such loans outstanding compared with $2.1 billion at the close of 1930. The reduction of $1.2 billion amounted to 30 percent of the decrease in farm mortgages held by private lenders; thus life insurance companies also relinquished a relatively large share of the mortgage market during the depression because they held 23 percent of the total debt in 1930. In 1940, farm real estate loans were only 15 percent of the mortgage portfolio of these institutions in contrast to 27 percent at the beginning of the decade. As a proportion of their total assets, such mortgages fell from 11 percent to 3 percent. The decline in the ratio was due partly to the absolute decrease in farm mortgage loans outstanding as well as to the reduced willingness of life insurance companies to lend against increasingly risky farm properties. On the other hand, a substantial share of the observed shrinkage in their mortgage holding was actually offset by a sizable rise in their ownership of farm real estate acquired through foreclosures. For example, at the end of 1940, life insurance companies owned $2.1 billion of real estate, and $658 million, or almost one-third of the total, represented farm properties. In 1930, they held only $548 million of real estate, of which farms constituted an insignificant fraction.[23] Moreover, the pre-World War II peak of $2.2 billion in real estate owned outright was set in 1938, and farms accounted for close to two-fifths of the total. Until they were resold as required by most state insurance laws, life insurance companies were usually able to rent these properties.

B. World War II Experience

No substantial headway was made in the disposal of these properties until World War II. The war years brought record prosperity to agriculture as well as to the rest of the economy. The unprecedented demand for farm output coincided with generally favorable weather, and by 1944 farm production was one-quarter above the 1940 level.[24] Despite the slower pace in 1945 as a whole, production was still 22 percent higher than that registered five years earlier. Prices received by farmers more than doubled during the war years; and while production costs rose sharply, farmers' net income was almost three times the amount realized in 1940. Thus, farmers were able to strengthen their financial position, Total farm assets rose from $53 billion in 1940 to $93 billion in 1945, and the largest share of the gain centered in assets other than real estate—although the value of the latter rose by $20 billion. Farmers' financial assets rose about three times and amounted to $12.5 billion at the end of 1945. Yet actual savings by farmers were even greater, because owners' equities rose from $43 billion to $85 billion over the war years. Non-real estate debt was unchanged over the period, but farm mortgages were reduced by $1.7 billion.[25]

The decreases in outstanding farm mortgage debt were widely distributed among holders, but more than 70 percent centered in federal lending agencies with Federal Land Banks accounting for about twice the proportion of other agencies. Among private lenders, individuals reduced their holdings in absolute terms somewhat more than financial institutions. However, because of the large drop in mortgage loans at federal agencies, all private lenders came out of the war with a bigger share of the market than they had in 1940. Individuals increased their relative share of the market from just over one-third to more than two-fifths. Life insurance companies and commercial banks registered only modest proportionate gains, and their holdings were, respectively, 16 percent and 11 percent of the total outstanding at the end of World War II.

C Investment Behavior in the Postwar Farm Mortgage Market

From the low point of $4.8 billion in 1946, farm mortgage debt rose consistently through 1959 by which date it was $12.3 billion. The rate of growth accelerated appreciably after 1950 and was especially sharp during the five years ending in 1959. Simultaneously, there was a significant realignment among mortgage lenders over the postwar period as a whole and within the three sub-periods demarcated by the substantially different growth rates mentioned above. However, before exploring the changing competitive position of lenders in the postwar farm mortgage market, it would be helpful to examine briefly the major factors underlying the demand for farm real estate loans.

Prices received by farmers, reflecting the continued strong demand (foreign as well as domestic) for agricultural output, continued to rise through the early postwar years. Realized net income of farm operators hit a record of $16.8 billion in 1947, an amount more than one-third above that registered during the last year of World War II. Because of the continued progress of technological changes in agriculture, many farmers found it increasingly possible to handle larger acreages as a means of expanding output and income. Their relatively large holdings of liquid assets (which in 1949 were more than one-quarter higher than in 1945) enabled them to translate this desire into a strong demand for farm real estate; by 1949 the aggregate value of farm land totaled $76.6 billion, an appreciation of over two-fifths compared with the value in 1945. After 1947, farmers were caught between declining prices for output and rising costs of production, and realized net income by the end of 1950 had fallen back to the level attained in 1945. This sharp decrease in farm income caused a reduction in farm real estate prices. The value of farm land was reduced slightly, but the decline was short and not severe. Nevertheless, this change marked the culmination of the first phase of the postwar market for such real estate. Apparently a large proportion of land transfers during this period was financed out of liquid assets because only moderate use was made of mortgage credit. By 1949, farm mortgage debt outstanding totaled $5.3 billion, a gain of slightly more than 10 percent from the trough reached in 1946.

The outbreak of the Korean War in mid-1950 brought renewed, although temporary, prosperity to agriculture. Prices received by farmers rose sharply during the last half of the year and reached an all time record in 1951. While farm costs also rose substantially during the same period, net income by the end of 1951 was 16 percent above that of the previous year. The advance in income stimulated a sharp rise in land values which subsided in 1952 as farm income began a steady slide which lasted without interruption until 1958. However, the index of farm real estate value turned up in 1954 and was still rising steadily through the close of 1959. When measured from March 1 to March 1, the value of farm land increased 3 to 8 percent annually from 1954 through 1959 and registered a total advance of almost one-third. The largest annual rise during the period was 8 percent in 1958—a rise partly generated by the jump of 19 percent (to $13.1 billion) in farmers' realized net income.[26]

Among the factors powering the rise in farm real estate values (against the general downtrend in farm income), two seem to have been of considerable importance. Increased competition among farmers to enlarge their operations placed heavy pressure on the relatively fixed supply of land. For example, the United States Department of Agriculture reported that in 1959 somewhat over two-fifths of all land purchases were made to expand farm size compared with only one-quarter of the total in 1950-53.[27] The incentive to enlarge acreage apparently sprang primarily from the desire to take advantage of rapidly improving technology as increased mechanization and bigger machines permitted farmers to manage larger acreages. The increased scale of production was, in many cases, the most convenient way to maintain farm income in the face of rising costs and falling prices for output.

The growing demand for land for nonfarm purposes also exerted pressure on real estate values. While the United States Department of Agriculture, in constructing the index of real estate values, attempts to minimize the effects of sales of farm land for nonfarm uses, such an impact cannot be eliminated entirely. The spreading of urban areas, road building, industrial expansion, flood control, and similar projects shaved a sizable share of the stock of farm land during the 1950's. Moreover, many people seem to have purchased farm land in an effort to hedge against inflation and this too was a further source of stimulation to farm real estate values. Toward the end of the 1950's, some of these pressures were weakening, but apparently few observers expected an appreciable ebbing in the land boom.

Farm mortgage debt paralleled the uptrend in land values. By the end of 1959, loans outstanding against farm real estate totaled $12.3 billion. This represented an increase of $7.5 billion since 1945, more than 80 percent of which occurred during the 1950's. In relation to the value of farm real estate, such debt continued to decline (with a slight interruption in 1950) until 1952 when the ratio had fallen to 7 percent. In that year, debt began to expand somewhat faster than land values, and by 1956 the ratio had climbed to 9 percent where it remained through 1959.

As mentioned above, the role of lenders in the farm mortgage market varied significantly during the postwar years. On the whole, life insurance companies made the only substantial gains, lifting their share of the outstanding debt from 16 percent in 1945 to 23 percent in 1959. But in the mid-1950's their share had been even larger. Commercial banks edged up a bit, but individual lenders simply maintained their relative position. Federal agencies experienced a sharp cutback in lending during the postwar period—although they still held slightly more than one-fifth of the farm mortgage debt in 1959.

Life insurance companies immediately returned to the farm mortgage market as large scale lenders once World War II was over. In fact, they began to acquire an expanding share of the market as early as 1943 when they were able to maintain their holdings against the shrinking stock of farm mortgage debt. From that year until 1953, the percentage of the total debt owned by these institutions rose without interruption. In the early postwar period, life insurance companies and commercial banks shared almost equally the entire net expansion of farm real estate loans, individuals barely maintained their position, and the federal agencies actually reduced their loans by almost one-fifth between 1945 and 1950.

The motivations of life insurance companies in concentrating more on the farm mortgage market in the early postwar years were apparently mixed. The growing pressure to find profitable outlets for their steadily accumulating funds undoubtedly induced many of them to look with favor on farm loans, and the continued advance in real estate values through 1949 greatly enhanced their attractiveness. Moreover, most companies had cleared up the backlog of farm real estate inherited from the Great Depression and began to view farm loans as a further means of diversification. Finally, many companies apparently began to recognize a possible tie-in between mortgage loans and life insurance sales which served as an added inducement to supply long-term funds to the farm sector.

Between 1950 and 1955, the growth of the farm mortgage market was supported more evenly by all types of important lenders, who shared the net increase in outstanding debt as follows: individuals, 39 percent; life insurance companies, 32 percent; Federal Land Banks, 18 percent; and commercial banks, 11 percent. The participation of lenders in the farm mortgage market during the Korean War period seems to have been primarily a response to the rising demand for funds by farmers seeking to expand production through a build-up of their capital stock. But in 1954 and 1955, several changes in the legal framework gave a boost to farm lending. In late 1954, Federal Land Banks were allowed to follow more liberal policies in appraising properties; in August, 1955, the Federal Reserve Act was changed to permit national banks to make larger real estate loans with longer maturities.[28] Both of these changes further sparked the growth of mortgage credit. The effects were quickly registered: the average size of farm mortgages recorded rose from $6,000 in 1954 to $7,000 in 1955, and the number of recordings increased from 316,000 to 335,000. At Federal Land Banks, the average size of new farm mortgage loans jumped even more sharply—from $6,000 to $8,000. The easier terms were transmitted to other lenders who responded vigorously in an effort to protect their share of the market. Life insurance companies also joined the trend, and the average size of farm mortgage recorded by them was $14,800 in 1955 compared with $14,700 a year earlier. By the end of 1955, these institutions held one-quarter of the outstanding farm mortgage debt, an amount which more than restored them to the relative position in the market which they had enjoyed on the eve of the Great Depression.

Life insurance companies and other major private lenders greatly reduced their participation in the farm mortgage market during 1955-59 compared with the previous five years. The relative cutback seems to have been related to expanding investment opportunities reflected in rising market yields over much of the period. While total farm mortgages outstanding rose by $3.2 billion (or 35 percent) between 1955 and 1959, new loans were made at generally advancing interest rates except in the first half of 1958. The sharpest rise occurred between 1955 and 1957. Federal Land Banks raised their posted rates from 5 percent to a range of 5.5 to 6.0 percent. Leading life insurance companies active in the field lifted the average rate quoted on new loans from a minimum slightly below 5 percent in early 1955 to 6 percent in the fall of 1957. At the latter date, the average contract rate on farm mortgages outstanding ranged from 4.40 percent for Federal Land Banks, through 5.21 percent for life insurance companies, to 5.86 percent at commercial banks and trust companies. From late 1957 through mid-1958, farm mortgage credit became somewhat easier, and interest rates declined slightly. However, during the last half of the year, the trend was again upward. By the end of 1959, most life insurance companies were making new farm loans at a minimum interest rate exceeding 6 percent, which lifted the average contract rate on their farm mortgage portfolio to 5.9 percent. On January 1, 1959, nine Federal Land Banks were charging 5 percent on new farm mortgage loans, and three were charging 5.5 percent. On December 31, 1959, all of them had posted the statutory limit of 6 percent.[29]

These swings in interest rates were clearly reflected in the flow of funds into the farm mortgage market. Over the period as a whole, federal lending agencies absorbed almost one-third of the net expansion in farm real estate debt in contrast to less than one-fifth in 1950-55. The shrinkage in the share of private lenders centered primarily in life insurance companies, who made only 18 percent of the net new loans against 32 percent in the previous five-year span. This relative withdrawal of life insurance companies from farm lending was in keeping with their behavior in the rest of the mortgage market; to a considerable extent, they substituted corporate securities for real estate loans and were a major source of funds to finance the business plant and equipment boom of 1955-57. Reflecting this reduced participation, the proportion of outstanding farm mortgage debt held by these institutions declined steadily after 1955, so that by the end of 1959 their share of the market was the same as in 1951. Nevertheless, life insurance companies as a source of farm mortgage loans were still second only to individuals, who have always advanced a major portion of such long-term credit.

The market for farm mortgages among life insurance companies since the end of World War II has centered primarily in the largest companies. As shown in Table VII-14, the fifteen largest institutions expanded their share of the market from 70 percent in 1945 to 84 percent in 1957. In the process, they absorbed almost 90 percent of the net increase in farm mortgages held by the 150 leading companies. This noticeable gain was at the

TABLE VII-14
FARM MORTGAGES HELD BY 150 LARGEST LIFE INSURANCE COMPANIES, BY SIZE GROUP OF COMPANIES, 1945 & 1957
(In Millions of Dollars)

Size Range of Companies:	1945		1957		Change: 1945-57	
Total Assets, 1957 ($ Millions)	Amount	Percent of Total	Amount	Percent of Total	Amount	Percent of Total Change
Group I (1,329-15,536)	520	70.0	2,094	83.8	1,574	89.5
II (514-1,273)	110	14.8	186	7.6	76	4.3
III (236-497)	53	7.1	99	3.8	46	2.8
IV (143-234)	30	4.0	45	1.8	15	0.8
V (100-141)	7	0.9	9	0.4	2	0.1
VI (82-99)	6	0.8	13	0.5	7	0.4
VII (59-81)	4	0.5	13	0.5	9	0.5
VIII (41-58)	7	0.9	18	0.7	11	0.7
IX (34-40)	5	0.7	17	0.7	12	0.7
X (25-33)	2	0.3	6	0.2	4	0.2
Total, 150 Companies	744	100.0	2,500	100.0	1,756	100.0

SOURCE: **Best's Life Insurance Reports**, 1946 and 1958.

expense of virtually all other size groups, but the loss in market share was especially heavy among medium-sized companies. While all of the groups shown expanded their ownership of farm mortgages, no other set of institutions even approached the threefold increase registered by the top life insurance companies.

Several factors help to explain the relatively faster rate of growth in farm mortgages of the largest companies. The somewhat higher rate of return on farm loans is certainly of some importance, because such loans typically yield one-half to three-quarters of a point more than urban loans. The average size of farm mortgages increased substantially over the postwar period to about $8,000 in 1959, but the average size of such mortgages held by life insurance companies was close to $15,000. Because the larger companies were generally more willing to meet the growing demand for bigger loans, this factor also gave them an edge. Moreover, many of these institutions have decentralized their operations by establishing regional and local offices to handle both the insurance and investment sides of the business. To keep their investment field staff fully employed, they find it necessary to generate a large volume of mortgage loans. This frequently induces them to concentrate on farm real estate loans to a greater extent than do most smaller companies when the demand for urban mortgages eases.

Section VII
Summary and Conclusions

The conclusions of this chapter can be summarized here to bring the discussion into sharper focus. It was shown that real estate mortgages have strong attractions as investment outlets for life insurance companies. While the relatively high yields are the main attraction, the diversification objective is also of considerable importance. Moreover, the increased liquidity of their mortgage portfolios provided by the amortization of loans further expands the demand for real estate mortgages. Significant structural changes in the mortgage market have brought about a number of major modifications in the extent and techniques of life insurance companies' mortgage lending practices. The spread of amortized repayment schedules is perhaps the most outstanding among these changes, but higher loan-to-value ratios and longer maturities have also exerted some influence. These features, combined with government insurance and guarantee provisions, have induced life insurance companies to expand their investment activities in the mortgage market. Although the vast majority of these institutions still prefer conventional mortgages to those underwritten by the federal government, a sizable group apparently feels that the reduced risk afforded by the latter type of mortgage is sufficient to compensate for the lower yields resulting from the interest rate ceilings on FHA and VA loans.

In order to place the companies' recent participation in the mortgage market in perspective, the pre-World War II record was examined. The survey indicated that the high level of mortgage lending in the 1920's was primarily a reflection of the construction boom rather than a fundamental change in life insurance companies' lending practices. However, an interesting aspect of their experience during this decade is that they continued to expand mortgage loans through 1929, although the construction of single-family dwellings declined after 1925. This was partly due to the rise of private nonresidential building to unusually high levels in 1928. Because life insurance companies are large-scale lenders in both of these sectors of the market, they did not experience a slackening in their rate of new lending activity until 1930. The Great Depression had a drastic impact on the mortgage market and on the participation of life insurance companies in this part of the capital market. As income and property values fell, defaults became widespread, and lenders found themselves reluctant owners of an ascending stock of both urban and farm real estate. On balance, the depression affected agriculture more than the rest of the economy, and the results were reflected in a decline of almost three-fifths in life insurance companies' farm mortgage holdings between 1930 and 1940. Their urban real estate loans, on the other hand, shrank by only 7 percent during the same decade.

During World War II, these institutions made considerable progress in liquidating their unwanted real estate and simultaneously built up their nonfarm mortgages against the general downtrend in the volume of such loans outstanding. Nevertheless, by the end of the war, most companies felt that their mortgage portfolios should be greatly expanded in relation to their total assets. In pursuit of this policy, they became major competitors for mortgages in the postwar period. In fact, to a large extent, the marked swings in the flow of mortgage funds in the capital market since 1945 (especially the swings in the availability of funds for borrowers against federally-underwritten properties) can be attributed partly to the investment behavior of life insurance companies.

Since the end of World War II, mortgage investments of life insurance companies have expanded with the demand for housing. A shortage of housing at the outbreak of the war, restricted construction during the conflict, and a substantial shift of population from rural to urban areas had already created a substantial housing shortage by the end of 1945. Subsequently, the spectacular rise in household formations and birth rates added further to the demand for housing. Because incomes registered sizable gains during most of the postwar years, families found it increasingly possible to acquire better homes. Moreover, the federal government, through its insurance and guarantee programs, sought to reduce the risk of mortgage lending and thereby expand the availability of funds to finance construction. On several occasions, these efforts were supplemented by considerable easing of terms of FHA and VA mortgages (reflected in lower down payments and longer maturities).

The interplay of supply and demand in the housing market was by no means uniform. In fact, the housing market after World War II displayed an extremely interesting pattern; the rate of residential construction varied widely and moved inversely with the rate of overall economic activity. Thus, housing was one of the main stabilizing forces in the economy. The explanation for this pattern seems to lie in the shifting availability of mortgage funds. The growing tightness in the capital markets toward the top of each postwar boom had an adverse impact on the mortgage market. The vigorous demand for funds by the business sector generated severe stringency through the capital market, and the brunt of the shortage of funds fell on the mortgage market. The impact was especially hard on the government-underwritten sector where relatively inflexible interest rates hampered the price adjustments necessary if such loans were to compete with other uses of funds. On the other hand, the easy money policies during each of the postwar recessions stimulated an increased flow of funds into mortgages and generated a boom of major proportions in residential construction.

In each of the three postwar housing booms, the role of life insurance companies varied. Although they swung into the mortgage market much later than other major lenders in 1949-50, they played a bigger part in the first boom than in those which followed. They absorbed almost one-third of the net increase in nonfarm mortgages outstanding over those two years and moved well ahead of their closest competitors (commercial banks and savings and loan associations) in carving out a share of the market. While outstanding commitments to lend against mortgages kept them in the market well after the start of the Korean War, life insurance companies turned increasingly away from residential mortgage lending in 1951-52 and concentrated on providing funds to industries in the process of building defense facilities. Furthermore, the relative cutback in mortgage funds was intensified by the unpegging of the government securities market in the spring of 1951; after this move, these institutions became increasingly unwilling to liquidate Governments to acquire mortgages because of the fear of capital losses. With the coming of the second postwar recession in the summer of 1953, the conditions were created from which the second housing boom developed. The decline of interest rates on corporate issues and the increased availability of funds forced life insurance companies and other lenders to scramble for mortgages. Given the pegged rates on federally-underwritten loans, and because of changes in terms on FHA and VA loans, this sector of the market experienced a spectacular expansion with most of the growth centering in VA mortgages. Again life insurance companies lagged behind other lenders in shifting to the mortgage market, but in September, 1953, their forward commitments began to climb with commitments for VA loans leading by a wide margin. By the time the peak in commitments was reached in the summer of 1954, those to buy VA mortgages had risen by twelve times from the level of the previous year. In terms of actual acquisitions, life insurance companies absorbed about three-tenths of the increase in VA mortgages outstanding, although they held only one-fifth in the third quarter of 1953. In terms of all types of nonfarm mortgages, their share of the market shrank slightly because they expanded their holdings of FHA and conventional loans at a rate somewhat less than that achieved by savings and loan associations and several other lenders.

The recession which began in the summer of 1957 produced a familiar pattern in the mortgage market. This time, however, FHA loans led the field in the rate of growth. To a considerable extent, the third housing boom was powered by an increase in demand for homes by middle and upper income groups in contrast to the previous booms when easing credit terms brought a substantial number of lower income families into the market. This possibility was clearly suggested by the heavier reliance on FHA mortgages. Life insurance companies made only a modest contribution to the growth of home financing during the housing expansion in 1958-59. This reduced participation in the mortgage market partly reflected the slower rate of growth in their total assets, which in turn was partly attributable to a relative shift to types of life insurance policies carrying smaller reserve provisions. Moreover, the companies were no longer willing to sell large quantities of government securities to make mortgage loans because their total holdings had been brought more or less into line with the rest of their portfolios. Finally, the vigorous competition of other lenders (especially savings and loan associations) severely restricted the volume of mortgages which life insurance companies were able to acquire. Nevertheless, these institutions at the end of 1959 remained a major source of mortgage funds, accounting for more than one-fifth of the total nonfarm mortgage debt outstanding.

The participation of life insurance companies in mortgage warehousing was examined in detail. It was concluded that, aside from the possibility of temporary overexpansion in commercial bank credit, this technique could probably be of considerable benefit in the stabilization of residential construction. The flow of funds into the mortgage market and the supply of available mortgages are imperfectly synchronized. In contrast to the generally steady inflow of funds to life insurance companies due to the regularity of mortgage repayments, the supply of mortgages reflects the seasonal pattern of residential building—in addition to the pronounced cyclical fluctuations. Sudden events, such as the outbreak of war in Korea, also exert a profound influence on the mortgage supply. Clearly, then, there is a need for a balancing mechanism to coordinate the demand for mortgages (exhibited as the supply of loanable funds) with the supply of mortgages. Mortgage warehousing, when conducted within limits set by judicious portfolio management, can serve this function. In the mid-1950's, however, there was some evidence that a few of the leading life insurance companies employed the warehousing technique in an injudicious manner, the result of which added to instability in the economy.

Life insurance companies provided the largest institutional market for farm mortgages in the postwar period. They moved far ahead of the commercial banks which are their traditional institutional rivals in this part of the mortgage market, and won a sizable piece of the market share relinquished by federal lending agencies. While their acquisition of farm real estate loans varied greatly from one sub-period to another, they absorbed almost three-tenths of the net increase in such loans outstanding between 1945 and 1959. Yet, the revival of large-scale farm lending by these institutions just about restored them to the relative position they held in the market in 1930.

The overriding conclusion to emerge from the study of life insurance companies' participation in the mortgage market is this: the most compelling motive directing their interest in mortgages is the desire to earn the relatively high yields available on real estate loans. It was also shown that the yield structure prevailing at any given time is primarily a reflection of the corporate demand for funds operating within the framework of the Federal Reserve System monetary policy. Life insurance companies' investment activities in the mortgage market demonstrate rather clearly the impact of changes in the structure of interest rates on the availability of mortgage funds at financial intermediaries. The most striking example of the response of life insurance companies to variations in interest rates in the mortgage market is provided in the periodic ebb and flow of funds into federally-underwritten mortgages from prosperity to recession.

Footnotes

1. Houghton Bell and Harold Fraine, "Legal Framework, Trends and Developments in Investment Practices of Life Insurance Companies," *Law and Contemporary Problems*, Winter, 1952, p. 47.
2. *1960 Life Insurance Fact Book*, pp. 10, 84.
3. J. F. Morton, *Urban Mortgage Lending: Comparative Markets and Experience*, a study sponsored by the National Bureau of Economic Research (Princeton: Princeton University Press, 1956) p. 74.
4. Saul B. Klaman, *The Volume of Mortgage Debt in the Postwar Decade.* Technical Paper 13. (New York: National Bureau of Economic Research, 1958), p. 54.
5. David L. Wickens, *Residential Real Estate* (New York: National Bureau of Economic Research, 1941), p. 198.
6. L. Douglas Meredith, "Real Estate Mortgages," *Investment of Life Insurance Funds*, p. 103.
7. R. J. Saulnier, *Urban Mortgage Lending by Life Insurance Companies* (New York: National Bureau of Economic Research, 1950), p. 49.
8. Meredith, *op. cit.*, p. 108.
9. Morton, *op. cit.*, p. 175.
10. The regulatory maximum interest rates on FHA mortgages secured by single-family houses have behaved as follows:

Date of Change in Rate	*Percent*
November 27, 1934	5 and 5½
June 24, 1934	5
August 1, 1939	4½
April 24, 1950	4¼
May 2, 1953	4½
December 3, 1956	5
August 5, 1957	5¼
September 23, 1959	5¾

In addition, insured borrowers are charged a premium of ½ of 1 percent of the principal outstanding.
The maximum interest rates under the VA program have behaved as follows:

Date of Change in Rate	*Percent*
June 22, 1944	4
May 5, 1953	4½
April 4, 1958	4¾
July 2, 1959	5¼

11. The limit on total borrowing was set in 1954 as an amount equal to ten times its capitalization and surplus. At the end of 1959, its capital (provided by the Treasury through purchase of preferred stock) totaled $143 million, and its surplus

was $52 million—giving it $195 million of funds to support its borrowing. Total borrowing at the end of 1959 amounted to $1,800 million. Source: Federal National Mortgage Association.

12. James J. O'Leary, "The Influence of Government," *Investment of Life Insurance Funds*, p. 232.

13. U. S. Department of Commerce, *Survey of Current Business*, April, 1960, pp. 16-20.

14. John C. Jewett, Testimony before Subcommittee on Housing, Committee on Banking and Currency, United States Senate, *Hearings, Investigation of Housing*, 1955, 84th Congress, 1st Session, 1955, p. 236. (Referred to hereafter as *Investigation of Housing*, 1955.)

15. Thomas P. Coogan, Testimony, *Investigation of Housing*, 1955, p. 115.

16. John J. Scully, Testimony, *ibid.*, pp. 105-6.

17. Letter to Hon. Albert Rains, dated September 12, 1955, and reprinted in *Investigation of Housing*, 1955, p. 119.

18. Jewett, *Investigation of Housing*, 1955, pp. 130-31.

19. R. B. Patrick, "1956 Mortgage Fund Supply and Determining Characteristics," *Commercial and Financial Chronicle*, May 24, 1956, p. 34.

20. Lawrence A. Jones and David Durand, *Mortgage Lending Experience in Agriculture*, a study sponsored by the National Bureau of Economic Research (Princeton: Princeton University Press, 1954), p. 10.

21. Glenn G. Munn, *Encyclopedia of Banking and Finance* (New York: Bankers Publishing Company, 1937), p. 275.

22. Jones and Durand, *op. cit.*, pp. 10-11.

23. *1946 Life Insurance Fact Book*, p. 44.

24. U. S. Department of Agriculture, Bureau of Agricultural Economics, *Impact of the War on the Financial Structure of Agriculture*, Misc. Publication No. 567, August, 1945, pp. 14-16.

25. U. S. Department of Agriculture, Bureau of Agricultural Economics, *The Farm Income Situation*, December 1952-January 1953, Table I, p. 4.

26. "The Balance Sheet of Agriculture," *Federal Reserve Bulletin*, August, 1955, pp. 872-73, and August, 1960, pp. 851-52.

27. "Balance Sheet of Agriculture," *Federal Reserve Bulletin*, August, 1960, p. 855.

28. "Balance Sheet of Agriculture," *Federal Reserve Bulletin*, August, 1956, p. 830.

29. "Balance Sheet of Agriculture," *Federal Reserve Bulletin*, August, 1957, p. 909; August, 1958, p. 900; July, 1959, pp. 730-31; August, 1960, p. 855.

CHAPTER VIII

Investment Behavior In The Market for State and Local Government Securities

SECTION I
DEMAND FOR STATE AND LOCAL GOVERNMENT SECURITIES

Life insurance companies have only a meager demand for state and local government securities. Traditionally, the burden of federal income taxes on them has been extremely light. Although a sizable increase in 1959 raised the average rate of taxation from about 8 to 12 percent, almost 90 percent of their investment income is still nontaxable. Consequently, life insurance companies, especially mutual institutions, are generally unprepared to pay the high prices or accept the correspondingly low yields, for municipal securities; they prefer taxable obligations of comparable risk and liquidity.[1] This price and yield structure, of course, is primarily the result of competition for state and local issues by individuals and institutions and especially commercial banks, which are subject to high tax rates. For the latter, the exemption from federal taxation of income earned on state and local securities is a matter of considerable importance, and they are willing to pay a substantial premium to obtain these issues.[2]

But it should be noted that here the marginal character of life insurance companies' demand for state and local securities is emphasized. Some of these institutions do acquire municipal issues on a continuous basis. Moreover, for reasons which will be examined in this chapter, their holdings are heavily concentrated in revenue bonds secured by receipts from business-type enterprises operated by local governments or special authorities created by the states. General obligations, backed by the taxing power of the issuer, have only moderate appeal to life insurance companies because of their relatively low yields.

Numerous factors motivate these institutions to hold state and local government debt. The advantage of tax-exempt income leads the list, but several other objectives are also important. Some indication of the order in which they rank different objectives is given in the replies to the BBER-MSU Survey in the spring of 1959. These are summarized in Table VIII-1. The first thing to note is that, while almost two-fifths of the companies emphasize tax-exempt income, this goal is strongest among the largest companies, and it loses some of its attraction among smaller institutions. This pattern is easily understood when one recalls that the larger companies are far more sensitive to yield differentials than the smaller ones. Moreover, the top companies have the technical staffs to watch the structure of interest rates and, within the limits imposed by considerations of portfolio balance, to steer their funds into investments offering higher rates of return. On the other hand, smaller companies tend to rely more than the large institutions on state and local securities as a means of portfolio diversification. This latter was the principal target for one-third of the smaller units but for less than 10 percent of the biggest firms. Again, the management of many small life insurance companies is not well equipped to analyze corporate obligations, but little difficulty is encountered in judging the investment qualities of municipal issues—especially general obligations which have been appraised by rating serv-

TABLE VIII-1

MAIN OBJECTIVES OF LIFE INSURANCE COMPANIES
IN HOLDING STATE AND LOCAL GOVERNMENT SECURITIES

Main Objective	All Companies	Group[1] I	Group II	Group III	Group IV
Tax-exempt Income	64	20	15	18	11
Portfolio Diversification	26	2	7	8	9
Accommodation to Home Areas	6	1	3	1	1
Other Objectives	9	3	3	0	3
State tax credits	3	—	1	—	2
Call protection	2	1	1	—	—
Capital gains on revenue bonds	4	2	1	—	1
Do Not Hold State and Local Government Securities	6	2	0	1	3
Total	111	28	28	28	27

1. Size groups are those shown in Table I-1.

SOURCE: BBER-MSU Survey, Spring, 1959.

ices. In addition, a few companies reported that they turn to state and local securities to diversify their holdings because their small size precludes their participation in direct placement of corporate bonds.

A few institutions concentrated in the intermediate sized range hold state and local issues principally as an accommodation to their home areas. They report that their prominence in a particular area makes them a beacon for local governments seeking funds. Because the companies have little need for tax-exempt income, they would prefer to avoid such debt and concentrate on higher-yielding business loans and real estate mortgages. Moreover, if their preference was shifted to municipals, they might prefer the obligations of governments for which a national market exists, but which are beyond their geographic area. Nevertheless, the necessity of maintaining local good will induces them to take up obligations of neighborhood borrowers. Of course, as one official pointed out, the companies' own self-interest would dictate some local accommodation because failure to do so might have an adverse effect on their insurance sales in the home market.

Some companies own state and local securities as protection against early redemption. Typically, general obligations are serial issues of which the nearest links in the series mature within a few years after offering. However, the longest maturities are not due (and are usually not callable) for at least a decade; even then they ordinarily must be called in the reverse order of maturity. A substantial proportion of revenue bonds have a fixed term, and these are almost always callable. In the case of both general obligations and revenue bonds, investors as a rule demand provisions which make it expensive for governmental units to redeem their issues before maturity. Thus, some life insurance companies hold state and local issues as a hedge against a sudden inflow of funds due to early redemption during a period of declining interest rates. A small number of companies reported they hold only revenue issues and do so mainly for capital gains. As discussed later in this chapter, many revenue bonds have been selling at substantial discounts in recent years. These discounts have made them attractive to life insurance companies and other investors who are only moderately concerned with the clouded short-run earnings prospects of some of the bond-financed projects whose long-run future seems promising. A small number of life insurance companies hold state and local issues because they gain tax credits in some states. Finally, some companies do not buy municipal obligations because the advantage of tax-exemption does not compensate for the extra effort associated with participating in the market.

While large life insurance companies have a tendency to select state and local securities purely on the basis of tax-exempt yields, smaller institutions are not so yield-conscious, although they generally hold a larger proportion of their assets in this form. Moreover, the biggest companies concentrate relatively more on revenue bonds while the market for general obligations is greater among smaller institutions. This is clearly illustrated in Table VIII-2 which shows the distribution of total assets and state and local securities held by the 150 largest companies in the United States at the end of 1957. The companies at the forefront of the industry held three-fourths of total assets but only two-fifths of general obligations and about three-fifths of revenue bonds. In all other size groups, the share of general obligations far exceeded that of total assets; the same is true for revenue bonds except for the two groups just short of the last. The explanation of this pattern is again evident. The leading companies have the facilities to search broadly in the capital market for various high-yielding outlets for their funds; they do not need to rely on state and local issues for diversification, and they are under less pressure for local accommodation. When they do turn to the municipal market, they take up revenue bonds because, aside from the tax factor, their yields are competitive with those on corporate bonds. For many small

TABLE VIII-2

DISTRIBUTION OF TOTAL ASSETS AND STATE AND LOCAL GOVERNMENT SECURITIES AMONG THE 150 LARGEST LIFE INSURANCE COMPANIES, BY SIZE GROUP, 1957

(Percent)

Size Group of Companies (Total Assets, 1957, $ millions)	Total Assets	State and Local Government Securities: General Obligations	State and Local Government Securities: Revenue Bonds
I(1,329-15,536)	74.6	43.7	57.6
II(514-1,273)	11.2	24.6	16.4
III(236-497)	5.3	10.6	8.0
IV(143-234)	2.8	5.4	6.6
V(100-141)	1.8	3.5	3.1
VI(82-99)	1.4	4.8	4.1
VII(59-81)	1.0	2.2	2.0
VIII(41-58)	0.8	2.4	0.6
IX(34-40)	0.6	1.5	0.6
X(25-33)	0.5	1.3	1.0
Total	100.0	100.0	100.0

SOURCE: Computed from data in **Best's Insurance Reports, Life Edition**, 1958.

institutions, the reverse of each of these propositions is frequently the case.

The pattern of ownership of state and local government securities by life insurance companies is examined in greater detail in this chapter. First, to place their participation in the market in perspective, their investment activities before World War II are reviewed in Section II. In Section III, the demand for funds by state and local governments during the years 1946-59 is analyzed because this has shaped the investment opportunities life insurance companies have found in the market. Also the competition among these and other investors for state and local issues is summarized. Section IV contains the core of the discussion relating to life insurance companies. It is shown that their holdings of state and local government issues are represented primarily by revenue issues, the supply of which has been greatly increased by the creation of special authorities to perform public services outside the framework of general government. Some of the main features of revenue bonds which make them attractive to life insurance companies are also examined.

Section II
Investment in State and Local Government Securities Before World War II

In the nineteenth century, life insurance companies' participation in the market for state and local government securities waxed and waned in accord with the two leading transport revolutions partly financed through the sale of municipal bonds. While municipal issues represented only a minor outlet for the companies' funds over the century as a whole, they absorbed sizable amounts in the periods 1825-40 and 1866-80.

The earlier period roughly straddled the boom in state bonds sold to finance internal improvements. Canal building perhaps generated the largest volume of debt, and life insurance companies acquired moderate amounts of such issues. After the panic of 1837, however, numerous states declared themselves bankrupt, and debt repudiation became widespread. Insurance companies, along with other investors, suffered substantial capital losses which virtually drove them away from state bonds for the remainder of the century.[3]

The railroad boom following the Civil War again stimulated heavy flotations of municipal bonds, but this time counties and cities took the lead. Apparently thousands of localities, which even the most cursory survey should have shown to be unpromising, cast an eye to the future and visualized themselves as great centers of commerce and industry—provided they could induce a railroad company to bypass their neighbors and could thus connect themselves with the expanding domestic and world markets. This vision persuaded hundreds of counties and municipalities to float bonds to subsidize railroads. Life insurance companies were caught up in the optimism and acquired this debt on a large scale. By 1880, municipal bonds accounted for about 15 percent of their total assets, which probably represented at least a threefold percentage gain from the previous peak set in the 1830's.[4] Moreover, the proportion was undoubtedly even greater on the eve of the panic of 1873. The depression which followed this crisis was extremely severe; as revenues fell, hundreds of development schemes were abandoned, and many municipalities repudiated their obligations. For example, over 100 cities in Illinois disowned their debts, and in Missouri more than 90 did likewise. In response to this wholesale rejection of claims, life insurance companies for practical purposes withdrew from the municipal bond market. By 1890, state and local government securities were only 7 percent of their assets, and the ratio fell steadily to 5 percent in 1900.

For the next quarter of a century, life insurance companies had little taste for municipal issues whose yields became increasingly unattractive compared with those obtainable on real estate mortgages and corporate securities. In 1917, the first year for which a firm estimate is available, these institutions owned $329 million of state and local obligations. (See Table VIII-3.) This represented 6 percent of their assets. While their

TABLE VIII-3

OWNERSHIP OF STATE AND LOCAL
GOVERNMENT SECURITIES, SELECTED DATES, 1917-1945
(In Millions of Dollars)

	1917	1920	1930	1940	1945
Total Outstanding[1]	6,290	7,746	17,985	19,891	16,293
Held by:					
Life insurance companies[2]	329	350	1,023	2,082	722
Commercial banks[2]	863	944	2,111	3,610	3,778
Individuals and others	5,098	6,452	14,851	14,199	11,793

1. As of June 30 of each year.
2. As of December 31 of each year.

SOURCE: Total Outstanding, **Bond Buyer**, "Special Convention Issue," November 26, 1956, insert between pp. 56-7; held by life insurance companies, **1960 Life Insurance Fact Book**, p. 69; commercial banks, U. S. Bureau of the Census, **Historical Statistics of the United States, Colonial Times to 1957** (Washington, D. C., 1960), p. 631.

holdings had climbed to $521 million by 1926, they accounted for only 4 percent of their total portfolio. In the late 1920's, however, these companies swung into the municipal market on a sizable scale; in fact, they almost doubled this part of their investment portfolio during the four years 1927-30. This growth is mainly explained by the purchase of substantial amounts of bonds sold by electric utilities owned by municipalities. As a result of these acquisitions, state and local government securities owned by life insurance companies rose to over $1 billion in 1930, an amount equal to 5.4 percent of their total assets.

During the depression of the 1930's, life insurance companies accelerated the acquisition of state and local issues. Over the decade they doubled their holdings although the volume of such debt outstanding rose by only 11 percent. They were able to make such deep inroads because many other investors, especially individuals, became increasingly uncertain about the future of these obligations.[5] While life insurance companies held approximately 6 percent of state and local debt outstanding in 1930, their share had risen to 11 percent at the close of the decade. Moreover, they absorbed almost three-fifths of the net expansion of the outstanding debt during the 1930's in contrast to only 7 percent in the previous decade. In fact, only commercial banks, for whom tax-exempt income became of increasing importance, surpassed life insurance companies as a market for municipal issues in this period. This confident buying was amply rewarded by the handsome capital gains which many companies realized during World War II. Numerous investors, primarily individuals, in search of tax-exemption, provided a vigorous demand for state and local government securities at the very time that the stock of such debt was shrinking. States and localities were using part of their swelling revenues to redeem outstanding issues while others matured; at the same time little new borrowing occurred. Moreover, the federal government, which previously had sold tax-exempt issues, no longer did so. Consequently, a large number of state and local obligations were quoted at premiums. Most life insurance companies quickly perceived the profit possibilities and promptly began to release their holdings to the market. This behavior is clearly seen in the shrinkage of their municipal portfolio by two-thirds over the years 1940-45 while the total volume of municipal debt declined by less than one-fifth. At the end of the war, they owned only 4 percent of the outstanding state and local bonds and were thus back to the relative position they held in this part of the capital market in 1920. Furthermore, such issues represented just slightly more than 2 percent of their total assets in 1945 compared with 8 percent in 1940.

SECTION III
STATE AND LOCAL GOVERNMENTS IN THE CAPITAL MARKET SINCE WORLD WAR II

A. DEMAND FOR FUNDS

Faced with the constantly increasing demand for public services, state and local governments spent about $110 billion for capital projects during the fourteen years ending in 1959. While a large proportion of these improvements was financed from current revenues, these governmental units also had to borrow almost $66 billion in the long-term capital market. Except for three years in which special factors were at work, the amount of bonds offered rose steadily, climbing from an annual total of $1.2 billion in 1946 to $7.5 billion in 1959. Within the period, however, there were sizable fluctuations in the volume of securities offered. Some of these reflected shifts in the structure of capital spending. But in general, state and local borrowing displayed a clearly contra-cyclical pattern—shrinking during periods of strong corporate demand for funds and expanding during recessions. On the other hand, these borrowers withdrew only relatively from the capital market as credit conditions tightened. Many of them were vigorous competitors for the available funds under even the most stringent terms, and at times they added further to market pressures.

Moreover, state and local governments became increasingly willing to grant concessions to stimulate investor demand. Aside from paying sharply higher interest rates (which in many cases required raising legal ceilings), they also accepted more severe call provisions and frequently pledged their full faith and credit as additional security for revenue bonds. The higher yields they offered and the resulting smaller spread between these and yields on other market instruments substantially broadened the market for municipal issues. This in turn enabled state and local governments not only to maintain their relative share in capital market flows during most of the postwar years, but at times they managed to enlarge it.

As shown in Table VIII-4, these borrowers raised $66.6 billion in the long-term capital market in the 1946-59 years.[6] Virtually all of this amount (97.5 percent) was for new capital, and refunding issues were negligible. In keeping with tradition, the bulk of these funds was raised to finance construction activities rather than to cover operating deficits. But, as explained more fully below, there were several exceptions, among which bond sales to provide veterans' benefits were the most important.

TABLE VIII-4

LONG-TERM BORROWING BY STATE AND LOCAL GOVERNMENTS, BY MAJOR PURPOSES, ANNUALLY, 1946-59

(In Millions of Dollars)

Purpose of Issue	1946	1947	1948	1949	1950	1951	1952	1953	1954	1955	1956	1957	1958	1959	1946-59 Amount	1946-59 Percent of Total
New Capital																
Total	1,047	2,311	2,798	2,896	3,579	3,188	4,093	5,473	6,788	5,911	5,383	6,760	7,315	7,389	64,931	97.5
Education	194	205	412	524	709	582	967	1,319	1,432	1,516	1,455	2,428	2,530	2,177	16,450	24.6
Transport facilities	234	249	530	587	578	606	998	1,635	2,224	1,464	835	1,219	1,358	1,184	13,701	20.6
Highways, bridges and tunnels	167	202	423	520	510	580	938	1,587	2,136	1,362	698	1,035	1,163	834	12,155	18.3
Ports and airports	67	47	107	67	68	26	60	48	88	102	137	184	195	350	1,546	2.3
Public utilities	181	475	438	545	618	640	642	803	1,270	881	1,398	1,503	1,378	1,940	12,712	19.1
Sewer and water	154	222	314	400	487	464	419	647	674	712	752	1,010	1,065	1,099	8,419	12.6
Other utilities	27	253	124	145	131	176	223	156	596	169	646	493	313	841	4,293	6.5
Social welfare	58	728	707	347	765	184	162	317	297	307	213	551	650	541	5,827	8.8
Hospitals and institutions	8	34	35	47	96	135	38	133	77	98	62	135	215	113	1,226	1.8
Veterans' aid	39	672	643	263	635	41	100	140	162	169	110	333	339	355	4,001	6.1
Recreation	11	22	29	37	34	8	24	44	58	40	41	83	96	73	600	0.9
Public housing	9	70	148	203	123	361	423	506	456	570	258	113	251	402	3,893	5.8
Industrial building	—	—	—	1	81	5	5	7	1	4	11	7	26	18	166	0.2
Other purposes	371	584	562	689	705	809	896	886	1,109	1,170	1,213	940	1,121	1,128	12,183	18.3
Refunding	155	42	192	107	114	90	314	82	180	65	63	50	86	108	1,648	2.5
Total Borrowing	1,202	2,353	2,990	3,003	3,693	3,278	4,407	5,555	6,968	5,976	5,446	6,810	7,401	7,497	66,579	100.0

SOURCE: **Bond Buyer,** 1946-56; Investment Bankers Association, **Statistical Bulletin,** 1957-59.

The single most important purpose of state and local government borrowing was the development of educational facilities. Bonds of this type amounted to $16.5 billion and represented one-quarter of the total. A substantial part of this huge expenditure, however, went primarily to reduce the backlog of postponed construction; at the end of the period the nation's schools were reported to be still inadequate, although conditions varied markedly among different jurisdictions. The volume of school bonds brought to market varied considerably from year to year around a generally rising trend. That school bond sales are extremely sensitive to changing credit conditions is clearly evident in Table VIII-4. In each period of credit ease associated with postwar recessions (1949-50, 1953-54, and 1957-58), sales of these obligations registered sizable gains. On the other hand, as credit became increasingly stringent in the subsequent periods of recovery and prosperity, the volume actually shrank or grew only moderately. In the early phase of the upswing, school bonds generally maintained their previous pace, but well before aggregate economic activity reached a crest the amount of such issues, postponed because of rising interest rates or unsettled markets, began to grow. The length of the postponement differed widely among borrowers, but the most frequent experience seems to have been less than six months. Moreover, a large proportion of the issues postponed was reoffered successfully before the advent of easier credit, and most of the remainder was quickly distributed once bond prices began to rise. Only minor quantities of bonds were completely withdrawn and the related projects actually cancelled.[7] In 1951, however, part of the drop in state and local bond sales was clearly attributable to the monetary policy of the Federal Reserve System. This policy centered in the Voluntary Credit Restraint Program designed to curb nondefense investment activities. Under it, state and local governments were prime targets, and many of them voluntarily reduced their capital expenditures; others encountered considerable difficulties in their search for lenders. To cyclical and policy influences on school bond sales should be added sporadic outbreaks of voter resistance to assuming heavier tax burdens to support schools. Such resistance became serious in the mid-1950's but eased steadily toward the end of the decade. Much of the decline in opposition was partly a reflection of the national outcry over the quality of education in the United States following the first Soviet space shot, but it was also partly due to a spreading conviction that increased investment in education is required to prepare the emerging generations for the new age of science and technology which seems to lie ahead.

Bonds sold to finance transport facilities followed school issues by a narrow margin. These include highway, bridge, tunnel, port, and airport bonds. State and local governments raised $13.7 billion for such projects, or one-fifth of total funds borrowed during 1946-59. This category was among the most volatile, and highway financing was the chief cause of instability. Behind the highway pattern were the short but spectacular turnpike movement and the advent of the long-range program to build a National Interstate Highway System. Aside from the Pennsylvania Turnpike built in the 1930's, the recent wave began in 1948 with the New Jersey Turnpike, and reached a crest in 1954. After the latter year, additional bonds were sold to complete construction of roads in progress and to begin a few roads previously planned. However, the national highway system was already casting a dampening shadow on the turnpike movement, and when the system actually got underway in 1956 the toll road era was effectively ended.

These developments stand out clearly in the figures of state and local borrowing for highways. From less than $200 million in 1946-47, annual sales of highway bonds more than doubled in 1948-51, climbing to an average of $500 million. During the next three years, the annual average was triple this latter figure, and actual sales in 1954 were a record $2.1 billion. For the following two years, the volume dropped sharply and settled around $700 million in 1956. Sales of highway obligations revived moderately in 1957-58 and exceeded $1 billion in each year. Very little of the increase was attributable to toll road financing, and the speed-up in the national highway program also added little. Rather, the chief stimulus was a concerted effort to mend existing roads and to build modern bypasses to relieve traffic congestion in large cities. The financing of several major bridges (including the Mackinac in Michigan) also boosted the total. Work on the interstate highway system was stepped up during the close of the decade, but its cost was paid largely out of the Federal Highway Trust Fund. The need to modernize ports and airports and to construct new ones led numerous local governments to the capital market. For these purposes, they raised $1.5 billion during the years 1946-59. The bonds appeared sporadically, but the volume was relatively steady in relation to total borrowing in 1956-58. In 1959, an appreciable jump occurred. The stimulus came from a variety of projects in widely scattered areas of the country, but the St. Lawrence Seaway provided a noticeable incentive to port development in the Great Lakes area.

The steady migration of the population to new suburbs combined with the growth of smaller urban areas generated a persistent demand for sewer and water systems, electric and gas works, and other public utilities. Because only a small part of the funds required for these facilities could be provided from current taxes or accumulated reserves, local governments and a few states had to borrow $12.7 billion during the period under review. About two-fifths of this amount was used for sewer and water projects, and most of the residual was devoted to traditional projects such as electric and gas establishments owned by municipalities or their agencies. However, as the years progressed, new types of ventures (including off-street parking facilities) accounted for a growing share of bonds sold under this heading. The volume of public utility bonds offered also displayed a contra-cyclical pattern, but the fluctuations seem to have been less marked than those characteristic of school bonds. Yet certain types of issues (especially electric and gas utility obligations) were more volatile than school issues. The long maturities involved make even a small change in interest rates a major consideration in the timing of such bond offerings. As market yields rise with growing credit stringency, issues of this type are increasingly postponed, and once the peak in rates is passed they are quickly brought forth. This behavior is amply illustrated in Table VIII-4.

State and local governments sold $5.8 billion for social welfare purposes. More than two-thirds of this amount went to veterans. Borrowing for this purpose was particularly large in 1947, 1948 and 1950, when, respectively, it accounted for 29, 22, and 17 percent of the total. From 1951 through 1956, funds raised for veterans' aid averaged between 1 and 3 percent of the total, but the ratio jumped to 5 percent during 1957-59. A major part of this was due to bonds offered periodically under a California program which occasionally involved bond sales of $50 million and above. Hospitals and recreation facilities accounted for the remaining one-third of social welfare issues. Public housing obligations amounted to $3.9 billion, and there were sizable year to year fluctuations. These bonds (offered periodically by the Public Housing Administration with the guarantee of the federal government) actually originate with numerous local housing authorities. The accumulation of small issues into a single large offering and the government's guarantee broaden the market and substantially reduce the interest cost. The proceeds are used primarily for slum-clearance and urban renewal projects. Although shifting credit conditions undoubtedly influenced the timing in the sale of these bonds, the changing public housing policy of the federal government also affected the pattern.

An essentially new form of borrowing by local governments appeared in 1949 and made noticeable strides in the next decade; this was borrowing to construct industrial buildings. Although the volume never assumed large proportions (it aggregated $166 million during 1949-59), the practice generated much heated debate over the appropriateness of using public credit for essentially private purposes. Municipal industrial bonds are usually sold by local governments to build plants, hotels, etc., as an inducement for private business firms to locate within their borders. The schemes frequently involve tax abatement and other concessions. The exact amounts and variety of municipal industrial financing are not known. However, at the end of 1960, local jurisdictions in eight states (Alabama, Arkansas, Kentucky, Louisiana, Mississippi, New Mexico, North Dakota and Tennessee) had sold 331 issues of this type aggregating $144 million. Communities in Mississippi accounted for 204 (or two-thirds) of the total number and $68 million (47 percent) of the total amount.[8] Opposition to the spread of this type of financing has sprung from a variety of sources, but the Investment Bankers Association (IBA), Municipal Finance Officers Association, and the Municipal Law Section of the American Bar Association have perhaps been the most vocal. Objections have been based on a number of considerations. Some (especially IBA) are afraid that the linkage of public credit to private, risky ventures may endanger confidence in municipal credit as a whole—and thus adversely affect the underwriting of state and local securities. It is also argued that this type of financing gives benefiting firms an undue advantage over their competitors; in addition to local tax concessions, the firms deduct from their income the rent paid to the municipality which results in lower federal income taxes. Moreover, it has been observed that if these businesses desire, they can buy the tax-exempt bonds sold by the municipality and reap still another gain. Proponents of municipal industrial financing answer that the practice is not only within the authority of local governments, but that they have an obligation to foster industrial development to improve the welfare of their citizens. Furthermore, they say that these new ventures are not essentially different from electric and gas utilities which provide services primarily for private users. While the debate is still in progress, more states are amending their constitutions to enable municipalities to sell bonds to finance industrial buildings. Thus, the prospect is for further expansion in this part of the capital market.

State and local governments borrowed $1.6 billion for refunding. The timing of refunding was primarily related to debt maturities. Although a few borrowers made some effort to take advantage of lower interest rates at times, the impact on the market was hardly noticeable.

While there is much variety in the types of state and local governments raising funds in the capital market, there is also a high degree of specialization. Table VIII-5 shows the pattern in 1959. State and local bonds sold in that year are cross-classified by level of government and proposed use of proceeds. It should be noted that borrowing is concentrated among special districts and special authorities, municipalities, states, and school districts. Each of these groups raised between one-fifth and one-quarter of the total in 1959. Counties obtained 6 percent of the total, but the presence of townships is barely detected. Similar figures are not available for the early postwar years. However, the distribution of borrowing among levels of government probably changed substantially over the period. State and local governments increasingly resorted to special districts and special authorities to provide public services which were outside the regular governmental framework. The latter played a steadily expanding role in the capital market. In 1959 they accounted for 28 percent of total borrowing, although they probably represented only about 14 percent of all governmental units in the United States. Moreover, these agencies are involved in the provision of all types of public services, but they tend to concentrate on toll roads, public utilities, and public housing.

The degree of specialization stands out clearly in the statistics. For example, in 1959, all levels of government borrowed to finance capital formation for education purposes, but school districts marketed three-fifths of the total and sold bonds for no other purpose except for a small amount of refunding. Municipalities sold $285 million of school obligations (representing 13 percent of all school issues) and used for school construction about 14 percent of all the funds they borrowed. States offered about 15 percent of all school bonds sold, with such issues accounting for more than one-fifth of their total borrowing. The states used the bulk of the proceeds to support educational institutions directly administered by them, but they probably passed along a sizable proportion to local governments as grants-in-aid. State governments are mainly responsible for the construction and maintenance of roads (except local streets). For this purpose, they borrowed $364 million in 1959, or more than two-fifths of all highway bonds sold. If borrowing by statutory authorities for highways is added, the proportion rises to two-thirds. Almost one-quarter of all state bond issues consisted of highway issues.

The financing of sewer and water systems is undertaken primarily by municipalities, which in 1959 floated well over one-half of all bonds of this type. These issues in turn represented about one-third of their total borrowing. On the other hand, utilities such as electric and gas works are financed chiefly through specially created agencies, although a small amount is done directly by municipalities. Borrowing for social welfare purposes (except veterans' aid) is widely distributed. Bonds sold to pay veterans' benefits are offered almost exclusively by the states. The major-

TABLE VIII-5

BONDS SOLD BY STATE AND LOCAL GOVERNMENT; BY TYPE OF ISSUER AND USE OF PROCEEDS, 1959[1]; NUMBER OF GOVERNMENTAL UNITS IN THE UNITED STATES

(In Millions of Dollars)

Use of Proceeds	Type of Issuer							
	States	Counties	Munici-palities	Town-ships	School Districts	Special Districts	Statutory Authorities	Total
New Capital								
Education	335	122	285	6	1,319	23	88	2,177
Transport Facilities	383	75	338	1	—	28	330	1,184
Highways, bridges and tunnels	364	62	153	1	—	11	214	834
Ports and airports	19	13	185	—	—	17	116	350
Public Utilities	61	87	779	3	—	446	544	1,940
Sewer and water	60	87	623	3	—	209	117	1,099
Other utilities	1	—	156	—	—	257	427	841
Social Welfare	361	50	68	—	—	22	44	541
Hospitals and institutions	36	42	16	—	—	12	7	113
Veterans' aid	323	—	—	—	—	—	32	355
Recreation	2	8	52	—	—	6	5	73
Public Housing	55	—	113	—	—	4	229	402
Industrial Building	—	3	13	—	—	3	—	18
Other Purposes	321	142	413	6	0	125	120	1,128
Total New Capital	1,512	479	2,009	17	1,319	667	1,386	7,389
Refunding	38	2	29	—	5	1	32	108
Total Borrowing	1,550	481	2,038	17	1,324	669	1,418	7,497
Number of Governmental Units, 1957	48	3,047	17,167	17,214	50,453	14,423		102,353

1. Excludes federal government loans.

Note: Columns may not add to totals because of rounding.

SOURCE: Investment Bankers Association, **Statistical Bulletin, March,** 1960, Table 6, p. 9, and U. S. Bureau of the Census, **Governments in the United States,** 1957.

ity of public housing issues originates with local housing authorities. However, a significant amount is backed by the full taxing power of cities, and a few states have also sold small amounts. As mentioned above, industrial financing through the issuance of tax-exempt bonds is done mainly by municipalities, and they account for virtually all of the obligations in this category.

B. SUPPLY OF FUNDS

These trips to the capital market in the postwar period resulted in a threefold rise in state and local government debt outstanding. As with the volume of new issues, there was considerable variation in the annual rate of debt expansion. Since there was no particularly distinctive pattern in debt maturities, most of the fluctuation arose from the pace of new bond sales. As mentioned above, these reflected cyclical factors as well as sharp changes in the composition of state and local expenditures. While local governments accounted for about three-fourths of the borrowing in the postwar years, their share in the net increase in debt outstanding was probably larger; this was due mainly to the growing use of special authorities which sell revenue bonds to finance public service facilities. The latter development was one of the main factors underlying the moderate growth of life insurance companies' role in the municipal sector of the capital market. The nature and extent of their interest in revenue bonds are discussed more fully in Section IV.

In the fourteen years ending in 1959, life insurance companies added $2.5 billion of state and local issues to their portfolio, representing 6 percent of the net increase in the amount outstanding. Their slowly expanding role in this part of the capital market is shown in Table VIII-6. The modest increase in these issues in relation to their total assets is also evident. At the end of 1959, they owned $3,200 million of bonds sold by state and local governments in the United States and $935 million offered by foreign governments (virtually all of which were in Canada). They held 5 percent of the domestic issues in 1959 compared with just under 4 percent in 1945. Thus, state and local governments in the United States received about 3.6 percent of the net amount of funds life insurance companies supplied to the capital market since World War II.

On several occasions, however, they had a noticeable impact on the state and local securities market—especially on the market for revenue bonds. In 1948, they acquired almost one-seventh of the net expansion of state and local debt, and this was the first time since 1940 that they increased their portfolio of tax-exempt issues. The main inducement ap-

TABLE VIII-6

STATE AND LOCAL GOVERNMENT SECURITIES
HELD BY LIFE INSURANCE COMPANIES, 1945-1959

Year	Total Outstanding in U. S. ($ Billions)	Held by Life Insurance Companies: Amount Held ($ Millions) Total	United States	Foreign	Percentage of U.S. Total Outstanding	Percentage of Total Life Insurance Companies' Assets
1945	19.5	1,047	722	325	3.7	2.3
1946	19.4	936	614	322	3.2	1.9
1947	20.7	945	609	336	2.9	1.8
1948	22.8	1,199	872	327	3.8	2.2
1949	25.2	1,393	1,052	341	4.2	2.3
1950	28.2	1,547	1,152	395	4.1	2.4
1951	30.3	1,736	1,170	566	3.9	2.5
1952	33.1	1,767	1,153	614	3.5	2.4
1953	37.0	1,990	1,298	692	3.5	2.6
1954	41.5	2,549	1,846	703	4.4	3.1
1955	45.0	2,696	2,038	658	4.5	3.0
1956	48.2	3,011	2,273	738	4.7	3.1
1957	52.8	3,163	2,376	787	4.5	3.1
1958	58.5	3,510	2,681	829	4.6	3.3
1959	63.4	4,135	3,200	935	5.0	3.7

SOURCE: Total outstanding, **Federal Reserve Bulletin,** August, 1959, p. 1059 and June, 1960, p. 695. Life insurance companies' holdings, **1959 Life Insurance Fact Book,** p. 69 and **The Tally of Life Insurance Statistics,** February, 1960.

parently was the substantial rise in sales of revenue bonds, which were enlarged by the offering of New Jersey Turnpike obligations. The heavy volume of turnpike financing in 1954 again stimulated life insurance companies' interest in municipal bonds. In that year, their share of the market rose to 11 percent compared with less than 2 percent in 1953. In 1951 and 1952, their state and local portfolio had remained virtually unchanged. The third time they swung into the municipal market on a fairly large scale was in 1959, when they acquired about 10 percent of the net bonds sold. This activity was apparently promoted by a mixture of objectives. Some institutions sought tax-exempt obligations as a hedge against increased federal taxes; others undoubtedly found the yield and capital gains on revenue bonds quite attractive for many were selling at sizable discounts. Moreover, new revenue issues rose substantially in relation to total flotations; they accounted for about one-third of the total in contrast to one-quarter in the previous year.

But, as shown in Table VIII-7, the influence of life insurance companies on the overall market for state and local government securities was small. Individuals continued to provide the major outlet for these bonds, but the postwar years also brought about a realignment in the sources of demand. Individuals, for whom the tax-exempt income is of considerable importance, absorbed slightly less than two-fifths of the net increase in state and local government debt during the years 1946-59. However, at the end of the period, they held about 44 percent of the total outstanding; in 1945 their share was 54 percent. Their lessened importance in the market was counterbalanced by the expanded role of commercial banks, life insurance companies, and other financial institutions. The banks also place a high value on tax-exemption, and they have registered a strong demand for municipal issues—especially for general obligations. At the end of 1945, they held about one-fifth of this type of debt outstanding; by 1959 their share had climbed to over one-quarter. This gain resulted from their acquisition of 30 percent of the net increase in indebtedness. More-

TABLE VIII-7

OWNERSHIP OF STATE AND LOCAL GOVERNMENT DEBT,
BY MAJOR HOLDERS, 1945-1959
(In Billions of Dollars)

		Major Holders				
Year	Total Outstanding	Life Insurance Companies	Individuals and Non-profit Organizations	Commercial Banks	Other Financial Institutions	State and Local Governments
1945	19.5	0.7	11.1	4.0	1.1	2.6
1946	19.4	0.6	10.9	4.4	1.1	2.4
1947	20.7	0.6	11.4	5.3	0.9	2.5
1948	22.8	0.9	12.4	5.7	1.2	2.6
1949	25.2	1.1	12.9	6.5	1.6	3.1
1950	28.2	1.2	13.4	8.1	1.9	3.6
1951	30.3	1.2	13.8	9.2	2.3	3.8
1952	33.1	1.2	15.0	10.2	2.7	4.0
1953	37.0	1.3	16.8	10.8	3.7	4.4
1954	41.5	1.8	17.8	12.6	4.6	4.7
1955	45.0	2.0	19.9	12.7	5.3	5.1
1956	48.2	2.3	21.6	12.9	5.8	5.6
1957	52.8	2.4	23.9	13.9	6.6	6.0
1958	58.5	2.7	25.4	16.5	7.4	6.5
1959	63.4	3.2	27.9	16.9	8.4	7.0

SOURCE: **Federal Reserve Bulletin**, August, 1959, pp. 1056-62, and June, 1960, p. 695. Board of Governors of the Federal Reserve System, "Flow of Funds Savings Estimates," Supplement # 4, March, 1961. **1960 Life Insurance Fact Book**, p. 69.

over, commercial banks were virtually the only source of short-term funds for state and local governments. Some of these frequently sold short-term tax anticipation notes to the banks in their area. Occasionally they also borrowed from commercial banks on a temporary basis when the capital market was unsettled, and subsequently repaid the loans from the proceeds of bond sales. Tax exemption is also a strong attraction for several other types of financial institutions. These include fire and casualty insurance companies, some mutual savings banks, and pension funds. Taken as a whole, this group took up about one-sixth of the net expansion in state and local debt in the postwar period, and this lifted their share of the total outstanding from 6 to 13 percent.

State and local governments themselves in the postwar years provided a somewhat smaller outlet for their own obligations than they did at the beginning of the period. Nevertheless, they still acquired approximately 10 percent of the net rise. This was done primarily through the investment of pension funds established for the benefit of their employees. Some state laws limited the investment of their funds to United States government securities or state and local issues; however, such restrictions were progressively eased during the latter part of the 1950's. In numerous instances, on the other hand, state officials turned to their pension funds to place their obligations when they could not find a favorable market elsewhere.

SECTION IV
INVESTMENT IN STATE AND LOCAL GOVERNMENT SECURITIES SINCE WORLD WAR II

A. PATTERN OF OWNERSHIP

Life insurance companies' holdings of state and local government securities are highly concentrated among bonds sold to finance business-type projects. On June 30, 1959, they owned $2,991 million of obligations marketed by state and local governments in the United States. Revenue bonds amounted to $2,174 million, or 72.5 percent of the total; general obligations backed by the issuers' full faith and credit represented the remaining $817 million, or 27.5 percent of the total.

When the holdings are cross-classified by type of issuer or purpose of borrowing, the same set of preferences is revealed. (See Table VIII-8.) Moreover, $1,200 million (or two-fifths) of their total holdings were in public utilities such as power, water, and sewer systems. While over half of these bonds had been sold by municipalities, they were almost entirely revenue issues. In addition, revenue bonds sold by special author-

TABLE VIII-8

HOLDINGS OF STATE AND LOCAL GOVERNMENT BONDS BY LIFE INSURANCE COMPANIES, BY PURPOSE OF BOND ISSUE AND TYPE OF ISSUER, June 30, 1959

(In Millions of Dollars)

Purpose of Bond Issue	Total Amount	Type of Issuer: States	Counties	Cities, Towns and Townships	Authorities	Other
Public Utilities						
Electric and gas	418	—	61	127	170	60
Sewer and water	726	—	90	497	102	37
Other	61	—	2	51	7	1
Total Public Utilities	1,205	—	153	675	279	98
Bridges, Roads, Tunnels	909	114	33	75	672	15
Terminals (Airline, Bus, Railroad, etc.)	117	4	3	70	37	3
Educational Facilities	500	67	32	37	64	300
Housing and Community Facilities	103	6	6	45	32	14
Hospitals	12	1	5	2	2	2
Flood Control, Irrigation, Water Conservation	36	2	11	2	6	15
General Purpose or Other	109	11	10	71	8	9
Total	2,991	205	253	977	1,100	456
	Percentage Distribution					
Public Utilities						
Electric and gas	14.0	—	24.1	13.0	15.5	13.2
Sewer and water	24.3	—	35.6	50.9	9.3	8.1
Other	2.0	—	0.8	5.2	0.6	0.2
Total Public Utilities	40.3	—	60.5	69.1	25.4	21.5
Bridges, Roads, Tunnels	30.4	55.6	13.0	7.7	61.1	3.3
Terminals (Airline, Bus, Railroad, etc.)	3.9	1.9	1.2	7.1	3.4	0.7
Educational Facilities	16.7	32.7	12.6	3.8	5.8	65.8
Housing and Community Facilities	3.4	2.9	2.4	4.6	2.9	3.0
Hospitals	0.4	0.5	2.0	0.2	0.2	0.4
Flood Control, Irrigation, Water Conservation	1.2	1.0	4.3	0.2	0.5	3.3
General Purpose or Other	3.7	5.4	4.0	7.3	0.7	2.0
Total	100.0	100.0	100.0	100.0	100.0	100.0

SOURCE: **The Tally of Life Insurance Statistics**, November, 1959, p. 1.

ities to finance public utilities represented about one-quarter of their total holdings. Another $909 million (or 30 percent) of their state and local government portfolio consisted of highway issues. Of these, two-thirds had been floated by special authorities operating turnpikes, toll bridges, and tunnels, and 12 percent were issues sold by states for the same purposes. If other bonds to finance terminals are added (including ports, airports, and terminals for buses and railroads), transportation issues climb to about one-third of all tax-exempt securities owned by life insurance companies. The overwhelming majority of these are revenue obligations.

On the other hand, in mid-1959, life insurance companies owned $877 million of state and local government bonds floated for other purposes, and this amount approximated rather closely their holdings of $817 million of general obligations. Of course, the approximation is only a rough one, because there is undoubtedly some overlapping of purpose and type of issues. Nevertheless, the picture is probably not distorted very much. As shown below, about half of their school bonds are general obligations, and a large proportion of the hospital and general purpose debt they hold would fall in the same category.

Life insurance companies' ownership of state and local government securities is further highlighted by the statistics in Tables VIII-9 through VIII-11. These tables summarize information on state and local government securities owned by 62 companies at the end of 1958. These companies are among the 111 reporting in the BBER-MSU Survey of 1959. In returning the questionnaire, they enclosed copies of their annual statements and schedules of investments covering 1958 which they submitted to state insurance officials. In Table VIII-9, the companies are divided into four groups of 16 companies each (except the last group which has 14 companies); the companies ranged in size of total assets from $9,298 thousand to $3,893,335 thousand. The combined assets of the 62 companies amounted to $28,096,806 thousand, and they held $1,059,417 thousand of state and local government securities. Thus, tax-exempt issues represented 3.8 percent of their total assets, or slightly more than for the industry as a whole. Moreover, such issues seem to appeal relatively more to smaller than to larger institutions. Tables VIII-10 and VIII-11, respectively, show the companies' holdings of state and local obligations by type of issue and level of issuing government.

Several distinguishing features are evident in the pattern of tax-exempt holdings by these 62 life insurance companies. Again their concentration on revenue bonds is clearly portrayed; the latter represented 70 percent of their total holdings compared with 30 percent for general obligations.

TABLE VIII-9

DISTRIBUTION OF TOTAL ASSETS AND STATE AND LOCAL GOVERNMENT SECURITIES AMONG 62 LIFE INSURANCE COMPANIES, BY SIZE GROUP, 1958

(In Thousands of Dollars)

Group and Number of Companies	Size Range of Companies (Total Assets)	Total Assets Held by Group		State and Local Government Securities Held by Group		State and Local Securities as Percent of Total Assets
		Amount	Percent of Total	Amount	Percent of Total	
I(16)	540,773-3,893,335	21,523,195	76.5	688,261	65.0	3.2
II(16)	162,894-450,665	4,129,936	14.7	246,530	23.3	6.0
III(16)	71,395-161,814	1,829,574	6.5	91,079	8.6	5.0
IV(14)	9,298-68,759	610,101	2.3	33,547	3.1	5.5
Total: 62 Companies	—	28,092,806	100.0	1,059,417	100.0	3.8

SOURCE: Compiled from Annual Statements and Schedules submitted by life insurance companies to state insurance commissioners.

Virtually all of their portfolio (99 percent) consisted of issues sold by local governments (political subdivisions or the special agencies of the states). This extremely skewed distribution partly reflects the fact that a large number of projects financed directly by the states are of a welfare nature and afford yields relatively unattractive to life insurance companies. On the other hand, it also partly reflects the growing tendency of state governments to set up special authorities to provide public services. These fall under the local government heading, and life insurance companies do purchase their issues on a substantial scale.

State and local government issues owned by these institutions are mainly utility-type obligations among which revenue bonds predominate. For example, revenue bonds accounted for 92 percent of their electric utility issues, 91 percent of other utilities (including gas), and 71 percent of water and sewer bonds. On the other hand, only one-half of education bonds held by them consisted of revenue issues. Bonds sold to finance utilities represented about two-thirds, and highway debt about one-quarter, of their total holdings of state and local government securities.

Their ownership of state and local obligations can also be differentiated by size of company. As already mentioned, the demand for tax-exempt issues appears to be slightly stronger among small and medium sized companies than among the largest institutions. For instance, the com-

TABLE VII-10

STATE AND LOCAL GOVERNMENT SECURITIES HELD BY 62 LIFE INSURANCE COMPANIES, BY TYPE OF ISSUE, 1958

(In Thousands of Dollars)

Size Group	Total	Education	Roads, Bridges, Tunnels	Water, Sewer	Electric Power	Other Utilities	Ports, Airports	Public Housing	Veterans' Aid	All Other
Total State and Local Government Securities										
I	688,261	143,066	196,062	158,782	49,894	52,942	12,286	4,345	1,740	69,144
II	246,530	67,301	32,026	83,389	17,353	17,014	3,246	3,826	1,240	21,135
III	91,079	12,326	21,468	28,547	8,231	9,589	1,409	732	—	8,777
IV	33,547	5,220	5,497	10,006	4,006	1,934	520	75	515	5,774
Total	1,059,417	227,913	255,053	280,724	79,484	81,479	17,461	8,978	3,495	104,830
General Obligations										
I	147,671	42,874	7,321	42,089	2,165	2,506	2,726	4,345	1,740	41,905
II	133,172	62,353	10,432	32,770	4,364	3,489	921	707	1,240	16,896
III	15,889	8,906	961	5,319	125	314	104	105	—	55
IV	8,441	3,011	364	977	150	—	95	65	515	3,264
Total	305,173	117,144	19,078	81,155	6,804	6,309	3,846	5,222	3,495	62,120
Revenue Bonds										
I	540,590	100,192	188,741	116,693	47,729	50,436	9,560	—	—	27,239
II	113,358	4,948	21,594	50,619	12,989	13,525	2,325	3,119	—	4,239
III	75,190	3,420	20,507	23,228	8,106	9,275	1,305	627	—	8,722
IV	25,106	2,209	5,133	9,029	3,856	1,934	425	10	—	2,510
Total	754,244	110,769	235,975	199,569	72,680	75,170	13,615	3,756	—	42,710

SOURCE: Compiled from Annual Statements and Schedules submitted by life insurance companies to state insurance commissioners.

TABLE VIII-11

STATE AND LOCAL GOVERNMENT SECURITIES HELD BY 62
LIFE INSURANCE COMPANIES, BY LEVEL OF ISSUING GOVERNMENT, 1958
(In Thousands of Dollars)

Size Group	Total	Education	Roads, Bridges, Tunnels	Water, Sewer	Electric Power	Other Utilities	Ports, Airports	Public Housing	Veterans' Aid	All Other
State Governments										
I	5,327	750	453	250	775	—	—	—	1,740	1,359
II	5,077	667	1,889	—	—	—	239	800	1,040	432
III	541	30	250	2	—	—	4	—	—	255
IV	670	—	100	25	—	—	—	—	265	280
Total	11,615	1,457	2,692	277	775	—	243	800	3,045	2,326
Political Sub-Divisions										
I	682,934	142,316	195,609	158,532	49,119	52,942	12,286	4,345	—	67,785
II	241,453	66,624	30,137	83,389	17,353	17,014	3,007	3,026	200	20,703
III	90,538	12,296	21,218	28,545	8,231	9,589	1,405	732	—	8,522
IV	32,877	5,220	5,397	9,981	4,006	1,934	520	75	250	5,494
Total	1,047,802	226,456	252,361	280,447	78,709	81,479	17,218	8,175	450	102,504

SOURCE: Compiled from Annual Statements and Schedules submitted by life insurance companies to state insurance commissioners.

panies in Group I had three-quarters of the assets held by the 62 companies but only two-thirds of the tax-exempt issues. The biggest share of municipal obligations relative to assets was held by the companies in Group II. The distribution of revenue bonds and general obligations among companies of various size also exhibits a mixed picture. In Groups I and III, revenue bonds approximate 80 percent of their total holdings. However, the type of revenue bonds held differs appreciably. The largest companies composing Group I tend to specialize in highway bonds (especially turnpikes) which accounted for 28 percent of their entire state and local portfolio; companies in Group III tend to hold primarily the revenue bonds floated by local utilities. The companies just below the top group in size have the smallest proportion of their holdings in revenue bonds.

When life insurance companies' holdings of state and local government securities are examined more closely in terms of the purpose of issue, the strong appeal of revenue issues is thrown into even sharper relief. About one-quarter of the total holdings of the 62 companies in the sample consisted of bonds sold to finance roads, bridges, and tunnels. Virtually all of these (93 percent) were revenue issues floated primarily by local governments, especially by statutory authorities or commissions operating turnpikes and toll bridges. Most of these issues enjoy a national market in which the largest life insurance companies are pre-eminent. The companies in Group I held over three-quarters of the bonds of this type owned by the 62 institutions, representing their largest share of any of the subsectors of the market. Revenue bonds accounted for 96 percent of their highway issues, and the latter in turn accounted for 29 percent of all their state and local government securities. Thus, highway obligations were the most important type of tax-exempt bonds owned by the largest companies. While revenue bonds were about the same proportion among highway securities owned by smaller institutions, the amount was much less in relation to their total assets. Road and bridge bonds owned by the companies in Group II were less concentrated in revenue issues (where the ratio was only two-thirds), and they represented only 13 percent of their total holdings of state and local government obligations.

The appeal of utility issues to life insurance companies varies greatly depending on the type of financing. Water and sewer bonds are purchased somewhat more heavily by intermediate and small sized companies than by larger institutions. Although almost one-third of such issues owned by the 62 life insurance companies consisted of general obligations, many of them do not enjoy a national market. The market for electric and gas utility obligations is considerably wider, but some offerings are still distributed chiefly in the local market. Consequently, the medium sized life insurance companies (whose investment activity is essentially regional in scope) are squeezed to some extent by both large and small competitors. The vast majority (95 percent) of utility issues held by the companies in the survey were revenue bonds, and the largest companies in Group I owned about three-fifths of the total. On the other hand, the smallest group of institutions owned close to 5 percent of utility issues, a proportion approximately twice their share in total assets and one and two-thirds times their share of all state and local government securities held by the 62 companies.

Education bonds represented about one-fifth of the tax-exempt obligations held by the life insurance companies in the sample. One-half of the education issues were general obligations, and this sharply reduces their appeal to the largest companies. For example, while the companies in Group I had two-fifths of all the education bonds owned by the firms in the sample, such issues accounted for only one-fifth of their municipal portfolio. Moreover, about 70 percent of their education bonds were revenue obligations. In contrast, 90 percent of the education bonds held by companies in Group II were general obligations, and they owned 55 percent of general obligation education bonds held by the 62 companies. In fact, education bonds represented the most important type of tax-exempt securities held by companies in Group II, for these amounted to 27 percent of their total state and local portfolio. Among the smallest group of companies, almost three-fifths of their education bonds were general obligations, but education issues constituted only one-sixth of their total state and local government holdings.

Little comment is required regarding the remaining statistics of Tables VIII-10 and VIII-11. The fact that the market for public housing issues among life insurance companies exists primarily among the largest institutions is easily understood. These obligations are sold mainly in the national market. Underwriters who acquire them at competitive auctions rely heavily on the leading life insurance companies and other large investors as ultimate buyers. Bonds sold for veterans' aid (all general obligations) have only a limited appeal to life insurance companies, and this is especially true of the largest institutions. This type of debt is sold almost entirely by the states, and the yields are relatively unattractive.

B. Rise of Special Authorities and Expansion of Revenue Bond Financing

The foregoing data have amply demonstrated the concentration of life insurance companies on revenue bonds—especially bonds sold by special authorities. The increased dependence of state and local governments on special authorities to meet the expanding demand for public services is one of the most striking developments in municipal finance since World War II. Almost without exception, these special purpose agencies have financed their capital outlays by the sale of bonds secured by revenue from the operation of business-type enterprises. The results have been a partial escape from the debt limitations imposed on state and local governments by outdated statutes, a smaller gap between the demand for and supply of services, and a substantial transformation in the structure and functioning of the municipal bond market.

In 1957, there were 14,423 statutory authorities and special districts in the United States.[9] Virtually all of these special authorities, many of the special districts, and a large number of municipalities and other governmental units had sold revenue bonds. No estimate exists of the volume of revenue bonds sold prior to 1938. For the years since then, the *Bond Buyer's* series and figures compiled by the Investment Bankers Association present a fair picture of the trend. The overriding conclusion obtained from these statistics is that revenue bonds during the postwar period have been about four times as important as a borrowing medium for state and local governments as they were before World War II. During the four years 1938-41, $383 million of revenue bonds were sold (including refunding); this amounted to only 10 percent of expenditures by state and local governments on new construction and represented about 8 percent of the total long-term bonds floated by them. In the fourteen years ending in 1959, around $19 billion of revenue bonds were sold by state and local governments, representing 28 percent of the total long-term debt marketed. Over roughly the same period, revenue issues grew from about one-tenth to approximately 28 percent of the outstanding long-term debt. Furthermore, revenue bonds accounted for well over one-third of the net increase in tax-exempt debt since 1948, the earliest year for which reliable estimates are available.[10] The share of revenue bonds in the net increase was larger than in new bond sales, because they typically have longer maturities than general obligations.

The volume and share of revenue bonds and general obligations sold since World War II are shown in Table VIII-12. The general uptrend in revenue bonds is clearly evident, but annual fluctuations have also been substantial. The first sizable jump occurred in 1948-49 and was primarily a reflection of the New Jersey Turnpike financing. The rest of the turnpike movement is also visible in the figures. This culminated with the record sale of $3.2 billion of revenue bonds in 1954, almost half the total

TABLE VIII-12

STATE AND LOCAL GOVERNMENT BOND SALES,
BY TYPE, 1946-1959
(In Millions of Dollars)

Year	Total	General Obligations		Revenue Bonds	
		Amount	Percent of Total	Amount	Percent of Total
1946	1,202	996	83.0	206	17.0
1947	2,353	1,967	84.0	386	16.0
1948	2,990	2,440	81.5	550	18.5
1949	3,003	2,320	77.4	683	22.6
1950	3,693	3,093	83.7	600	16.3
1951	3,278	2,548	77.7	730	22.3
1952	4,407	2,944	66.6	1,463	33.4
1953	5,555	3,988	72.0	1,567	28.0
1954	6,968	3,754	53.6	3,214	46.4
1955	5,976	4,266	71.2	1,710	28.8
1956	5,446	3,786	69.5	1,660	30.5
1957	6,810	4,850	71.2	1,960	28.8
1958	7,401	5,629	76.0	1,772	24.0
1959	7,497	5,100	68.0	2,397	32.0

SOURCE: **Bond Buyer**, 1946-56 and Investment Bankers Association, **Statistical Bulletin**, 1957-59.

floated. Moreover, about three-fifths of the revenue bonds sold in that year were for toll roads.

Another broad measure of the increased reliance of state and local governments on revenue bond financing is given in the multiplication of such securities in the postwar period. As shown in Table VIII-13, in 1946 approximately 1,642 separate issues were recorded by Moody's Investors Service. By the end of 1959, the number had almost doubled. Furthermore, the growth was particularly marked among bonds secured entirely by revenue from fees charged for the use of toll roads, gas, and multiple purpose projects. In 1946, no bonds were reported outstanding against off-street parking facilities, but by 1959 there were 135 issues. The expansion in the number of traditional revenue issues (local transportation, water, and sewer systems) was rather moderate. The number of revenue bonds of a quasi-utility nature (secured partly by fees and partly by general taxes) also experienced moderate growth—except for those sold to finance airports. School bonds, backed almost exclusively by rents collected on publicly-owned school buildings, continued to account for the bulk of nonutility issues. Most of these bonds have been sold by school

TABLE VIII-13

NUMBER OF OUTSTANDING REVENUE BOND ISSUES
IN THE UNITED STATES, BY SOURCE OF PAYMENT, 1946 AND 1959

Source of Payment	1946	1959
Utility	1,373	2,864
Bridge, tunnel, toll highway	63	134
Electric light and power	157	209
Gas	36	95
Public transportation	5	8
Off-street parking facilities	—	135
Water	825	1,216
Sewer	185	280
Multiple purpose	102	787
Quasi-Utility	42	90
Airport	4	28
Dock and terminal	11	19
Hospital	22	34
Public market	5	9
Nonutility	185	256
Rentals of public buildings:		
To the general public	185	235
Educational facilities	165	172
Recreational facilities	20	63
To private persons or corporations	—	21
Miscellaneous	42	59
Total	1,642	3,269

SOURCE: Compiled from Moody's Investors Service, **Municipals,** 1960.

districts in Pennsylvania, Indiana, and Kentucky, where special authorities are mainly responsible for the construction of educational facilities.

Of all the governmental units selling revenue bonds, the statutory authorities are the most important in terms of volume. As a rule, these agencies are created by a special act of state legislatures to construct and operate utilities (such as a toll highway, bridge, or tunnel), but commissions to perform the same functions have also been established by municipalities under their general charters. Water, sewer, electric and gas systems, and local transportation networks are typical of the facilities operated by municipal commissions. Most authorities are autonomous bodies, free of supervision by either the general electorate or regulatory agencies. While they usually possess power of eminent domain (similar to that of other governmental units), the exemption of revenue bond income from federal income taxation is the feature of most importance to the capital market. Until the mid-1920's, statutory authorities were very few, and revenue bonds had been resorted to by only a few municipalities: Seattle was perhaps the largest among them. But in 1926, the statutory authority and revenue bond financing were securely joined when the Port of New York Authority sold $34 million of bonds to meet outlays on its Staten Island bridges and to initiate construction of the George Washington Bridge. The authority used the same technique to finance its airports, docks, and tunnels and thoroughly demonstrated the advantages of both the special authority and revenue bond financing. Since then, the combination has been increasing in popularity.

Several main reasons explain the accelerated growth of statutory authorities and revenue bond financing. In the first place, municipalities early recognized the need to provide services which could not be readily supplied by private enterprise—or which the latter could supply only at excessively high cost. It was felt that if the local government entered the field, it could grant tax exemption, and this would result in lower borrowing cost—some of which could be passed on to consumers in the form of lower rates. Local utilities typify this sort of consideration.

Secondly, the demand for still other services was recognized but held to be of a specific nature. For these, most governments were unwilling to tax the general public or stake their full faith and credit on a risky business-type venture. In this category fell toll roads, bridges, tunnels, ports, airports, off-street parking facilities, college dormitories, and similar projects. Another factor which became increasingly prominent in the postwar years was the fact that many states and local governments were pressing against debt limitations and were unable, even if they had been willing, to finance required services by directly assuming additional debt. The remedy was found in special authorities empowered to borrow money and carry out governmental functions clearly defined but outside the structure of general government. School building authorities (of which the examples found in Pennsylvania, Indiana, and Kentucky are the most highly developed) illustrate this principle. These are public corporations set up to construct buildings which are then rented to local school districts on the basis of a long-term lease. The annual rent, after operating costs are covered, pays the interest on the bonds and provides for their retirement; the lease arrangement is hardly distinguishable from an ordinary tax dedication.

C. Advantages of Revenue Bonds for Life Insurance Companies

The rise of special authorities described above, and their borrowing through the use of revenue bonds, has created a capital market instrument admirably suited for the investment of life insurance funds. The relatively high yield on revenue bonds (even aside from the tax exemption feature) is the chief attraction for these institutions. The lack of a government guarantee behind most of these issues is the main factor underlying the higher yield on revenue issues compared with general obligations, but part of the differential also reflects the greater risk inherent in a business-type enterprise. In general, the state or local government does not pledge its full faith and credit (derived from its taxing power) to support borrowing by special authorities as it does when bonds are floated directly by the government involved.[11]

In many instances, the coupon required for the successful marketing of an unrated revenue bond may be as much as 2 percentage points above that for high grade general obligations. Of course, some widely known users of revenue bonds can finance their projects at a much smaller differential. But in general, interest rates on revenue bonds are quite close to those on taxable obligations. For example, of ten new toll road bond issues sold in 1954 (the year of heaviest flotations) five were offered to yield from 3.30 to 4.30 percent; four afforded a 3.00 percent yield, and only one went as low as 2.75 percent. Thus, the average yield on these new issues was about 3.38 percent. During the same year, according to the Dow-Jones index, yields on seasoned revenue bonds averaged about 2.80 percent; the interest rates on outstanding general obligations averaged about 2.40 percent (Moody's figures). On the other hand, new issues of corporate bonds rated Aa by Moody's were marketed at yields between 2.98 and 3.19 percent and averaged 3.02 percent in 1954; the index for similar seasoned corporate bonds ranged between 3.00 and 3.22 percent with an average of 3.06 percent in the same year. Thus, if these rates were typical, new revenue bonds (even without considering their tax status) provided investors about $\frac{1}{12}$ more than they could get on new high grade corporate bonds entailing approximately the same risk. Seasoned revenue issues yielded around 90 percent of the return on corporate obligations. After adjusting for the tax advantage, the differential in favor of seasoned corporate debt is entirely erased. Given the federal income tax rates to which life insurance companies were subject in 1954, tax exemption was worth about 25 basis points; this made even seasoned revenue bond yields equal to those on taxable high grade corporates. Furthermore, the differential in favor of newly offered revenue securities was widened to about one-fifth.

Another illustration of the high yields on revenue bonds and their attraction for life insurance companies is exhibited in Table VIII-14. This compares changes in prices and yields on ten highway revenue bonds

TABLE VIII-14

COMPARISON OF CHANGES IN PRICES AND YIELDS
FOR SELECTED HIGHWAY REVENUE BONDS,
October 30, 1957-April 29, 1958

Issuer	Amount Outstanding[1] ($ Millions)	Coupon and Maturity	October 30, 1957			April 29, 1958			Change in Yield Oct. '57-April '58
			Bid	Asked	Yield[2] (Percent)	Bid	Asked	Yield[2] (Percent)	
Illinois Toll Road	415	3¾-95	68	69	5.70	80	81	4.86	—.84
Indiana Toll Road	280	3½-94	81½	82½	4.44	91½	92¼	3.88	—.56
Jacksonville Express	60	4¼-92	92½	93½	4.59	103	104	4.03	—.56
Kansas Turnpike	160	3⅜-94	67½	68½	5.21	79	80	4.45	—.76
Maine Turnpike	75	4-89	82	83½	5.00	92	93	4.40	—.60
Massachusetts Turnpike	239	3.30-94	85	86	4.04	91	91¾	3.72	—.32
New Jersey Turnpike	150	3⅜-88	94	95	3.61	100⅜	101½	3.30	—.31
New York Thruway	235	3.10-94	90	91	3.52	98½	99½	3.12	—.40
Ohio Turnpike	326	3¼-92	83½	84½	4.04	92¾	93½	3.55	—.49
Pennsylvania Turnpike	233	3.10-93	78½	79½	4.18	88¼	89	3.67	—.51

1. Amount outstanding is for a particular issue and does not necessarily represent the total indebtedness of the issuer.

2. Based on offering price.

SOURCE: Compiled from market quotations reported in the **Bond Buyer**.

between October 1957, and April 1958. These toll road issues are highly favored by life insurance companies because of their long maturities (averaging close to 40 years) and broad market as well as high rate of return. In October 1957, during the peak in interest rates just prior to the shift to an easier monetary policy to counter the 1957-58 recession, all of the toll road bonds were selling at discounts, and yields ranged from 3.52 to 5.70 percent. While bonds of the strongest roads experienced the smallest discounts, even these provided an opportunity for sizable capital gains, and market yields on some issues exceeded those on corporate obligations of approximately the same credit risk. By the end of April, 1958, the competition for investment outlets during the period of credit ease had raised prices of highway revenue bonds by an average of ten points, and yields had fallen by an average of 54 basis points. Nevertheless, eight of these issues were still quoted below par; all of them were priced to yield from 3.12 to 4.86 percent, and the average was 3.90 percent. In the same month, Moody's Aa corporate index averaged 3.85 percent for new flotations and 3.78 percent for outstanding issues. Thus, again the substantial yield advantage of revenue bonds is evident. Furthermore, it tends to persist despite sharp changes in the level and structure of interest rates.

The form and maturities of revenue bonds also enhance their appeal to life insurance companies. Revenue issues are sold in both term (single payment) and serial form, but about three-quarters of the offerings are of the latter type.[12] However, the proportion varies widely depending on the purpose of the issue. Serial bonds are almost always used in the financing of water and sewer projects and school buildings. Term issues are characteristic of most toll roads, many ports, airports, bridges, and some electric utilities. Life insurance companies, given their interest in minimizing return cash inflow arising from loan repayments, see considerable advantage in the acquisition of fixed term revenue bonds. Virtually all of the term bonds are callable, and call of bonds by lot to be retired from earnings is generally permitted. In fact, many projects presuppose a margin of coverage which would retire the whole issue well before maturity. On the other hand, a penalty is usually imposed on calls for refunding, and this too offers life insurance companies some protection against a sudden return of cash.

Revenue bonds typically have far longer maturities than general obligations. The IBA found that for about three-quarters (by value) of revenue bonds sold in 1956-57 the final maturity exceeded 20 years, and for about two-fifths the maturities were in excess of 30 years. In terms of the number of issues, both of these percentages were lower; this suggests that the smaller flotations tend to have shorter maturities. Life insurance companies, however, are primarily interested in the longer issues whose long maturities are ideally suited to their investment needs.

The specialized and narrow market for revenue bonds gives life insurance companies a slight edge in the competition with other investors. Revenue bond issues are typically larger than general obligations, averaging \$2.1 million compared with \$700 thousand,[13] but supply and demand are rather thin in the neighborhood of bid and ask quotations. A few of the larger issues, however, are popular market items, the spread between bid and ask prices is small, and their marketability approaches that of the direct debt of the parent government. Other less marketable issues also have considerable appeal to life insurance companies who purchase such obligations primarily to hold to maturity to obtain the high returns. Because they are traders to a far less extent than most other investors, these institutions are not quite so concerned with the narrowness of the market for revenue bonds.

Most revenue bonds are not rated at the time of issue, and this also adversely affects their marketability. Again, however, this does not greatly hinder life insurance companies. For example, of the revenue bonds sold in the year ending in June, 1957, about three-quarters of the total number were not rated by Moody's. Among the rest, 18 percent were rated A or better, and 6 percent were rated Baa. On the basis of dollar volume, Moody's rated about 30 percent of the issues Aa and another 30 percent were rated A; 8 percent drew Baa, and the remaining one-third were not rated at all.[14] Nevertheless, in general Moody's prefers to wait until a project has demonstrated its earning potential during several years of successful operation before a rating is made. Other rating agencies tend to view revenue bonds primarily as obligations of a business-type undertaking. Because issuing authorities usually cannot show an earnings record, analysts in rating agencies rely on the engineers' estimates and the long-run economic outlook for the project. While most sewer and water projects (and to a certain extent electric and gas works) already have established market areas as a backstop, this is far from true of toll roads, bridges, and similar ventures. These types of revenue bonds entail much greater risk for investors. But it is exactly in appraising this type of risk that the large life insurance companies have an advantage. They already have the technical personnel skilled in the investigation of bonds offered by corporate enterprises, and the revenue obligations described above are not essentially different. Moreover, because many of these institutions have accumulated considerable experience with direct placement of corporate securities, the absence of ratings does not pose a serious obstacle in the valuation process.

The actual ownership of revenue bonds by life insurance companies and other investors cannot be delineated in detail. Yet the market for these issues appears to be somewhat separate from the market for other tax-exempt securities. Individuals, the leading buyers of general obligations, also acquire the largest share of revenue bonds. However, the critical difference between the two sectors of the municipal market is the role of commercial banks in each. Since 1933, these institutions (whose sustained interest in general obligations considerably strengthens the latter) have been prohibited from underwriting revenue bonds. Moreover, because of the long maturities and thin market for most revenue issues, they have lacked the liquidity required of commercial bank portfolios. Consequently, they participate in only a limited way in the secondary market for revenue bonds. In mid-1956, they held about $1,850 million of revenue bonds; this represented about one-sixth of the estimated total outstanding. At the same time, they held nearly $13 billion of state and local general obligations, or approximately 30 percent of the total. Mutual savings banks also acquire a sizable amount of revenue issues. Many of them place a high premium on tax-exempt income; while their relative tax burden is much less than that of commercial banks, it is still substantial for some of them. Prospects of capital appreciation have also attracted many of these institutions.

As already mentioned, life insurance companies have a much larger share of the market for revenue bonds than of the municipal market as a whole. At the end of 1959, they owned $2,316 million of revenue bonds. Since revenue bonds at that time probably represented about 28 percent of the state and local government debt, the volume of revenue bonds outstanding was approximately $17.8 billion. Thus, life insurance companies held roughly 13 percent of the revenue issues compared with 5 percent of all state and local obligations.

Section V

Summary and Conclusions

From the above discussion, it is evident that despite the vigorous expansion of the state and local government securities market since World War II, life insurance companies have been a minor source of funds in this part of the capital market. In the fourteen years ending in 1959, they added $2.5 billion of such obligations to their portfolios, representing about 6 percent of the increase in the amount outstanding. State and local governments thus received around 4 percent of the net volume of funds life insurance companies supplied to the capital market as a whole.

The accelerated pace of state and local spending in the postwar period generated a persistent increase in the long-term demands on the capital market. Their increased spending in turn was stimulated by factors such as general population growth, expansion of school enrollment, and the migration from cities to suburbs. All of these trends boosted public capital outlays on new school buildings, streets, water and sewer systems, and electric and gas facilities. Moreover, municipalities began to branch out into entirely new types of ventures as the nature of public needs changed. Simultaneously, to find a market for their high volume of debt, they found it necessary to make significant concessions to investors along the traditional lines of higher yields and greater call protection; they also had to devise essentially new techniques of bond financing, exemplified in the rise of the special authority and the growth of revenue bond flotations.

The increased reliance on special authorities was the result of a combination of factors, among which three were perhaps most important. The necessity to provide services (offered mainly by public utilities) at prices below what private firms would have to charge was the first stimulus. While this type of project had existed long before World War II, it served as a ready model for ventures into new activities. Some of these activities were undertaken to provide services the demand for which was so specialized that most governments did not feel justified in taxing the general public to finance them. Toll roads are the most prominent example, although parking lots and similar business-type enterprises should also be included. The special authority was the ideal vehicle to operate such projects, and revenue bonds were the ideal means of borrowing the funds required to finance capital formation. Finally, outmoded debt ceilings, a legacy of depressions and other periods of crises in public finance, prevented many governments from borrowing funds for capital expenditures; the solution was again found in the use of special authorities outside the framework of general government. School authorities found in several states are typical examples of this technique.

The interest of life insurance companies in state and local government securities centers primarily in revenue bonds floated by special authorities operating business-type enterprises. For the industry as a whole, almost three-fourths of the municipal securities owned at the end of 1959 consisted of revenue bonds compared with just over one-quarter of general obligations. Considerable disparity exists among companies of various sizes in their preference for revenue bonds, and demand is particularly strong among large institutions. Numerous factors explain this priority given to revenue bonds. First, of course, is the relatively higher yield resulting from the lack of a government guarantee and the greater risk inherent in business-type ventures. However, for most large institutions this type of risk can be readily appraised since it is essentially the same as that with which they must cope in corporate lending. In addition, the long maturities, call provisions, and other features of revenue bonds enhance their appeal to life insurance companies. Furthermore, the narrow and specialized market for revenue bonds does not hamper life insurance companies' participation; their experience with direct placements of corporate issues has conditioned the larger companies to handle investment problems associated with buying securities primarily to hold because of the lack of a secondary market.

Life insurance companies' concentration on revenue bonds has given them a much larger share of this market than of the municipal market as a whole. In 1959 they owned about 13 percent of revenue issues compared with 5 percent of all state and local obligations outstanding. On balance, however, it seems that life insurance companies are not likely to become a major source of funds for state and local governments. The rate of federal taxation applicable to them remains relatively light—despite the substantial percentage increase in 1959. Thus, they will most likely continue to refrain from paying the premium on tax-exempt income which is so highly valued by individuals, commercial banks, and others subject to heavier tax burdens.

Footnotes

1. State and local government securities are frequently referred to as "municipal" issues in the language of the capital market. The term when used in this chapter has the same meaning.

2. The income is not usually exempt from state income taxes except in the state of issue. For example, in 1952, there were 34 states with a corporate income tax, and 33 had a personal income tax. In 31 states, the corporate tax was levied against the income from securities of other states and local governments, and the personal income tax was applied in 30 states. Moreover, 16 states taxed corporate income from their home state securities, and 8 states treated personal income in the same way. See Roland I. Robinson, *Postwar Market for State and Local Government Securities,* a study sponsored by the National Bureau of Economic Research (Princeton: Princeton University Press, 1960), p. 67.

3. George T. Conklin, Jr., "A Century of Portfolio Management," *Investment of Life Insurance Funds,* pp. 274-75.

4. *Ibid.*

5. Robinson, *op. cit.,* p. 93.

6. Loans from the federal government are excluded.

7. Investment Bankers Association, *Statistical Bulletin,* April, 1957, pp. 1-4.

8. Investment Bankers Association, *Municipal Industrial Financing*, May, 1961, p. 9.

9. U. S. Bureau of the Census, *Governments in the United States*, 1957.

10. Robinson, *op. cit.*, p. 202.

11. While this is generally true, some governmental units have guaranteed the obligations of special authorities. The IBA found that about 20 percent of revenue bonds sold in the year ending in June, 1957, were in this category. Moreover, bonds of some major toll roads (including the New Jersey Turnpike and New York Thruway) have state backing.

12. IBA *Statistical Bulletin*, October, 1957, p. 4.

13. *Ibid.*, p. 2.

14. *Ibid.*, p. 3.

CHAPTER IX

Small Business and Equity Financing

SECTION I
INTRODUCTION

With the growing institutionalization of savings, many businessmen, economists, government officials, and other observers have anxiously raised the question of the adequacy of equity capital. Some of this attention has sprung from the concern with the more narrow problem of the availability of funds for small businesses, but a more fundamental issue is also involved. The leading financial institutions, such as life insurance companies and other savings intermediaries, are mobilizing an increasing share of savings which they invest almost exclusively in debt instruments. In view of this trend, some students of economics and finance are doubting whether firms seeking risk capital have, and will continue to have, reasonable access to the nation's savings stream. While the perception and analysis of the problem vary greatly, one thread is visible in most discussions: how can a greater proportion of the savings flowing into nonbank financial intermediaries be channeled into equity investment?[1]

In this chapter, the role of life insurance companies in small business financing is examined first. Attention is then given to their participation in the stock market and the appropriateness of common stocks as investments for these institutions.

SECTION II
SMALL BUSINESS FINANCING

A. PROBLEMS OF SMALL BUSINESS LENDING

A complex of legal, institutional, and objective factors makes life insurance companies rather unpromising as a source of funds for small businesses. Spokesmen for the industry frequently emphasize that the life insurance community is sensitive to the needs of small firms and contributes in an important way to the supply of long-term funds available to them. Nevertheless, even the meager amount of statistical evidence relating to their investments in enterprises of various sizes demonstrates the validity of the above proposition.

As noted in Chapter II, most state insurance laws impose severe restraints on the ability of life insurance companies to supply nonmortgage credit to unincorporated businesses. In the late 1940's, it was estimated that 90 percent of the country's small businesses were unincorporated,[2] and the strong pull of income tax and other advantages probably has maintained the proportion. But the advantages of the noncorporate form of business organization have been far from costless, because these concerns have generally been handicapped in trying to raise long-term funds through the sale of bonds. Moreover, the five-year earnings requirement, or a similar provision, as a standard of eligibility contained in most state laws governing life insurance investments also precludes these institutions from purchasing bond issues of many small corporate businesses. These restraints have been easing in recent years through the adoption of leeway clauses in several states. The provision added in New York State in 1958 is typical; it allows life insurance companies to invest 2 percent of their total assets in a form not otherwise prohibited or limited. Through this opening, more life insurance funds may reach the small business area, but the volume is not likely to be greatly enlarged.

Even if legal limitations were relaxed appreciably, the risk inherent in small businesses would remain an obstacle to life insurance company lending to such firms. Portfolio managers report that small businesses typically are weak in managerial capacity and do not have the equity base to support a loan of the size for which they apply. In many instances, a single individual manages the entire range of business activity, including finance, production, and sales, as well as day to day administration. Moreover, their interest in maintaining this control makes them unwilling to share ownership with others who would expand the equity of the firm. The smaller the business the greater the likelihood that it will be plagued by these weaknesses. Given this increasing risk as one descends the array of firm size, life insurance companies are unprepared to expose policyholders' funds to the hazards which most small businesses encounter. Aside from the extra risk, the higher administrative cost per dollar of investment also dampens these investors' interest in lending to small enterprises. According to officials in the insurance community, legal, administrative, and other costs vary inversely with size of borrower and would quickly become prohibitive if numerous loan applications from small businesses scattered about the country were handled. This aversion to getting involved with such difficulties is illustrated by the case of a large New England life insurance company which has a standing rule that no loans of less than $500,000 are to be made outside the New England region.

On the other hand, life insurance companies are favorably situated to finance small businesses through mortgage loans. Compared with the constraints on bond acquisitions, the legal barriers to mortgage lending are less formidable; the administrative machinery is less cumbersome, the cost per dollar of business is lower, and above all the inherent risk is smaller. Most legal standards relate to mortgage terms (such as maturities and loan-to-value ratios) which many small enterprises can meet. Except in rare instances, business and commercial mortgage applications can be processed through the correspondence system which originates other types of mortgages, and these can be readily evaluated by the company's mortgage staff. Because of the built-in facilities for handling other types of mortgages, the extra cost of extending nonresidential loans is slight. Finally, with respect to risk, life insurance companies in mortgage lending rely mainly on property values and the expected income stream for security and to a much less extent on management ability or assets of the borrower. Given this setting, life insurance companies find relatively few investment opportunities among small businesses, and these are tapped primarily through the extension of mortgage credit.

The one substantial block of information available on life insurance companies' lending to business by type of financing and size of borrower was developed in 1957 by the Life Insurance Association of America (LIAA) at the request of a congressional committee examining some of the basic problems faced by small firms in the economy.[3] In the survey, LIAA polled 67 member companies whose $74 billion of assets in 1956 represented 77 percent of the industry total. Cooperating companies were asked to provide details on their loans to business and industry during the four years 1953 through 1956. Data gathered in the survey included the number of loans and dollar amounts authorized in each year to acquire public utility obligations, business and industrial bonds, and mortgage loans secured by business and industrial property. The statistics were classified in terms of the total size of loan, the asset size of the borrowing firm, the principal business of the borrower, and the average rate of interest.

Data from the LIAA Survey were supplemented by qualitative information obtained by Federal Reserve interviewers in 1958 who contacted officials in a few leading life insurance companies.[4] From the combined results of these studies emerged the following picture of small business lending by life insurance companies:

> Real estate mortgages account for virtually the entire amount of such financing.
>
> Of all business loans made by life insurance companies, those to small businesses represent a large proportion of the number but only a minor share of the amount.
>
> Interest rates on long-term loans to small enterprises are higher than to large businesses and are also more inflexible.
>
> Small businesses obtain mortgage funds primarily to finance construction or to acquire real estate.
>
> Many small firms may be ignorant of the lending standards established by life insurance companies, and the actual, effective demand of small businesses for the institutions' funds may be less than it appears on the surface.

Before examining the statistics on the pattern of life insurance lending to small businesses, it would be useful to have a rough guideline differentiating small from large business enterprises. In the LIAA Survey, small business loans were assumed to be those for $250,000 or less. This definition, which LIAA recognized as quite arbitrary, was chosen because it was the limit on the size of loan which the Small Business Administration could make. In terms of the size of borrower, the definition of small business varies depending on the type of activity; the Federal Reserve System in its business loan surveys classifies a small business in the retail and real estate fields as one whose total assets are less than $50,000; in manufacturing the ceiling is $1,000,000. In the present discussion, the Federal Reserve's definition of size of firm is adopted, and the Small Business Administration's limit on the size of loans is accepted.

B. Mortgage Loans to Small Businesses

Within these boundaries, it is evident that life insurance companies' mortgage lending to small businesses is done through numerous small loans and is highly concentrated among real estate outlets. As Table IX-1 shows, in the period 1953-56, between two-fifths and one-half of the number of loans were under $50,000; if loans of $50,000 to $100,000 are included (and because of the rough definition of small business which is being used these should be included), the proportion climbs to between

TABLE IX-1

DISTRIBUTION OF NUMBER AND AMOUNT OF BUSINESS MORTGAGE LOANS OF LIFE INSURANCE COMPANIES, BY SIZE OF LOAN

(Percent)

Amount of Loan (Thousands of Dollars)	1953	1954	1955	1956
		Number		
Under $50	48.6	44.0	41.8	39.1
$50 to $100	19.4	19.3	19.6	21.1
$100 to $250	19.4	20.7	21.7	22.4
$250 to $1,000	9.1	11.8	12.6	12.5
Over $1,000	3.5	4.2	4.3	4.9
All Sizes	100.0	100.0	100.0	100.0
		Amount		
Under $50	6.4	4.7	4.2	3.9
$50 to $100	7.3	5.8	5.5	5.7
$100 to $250	15.6	13.6	13.8	13.5
$250 to $1,000	21.8	23.4	22.9	21.7
Over $1,000	48.9	52.5	53.6	55.2
All Sizes	100.0	100.0	100.0	100.0

SOURCE: Life Insurance Association of America, **Survey of Life Insurance Loans to Business and Industry,** reported in U. S. Congress, House, Select Committee on Small Business, "Problems of Small Business Financing," **Hearings,** 85th Congress, 1st Session, November 1957, Pt. I, pp. 142-70. (Referred to hereafter as LIAA Survey, 1957.)

60 and 70 percent. However, the distribution of mortgage loans in terms of amount was the reverse. Loans for less than $50,000 accounted for 4 to 6 percent of the total, and the proportion was only 6 to 7 percent if mortgages up to $100,000 are registered as going to small business. Moreover, the share of small concerns in the number and amount of life insurance companies' funds advanced to business and industry declined steadily over the four years surveyed while the largest enterprises (which presumably borrowed the amounts exceeding $1,000,000) received an increasing share. To some extent, the shrinkage in the proportion of loans granted in the smallest categories may reflect the effects of the general uptrend in prices, but the changing use of loan proceeds may also be partly responsible. For example, shopping centers were spreading rapidly during these years, and life insurance companies are among the major suppliers of funds to builders of these retail outlets.

Retailers as a group are the main borrowers of funds from life insurance companies against nonresidential mortgages. They are followed by real estate firms and manufacturers. In 1956, retailers accounted for more than two-fifths of the total number of business mortgages. Office buildings and manufacturing plants were security for one-seventh and one-ninth, respectively, of the total number. By type of property, loans secured by office buildings topped the list as a percentage of the total amount of business mortgages, because individual building loans are typically much larger than those on retail outlets and manufacturing facilities.

When borrowers are considered from the point of view of size of firm, the LIAA study shows that in 1956, only a small percentage of life insurance companies' business and industrial mortgages went to enterprises with assets below $50,000 or even below $100,000. (See Table IX-2.) On the other hand, as already observed, the bulk of such loans was for amounts less than $100,000, and it seems reasonable to assume that the respective borrowers had assets of under $500,000. The latter accounted for more than one-half of the number of business mortgages in 1956. Manufacturers got almost one-tenth of the total number of loans, and in this sector firms with assets under $1,000,000 are classed as small businesses. When they are included, small enterprises received about three-

TABLE IX-2

DISTRIBUTION OF NUMBER AND AMOUNT OF BUSINESS MORTGAGE LOANS OF LIFE INSURANCE COMPANIES, BY SIZE OF BORROWER

(Percent)

Assets of Obligor	1953	1954	1955	1956
		Number		
Under $50,000	7.3	7.5	5.3	5.2
$50,000 to $100,000	15.7	11.9	10.4	10.5
$100,000 to $500,000	35.2	41.7	40.5	38.1
$500,000 to $1,000,000	19.1	17.0	19.4	22.6
Over $1,000,000	22.7	21.9	24.4	23.6
All Sizes	100.0	100.0	100.0	100.0
		Amount		
Under $50,000	1.3	1.6	0.8	1.4
$50,000 to $100,000	2.8	2.3	2.2	1.8
$100,000 to $500,000	16.6	16.2	12.7	12.9
$500,000 to $1,000,000	16.4	17.1	12.9	16.4
Over $1,000,000	62.9	62.8	71.4	67.5
All Sizes	100.0	100.0	100.0	100.0

SOURCE: LIAA Survey, 1957.

fourths of the total number and one-third of the total amount of business and industrial mortgage funds extended by life insurance companies in 1956.

Federal Reserve interviewers found that most small businesses use the proceeds from mortgage loans to finance new construction, existing real estate, or to purchase plant and equipment.[5] While some mortgages are taken out to provide working capital or to carry inventories, the proportion is exceptionally small. One aspect of life insurance company lending to real estate firms complicates the picture of small business financing by these institutions. While most industrial mortgage loans are made directly to firms occupying the facilities, this is true to a much smaller extent of commercial loans. On the basis of the LIAA Survey, it appears that between one-third and two-fifths of the number of life insurance companies' business mortgage loans in 1956 went to real estate investors.[6] Within several areas, the proportion was much higher; they probably accounted for about one-half of the number of mortgages on retail properties and for virtually all of those on office buildings. In one sense then, in so far as small businesses occupy the facilities constructed or financed by large-scale real estate operators, life insurance company funds contribute indirectly to meeting the needs of small enterprises.

C. Other Loans to Small Businesses

Aside from mortgage loans, all other types of borrowing by small businesses from life insurance companies are relatively insignificant. However, a certain amount of life insurance funds do reach small enterprises through the acquisition of bond issues. It is also reported that proceeds of a substantial proportion of policy loans are used for business purposes, and a somewhat smaller percentage of residential mortgages serves the same purpose.

Data on life insurance companies' purchases of bond issues reported in the LIAA Survey are summarized in Table IX-3 according to size of borrowers. Of total business and industrial bond investments authorized in 1956, less than 6 percent of the number and only 1 percent of the amount went to firms with assets below $2,000,000. Even if the size boundary of small businesses were stretched to include firms with assets of $5,000,000, it would encompass less than one-sixth of the number and 5 percent of the amount. In contrast, in all four years, bonds offered by firms with assets over $10,000,000 represented from two-thirds to three-fourths of the total number of bond issues and about 90 percent of the total amount. The degree of life insurance companies' concentration on

TABLE IX-3

DISTRIBUTION OF BUSINESS AND INDUSTRIAL BOND INVESTMENTS AUTHORIZED BY LIFE INSURANCE COMPANIES, BY ASSET SIZE OF OBLIGOR

(Percent)

Assets of Obligor	1953	1954	1955	1956
		Number		
Under $1,000,000	3.6	4.5	2.5	2.0
$1,000,000 to $2,000,000	5.3	3.9	4.9	3.6
$2,000,000 to $5,000,000	10.0	13.6	10.5	9.9
$5,000,000 to $10,000,000	10.4	14.0	10.3	9.9
Over $10,000,000	70.7	64.0	71.8	74.6
All Sizes	100.0	100.0	100.0	100.0
		Amount		
Under $1,000,000	0.2	0.3	0.2	0.2
$1,000,000 to $2,000,000	1.1	0.8	0.9	0.7
$2,000,000 to $5,000,000	3.1	3.4	4.1	3.9
$5,000,000 to $10,000,000	5.3	5.4	5.6	5.4
Over $10,000,000	90.3	90.1	89.2	89.8
All Sizes	100.0	100.0	100.0	100.0

SOURCE: LIAA Survey, 1957.

bonds of large corporations is even more pronounced when loans are distributed by size of bonds. Issues of less than $50,000 absorbed about 3 percent of the total number in 1953, and the proportion shrank steadily to only ½ of 1 percent in 1956. The corresponding figures for bonds under $250,000 were 15 percent and 11 percent, respectively, in 1953 and 1956. In fact, if one were to rank by size the business, industrial, and public utility bonds acquired by life insurance companies and proceed from the largest downward, he would account for considerably more than one-half of the total number well before he encountered an issue as small as $1,000,000. Thus, the view that small corporate bond flotations are of little interest to life insurance companies seems well founded.

The reliance on residential mortgages as a means of financing for small business is said to be widespread, but the evidence is meager. In 1957, the LIAA asked the Prudential Insurance Company to examine its own lending records covering 1953-1956 to see if it could detect the extent to which proceeds of residential mortgages were channeled into business activity. Prudential found that it made as many loans to business and industry through the vehicle of residential mortgages as through strictly business loans.[7] Furthermore, Federal Reserve interviewers were told by Prudential officials that in 1956 approximately one-quarter of its refinancing of residential mortgages in one small urban area went to support small business. Life insurance companies also report that a sizable proportion of the money from policy loans is employed in the same way. Yet, because these institutions do not ask the purpose of policy loans, it is impossible to trace the scope of this method of financing small enterprises.

D. Terms of Loans to Small Businesses

As one would normally expect, small businesses obtain funds from life insurance companies on interest rate terms that are less favorable than those available to the largest concerns. Data in Table IX-4 from the LIAA Survey show clearly that interest rates vary inversely with size of loan. In 1953-56, firms in the largest size group paid from one-eighth to one-quarter less than those in the smallest group when they raised funds through the sale of bonds. On mortgage loans, the differential in favor

TABLE IX-4

INTEREST RATES ON BUSINESS SECURITIES AND MORTGAGES MADE BY LIFE INSURANCE COMPANIES, BY SIZE OF LOAN

(Percent)

Amount of Loan	1953	1954	1955	1956
	Business and Industrial Bonds			
Under $50,000	4.36	4.38	4.09	5.53
$50,000 to $100,000	5.19	4.87	4.72	4.99
$100,000 to $250,000	5.07	4.54	4.63	5.27
$250,000 to $1,000,000	4.79	4.59	4.67	5.04
$1,000,000 to $5,000,000	4.50	4.23	4.34	4.77
$5,000,000 to $10,000,000	4.44	4.10	4.20	4.55
$10,000,000 and over	3.88	3.74	3.95	4.36
	Business Mortgages			
Under $25,000	5.11	5.12	5.11	5.29
$25,000 to $50,000	4.91	4.90	4.88	5.10
$50,000 to $100,000	4.80	4.81	4.75	5.00
$100,000 to $250,000	4.73	4.69	4.67	4.92
$250,000 to $1,000,000	4.63	4.56	4.62	4.88
$1,000,000 to $5,000,000	4.52	4.50	4.56	4.87
$5,000,000 to $10,000,000	4.52	4.32	4.47	4.72
$10,000,000 and over	4.45	4.50	4.68	4.68

SOURCE: LIAA Survey, 1957.

of the largest borrowers ranged from one-tenth to one-sixth. Furthermore, interest cost to small firms is quite inflexible compared with the cost to the largest establishments. This is clearly illustrated in the behavior of interest rates during the 1953-54 recession and subsequent recovery. Rates charged on the smallest loans were virtually unchanged during the downturn and rose less during the recovery. The failure of small borrowers to benefit substantially from reduced interest cost in a period when rates in general were declining is due primarily to the rigidity imposed by the high administrative cost of handling small loans as well as to the greater risk inherent in such loans. On the other hand, maturities of both bonds and mortgages, according to the LIAA Survey, do not differ appreciably by size of borrower. The longest terms for bonds are found among public utilities where the average is about 30 years, but small business almost never appears in this industry. Maturities of industrial and commercial bonds typically range between 20 and 25 years, and the range for mortgages is about 15 to 25 years.

Apparently the terms of bond agreements are frequently more stringent for small than for large firms, but there is no published evidence on the basis of which this question can be examined. Nevertheless, if this is the case, the reasons underlying it can be easily understood. Because of the tenuous footing of many small businesses within their industries, most life insurance companies would naturally seek extra safeguards which are unnecessary when lending to larger, more solidly entrenched corporations. On balance, however, as already mentioned, the majority of these investors would prefer to stand aside from the market for small business bonds rather than attempt to hedge their positions with unusual provisions.

E. Special Programs for Small Business Financing

There is some evidence suggesting that small corporations generally do not look to life insurance companies as a market for bonds. This may be attributable partially to ignorance on their part and partially to an acceptance of the fact that they probably could not qualify as good credit prospects. The relative lack of knowledge among small businessmen about life insurance companies' lending practices and standards is strongly suggested in the experience of Metropolitan Life Insurance Company with its specially developed small loan plan. In 1950, Metropolitan set up a scheme in which it offered to finance 90 percent of small business loans up to $250,000 each with maturities running between three and ten years—provided loan applications originated through local banks which agreed to assume the remaining 10 percent. In the first eight years of the plan's operation, Metropolitan received 228 applications involving an aggregate of $28 million. Eighty-six loans were approved amounting to $12 million, but twelve requests for a total of $2 million were withdrawn after the insurance company agreed to lend the money. Default had not occurred on any of the loans. The fact that Metropolitan accepted such a minor proportion of the applications does not speak well of small businessmen's, or local banks', understanding of life insurance companies' lending standards. A similar conclusion emerges from the experience of Prudential Insurance Company's small and medium loan program instituted in 1956. Through its numerous branch offices, Prudential has vigorously pushed the program, but it too has rejected a large percentage of applications because they were submitted by firms with insufficient capital, or would have exposed Prudential to an undue amount of risk.[8]

Some life insurance companies have participated in business development corporations designed to expand the supply of funds for small businesses. These corporations sell stocks to the public and also obtain loans from financial institutions which may not be quite as willing to lend directly to small enterprises. Some insurance companies have also helped to solve the corporations' management problems. For example, New England Mutual and John Hancock frequently assign some of their senior officers as board members of the Massachusetts Business Development Corporation. While these corporations have made some contribution to small business, it seems, on balance, that they are not likely to overcome the inherent risk in small enterprises which severely limit the desire of life insurance companies to venture policyholders' funds in this area.

SECTION III
LIFE INSURANCE COMPANIES IN THE STOCK MARKET

A. POSTWAR STOCK MARKET

Before examining the role of life insurance companies, a brief survey of the postwar behavior of the stock market would be helpful. While the secondary market for stocks has gone through periods of sustained and vigorous activity since World War II, only a meager supply of new issues has been offered in the primary sector. Some indication of the relatively insignificant role of equity financing in the postwar period can be obtained from an analysis of the sources and uses of corporate funds since the end of the second World War. In Table IX-5 these data are shown. Between 1946 and 1959, nonfinancial corporations used on a net basis

TABLE IX-5

SELECTED SOURCES AND USES OF CORPORATE[1] FUNDS, 1946-1959

(In Billions of Dollars)

	1946-59	1946	1947	1948	1949	1950	1951	1952	1953	1954	1955	1956	1957	1958	1959
Uses of Funds															
Plant and equipment outlays	312.7	12.5	17.0	18.8	16.3	16.9	21.6	22.4	23.9	22.4	24.2	29.9	32.7	26.4	27.7
Change in inventories	58.4	11.2	7.1	4.2	–3.6	9.8	9.8	1.3	1.8	–1.6	6.7	7.6	2.1	–3.3	5.3
Other working capital	114.6	–0.5	8.6	5.3	3.8	18.6	8.1	6.3	2.9	3.0	19.7	7.5	5.5	7.2	18.6
Total Uses	485.7	23.2	32.7	28.3	16.5	45.3	39.5	30.0	28.6	23.8	50.6	45.0	40.3	30.3	51.6
Sources of Funds															
Internal: total	298.1	11.4	16.6	18.8	14.9	20.8	19.0	17.8	19.7	19.8	26.6	27.8	28.0	26.3	30.6
Retained profits	129.1	7.2	11.4	12.6	7.8	13.0	10.0	7.4	7.9	6.3	10.9	10.5	8.9	6.1	9.1
Depreciation	169.0	4.2	5.2	6.2	7.1	7.8	9.0	10.4	11.8	13.5	15.7	17.3	19.1	20.2	21.5
External long-term: total	109.5	4.2	6.3	7.2	4.3	4.2	7.8	9.4	7.6	6.4	8.6	11.1	11.9	10.8	9.7
Stocks	34.0	1.3	1.4	1.2	1.6	1.7	2.7	3.0	2.3	2.1	2.7	3.2	3.5	3.6	3.7
Bonds	57.2	1.1	3.0	4.7	3.3	2.0	3.6	4.9	4.8	3.8	4.2	4.7	7.0	5.8	4.3
Other debt	18.3	1.8	1.9	1.3	–.6	.5	1.5	1.5	.5	.5	1.7	3.2	1.4	1.4	1.7
Short-term sources: total	82.9	6.3	9.5	3.1	–3.7	19.2	12.8	3.6	3.1	–4.0	15.1	9.0	2.6	–6.4	12.7
Total Sources	490.5	21.9	32.4	29.1	15.5	44.2	39.6	30.8	30.4	22.2	50.3	47.9	42.5	30.7	53.0
Discrepancy (Uses Less Sources)	–4.8	1.3	.3	–.8	1.0	1.1	–.1	–.8	–1.8	1.6	.3	–2.9	–2.2	–.4	–1.4

TABLE IX-5 (cont.)

SELECTED SOURCES AND USES OF CORPORATE[1] FUNDS, 1946-1959

(In Billions of Dollars)

	1946-59	1946	1947	1948	1949	1950	1951	1952	1953	1954	1955	1956	1957	1958	1959
Ratios (Percent)															
Stocks to external long-term sources	31.1	31.0	22.2	16.7	37.2	40.5	34.6	31.9	30.3	32.8	31.4	28.8	29.4	33.3	38.1
Stocks to total sources	6.9	5.9	4.3	4.1	10.3	3.8	6.8	9.7	7.6	9.5	5.4	6.7	8.2	10.8	9.7
Stocks to plant and equipment	10.9	10.4	8.2	6.4	9.8	10.1	12.5	13.4	9.6	9.4	11.2	10.7	10.7	13.6	13.4
Bonds to external long-term sources	52.2	26.1	47.6	65.3	76.7	47.6	46.2	52.1	63.2	59.4	48.8	42.3	58.8	53.7	44.3
Other debt to external long-term sources	16.7	42.9	30.2	18.0	–13.9	11.9	19.2	16.0	6.5	7.8	19.8	28.9	11.8	13.0	17.6
Bonds to total sources	11.7	5.0	9.3	16.1	21.3	4.5	9.1	15.9	15.8	17.1	8.3	16.3	16.5	18.9	8.1
Bonds to plant and equipment	18.3	8.8	17.6	25.0	20.2	11.8	16.7	21.9	20.1	17.0	17.4	15.7	21.4	22.0	15.5
Internal sources to plant and equipment	95.3	91.2	97.6	100.0	91.4	123.1	88.0	79.5	82.4	88.4	110.0	93.0	85.6	99.6	110.5
Internal sources to total sources	60.8	52.1	51.2	64.6	96.1	47.1	48.0	57.8	64.8	89.2	52.9	58.0	65.9	58.7	57.7

1. Excludes banks and insurance companies. Note: These figures differ from those in Table VI-2 because of differences in coverage by reporting agencies.

SOURCE: U. S. Department of Commerce, **U. S. Income and Output,** 1958, p. 195, and **Survey of Current Business,** July, 1960, p. 24.

about $486 billion of funds. Plant and equipment expenditures absorbed $313 billion; $58 billion represented an increase in inventories, and the remaining $115 billion were employed as working capital. Funds from the corporations' own operations, amounting to $298 billion, were sufficient to meet three-fifths of the total required and 95 percent of expenditures on plant and equipment. When these business firms did go outside to obtain funds, they relied on stocks for 7 percent of their total needs, and the amounts raised were only 11 percent of plant and equipment outlays. In contrast, corporate bonds constituted 12 percent of all sources and 18 percent of plant and equipment purchases. When other long-term debt (primarily mortgages) is included, total long-term borrowing by corporations is lifted to $76 billion or more than two-thirds of the total new long-term funds demanded by them.

In addition to the large internal flow of funds, the cost factor has worked in favor of bond flotations and against stock sales as a method of financing capital formation. As mentioned in Chapter VI, the relatively high corporate income tax levied by the federal government appreciably reduces the effective net cost of bond financing. Because most firms pay the 52 percent rate, the annual net burden is slightly more than half the cost before the interest is deducted. This means that a corporation could afford to pay interest rates about twice as high as dividend yields before stocks would have a clear cost advantage. Of course, some of the exceptionally blue chip corporations (the price of whose stock in 1959 ranged between 30 and 40 times earnings compared with 17 times earnings for all industrial stocks) have been able to raise equity capital at a cost only moderately above the after-tax cost of bond financing.[9]

The internal generation of such a large share of corporate funds is a mirror of the basic transformation of corporate dividend policies. In the heyday of stock financing in 1929, all corporations in the United States paid out in dividends 70 percent of their profits after taxes. In the prosperous years 1955-57, paid dividends accounted for only 52 percent of after-tax profits. If the 1929 ratio had governed dividends in 1955-57, corporations would have distributed an additional $12 billion to stockholders in these three years.[10] But this was not done, and these funds were retained to strengthen the companies' equity position.

This aspect of internal finance should be kept in mind. It indicates that for profitable corporations the real supply of equity capital is not as inadequate as one may conclude from the relatively small volume of stock sales in recent years. At the same time, however, the spread of internal financing may distort the pattern of savings flow and through this the allocation of resources in the economy. If corporations had to submit their expansion plans to the judgment of the capital market, a quite different structure of real investment might well emerge. In the meantime, it is clear that corporations do bank heavily on retained earnings as the chief source of their new equity capital. This has seriously restrained the supply of new stocks offered to the market.

The annual net additions to outstanding corporate stock have displayed a mixed pattern. The dominant influence has clearly been the fluctuation in plant and equipment expenditures which were the main source of the demand for new financial resources. In connection with reconversion to peacetime activity in 1946, corporations raised through the sale of stock about 6 percent of the funds spent on plant and equipment, but the proportion dropped to 4 percent in the next two years. The sharp recovery in stock prices from the summer of 1949 induced some corporations to float new issues, and the net amount offered was one-third above that of the previous year. In fact, such stock sales accounted for 37 percent of the corporations' total external long-term funds in contrast to 17 percent in 1948. During the Korean War boom, the volume of net stock sales mounted steadily in absolute terms and in relation to plant and equipment outlays. At the peak in 1952, corporations raised $3 billion through net stock flotations which amounted to 13 percent of their spending for fixed capital. With the onset of the 1953-54 recession, however, corporations' investment plans were pared, and stock offerings subsided. But again in 1954, stock prices anticipated the recovery in the general economy, and substantial gains were registered during the year. In this favorable environment, corporations began an expansion in new stock sales which was still in progress at the end of 1959. The ratio of proceeds from stock sales to total long-term external funds advanced steadily from 31 percent in 1955 to 38 percent in 1959. On the other hand, such proceeds still represented less than 10 percent of corporations' total funds.

B. Stock Market Participation

Against this background, the activities of life insurance companies in the stock market can be examined. At the end of 1959, these companies owned $4.6 billion of preferred and common stock. This represented an increase of $452 million during the year and a gain of $3.6 billion since 1945. A substantial part of the gain in their stock holdings reflected price advances; for example, about one-third of the total increase in 1959 represented higher market values.[11] But after allowing for price changes, the expansion has been appreciable in absolute terms. At the end of 1959, stocks accounted for 4 percent of life insurance companies' total assets

CHART IX-1

Stocks Owned By United States Life Insurance Companies

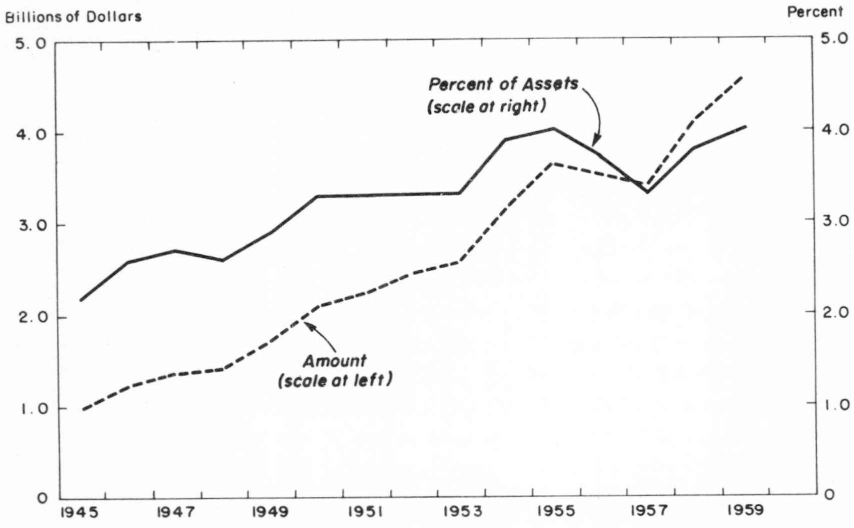

SOURCE: *1960 Life Insurance Fact Book*, p. 80.

compared with 2.2 percent at the close of 1945. Trends in these holdings in dollar amounts and in relation to total assets are drawn in Chart IX-1. In interpreting these trends, it should be recalled that stocks have never been a major investment outlet for life insurance funds. The highest ratio of stocks to total assets was in 1903 when they amounted to about 7.5 percent. Since the turn of the century, the trough was set at 0.6 percent in 1922-24. More than two-thirds of the postwar rise in the companies' stock holdings occurred after 1950 and was due primarily to two factors. As mentioned above, valuation increases based on market prices were responsible for a major share of the boost. Of more importance, however, were the 1951 amendment to the New York insurance law and its further liberalization in 1957. The 1951 modification permitted life insurance companies to invest in common stock the smaller of 3 percent of total assets or one-third of surplus, where surplus in turn was restricted to 10 percent of total assets; the limit on common stocks was raised in 1957 to 5 percent of total assets or 50 percent of surplus. On the other hand, while these changes provided a stimulus to life insurance companies' purchase of common stock, they certainly did not spark a run by these institutions on the stock market.

The New York law was amended in March, 1951, so companies had the benefit of the more liberal provisions for most of the year, but the response was not spectacular. Their stock purchases in 1951 totaled $298 million, only three-fifths of the volume in the previous year. Furthermore, while acquisitions of common stocks exceeded those of preferred issues for the first time, the amount of common stock purchased ($159 million) was actually smaller than in 1950. The purchase of preferred stock declined even more, and the $139 million acquired was less than one-half the amount a year earlier. The moderate interest of life insurance companies in the stock market during this period is clearly shown by the fact that stocks remained 3.3 percent of their total assets from 1950 through 1953. Finally, in 1954, the value of life insurance companies' holdings of stocks rose by $695 million, the largest annual increase on record. More than 70 percent of the increase ($494 million) centered in common stocks, primarily of industrial companies. Some of the sharp rise was due to changes in market values, but the shrinkage in the supply of corporate bonds during the recession was also a factor. With the resumption of corporate demands for funds in 1955, and given the large backlog of commitments for mortgages made in the recession, stock purchases by life insurance companies again ebbed to the normally modest level. Moreover, the decline in stock prices more than offset the small volume of new purchases, and the value of their portfolio was actually reduced in 1956 and 1957. But the net depreciation in value was not serious, amounting to 3.7 percent and 3.3 percent, respectively. The stock market boom of 1958 sharply reversed the trend, and life insurance companies' holdings jumped by $718 million, more than half of which was attributable to increased market values of common stocks. But stock acquisitions of $365 million were about one-quarter higher than in the previous year. In 1959, acquisitions rose by more than one-third to $498 million; this was the second largest volume registered in the postwar years. The combined price and net purchases returned the companies' stock holdings to 4 percent of total assets, the same proportion reached in 1955 for the first time since 1909.

The postwar gain in life insurance companies' stock holdings has centered mainly in common stock. For example, between 1947 and 1959, the value of their common stock rose by $2.6 billion, equal to more than three-quarters of the increase in their total stock portfolio. (See Table IX-6.) This expansion lifted common stocks from about one-quarter of the total in 1947 to two-thirds in 1959. Within the common stock category, those of industrial and commercial concerns led the list, climbing from under one-fifth to about one-half of the value of all stocks owned. In con-

TABLE IX-6

TYPES OF STOCKS OWNED BY U. S.
LIFE INSURANCE COMPANIES
(In Millions of Dollars)

Year	Total	Railroad	Public Utility	Industrial and Miscellaneous	Total: Common and Preferred
Preferred					
1947	1,033	71	302	660	1,390
1948	1,055	75	295	685	1,428
1949	1,258	79	413	766	1,718
1950	1,454	93	529	832	2,103
1951	1,401	91	527	783	2,221
1952	1,483	106	595	782	2,446
1953	1,531	102	668	761	2,573
1954	1,732	98	862	772	3,268
1955	1,744	80	944	720	3,633
1956	1,551	64	868	619	3,503
1957	1,524	62	878	584	3,391
1958	1,561	61	932	568	4,109
1959	1,607	59	1,005	543	4,561
Common					
1947	357	22	73	262	
1948	373	24	77	272	
1949	460	25	100	335	
1950	649	35	143	471	
1951	820	31	197	592	
1952	963	38	246	679	
1953	1,042	34	279	729	
1954	1,536	64	386	1,086	
1955	1,889	70	449	1,370	
1956	1,952	56	447	1,449	
1957	1,867	37	464	1,366	
1958	2,548	57	618	1,873	
1959	2,954	47	661	2,246	

SOURCE: **1960 Life Insurance Fact Book,** p. 79.

trast, the composition of their preferred stock holdings swung substantially to public utilities where the proportion rose from one-third in 1947 to two-thirds in 1959. Throughout the postwar years, life insurance companies showed little interest in railroad stocks because of the generally indifferent performance of the industry. Their holdings of preferred railroad issues dropped slightly between 1947 and 1959, and, although their holdings doubled in percentage terms, only small dollar gains were made in railroad common stock.

C. Impact on the Stock Market

In view of the meager position of stocks in life insurance companies' investment portfolios, one is not surprised to find that they have had virtually no impact on the stock market. Because even their relatively small stock holdings are concentrated among high-grade issues, stocks listed on the New York Stock Exchange (NYSE) probably give a fair measure of that part of the market in which they are active. For example, in 1959, their ownership of listed stocks represented about two-thirds of the total value of their stock portfolio. Taking as a benchmark the market value of all NYSE-listed stock in 1949 and 1959, one can clearly trace the erosion in the relative importance of life insurance companies in the market—although their influence was already quite weak at the beginning of the decade. As shown in Table IX-7, life insurance companies in 1959 owned about 7 percent of the listed stock held by all savings-type institutions and about 1 percent of the market value of all listed issues. In 1949, their shares had been 12 percent of the amount owned by savings institutions and 1.4 percent of the total. Moreover, among savings institutions (which as a group lifted their stake in the market from 12 percent to 17 percent), the relative decline of life insurance companies was equally marked. Although they held 7 percent of all institutionally-owned stocks in 1949, they absorbed only 5 percent of the net increase in such holdings over the next decade.

In terms of the annual growth in stock holdings, life insurance companies were surpassed by all other institutions except college and university endowments with whom they tied. The undisputed leaders, when measured by the absolute and percentage change, were investment companies and noninsured corporate pension funds. Open-end investment companies (mutual funds) place from 80 to 90 percent of their rapidly expanding assets in equities, and this has given them a premier role in the stock market. Moreover, they have far overshadowed the older closed-end investment companies. During the decade of the 1950's, their total assets rose fourfold, and the number of shareholders more than tripled. A substantial part of the greater value of mutual funds' stock portfolios reflects price advances, but a large and increasing stream of new savings has flowed through them into the market. For example, in 1952, net sales of new shares (sales less redemptions) amounted to $600 million, and this rose to $1.5 billion in 1958. By the end of 1959, open-end

TABLE IX-7

ESTIMATED INSTITUTIONAL OWNERSHIP OF STOCKS
LISTED ON THE NEW YORK STOCK EXCHANGE
(In Billions of Dollars)

Type of Institution	1949	1959	Change, 1949-59 Amount	Change, 1949-59 Percent	Percentage Distribution of Change, 1949-59
Insurance Companies					
Life	1.1	3.1	2.0	181.8	4.8
Non-life	1.7	6.0	4.3	252.9	10.4
Investment Companies					
Open-end	1.4	12.8	11.4	814.3	27.5
Closed-end	1.6	5.2	3.6	225.0	8.7
Non-profit Institutions					
College and university endowments	1.1	3.1	2.0	181.8	4.8
Foundations	1.1	3.9	2.8	254.5	6.7
Other	1.0	4.4	3.4	340.0	8.2
Non-insured Corporate Pension Funds	0.5	10.8	10.3	2,060.0	24.8
Common Trust Funds	—	1.4	1.4		3.4
Mutual Savings Banks	—	0.3	0.3		0.7
Total	9.5	51.0	41.5	436.8	100.0
Market Value of all NYSE Listed Stocks	76.3	307.7	231.4	303.3	
Estimated Percent Held by Institutions	12.4	16.6			

SOURCE: New York Stock Exchange, **Fact Book,** 1960, p. 29.

investment companies owned $12.8 billion of stock listed on the NYSE; this amount was 4 percent of the value of all listed stock and one-quarter of that held by savings institutions. Finally, they were responsible for about 28 percent of the net acquisitions of all savings institutions between 1949 and 1959.

However, while mutual funds made the largest absolute gains in stock holdings during the 1950's, the relative growth in stock ownership by noninsured corporate pension funds was the most striking. In 1949, they held only $500 million of NYSE-listed issues; by the end of 1959, their portfolio, at market prices, was valued at $10.3 billion, representing one-quarter of the net increase in the value of all institutional holdings. As discussed in Chapter II, the emergence of these institutions has posed a serious competitive problem for life insurance companies. Their assets have expanded enormously, from $5 billion in 1950 to $25.3 billion in 1959—both at book values, mainly because of the introduction of pension provisions in collective bargaining agreements and their further spread among managerial and nonunion corporate employees. A substantial part of their new resources has been concentrated in common stocks, which climbed from 12 percent of their total assets in 1950 to 30 percent in 1959. Although pension fund trustees are generally far more venturesome than life insurance officials in common stock purchases, they too focus principally on high-grade issues. Of their stock holdings in 1959, valued at market prices, NYSE-listed stock accounted for 84 percent of the total. For practical purposes, the ability of the pension fund trustees to invest in common stock is limited only by the requirements of prudence, and this puts life insurance companies to a considerable disadvantage. Because they are basically restricted to debt issues, life insurance companies cannot guarantee to corporations returns as high as those pledged by pension fund trustees. The liberalization of insurance investment laws in recent years has partially reduced this disability, but life insurance companies still feel that their ability to compete for corporate pension funds is impaired. Other institutions have also been achieving larger gains in stock ownership than life insurance companies, but their activities have little bearing on the latter.

The year to year experience of life insurance companies in the stock market is shown in Table IX-8, which traces net changes in stock ownership among major groups since 1952. The figures have been corrected for appreciation and depreciation in market value and thus reflect actual net purchases. Here again life insurance companies' relative lack of interest in stocks is clear. Only in 1954 did they play a noticeable part in the market by absorbing about 17 percent of the net increase in the value of stocks outstanding. But this improvement in their share of the market was partly a reflection of the recession-induced drop in net stock offering and partly a reflection of the companies' search for alternative investments. On the other hand, the vigorous participation of corporate pension funds in the market is also evident.

Life insurance companies purchase stock primarily to hold and are among the lightest traders in the market. This picture is sharply etched in the NYSE's public transactions studies. Data from the tenth study, covering the five days September 26-30, 1960, are summarized in Table IX-9. It will be noted that the ratio of life insurance companies' net purchases to their total purchases (86 percent) was the highest for all groups shown. In absolute amount, commercial banks were the heaviest traders

TABLE IX–8

CHANGES IN OWNERSHIP OF STOCKS[1] BY SAVINGS INSTITUTIONS AND OTHER HOLDERS, 1952-59
(In Billions of Dollars)

Type of Holder	1952	1953	1954	1955	1956	1957	1958	1959
	Amount							
Savings Institutions								
Life insurance companies	.1	.2	.3	.2	—	.1	.1	.2
Other insurance companies	.2	.2	.2	.2	.2	.2	.1	.1
Corporate pension funds	.5	.5	.7	.7	.9	1.0	1.3	1.6
Mutual savings banks	.1	.1	.1	.1	.1	.1	.1	.1
State and local government retirement funds	—	—	—	—	—	—	.1	.1
Total Savings Institutions	.9	1.0	1.3	1.2	1.2	1.4	1.7	2.1
Other Holders								
Foreign investors	—	—	.2	.1	.3	.1	–.1	.4
Individuals and others	1.5	1.0	.3	.6	1.1	1.2	.5	–.2
Total Stocks	2.4	2.0	1.8	1.9	2.6	2.7	2.1	2.3
	Percentage Distribution of Changes							
Savings Institutions								
Life insurance companies	4.2	10.0	16.7	10.5	—	3.7	4.8	8.7
Other insurance companies	8.3	10.0	11.1	10.5	7.7	7.4	4.8	4.3
Corporate pension funds	20.8	25.0	38.9	36.8	34.6	37.0	61.8	69.6
Mutual savings banks	4.2	5.0	5.5	5.3	3.8	3.7	4.8	4.3
State and local government retirement funds	—	—	—	—	—	—	4.8	4.3
Total Savings Institutions	37.5	50.0	72.2	63.1	46.1	51.8	81.0	91.2
Other Holders								
Foreign investors	—	—	11.1	5.3	11.5	3.7	–4.8	17.5
Individuals and others	62.5	50.0	16.7	31.6	42.4	44.5	23.8	–8.7
Total Stocks	100.0	100.0	100.0	100.0	100.0	100.0	100.0	100.0

1. Net of Appreciation or depreciation in market value.

SOURCE: Bankers Trust Company, **The Investment Outlook, 1960,** Table 9.

although estates were the most active in percentage terms. The behavior of commercial banks is probably more a reflection of orders transmitted for customers than of transactions for the banks' own accounts. It will also be observed that corporate pension funds, whose liabilities and investments objectives are similar to those of life insurance companies, also purchased stocks primarily to hold. During the five-day survey, life in-

TABLE IX-9

PURCHASES AND SALES OF NYSE-LISTED STOCK
BY SELECTED TYPES OF INSTITUTIONS AND INTERMEDIARIES
September 26-30, 1960
(In Thousands of Shares)

Type of Institution	Purchases	Sales	Net Purchases or Sales(-)	Percent of Purchases Retained
Life Insurance Companies	147	21	126	85.7
Other Insurance Companies	153	90	63	41.2
Commercial Banks	1,449	1,575	−126	−8.7
Mutual Funds	683	638	45	6.6
Colleges and Universities	65	44	21	32.3
Corporate Pension or Profit Sharing Funds	288	68	220	76.4
Personal Trusts[1]	78	121	−43	−55.1
Estates	24	94	−70	−291.7
Foundations	52	38	14	26.9
Non-member Broker/Dealers	371	458	−87	−23.5
Non-financial Corporations	236	112	124	52.5
Personal Holding Corporations	59	83	−24	−40.7
All Other	323	277	46	14.2
Total	3,927	3,618	309	

1. Non-bank Administered.

SOURCE: New York Stock Exchange, **The Institutional Investor and the Stock Market,** Part II, **Tenth Public Transaction Study, September 26-30, 1960,** p .11.

surance companies undertook transactions in 168,000 shares; these were divided between purchases of 147,000 shares and sales of 21,000. They accounted for 2.2 percent of total transactions of 7,546,000 shares, which is still another index of their minor impact on the market for equity capital.

SECTION IV
INVESTMENT POLICIES, ATTITUDES, AND THE OWNERSHIP OF COMMON STOCK

A. CURRENT INVESTMENT PRACTICES

Taken as a group, almost one-third of all United States life insurance companies do not invest in common stocks, but there is, of course, considerable diversity in practice. Several broad patterns are evident in both their current policies and their attitudes toward the appropriateness of owning common stocks. The main contours of common stock investment practices reported by companies in the BBER-MSU Survey are sketched in Table IX-10, which shows the distribution of companies by size and type, whether they invest in common stocks, and the extent to which they rely on dollar averaging or similar formula plans.

Behind the overall pattern of the companies' common stock investment policies, there is considerable divergence. The large institutions are more prone to own stocks than are smaller companies, but the differential in behavior tends to disappear about midway in the size distribution of companies. For example, about 82 percent of the companies in Group I invest in common stocks. The proportion drops to 72 percent in Group II. On the other hand, there is virtually no difference between the proportions in Groups III and IV where the ratios are 61 and 63 percent, respectively. Life insurance companies owned by stock holders have a much greater interest in investing in common stocks than have mutual institutions, and the discrepancy is particularly marked among smaller units in the industry. About three-quarters of all life insurance companies organized on a stock-ownership basis are active purchasers of equity shares compared with three-fifths of the mutual companies. Approximately 80 to 90 percent, respectively, of mutual and stock companies in Group I participate in the market for common stocks. On the other hand, while the propor-

TABLE IX-10

COMMON STOCK INVESTMENT PRACTICES OF LIFE INSURANCE COMPANIES, BY SIZE GROUP AND TYPE OF COMPANY

	Total		Size Group[1] I		II		III		IV	
	Mutual	Stock	Mutual	Stock	Mutual	Stock	Mutual	Stock	Mutual	Stock
No Answer	1	2	—	—	—	—	1	2	—	—
Do Not Purchase Common Stocks	19	15	4	1	2	6	7	4	6	4
Purchase Common Stocks	29	45	15	8	7	13	3	11	4	13
Rely on Dollar Averaging or Other Formula Plan										
Yes	10	13	6	3	2	4	1	3	1	3
No	19	32	9	5	5	9	2	8	3	10
Total	49	62	19	9	9	19	11	17	10	17

1. Size groups are those shown in Table I-1.

SOURCE: BBER-MSU Survey, Spring, 1959.

tions are generally lower for all companies in Groups III and IV, the shrinkage is much smaller for stock companies among whom three-quarters are active in the market compared with two-fifths of mutual institutions.

Numerous factors contribute to these divergent patterns, but several seem to stand out. The less active participation of small companies in the market clearly reflects their lack of adequate investment staffs to manage a portfolio of common stocks, but (as explained more fully below) many of the small companies are opposed to such investments on principle. As mentioned in Chapter III, some of the smaller life insurance companies employ investment advisory firms, and this device probably accounts for much of even the limited presence of small life insurance companies already observed. In contrast, most of the companies in the forefront of the industry can undoubtedly muster the experts required if they wish to accumulate a portfolio of common stocks. The greater propensity of stock companies to concentrate on equity securities appears to be related to the high priority most life insurance firms of this type attach to profits available to stockholders. This is not intended to imply that most of these enterprises, in the pursuit of profits, neglect the interest of policyholders; in fact, the structure of assets in some stock companies, especially among the larger ones, is indistinguishable from that in mutuals of comparable size. Moreover, many stock companies sell participating policies, and some of their policyholders thus enjoy some of the same advantages as those who own policies in mutual companies. Nevertheless, the fact remains that owners of shares in stock life insurance companies expect a rate of return in line with alternative investments entailing similar risks. Reflecting this profit motive, stock companies have a strong preference for equities. The results of this preference are revealed in Table IX-11 which shows the ownership of stock by the 150 largest life insurance companies in the United States by class of stock and type of company in 1957. First, it will be noted that stock companies are concentrated among the smaller units in the industry, for they represented two-thirds of the number of companies but accounted for less than one-quarter of total assets. On the other hand, the value of equities owned by stock companies was three-tenths of that for all life insurance companies. Moreover, they held two-fifths of common stocks and only one-sixth of preferred issues on which the rate of return is much lower. The same divergent pattern of stock ownership among mutual and stock companies is seen in the ratio of stocks to their total assets. For all companies combined, equities represented 3.2 percent of total assets, but the ratio was 2.9 and 4.0 percent, respectively, for mutual and stock companies. In

TABLE IX-11

OWNERSHIP OF STOCKS BY 150 LARGEST COMPANIES,
BY CLASS OF STOCK AND TYPE OF COMPANY, 1957
(In Millions of Dollars)

	All Companies		Mutual Companies		Stock Companies	
Type of Stocks	Amount	Percent of Total	Amount	Percent of Total	Amount	Percent of Total
Preferred	1,438	45.8	1,211	54.6	227	24.6
Railroad	60	1.9	53	2.4	7	0.8
Public utility	845	26.9	712	32.1	133	14.4
Industrial and commercial	527	16.8	443	20.0	84	9.1
Banks	1	—	1	0.1	—	
Insurance companies	5	0.2	2	0.1	3	0.3
Common	1,704	54.2	1,008	45.4	696	75.4
Railroad	36	1.1	24	1.1	12	1.3
Public utility	442	14.1	288	13.0	154	16.7
Industrial and commercial	812	25.8	607	27.4	205	22.2
Banks	203	6.5	71	3.2	132	14.3
Insurance companies	211	6.7	18	0.7	193	20.9
Total Stocks	3,142	100.0	2,219	100.0	923	100.0
Total Assets	97,585		74,701		22,884	
Total Companies (Number)	150		51		99	
Stocks as Percent of Total Assets						
Preferred	1.5		1.6		1.0	
Common	1.7		1.3		3.0	
Total	3.2		2.9		4.0	

SOURCE: Compiled from **Best's Life Insurance Reports, 1958.**

mutual companies and in the industry as a whole, the portfolios were about evenly divided between preferred and common stock. In stock companies, however, there was a marked concentration on common stock which accounted for two-thirds of the value of total stocks owned.

Finally, many of the stock companies are located in states with liberal investment laws which allow considerable latitude for the acquisition of common stock. The effects of this relatively greater freedom are illuminated in Table IX-12 showing the percentage distribution of assets and rates of return on types of assets held by life insurance companies in New York, Illinois, Massachusetts, and Texas. It will be recalled that New York's law is among the most restrictive in the matter of common stock investments while Texas' is among the most liberal. The Illinois and Massachusetts laws fall between these extremes while the Massachusetts

TABLE IX-12

DISTRIBUTION OF ASSETS AND RATES OF RETURN ON TYPES OF ASSETS IN LIFE INSURANCE COMPANIES: NEW YORK, ILLINOIS, MASSACHUSETTS, AND TEXAS, 1957

(Percent)

Type of Asset	New York	Illinois	Massachusetts	Texas
Cash	0.8	1.8	0.9	3.2
Government Securities	7.4	12.5	8.5	16.1
United States	5.6	8.9	4.8	9.0
State and local	1.4	3.4	3.7	7.0
Other	0.4	0.2	—	0.1
Corporate Bonds	49.2	35.9	47.6	13.1
Mortgages	29.9	35.1	29.1	46.9
Stocks	2.5	2.7	8.7	9.7
Preferred	1.9	0.9	1.6	1.8
Common	0.6	1.8	7.1	7.9
Real Estate	3.8	3.1	2.4	1.8
Other Assets	6.4	8.9	2.8	9.2
Total Assets	100.0	100.0	100.0	100.0
Rates of Return on Type of Asset (Percent)				
All Assets	3.67	3.72	3.69	4.25
Bonds	3.50	3.30	3.57	3.11
Stocks	4.83	4.33	4.37	4.24
Mortgages	4.20	4.55	4.30	4.83
Real Estate	2.50	4.23	3.79	4.04

SOURCE: Compiled from **Best's Life Insurance Reports,** 1958.

provision (essentially the prudent man rule) is perhaps closer to Texas than to New York. Figures in the table are for the 150 largest life insurance companies previously mentioned; thirteen are in New York, and ten each in Illinois, Massachusetts, and Texas. Mutuals are dominant among the New York and Massachusetts companies, numbering eight and seven, respectively; on the other hand, nine of the Illinois companies are owned by stockholders, and this is true of all of the Texas firms. The Texas companies held about 10 percent of their total assets in stocks in 1957, and in Massachusetts companies the proportion was 9 percent; in both New York and Illinois, the ratio was less than 3 percent. Moreover, stock holdings of Texas and Massachusetts companies were heavily concentrated in common stocks; preferred issues represented the bulk of stock holdings in New York companies, and again the Illinois institutions were in the intermediate category. The greater concern for profit among the Texas companies is also emphasized in their holdings of state and local government securities; these represented 7 percent of their total assets, compared with 1 percent for the New York companies and between 3 and 4 percent for companies in Illinois and Massachusetts. To some extent, this preference of Texas institutions for tax-exempt obligations may reflect a peculiarity of the Texas investment law requiring companies to invest in Texas securities 75 percent of the reserves against Texas policies, but the profit advantage of tax-exempt securities is also probably a factor. Table IX-12 also shows a considerable advantage in the average rate of return of Texas companies over those in New York, Massachusetts, and Illinois. Some of the differential in favor of Texas institutions may be due to the generally higher levels of interest rates in the southwest, but the composition of their portfolios also seems to have some influence. About half of total assets in New York and Massachusetts companies is concentrated in corporate bonds, but mortgages account for approximately the same proportion of assets in Texas companies. The large share of mortgages combined with their higher yields give the latter institutions an edge in the net earnings rate. The lower return on bonds of Texas companies is probably a reflection of their sizable holdings of relatively low-yielding tax-exempt issues. Texas companies in 1957 had the lowest return on stocks, but this is partly due to the fact that some companies made heavy purchases of stocks at relatively high prices compared with earnings. Apparently they were more interested in capital gains than in immediate yields.

Among life insurance companies which do invest in common stock, there is a slightly greater tendency for mutual than for stock companies—and for larger than for smaller institutions—to rely on dollar averaging or some other formula plan as a guideline in stock purchases. However, in every category, most of the companies active in the stock market do not employ any kind of formula. (See Table IX-10.) The simple principles of dollar averaging are generally known and need not be discussed here.[12] The main element is the more or less constant investment of the same dollar amount in stocks per time period. The objective is to buy the largest number of shares at the lowest average price. Basic to the theory is the assumption that the stock market is cyclical and is not subject to a secular rise or fall in prices. The steady cash inflow of life insurance companies makes it fairly easy for them to employ the scheme. The typical planning period reported is one month, although a few companies say they average over a quarter with considerable variation within the quarter. Most companies specialize in a relatively narrow range of stocks, not necessarily blue chip issues. Nevertheless, several replied that they select specific stocks from a relatively long list of promising corporations at the time the investment is to be made. Virtually none of the companies reported using dollar averaging in timing stock sales from their existing portfolio. A few companies said they use a modified "constant ratio" plan in administering their stock investments. In each case, they strive to maintain a given ratio between new dollar investments in stocks, bonds, and mortgages, but none of them indicated that they shift funds from stocks into bonds or mortgages as stock prices rise, or back into stocks when stock prices fall. The few small companies which explained why they adhere to some kind of formula plan said they do not have the personnel to devote to detail management of the stock portfolio. Yet among the largest companies, where two-fifths of those who are active in the stock market employ dollar averaging, the shortage of staff appears not to be the chief reason for adopting some sort of mechanical investment guide. Rather, they seem to be much more conscious of the potential gains inherent in concentrating their buying, in terms of the number of shares, when stock prices are low and easing off as the market rises. One or two life insurance officials hastened to explain that this is not speculation and emphasized the benefits to policyholders arising from this type of perceptive portfolio management.

B. Attitudes Relating to Common Stock Investments

A large number of life insurance companies reported that they do not invest in common stocks and are not likely to acquire any as long as they are required to carry them at market prices in their annual statements to state insurance commissioners. They hold that wide year to year fluctuations in the value of the common stock portfolio have too great an impact on their surplus accounts. The use of special reserves to absorb these variations has little appeal to these companies. This question is discussed further below, but it seems evident that there is no prospect in the near future of the companies being able to adopt book values, or some other constant values, as the unit in which to record their stock holdings. Thus, most of these institutions for whom price fluctuations are a deterrent are unlikely to provide a new market for equities.

Other facets of life insurance companies' attitudes toward common stocks as investment outlets as reported in the BBER-MSU Survey are summarized in Table IX-13. The companies were asked whether they believe the present legal restrictions (in their states of domicile or in New York State if they are domiciled elsewhere but licensed to do business there) on investment in common stocks should be liberalized. Virtually

TABLE IX-13

SELECTED ATTITUDES OF LIFE INSURANCE COMPANIES RELATING TO THE OWNERSHIP OF COMMON STOCKS, BY SIZE GROUP

Question	All Companies	Size Group[1] I	Size Group II	Size Group III	Size Group IV
Liberalization of Restrictions					
State of domicile					
No answer	9	2	3	3	1
Favor	27	7	6	8	6
Against	75	19	19	17	20
New York State					
No answer	63	13	19	14	17
Favor	23	9	1	8	5
Against	25	6	8	6	5
Specific Limit on Ownership of Common Stock					
No answer	46	14	13	10	9
Limit recommended	59	12	14	16	17
Opposed to a limit	6	2	1	2	1
Limit as percent of assets					
Under 10	10	5	2	1	2
10	23	5	7	7	4
15	5	—	1	1	3
20	3	1	1	1	—
Other	18	1	3	6	8
Extension of Prudent Man Rule to Life Insurance Companies					
No answer	7	1	2	3	1
Favor	16	8	2	4	2
Against	88	19	24	21	24
Restriction of Common Stock Purchases to Blue Chip Issues					
No answer	7	1	2	2	2
Favor	30	6	5	6	13
Against	74	21	21	20	12
Number of Companies	111	28	28	28	27

1. Size groups are those shown in Table I-1.

SOURCE: BBER-MSU Survey, Spring, 1959.

all of the companies commented on their home states, but a large proportion failed to do so regarding New York State. As shown in the table, the vast majority of the companies felt no liberalization is required in their home state legislation. Moreover, this attitude is rather uniform among companies of all sizes. With respect to further liberalization in New York State, the larger institutions seem slightly more anxious to see this change than are smaller life insurance companies. One can easily understand the position of the top companies in the industry. They sell insurance in a national market, and virtually all of them must substantially comply with the New York statute. On the other hand, a number of companies emphasized the need for caution in pressing for greater relaxation of restrictions. This attitude is exemplified in the observations of the chief investment officer in a large New England company:

> As a practical proposition any increase in the maximum amount of common stock permitted legally by certain states will probably come only gradually. Companies like my own which would like to see the percentage allowed by the State of New York increased would probably suggest a relatively modest increase rather than their ultimate objective since the former would be more likely to meet political support. (I mention New York because its common stock statutes are probably the most important to any company licensed to do business in that state unless the statutes in the state of domicile are more restrictive than the New York statutes.)

Companies were also asked whether they thought a limit should be set on the ownership of common stock by life insurance companies, and if so what the limit (defined as a percentage of admitted assets or surplus) should be. Of the companies answering the question, the vast majority felt a ceiling should be set and generally expressed it as a certain percentage of assets. The most popular figure was 10 percent recommended by over one-third of those replying. A few set the ceiling as 100 percent of surplus; but because surplus in a number of states is limited to 10 percent of assets this ceiling is also equivalent to 10 percent. A few would go up to 20 percent. Those life insurance companies which felt that no maximum limit on common stock holdings is required typically based their case on the argument that most investment officers in these institutions are sufficiently prudent to manage their assets without such restrictions.

However, the overwhelming majority of life insurance companies strongly disagree. In the survey, companies were asked whether detailed legal restrictions on life insurance companies' investment activities should be eliminated and such activity left to each company to be guided by the so-called prudent man rule. Virtually all of the companies replying answered this question, and 85 percent of them would oppose a change in this direction. The opposition is slightly weaker among the large companies, but even here 70 percent of them would stand against it. The prudent man rule has been adopted by over three-quarters of the states (including New York, Massachusetts, Illinois, Michigan, and California) as a guide to uninstructed trustees in the management of trust funds. The rule affords considerable discretionary authority to invest in assets of any type, including common stocks, which an ordinarily prudent man would judge to be appropriate in the case at hand. However, only a few states give life insurance companies the same privilege enjoyed by other trustees, although most do not restrict them to detailed "legal lists" prescribed for trustees by about one-quarter of the states. Objections to having the rule extended to life insurance companies turned primarily on the fear that many small institutions would abuse it. Most of these are new, and numerous officials in the industry are afraid that inexperienced managements might engage in unwise investment practices which would harm the industry as a whole. A number of companies, including some small ones, believe most of the largest institutions would follow essentially the same investment practices they do now if the prudent man rule were extended, but none of the respondents thought their example would be persuasive enough to prevent speculation by many newly launched companies. An official of a medium-sized Illinois company observed:

> Practically all life insurance failures are due to poor investment policies. Restrictions to prevent new and small companies from speculating or investing substantially all their assets in real estate or oil leases, etc., are necessary. The failures in Texas are an example of results of these policies. Prudent man rule would be ineffective in preventing losses to the policyholders. Financial responsibility for failure to follow prudent man rule would not be as effective as in trust institutions.

On the other hand, about three-quarters of the companies feel that life insurance companies should not be restricted, by either law or custom, to investing in so-called blue chip stocks. In fact, a substantial number of companies feel they should make a special effort to discover companies well on the way to becoming blue chip. According to another large New England company:

> A portion of any equity program definitely belongs in the smaller, less well-recognized companies. The best of these will grow faster than the giant companies, and will eventually attain more wide-spread investment recognition. The combination of faster earnings growth plus increasing multiples produces an obvious effect on profitability of the investment. The conditions precedent to each such investment are substantially identical to those precedent to investment in "blue chips." Each situation must be examined as to its industry, markets, products, research activities, finances, management capabilities, etc. Its earnings and dividend potential must bear a reasonable relationship to its market price.

This view is typical among life insurance companies except those in the smallest size group. About half of the latter replied that, if life insurance companies are to invest in common stocks at all, they should be restricted to the issues of the strongest corporations. Again the primary concern seems to be with the dangers of speculation if life insurance companies are given substantial latitude in selecting investment outlets.

In summary, it is evident that most large life insurance companies would like further liberalization in investment laws to permit an increase in common stock holdings; a substantial number of them would like to see the New York ceiling raised to 10 percent of assets, or twice the proportion currently allowed. Also, many companies in the industry would readily authorize the largest institutions to follow such a policy, but they are apprehensive about empowering small and new companies to do likewise; they are afraid this would lead to speculation and ultimately to the public's loss of confidence in the entire industry. For the same reason, they are almost universally opposed to the extension of the prudent man rule as a guide to life insurance companies' investment activities. Simultaneously, most institutions feel they should not restrict their common stock purchases to issues offered by the strongest corporations, but should search for stocks of promising enterprises on the verge of entering the rare blue chip category.

Section V
In Support of Common Stock Ownership by Life Insurance Companies

A. Changes in Attitudes

While a substantial number of life insurance company officials still have serious doubts about the appropriateness of common stocks as investment outlets, one should remember that until recent years this attitude was almost universal in the industry. But several factors have gradually brought about a modification in views, and many companies see considerable advantages in owning common stocks. One of the most compelling forces inducing the change was the low level of interest rates during the late 1930's and all of the 1940's. The rate of earnings on invested life insurance funds dropped from a little over 5 percent in 1930 to a trough of 2.88 percent in 1947. Behind this latter rate average, many assets were earning less than was required to build up policy reserves at the minimum pace projected in contracts. Thus, the chief investment problem of life insurance companies during most of the 1940's was to find outlets for their funds that would give a reasonable rate of return. Quite naturally, preferred and common stocks became more alluring under these conditions.

A further important reason for the change in attitude was the continued scarcity of equity finance, and it was frequently suggested that savings institutions should fill the gap. The case for life insurance companies' investing a larger share of their resources in common stocks was forcefully argued by Thomas B. McCabe, former Chairman of the Board of Governors of the Federal Reserve System, in a statement prepared at the request of a Subcommittee of the Committee on Banking and Currency of the United States Senate in August, 1949. He said in part:

> My second major suggestion for alleviating the equity capital problem would be that consideration be given to a liberalization of the investment opportunities open to fiduciary institutions, particularly the life insurance companies. In view of the large volume of individual savings flowing into private pension and insurance reserves, the legal restrictions on insurance companies and other fiduciaries which prohibit them from investing in corporate stocks should be reviewed. These restrictions, rightly established many years ago as safeguards needed at that time, may, in the light of changed savings and investment patterns, now be out of date. I recommend that the life insurance companies, in cooperation with the proper State authorities explore fully the opportunities for investing in common stock with the aim of modifying these restrictions.
>
> Two of the most common arguments against relaxing the legal restrictions on the investment opportunities of life insurance companies and fiduciaries are:
>
> (1) The risks of equity investments.
>
> (2) Possibility of a concentration of industrial control in large life insurance companies.
>
> I agree that there is a certain element of risk involved in the ownership of equity shares. Yet there is little ground in past experience to support the broad premise that many permitted bond investments involve less risk than carefully selected common stock. In general, I feel that informed and flexible investment policy together with sound judgement are much to be preferred to rigid legal restrictions. The experience of endowment funds of educational institutions, as well as of the fire insurance industry, which operate under more liberal investment regulations, has demonstrated that diversified investment in common stocks along with other types of securities can produce better than average return.
>
> In order to prevent domination by the life insurance companies of individual companies or industries, or unwarranted risks of investment loss through common stock ownership, such investment should be carefully prescribed by appropriate legislation. Some such formula as the following might be employed, e.g., investment of any one life insurance company in the common stock of a business enterprise might be limited to one per cent of the outstanding voting shares or $1,000,000, whichever is larger.[13]

The Congressional hearings, of which Mr. McCabe's testimony is a part, stimulated much discussion of common stock investments for life insurance companies. One outcome was the 1951 amendment to the New York State law previously mentioned. Since then numerous portfolio managers have begun to accept the validity of the above argument. The heart of the issue seems to rest on three points. First, are common stocks suitable investment for a fiduciary institution if its contractual liabilities are expressed in a fixed number of dollars? To put it another way, might investment in common stocks, with their fluctuating values and lack of maturity date, jeopardize a life insurance company's ability to meet its insurance contracts? Second, might the ownership of common stocks impair public confidence in the stability and strength of life insurance companies as a whole? Third, what legal and technical impediments need to be overcome if common stocks are to be owned in large amounts by life insurance companies?

B. Suitability of Common Stocks as Investments for Life Insurance Companies

Before attempting to answer whether common stocks are suitable investments for life insurance companies, it would be well to stress again a few of the unique features which distinguish the investment opportunities and objectives of these institutions from those of virtually all other investors. Because their liabilities are exceptionally long-term, they make an effort to acquire investments of comparable maturities. This fact is illustrated by a case reported by New England Mutual Life Insurance Company. It held one security for 101 years, and the company is reported to have many investments in its portfolio which have been owned for over 30 years. Moreover, a growing life insurance company virtually always has a large net cash inflow. This was true even in the depths of the 1930's depression; thus they are almost, if not entirely, free of pressure to liquidate investments to meet liabilities. Finally (and perhaps this is the most relevant issue), unlike individuals or other investors, life insurance companies retain the bulk of their income and reinvest it at compound interest. The results of this practice are quite striking and amply illustrated by the experience of New England Mutual.

One of the first three investments of that company was the stock of a railroad. The stock was purchased in 1844 when the railroad was still in the construction stage. The investment was sold in 1945—101 years later—after the railroad had gone into receivership, and New England Mutual suffered a capital loss of 57 percent on the original investment. During the 101 years of ownership, however, the company received dividends totaling 839 percent of the original investment, and most of this was retained and reinvested. Clearly, the 57 percent capital loss was of no consequence compared to the income received. Even after absorbing the capital loss, the annual rate of return over the 101 years was 7.7 percent.

From the foregoing discussion, it should be clear that the investment characteristics of life insurance companies are quite different from those of other investors. Because of this, their investment objectives and techniques are also different. What then should be the target of a life insurance company if it invests in common stocks? Among industry officials who favor common stock investments the typical answer is that either present or perspective income should be the fundamental objective; furthermore, it should not be subordinated to any desire to achieve capital appreciation or make capital profits.[14] The advantages of concentrating on income rather than expected capital gains are also demonstrated by data from New England Mutual.

The company's portfolio of common stocks was yielding in 1953 about 7.5 percent on its cost, and the average yield from 1929 to 1953 was approximately 6 percent, almost double the rate which could have been obtained on bonds during that period. If one compares the results of compounding income at 6 percent to compounding at 3 percent, one finds that the excess return at 6 percent in a ten-year period amounts to $466 per thousand dollars invested. In a fifteen-year period, the difference between the two rates results in $878 more income per thousand dollars of original investment, while over twenty years the figure is $1,473 of additional income. Although the company's investment plan was not established with capital appreciation in view, the results for a ten-year period were equivalent to an appreciation of 47 percent in original principal; and for a twenty-year period it was about as good as a capital gain of 147 percent.

An even stronger observation can be drawn from this experience. The additional income was actually more desirable than the same amount of capital appreciation. The reason for this is obvious, since a capital gain remains uncertain until the profit is actually taken. But a life insurance company is unlikely to liquidate its common stock portfolio in order to take its profits. Theoretically, the company may take a profit by selling a particular investment that has appreciated. However, there is a high probability that the proceeds from the sale (including the profit) will be immediately reinvested in a similar asset. Thus, the funds remain at risk exactly as before, although after the sale they may be in the stock of a different company. Of course, the switch to another company may occasionally be necessary to avoid an actual loss, but this prospect is not likely to occur frequently because nearly all common stocks held by life insurance companies are concentrated among issues of the most substantial corporations.

The principle of reinvesting for income is illustrated still further by statistics from New England Mutual. During the 21 years, beginning in 1930 (close to the peak in the predepression expansion of the economy) and ending with December, 1950, the company received total dividend income from its stocks of approximately $10,400,000. During those 21 years, the institution's total realized gains on common stocks were little over $1,000,000, or about one-tenth the amount of dividends received in the period. This profit was not put into bonds or retained as cash; instead it was reinvested in other common stocks. During the 1929-50 period as a whole, the appreciation on the company's total common stock portfolio amounted to about $8,300,000, almost as much as total dividends received over the same years. Apparently, it was never suggested by any officer of the company that this profit actually be taken and reinvested in an alternative outlet. On the contrary, the company followed, and continues to follow, a policy of adding periodically to common stock holdings. In other words, the company's paper profits have remained paper profits, and little attention is given to the market prices of particular issues (other than for year-end valuation purposes) as long as other evidence suggests the corporation in question is performing well. If this experience can be generalized, it seems that (unless a life insurance company contemplates liquidation at some specified time) the market price of the common stocks owned by the institution is really of no great significance, no greater in fact than the day to day market value of its home office building. What is significant is the income the company receives from its stocks and reinvests over a period of time.

In its investment activities, as in other parts of its operation, a life insurance company has to make some estimate of the probability of occurrence of both favorable and unfavorable events. Portfolio managers know that dividends paid by most corporations on their common stock fluctuate from year to year, but it is not too difficult nor too impractical to predict within a reasonable range the minimum dividend rates on a widely diversified portfolio of seasoned issues. Over a period of years, errors are likely to cancel out. By contrast, despite the massive amount of work that has been done to predict prices of particular stocks, no method has been found that is even moderately reliable. It seems to follow that, if a life insurance company is to buy common stocks, it should do so on the basis of the income it can reasonably expect to receive over a rather long period and not on the assumption that it may enjoy a large appreciation. While the latter may in fact occur, it should be attributed primarily to the vagaries of the stock market and it is therefore transitory.

Another question relating to life insurance companies' purchasing common stocks stems from the fear that large holdings of such issues might jeopardize public confidence in these institutions during times of general economic stress. It should be noted that this question does not arise from the fear of internal mismanagement discussed above in connection with apprehension about the behavior of new and small companies. While this question is certainly a relevant one, it is perhaps misleading to concentrate on it in regard to stocks apart from other types of investments. As already emphasized, most life insurance companies purchase primarily the stocks offered by the strongest corporations; in many instances they also own the bonds of the same firms. If a generalized depression occurs, even the strongest firms may have to default on bonds as well as forego dividends. While dividends, of course, would be passed before interest payments, it is quite likely that both types of yields would shrink during a deep and sustained depression. It is difficult to see why the companies' loss of dividends under these circumstances would be more damaging to public confidence in the life insurance industry than the loss of interest income. But, as discussed above, it is unlikely that these institutions will become overly burdened with common stocks; investment laws most certainly will not become so liberal that stocks might become a large enough percentage of the total assets of life insurance companies to expose them to serious difficulties.

A technical difficulty also poses a formidable obstacle to any considerable expansion of the companies' common stock holdings. This is the problem of valuation of equities for balance sheet purposes previously mentioned. For many years, under the rulings of the National Association of Insurance Commissioners, common stocks have been carried at their market value as of the year end.[15] This means that any appreciation or depreciation has been reflected in surplus, which is one of the most prominent items in a company's balance sheet. Moreover, unlike fire and casualty companies, life insurance companies are limited by law to accumulating a relatively small amount of surplus in relation to assets (usually 10 percent). Consequently, fluctuations in market values of common stocks have had an exaggerated effect on surplus. Beginning with the statement for December 31, 1951, however, the commissioners adopted a valuation method which was designed to remedy this, at least in part. They ruled that any appreciation in common stocks during the year (whether or not realized) must be offset by a reserve carried as a liability and not as a part of surplus. The intention of the commissioners was to start a system of investment reserves which eventually could be a buffer against swings in market prices. While most company officials apparently think the scheme has introduced some stability and eased the impact on surplus, they feel it should be supplemented by some method of using average market prices for valuation purposes. But as mentioned above, it seems unlikely that this development is in prospect in the near future. Consequently, the valuation problem will remain a hindrance to many companies which otherwise might consider acquiring common stocks.

The possibility that life insurance companies' ownership of common stock may place them in a position to control the management of leading corporations is another argument sometimes used to support limiting their ownership of such issues. But this argument too can be discounted. In the first place, most state insurance laws which do permit them to own common stock fix a ceiling of some sort. For example, in New York the limit is set as 2 percent of the total issued and outstanding common shares of any corporation, and the amount must not exceed one-tenth of 1 percent of the admitted assets of the insurance company. Secondly, given the acute sensitivity of life insurance managements to public opinion (and the constant recognition of the possibilities of more intensive regulation), the companies would probably never allow themselves to get into a situation where their ownership of common stocks in a given corporation could provide influence, real or imagined, over a corporation's affairs. Numerous examples suggest that even the suspicion of questionable behavior is sufficient to produce immediate corrective action.[16] In the recent past, life insurance companies have generally preferred to sell their stock holdings when corporate performance fell short of expectations rather than engage in extensive efforts to reform or replace existing management. While this behavior may well have left less informed investors to bear the consequences of managerial shortcomings, it has freed the insurance companies of possible involvement in struggles for corporate control. There seems to be no reason to anticipate a substantial change in their attitudes and behavior, so one need not devote much thought to the possibility of their exerting an undue influence in corporate affairs.

SECTION VI
OTHER AREAS OF EQUITY FINANCING

A. RESIDENTIAL REAL ESTATE

Two other areas of equity investment by life insurance companies require brief discussion. These are housing and income-producing real estate.

In 1938, a new section was added to the New York State insurance law permitting life insurance companies to acquire and construct housing projects. Although investment in public housing companies had previously been allowed, this marked an innovation because it permitted direct ownership of housing projects with no element of subsidy or rent limitations involved. Under it a number of projects have been constructed. Other amendments have broadened the provision to include investment in housing projects either directly or through the ownership of stock. In many of these cases, the power of the state or municipality in assembling the required land (often involving slum clearance) through eminent domain and a limitation on taxes were provided, together with a maximum return to the investor about equal to the return which could be expected from mortgage loans.

The peak in life insurance companies' ownership of residential real estate came in 1949, and activity in this area was sluggish throughout the decade of the 1950's. In the middle of 1949, they had completed or had underway housing projects designed to provide rental housing for 47,000 families and entailing an investment of $475 million.[17] Of these, 41 projects, housing 34,500 families and representing an expenditure of $275 million, had been completed by mid-1949. Additional housing for 12,000 families was under construction, and the projected cost was estimated at $185 million. The remaining developments were still in the planning stage. At the end of 1949, the value of housing schemes actually completed and owned by life insurance companies totaled $302 million, representing 24 percent of their total real estate holdings. Through 1952, construction continued to expand in line with other types of real estate. At the end of that year, the value of residential properties owned ($461 million) was the highest on record, and the ratio to total real estate was the same as in 1949. Subsequently, however, life insurance companies' interest in housing developments waned. The pace of construction slowed appreciably, and depreciation and amortization of existing units steadily shaved the dollar values of the companies' holdings. By the end of 1959, these were recorded at $414 million, or only 11 percent of total real estate owned.

B. Purchase or Leaseback Agreements

In the early postwar years, several states amended their insurance laws to allow life insurance companies to acquire income-producing real estate in addition to housing. The limit was generally set between 3 and 5 percent of a company's assets.[18] Such provisions are now almost universal. Some of these laws require that the acquisition be made only in conjunction with a long-term lease, but for the most part this restriction does not hold. Nevertheless, many life insurance companies have found purchase-leaseback arrangements of considerable advantage. Under such an agreement, the insurance company usually purchases the property either from a prospective tenant or after an arrangement has been worked out with a tenant. It then enters into a lease with the tenant providing for an absolute net rental, the tenant undertaking to assure all of the expenses and real estate taxes on the property. Tenants are usually corporations which have sufficiently high credit ratings to justify the expectation that they will survive long enough to allow the investment to be recovered. The investor looks to both the tenant's credit and the intrinsic value of the real estate purchased. The investor's relative reliance on the two varies from case to case, but where the intrinsic value of the property, except to the particular tenant, is relatively small, the tenant must possess a credit rating which would justify the extension of unsecured credit during the normal period of a debenture issue or even longer, since the leases generally run from five to ten years beyond the usual term of a debenture issue.

The principal incentives to the tenant for this type of transaction in preference to a security issue are threefold. In the first place, it lends itself to the piecemeal financing involved in constructing a series of buildings much better than does the ordinary security issue where the sale of the entire issue typically takes place at one time. More important, however, is the fact that the credit of the tenant corporation is less directly engaged than in a debenture issue and the tenant can generally obtain additional financing through the issuance of securities more easily than if he had long-term debt outstanding. Finally, under existing tax laws, many corporations have considered it more advantageous to rent than to own property. Under a rental arrangement the full amount of the rental can be deducted and the taxable income reduced; if they own the property they are limited to depreciation on the improvements plus interest on any indebtedness incurred in the acquisition.

Section VII
Summary and Conclusions

The discussion in this chapter clearly suggests that life insurance companies are an unpromising source of small business and equity finance. In the small business area, both legal restrictions and high credit risks impose severe constraints on the ability of life insurance companies to extend loans to new or small-scale enterprises through the purchase of bonds. On the other hand, these investors do acquire a sizable numb of real estate mortgages secured by business and commercial properti Thus, numerous small businesses are able to tap life insurance funds this manner. Moreover, a large share of the proceeds of policy loans and residential mortgages is reportedly used for business purposes. But, given the legal framework, the relatively heavy administrative costs, and the high probability of loss inherent in small business lending—and considering the variety of alternative investment opportunities open to life insurance companies—it is easily understood why small businesses get such a meager portion of life insurance funds.

Equity financing by life insurance companies is even more limited. Since shortly after the turn of the century, they have played an insignificant role in the stock market, and equities have been only a minor investment outlet. Until recent years, the investment laws in most states prohibited their investment in common stocks, but in states where they were allowed to hold this type of asset they showed little interest in exploiting the privilege. With the amendment of the New York State law in 1951 (which was further liberalized in 1957), some observers thought the companies' demand for common stocks would greatly expand. These expectations have been gravely disappointed. While life insurance companies' participation in the stock market registered a noticeable increase in the few years immediately following the easing of the law in New York, this was not sustained at the same high level through the decade. Furthermore, life insurance companies tend to concentrate on a relatively narrow list of high-grade stocks, so their activity in the market is even more limited than suggested by the small volume.

The reasons underlying life insurance companies' moderate interest in the market are easily understood. Because their liabilities to policyholders are fixed in dollar terms, many officials feel that (completely aside from the legal requirement) prudence would dictate the avoidance of assets whose values vary erratically with stock market prices. Common stocks for annual statement purposes must be carried at year-end prices, and book losses must be charged against a special reserve or surplus. Many companies feel this is an unreasonable burden, and consequently have refrained from investing in common stocks. Many also emphasize that considerable risk is still involved in the ownership of stocks despite the great improvements in the economic environment since the 1930's. They recognize that government regulation of certain crucial aspects of market activity reduces the prospect of a recurrence of a widespread collapse similar to that of 1929-30. They agree that the greater stability of the economy and the stronger financial position of corporations also lend substantial support to market prices. The stabilizing role of savings institutions in the market is another factor enhancing the appeal of common stocks to some life insurance companies. Nevertheless, swings in market prices are still substantial, and these frequently affect even the highest grade issues. Finally, although the likelihood of failure among the leading corporations is extremely remote, many cautious portfolio managers do not completely rule it out. For these and other reasons, life insurance companies as a group have been extremely circumspect in approaching the stock market. Furthermore, given the pessimistic attitudes of many companies, the situation is not likely to change in the near future.

On the other hand, the appropriateness of much larger holdings of common stocks by life insurance companies was strongly defended in this chapter. It was pointed out that in limited amounts, and provided seasoned and amply diversified stocks (although not necessarily blue chip issues) are selected, common stocks are an advantageous investment outlet for life insurance companies. Because of the long-term nature of their liabilities and the steady cash inflow, these institutions are probably never forced to liquidate assets to meet claims. Thus, they are free to hold common stocks primarily as a source of income. Over a period of time, and after allowing for reasonable yearly variation in dividends and for occasional small capital losses, common stocks can make a major contribution to building up the net earnings of life insurance companies and, thereby, to keeping down or reducing the net cost of insurance. While an increasing number of companies will undoubtedly enter the market and others will add further to their existing holdings, it is unlikely that life insurance companies will become an important factor in the market. But on the whole, the change in the legal environment and the shift in attitude among industry officials are both developments which in the long run will stimulate growth in the supply of equity capital. This will clearly be of benefit to the economy as a whole as well as to the life insurance industry.

Footnotes

1. Joint Committee on the Economic Report, *Volume and Stability of Private Investment, Hearings,* 81st Congress, 2nd Session, 1950.
2. A. D. H. Kaplan, *Small Business: Its Place and Problems* (New York: McGraw-Hill, 1949), p. 22.
3. United States Congress, House, Select Committee on Small Business, *Problems of Small Business Financing, Hearing,* 85th Congress, 1st Session, November, 1957, pp. 125-85. (Referred to below as LIAA Survey, 1957).
4. Federal Reserve System, *Financing Small Business,* "Report to the Committees on Banking and Currency and the Select Committees on Small Business, United States Congress" (Washington, D. C., 1958), pp. 512-24.

5. *Ibid.*, p. 516.
6. *Ibid.*, p. 517.
7. LIAA Survey, 1957.
8. Gordon W. McKinley, "Life Insurance Company Lending to Small Business," *Journal of Finance*, May, 1961, pp. 300-3.
9. It should be borne in mind that, while equity financing does not impose the same contractual commitment involved in bond financing, dividends are a cost to corporations with alternative uses of their funds.
10. *The Morgan Guaranty Survey*, July, 1959, p. 6.
11. Life insurance companies' common stock portfolios are carried at year-end market values.
12. See C. Sidney Cottle and W. Tate Whitman, *Investment Timing: The Formula Plan Approach* (New York: McGraw-Hill, 1953).
13. "The Equity Capital Situation," The Board of Governors of the Federal Reserve System, Washington, D.C., August, 1949, p. 5.
14. This point was emphasized by numerous respondents in the BBER-MSU Survey. Similar views have also been reported by another writer; see G. Wright Hoffman, "Preferred and Common Stocks," *Investment of Life Insurance Funds*, pp. 190-91.
15. For a fuller discussion, see Harold G. Fraine, "The Valuation of Security Holdings of Life Insurance Companies," *Journal of Finance*, March, 1951, pp. 124 ff.
16. See the discussion in Adolf A. Berle, *The 20th Century Capitalist Revolution* (New York: Harcourt, Brace & Co., 1954), pp. 80-81. The resignation of the president of the Prudential Insurance Company in 1960 in connection with a wholly legal private transaction with a firm which had previously obtained a loan from the company is another illustration of the same point.
17. Press release by the Institute of Life Insurance, May 19, 1949.
18. See John W. McPherson, "Some Economic and Legal Aspects of the Purchase and Lease of Real Estate by Life Insurance Companies," a paper read before the Association of Life Insurance Counsel, December, 1948.

CHAPTER X

Summary and Conclusions

The main conclusions emerging from this examination of the role of life insurance companies in the capital market have been stated in each chapter. However, the brief summary in Section I may be helpful in placing the study as a whole in sharper focus. In Section II, the bearing of these conclusions on several broader questions of economic analysis and public policy is considered.

Section I
Record of Life Insurance Companies' Participation in the Capital Market

A. Framework of Investment Activities

Until recent years, life insurance companies have been one of the leading growth sectors of the American economy. While the rate of growth in their assets has slowed slightly since the mid-1950's, they remain at the forefront in the mobilization of savings and continue to be a major source of funds for corporations and home buyers. In addition, they supply a substantial amount of funds to some small businesses through real estate mortgages, and state and local governments (primarily through the sale of revenue bonds) also tap life insurance funds to some extent. Moreover, life insurance companies, from time to time, exert considerable influence on the market for United States government securities and are in turn greatly influenced by developments in the heart of the capital market.

The strategic place of life insurance companies in the capital market rests on the accumulation of a vast and steadily expanding amount of savings owned by policyholders. At the end of 1959, these institutions held $114 billion of total assets, of which $108 billion represented savings. Thus, since the end of World War II, their assets rose more than two and one-half times. This rising trend was supported by the increasing demand for life insurance protection; between 1945 and 1959, this demand advanced insurance in force by three and one-half times. However, toward the end of the 1950's the rate of savings through life insurance was adversely affected by several factors; some of these were internal to the industry, others resulted from developments in the economy as a whole.

There was a substantial shift to group and term (as opposed to ordinary) insurance policies, necessitating a smaller accumulation of reserves.

Policyholders began to draw more heavily against the liquidity of their policies as shown in the acceleration of policy loans and the increase in surrender values.

Partly because of the uptrend in interest rates during most of the decade, beneficiaries became increasingly reluctant to leave dividends and proceeds of policies on deposit with insurance companies.

Operating expenses of insurance companies rose sharply.

All of these developments dampened the expansion of savings mobilized by life insurance companies.

This slowdown in the flow of savings through life insurance companies was also reflected in a weakening of their competitive position relative to some of the other savings institutions. They lagged appreciably behind non-insured corporate pension funds and savings and loan associations. However, the deterioration in their status was far less than that experienced by commercial and mutual savings banks. Life insurance companies held slightly more than two-fifths of the total assets owned by the six leading types of savings institutions in 1945; this proportion was 37 percent in 1959, and they accounted for only one-third of the net expansion in total assets of the group as a whole over the same period. This comparative lag has serious implications for the capital market because life insurance companies are the only major savings institutions able to invest in a wide range of financial instruments. Some of these are discussed more fully below.

It was pointed out in Chapter III that while life insurance companies have more investment choices than commercial banks and a few other types of institutions, legal and customary restrictions still confine them primarily to the acquisition of high grade debt. The regulation of life insurance companies is left to the states, but through voluntary cooperation (channeled principally through the National Association of Insurance Commissioners) a basically common framework has evolved. Moreover, the high degree of concentration in the life insurance industry makes the bulk of life insurance assets subject to the laws of a few states. For example, the investment laws of six states (New York, New Jersey, Massachusetts, Connecticut, Wisconsin, and Pennsylvania) govern directly the disposition of more than three-quarters of the industry's total assets. Furthermore, the New York law (which has traditionally been the strictest) requires that all companies licensed to do business within its borders must comply in substance with the investment regulations and limitations imposed on domestic insurers. The details of these laws were examined in Chapter III and need not be repeated here. It is sufficient to recall that they in effect limit the investment of life insurance funds to public debt, the obligations of the strongest business firms, and loans secured by real estate with an ample margin of safety. Although the New York State law was amended in 1951 to permit companies to hold three percent of their assets in common stocks (and it was further liberalized in 1957 to allow up to 5 percent), the legal framework of life insurance investment activities remains extremely restrictive. The attitudes of company officials toward these restrictions were reported in Chapter IX and will be mentioned again below.

But given this legal framework, it was shown in Chapter IV that investment decisions in life insurance companies are guided by a few clearly defined principles and respond in a systematic way to changes in the level and structure of interest rates. These institutions strive for the highest net yields obtainable consistent with reasonable standards to ensure the safety of policyholders' reserves. Most of them try to remain fully invested while making forward commitments to deliver funds at currently prevailing interest rates; such a policy, it is believed, provides an assured outlet for funds and protection against future declines in market yields. While the steady cash inflow from new savings and from loan repayments virtually eliminates the necessity of holding liquid assets to meet policyholders' withdrawals, nevertheless they do require working balances in order to manage their investment portfolios. In an attempt to keep fully invested, they extend loans on an advanced commitment basis. They do not, as a rule, explicitly accumulate idle funds in anticipation of interest rate increases nor borrow or otherwise overcommit themselves in expectation of rate declines. Nevertheless, the backlog and length of commitments seem to increase with advancing rates and to decrease when yields decline. Moreover, the companies' holdings of short-term liquid assets exhibit a similar accordion-like pattern. Thus, one cannot escape the inference that investment decisions in life insurance companies respond in a systematic way to variations in interest rates.

It was demonstrated that the quantity of funds supplied by life insurance companies to the capital market is primarily a function of the structure of interest rates. As a rule, in a period of rising interest rates, life insurance companies, while first attracted by the higher yields available on assets of greater credit risk, gradually become more restrictive and selective in their investment activities. They become less willing to sell government securities to acquire higher yielding, but more risky, private debt (such as corporate bonds and mortgages). This is due partly to the fact that discounts on Governments deepen progressively with an uptrend in rates, and they become hesitant to accept the increasing capital losses. Also they become more interested in retaining the more liquid types of assets, or in adding them to their portfolios. This motivation springs from concern over the decline in the market value of a substantial share of their investment portfolio as well as from the general uncertainty about the future course of interest rates. Finally, the higher interest rates on government securities in a period of tightening credit approximate more closely the average rate of return which life insurance companies must obtain on their earning assets to meet the interest rates guaranteed in contracts with policyholders. On the other hand, it was also pointed out that much of the observed response of life insurance companies to changes in interest rates is attributable to customary practices rather than to an objective appraisal of capital gains and losses. Some of these customary practices arise from the conventions of life insurance accounting, but perhaps of greater importance are the attempts of many company officers to conform to the prejudices of state supervisory personnel.

The response of life insurance companies to changes in interest rates is clearly shown in the behavior of forward commitments. Swings in commitments to buy securities are not only clearly pro-cyclical, but they actually lead cyclical variations in interest rates. New commitments to buy nonresidential mortgages show a mixed pattern with respect to business cycles and interest rate trends. Those for conventional mortgages are characterized by a relatively mild contra-cyclical profile. In contrast, commitments to acquire federally-underwritten mortgages have the strongest tendency of all life insurance companies' investment outlets to run against the cycle. Most of this instability derives from the critical role of VA-guaranteed mortgages, but those insured by FHA are also less stable than conventional loans. The pegged interest rates on federally-underwritten mortgages enhance their appeal to life insurance companies and other investors when other open market yields are declining; the reverse is also true. In fact, the inverse movements of corporate bond yields and the companies' new commitments for FHA and VA mortgages are almost perfectly synchronized. With few exceptions, peaks in bond yields coincide with troughs in new commitments for these types of mortgages.

Although the pattern is somewhat blurred, one can detect a systematic relationship among movements in interest rates, securities commitments, and securities acquisitions. There is also a suggestion of a definite sequence among the mortgage series, but it appears to be somewhat weaker than that outlined for securities. New securities commitments seem to lead changes in interest rates by at least one quarter and in some instances as much as six months. Turning points in interest rates and new commitments for mortgages seem to occur simultaneously and to move in opposite directions. With respect to acquisitions, a divergent pattern is also evident. The time lag between securities commitments and acquisitions seems to be at least six months and that for mortgages about three months.

B. Investment Activities in the Main Sectors of the Capital Market

Against the background fixed by economic, legal, and interest rate considerations, the investment activities of life insurance companies in five sectors of the capital market were examined in some detail. These sectors are the United States government securities market, the corporate bond market, the market for real estate mortgages, the state and local government securities market, and the market for equity capital.

It was shown in Chapter V that the market for United States government securities is the central platform from which to observe their role in the capital market as a whole. First, the yields on federal government obligations are the key interest rates in all maturity sectors of the financial markets. These key rates serve as anchors to yields on private instruments while the latter are generally higher. The differentials are based on the higher credit risk attached to private or nonfederal issues, their lower marketability, the higher cost of investigation. By each of these standards, Governments are superior investment outlets for life insurance companies. On the other hand, the lower yields on Governments make it necessary for portfolio managers to search elsewhere for assets whose rates of return are more in line with the rates guaranteed in insurance policies. Nevertheless, most life insurance companies have a basic demand for small amounts of Governments to satisfy liquidity needs and to provide portfolio diversification.

Secondly, government securities, in excess of the amounts held for liquidity and diversification, also serve as residual investments for life insurance companies. A theme running throughout their experience is that these institutions generally prefer higher-yielding corporate bonds and mortgages to holding Governments. It is only if they have long-term funds in excess of the amounts they are able to invest in loans and securities that they will buy Governments on a large scale. On the other hand, when they can find alternative investment opportunities providing yields more than sufficient to compensate for the additional risk assumed, life insurance companies seem generally willing to sell Governments to acquire the more profitable investments.

This pattern of behavior is basically a reflection of the legacy of depression and war finance. During major depressions and war years when private demands for funds shrank relative to the demand arising from the federal government, these institutions built up their holdings of government securities; each period of peace and prosperity brought the opposite behavior. The depression of the 1930's and World War II provided an exceptionally clear demonstration of this tendency. Although it was in the 1930's that life insurance companies became virtually the only purchasers of corporate bonds, they also put almost half of the net increase in their assets in government securities. In World War II, they provided 12 percent of the total funds borrowed by the federal government, but their acquisition of long-term issues accounted for more than one-third of the total offered during the war loan drives. Furthermore, federal obligations compensated for the decline in their holdings of other types of assets, because their government portfolio rose by slightly more than the growth in their total assets. Within the war years, however, the life insurance companies sold a considerable amount of the bank-eligible bonds purchased in the early war loan drives and thus to some extent facilitated commercial bank financing of a larger share of the war effort than the monetary authorities felt desirable. Simultaneously, some of the life insurance companies borrowed directly from the banks to buy government securities in excess of the amount of funds they had available through new savings and loan repayments; subsequently some of these issues were sold at sizable profits which were assured by the pegged prices on Governments. But on the whole, life insurance companies seem to have engaged in this type of speculation to a far smaller degree than individuals, nonfinancial corporations, and several other types of financial institutions.

Just as Governments constituted a residual use of life insurance companies' funds during the depression and war years, they were a residual source of funds in much of the prosperous postwar period. Savings through life insurance remained the primary source of funds supplied to the capital market, but the companies sold Governments and reinvested the proceeds in private obligations (principally corporate bonds and real estate mortgages) when the volume of savings was insufficient to meet the acceptable requests for loans. As a rule, the rate of liquidation of Governments was dampened during periods of declining bond prices. The pace of liquidation was especially heavy in 1947-48 and 1950-51. In fact, the liquidation of Governments by life insurance companies and other investors in the early months of the Korean War was one of the major factors prompting the accord between the Treasury and the Federal Reserve System in March, 1951. As part of the agreement for the conduct of monetary policy, pegged prices for government securities were eliminated. After this, Governments were no longer the equivalent of cash; and while sales continued during the post-accord period, they were made with hesitation. In fact, by the end of the 1950's, life insurance companies had generally brought their government holdings into balance in relation to the rest of their portfolio and were frequently found on the buying side of the market.

The participation of life insurance companies in the corporate bond market was analyzed in Chapter VI. This type of debt was shown to be especially attractive to these institutions. Over the years, life insurance companies have come to hold around two-fifths of the long-term corporate debt outstanding, although the rise of corporate pension funds in recent years has seriously challenged their hegemony in this part of the capital market. The expansion in the role of life insurance companies in the market for corporate bonds is the result of several factors. Primarily, of course, it is a reflection of the pace of growth of the life insurance industry itself and of the special qualifications of corporate long-term debt as an investment outlet. In addition, however, it is partly due to fundamental changes in the economic environment induced by the monetary and fiscal policies followed by the federal government at different times. Thus, declining interest rates and the rising tax burden, both the result of federal policy, seem to have persuaded many individuals and certain types of financial institutions to leave the corporate bond market during the 1930's. Because of the constant pressure to find employment for their funds, life insurance companies willingly filled the gap.

The corporate bond market itself experienced basic changes which facilitated the expansion of life insurance companies' lending to corporations. Internal funds satisfied an increasing proportion of corporate capital requirements, and when corporations did seek outside finance they relied heavily on debt rather than equity securities. This behavior in turn reflected the greater tax advantages of debt over equity financing. Life insurance companies were able to enhance their position as suppliers of corporate funds through direct placement of securities. The spread of direct placements was stimulated partly by the desire to avoid the problems associated with registration under the Securities and Exchange Act, but several positive advantages also played a part. Since loans are negotiated directly with corporate management, they can be tailored to meet the needs of the borrower and lender. Conditions under which loans are granted are quite flexible, and desired changes in the agreement can be made more easily than in the case of securities offered publicly. The borrower gets an immediate commitment of funds thus avoiding the risk that the market will take an unfavorable turn before a public offering can be made. While the interest costs of direct placements are usually higher than those which public auction would produce, the differential is said to be justified by the assumption of a nonmarketable obligation. On the other hand, while these advantages of direct placement are evident, there is another side to the story, and this will be explored below.

The corporate bond market absorbed a major share of the funds life insurance companies obtained through both new savings and sales of government securities. The substitution of corporate for government debt was stimulated partly by the rise in corporate bond yields in relation to those on Governments and partly by the desire of portfolio managers to correct the imbalance in their holdings resulting from the dearth of corporate bond financing during the 1930's and the World War II period. In switching from Governments into corporate issues, life insurance companies exhibited a clearly defined pattern which was virtually a retracing of the corporate demand for funds. Thus, the rate of growth of the corporate sector to a large extent determined the availability of life insurance funds to other sectors of the capital market.

This was especially true with respect to the mortgage market, as shown in Chapter VII. While the relatively high yields on mortgages keep most life insurance companies in the market at all times, their extension of such loans has a sharply defined contra-cyclical pattern. The main force underlying this, of course, is the contra-cyclical character of residential construction, but life insurance companies have had a major influence on the behavior of construction through varying the amount of mortgage funds made available. A shortage of housing at the outbreak of World War II, restricted building during the conflict, and a substantial shift of population from rural to urban areas had already created a substantial housing shortage by the end of 1945. Subsequently, the spectacular rise in household formations and birth rates added further to the demand for housing. Because incomes registered sizable gains during most of the postwar years, families found it increasingly possible to acquire better homes. Moreover, the federal government, through its insurance and guarantee programs, sought to reduce the risk of mortgage lending and thereby expand the availability of funds to finance construction. On several occasions, these efforts were supplemented by considerable easing of terms of FHA and VA mortgages (reflected in lower down payments and longer maturities).

The interplay of supply and demand in the housing market was by no means uniform, but in general the rate of residential construction varied inversely with the rate of overall economic activity. Thus, housing was one of the main stabilizing forces in the economy, although the instability in the flow of mortgage funds generated considerable instability in the housing sector itself. Some of the implications of this development will be examined below. In each of the three postwar housing booms, the role of life insurance companies varied. Although they moved into the mortgage market much later than other major lenders in 1949-50, they played a bigger part in the first boom than in those which followed. They absorbed almost one-third of the net increase in nonfarm mortgages outstanding over those two years and moved well ahead of their closest competitors (commercial banks and savings and loan associations) in carving out a share of the market. While outstanding commitments to buy mortgages kept them in the market well after the start of the Korean War, life insurance companies turned increasingly away from residential mortgages in 1951-52 and concentrated on providing funds to industries in the process of building defense facilities. Furthermore, the relative cutback in mortgage funds was intensified by the unpegging of the government securities market.

With the advent of the second postwar recession in the summer of 1953, the conditions were created from which the second housing boom developed. The decline in interest rates on corporate issues and the increased availability of funds forced life insurance companies and other lenders to scramble for mortgages. Given the pegged rates on federally-underwritten loans, and because of changes in terms on FHA and VA loans, this sector of the market experienced a spectacular expansion with most of the growth centering in VA mortgages. Again life insurance companies lagged behind other lenders in shifting to the mortgage market, but in September, 1953, their forward commitments began to climb with commitments for VA loans leading by a wide margin. By the time the peak in commitments was reached in the summer of 1954, those to buy VA mortgages had risen twelve times from the level of the previous year. In terms of actual acquisitions, life insurance companies absorbed about three-tenths of the increase in VA mortgages outstanding, although they held only one-fifth in the third quarter of 1953. In terms of all types of nonfarm mortgages, their share of the market shrank slightly because they expanded their holdings of FHA and conventional loans at a rate somewhat less than that achieved by savings and loan associations and other lenders. The recession which began in the summer of 1957 produced the same familiar pattern in the mortgage market. This time, however, FHA loans led the field in the rate of growth. To a considerable extent, the third housing boom was powered by an increase in demand for homes by middle and upper income groups in contrast to the previous booms when easing credit terms brought a substantial number of lower income families into the market. Life insurance companies made only a modest contribution to the growth of home financing during the housing expansion in 1958-59. This reduced participation in the mortgage market partly reflected the slower rate of growth in their total assets for the reasons described above. Moreover, the companies were no longer willing to sell large quantities of government securities to make mortgage loans. Finally, the competition of other lenders, particularly savings and loan associations, severely restricted the volume of mortgages which life insurance companies were able to acquire. Nevertheless, these institutions at the end of 1959 remained a major source of mortgage funds, accounting for more than one-fifth of the total nonfarm mortgage debt.

From the study of life insurance companies' participation in mortgage warehousing, it was concluded that aside from the possibility of temporary overexpansion in commercial bank credit, this technique could probably be of considerable benefit in the stabilization of residential construction. In the mid-1950's, however, there was some evidence that a few of the leading life insurance companies employed the warehousing technique in a manner which added to instability in the economy. Toward the end of the decade, the reliance on warehousing had shrunk to only minor proportions.

Life insurance companies provided the largest institutional market for farm mortgages in the postwar period. They moved far ahead of the commercial banks, which are their institutional rivals in this part of the mortgage market, and won a sizable piece of the market share relinquished by federal lending agencies. While their acquisition of farm real estate loans varied greatly during the postwar years, they absorbed almost three-tenths of the net increase in such loans outstanding between 1945 and 1959. Yet, the revival of large-scale farm lending by life insurance companies just about restored them to the relative position they held in the market in 1930.

The above three sectors of the capital market were the focus of most life insurance companies' investment activities, but two other sectors also attracted them to some extent. As shown in Chapter VIII, the state and local government securities market received only 4 percent of the net amount of funds the companies supplied to the capital market. In the fourteen years ending in 1959, they added $2.5 billion of such obligations to their portfolios, representing about 6 percent of the increase in the amount outstanding. When they did enter the market, they concentrated on revenue bonds whose yields, even before taking account of tax exemption, are quite competitive with corporate obligations. The rise of special authorities to operate essentially business-type facilities has considerably expanded the supply of revenue bonds, and life insurance companies have found them an ideal investment outlet. In 1959, they owned about 13 percent of revenue issues compared with 5 percent of all state and local obligations outstanding. On balance, however, it seems that life insurance companies are not likely to become a major source of funds for state and local governments. The rate of federal taxation applicable to them remains relatively light despite the substantial percentage increase in 1959. Thus, they will most likely continue to refrain from paying the premium on tax-exempt income which is so highly valued by individuals, commercial banks, and others subject to heavier tax burdens.

The evidence in Chapter IX demonstrates that life insurance companies are an unpromising source of small business and equity finance. In the small business area, both legal restrictions and high credit risks impose severe constraints on their ability to extend loans to new or small-scale enterprises through the purchase of bonds. On the other hand, life insurance companies do acquire a sizable amount of real estate mortgages secured by business and commercial properties. Moreover, a large share of the proceeds of policy loans and residential mortgages is reportedly used for business purposes. But, given the legal framework, the relatively heavy administrative costs, and the high probability of loss inherent in small business loans—and considering the variety of alternative investment opportunities open to life insurance companies—it is easily understood why small businesses get such a meager portion of life insurance funds.

Equity financing by life insurance companies is even more limited.

Since shortly after the turn of the century, they have played an insignificant role in the stock market, and equities have been only a minor investment outlet. Until recent years, the investment laws in most states prohibited their investment in common stocks, but in states where they were allowed to hold this type of asset they showed little interest in exploiting the privilege. With the amendment of the New York State law in 1951 and 1957, some observers thought the companies' demand for common stocks would greatly expand. These expectations have been gravely disappointed. While their participation in the stock market registered a noticeable increase in the few years immediately following the easing of the New York law in 1951, this was not sustained at the same high level through the decade. Furthermore, life insurance companies tend to concentrate on a relatively narrow list of high-grade stocks, so their activity in the market is even more limited than suggested by the small volume. Despite this pessimistic record, it was argued that life insurance companies could appreciably expand their common stock holdings without an undue amount of risk, and the benefits would accrue to the economy as a whole as well as to policyholders. This issue is taken up again in the next section.

SECTION II
FUTURE ROLE OF LIFE INSURANCE COMPANIES IN THE CAPITAL MARKET

The record of investment experience suggests that life insurance companies are likely to play essentially the same role in the capital market during the next decade which they played in the recent past. However, several questions arise.

In the first place, unless the slower pace of growth in their assets which has been evident since the mid-1950's is purely temporary, and this seems unlikely, they will probably command a smaller share of savings. These savings will be increasingly mobilized by savings institutions. The result will be that the volume of loanable funds flowing from the life insurance companies to the capital market will decrease. On the other hand, if demand for houses eases somewhat, one group of the companies' competitors, savings and loan associations, may not be quite so successful in the future as in the recent past in attracting savings; this would enhance the companies' chances in the bid for savings. Moreover, since life insurance as a form of savings has been losing ground to some extent because of the fear of creeping inflation, any success toward achieving reasonable price stability may also help to restore to life insurance companies their previous position as premier savings institutions.

But whatever volume of savings they will have, the uses to which they can put such savings remains the central question. Unless the investment laws in a few key states are further liberalized, the investment activities of life insurance companies will be confined primarily to high-grade debt. On the other hand, it was argued that a good case can be made for their being allowed to invest in equities on a much larger scale without exposing themselves to excessive risk. It was pointed out that in limited amounts (perhaps as much as 10 percent of assets), and provided seasoned and amply diversified stocks are selected (although not necessarily blue chip issues), common stocks are an advantageous investment outlet for life insurance companies. Because of the long-term nature of their liabilities and the steady cash inflow, these institutions are probably never forced to liquidate assets to meet claims. Thus, they are free to hold common stocks primarily as a source of income. Over a period of time, and after allowing for reasonable yearly variation in dividends and for occasional small losses, common stocks can make a major contribution to building up the net earnings of life insurance companies and thereby keeping down, or reducing, the net cost of insurance. While an increasing number of companies will undoubtedly enter the market even under existing regulations, it is unlikely that life insurance companies as a group will become so important as to exert a major influence in the market. Many companies, because of lack of staff and the unwillingness to take even moderate risks, will refrain from participating in the market at all. On the other hand, a further easing of restrictions would permit some of the larger institutions to enter the market on a much larger scale. The change in legal environment and the shift in attitudes among industry officials would stimulate the supply of equity capital. This would clearly be of benefit to the economy as a whole as well as to the life insurance industry.

Life insurance companies will undoubtedly continue to play a dominant role in the market for corporate bonds, although corporate pension funds may offer a major challenge. They will most likely remain the chief outlet for securities placed directly by the leading corporate borrowers. At the same time, their mastery of the direct placement technique of financing may not be entirely an advantage. The method has a serious shortcoming for both small borrowers and small lenders. For example, small life insurance companies are not equipped to make direct loans and do not have the opportunity to participate in the larger loans. Thus, these institutions are cut off from a large portion of the modern capital market. This situation cannot be alleviated by turning to the public sector of the market because here also the larger life insurance companies have a much stronger competitive position. A similar obstacle must be faced by small enterprises seeking funds. For the most part, they do not have access to the private placement market because their requirements are generally not large enough to induce life insurance company officials to expend the resources necessary for a credit analysis and appraisal. When small companies do obtain funds directly from life insurance companies, the cost to them is necessarily high in relation to the amount borrowed. Also, when viewed from the point of view of the society as a whole, the direct placement technique has a shortcoming. Namely, that such new financing circumvents the traditional mechanisms of the market place and may well result in a misallocation of resources. Nevertheless, the method of financing seems firmly entrenched, and in the short run its advantages seem to outweigh its disadvantages.

The investment behavior of life insurance companies in the mortgage market in the future is not likely to be the source of as much instability in financial flows as it was in the past. But this is likely to be more attributable to changes in the market than to shifts in the companies' attitude toward mortgages. As mentioned in the text, much of the fluctuation in the flow of life insurance funds into mortgages reflected the influence of pegged rates on federally-underwritten mortgages. This influence is likely to diminish further because of a number of factors. In the first place, the volume of VA mortgages outstanding will shrink, even if Congress broadens the program to include more peacetime veterans, as the backlog of eligible applicants declines. Thus, the availability of these mortgages as an emergency outlet for funds will lessen. But of perhaps more importance will be the spread of discounts on FHA and VA mortgages. The effect of such discounts is to bring the effective yield to investors closer into line with the rates the market would demand. As this happens, FHA and VA rates will lose their rigidity and will rise and fall in tune with other open market rates, and the yield differential in their favor which attracted life insurance companies and other investors during periods of recession would be narrowed and perhaps eliminated. This pattern does not depend on the removal of the statutory ceiling nor on raising it to the level of rates on conventional mortgages. In fact, the latter action may be seriously questioned in light of the federal government's underwriting of most of the risk on FHA and VA mortgages. But this issue aside, it seems that the behavior of life insurance companies in the market will be far less destabilizing than in the past.

In the market for state and local government securities, one can expect life insurance companies to continue to play only a minor role. However, this may be strengthened somewhat as special authorities assume more of the responsibility for capital construction on behalf of other governmental units. This trend would generate a growing volume of revenue bonds, and life insurance companies would probably remain a major outlet for such obligations. Moreover, their interest may be intensified if the burden of federal taxation on life insurance companies becomes heavier.

A final comment may be made on the companies' future role in the market for United States government securities. Unless the future is plagued by long depressions or war periods, the demand for Governments is likely to remain weak. They will undoubtedly use Governments to provide balance and liquidity to their total investment portfolios, but this will not have a major impact on the market. On the other hand, if alternative private investment opportunities shrink appreciably, these institutions will again turn to Governments as a residual outlet for their surplus funds. If this happens, then one can look forward to a subsequent period of liquidation, which may have serious implications for the maintenance of monetary stability.

In the meantime, the immediate outlook suggests that life insurance companies will remain the dominant source of funds in the corporate bond market; they will continue to do a large but perhaps gradually declining share of mortgage financing, and they may even expand their modest role in the state and local government securities market and in the market for equities.

Appendix Tables

APPENDIX TABLE II-1

ANNUAL PERCENTAGE CHANGES IN DISPOSABLE PERSONAL INCOME, LIFE INSURANCE IN FORCE, AND ASSETS OF LIFE INSURANCE COMPANIES, 1930-1959

Year	Disposable Personal Income	Life Insurance in Force	Life Insurance Assets
1930	−10.5	4.2	8.0
1931	−14.2	0.6	6.9
1932	−23.7	−5.0	3.0
1933	− 6.2	−5.3	0.5
1934	13.8	0.5	4.3
1935	12.1	1.9	6.4
1936	13.6	4.3	7.3
1937	7.3	5.0	5.2
1938	−7.5	1.0	6.1
1939	7.2	2.5	5.0
1940	8.1	3.5	5.5
1941	22.2	5.8	6.2
1942	26.3	4.5	6.7
1943	13.6	7.4	8.3
1944	10.0	6.3	8.7
1945	2.5	4.1	9.0
1946	6.8	12.1	7.6
1947	5.9	9.3	7.3
1948	11.3	8.2	7.4
1949	0.2	6.2	7.4
1950	9.5	9.6	7.4
1951	9.5	8.1	6.7
1952	4.9	9.3	7.5
1953	5.8	10.0	6.9
1954	1.7	9.7	7.6
1955	6.8	11.6	7.0
1956	6.7	10.8	6.2
1957	5.1	11.1	5.5
1958	2.8	7.7	6.2
1959	5.7		5.6

SOURCE: U. S. Department of Commerce and Institute of Life Insurance.

APPENDIX TABLE II-2

GROWTH OF SAVINGS THROUGH LIFE INSURANCE AND THE ACCUMULATION OF POLICY RESERVES, 1896-1959
(In Millions of Dollars)

Year	Accumulated Savings at Year End	Net Savings During Year	Rate of Annual Increase (Percent)	Policy Reserves
1896	1,244	M.A.	M.A.	1,048
1897	1,327	83	6.67	1,119
1898	1,429	102	7.69	1,203
1899	1,538	109	7.63	1,322
1900	1,659	121	7.87	1,443
1901	1,800	141	8.50	1,584
1902	1,959	159	8.83	1,738
1903	2,127	168	8.58	1,916
1904	2,307	180	8.46	2,101
1905	2,502	195	8.45	2,295
1906	2,708	206	8.23	2,473
1907	2,868	160	5.91	2,651
1908	3,040	172	6.00	2,829
1909	3,248	208	6.84	3,029
1910	3,453	205	6.31	3,226
1911	3,691	238	6.89	3,473
1912	3,915	224	6.07	3,695
1913	4,140	225	5.75	3,934
1914	4,342	202	4.88	4,166
1915	4,595	253	5.83	4,399
1916	4,930	335	7.29	4,696
1917	5,303	373	7.57	5,033
1918	5,822	519	9.79	5,407
1919	6,150	328	5.63	5,830
1920	6,643	493	8.02	6,338
1921	7,136	493	7.42	6,903
1922	7,745	609	8.53	7,449
1923	8,504	759	9.80	8,130
1924	9,286	782	9.20	8,939
1925	10,295	1,009	10.87	9,927
1926	11,530	1,235	12.00	11,061
1927	12,765	1,235	10.71	12,279
1928	14,101	1,336	10.47	13,596
1929	15,251	1,150	8.16	14,948
1930	16,299	1,048	6.87	16,231
1931	17,083	784	4.81	17,384
1932	17,357	274	1.60	17,839
1933	17,887	530	3.05	18,077
1934	19,122	1,235	6.90	19,030
1935	20,667	1,545	8.08	20,404

APPENDIX TABLE II-2 (cont.)

GROWTH OF SAVINGS THROUGH LIFE INSURANCE AND THE ACCUMULATION OF POLICY RESERVES, 1896-1959

(In Millions of Dollars)

Year	Accumulated Savings at Year End	Net Savings During Year	Rate of Annual Increase (Percent)	Policy Reserves
1936	22,389	1,722	8.33	21,800
1937	24,023	1,634	7.30	23,202
1938	25,614	1,591	6.62	24,495
1939	27,329	1,715	6.70	25,827
1940	29,152	1,823	6.67	27,238
1941	31,314	2,162	7.42	28,945
1942	33,775	2,461	7.86	30,797
1943	36,643	2,868	8.49	33,049
1944	39,829	3,186	8.69	35,577
1945	43,277	3,448	8.66	38,667
1946	46,679	3,402	7.86	41,702
1947	50,287	3,608	7.73	44,882
1948	53,910	3,623	7.20	48,158
1949	57,828	3,918	7.27	51,498
1950	61,818	3,990	6.90	54,946
1951	65,964	4,146	6.71	58,547
1952	70,761	4,797	7.27	62,579
1953	75,761	5,000	7.07	66,683
1954	80,979	5,218	6.89	70,903
1955	86,490	5,511	6.81	75,359
1956	92,059	5,569	6.44	79,738
1957	97,260	5,201	5.65	84,075
1958	102,599	5,339	5.49	88,604
1959	108,000	5,400	5.26	93,975

Note: Column 1 is the accumulated total of net savings through life insurance beginning in 1896. Life insurance savings shown in Column 2 represent the net increase in total admitted assets of all U. S. life insurance companies, less the increase in policy loans, and after adjusting for net capital gains and losses.

Source: (a) Savings figures: Raymond W. Goldsmith, **A Study of Savings in the United States**, Vol. I, p. 450 (for 1896-1947 data); Life Insurance Association of America (for 1948-1959 data, derived on the basis of definitions consistent with Goldsmith's). (b) Policy reserves are from **1960 Life Insurance Fact Book**, p. 59.

Index of Subjects

Index of Names